Svein Linge • Hans Petter Langtangen

# Programming for Computations - Python

## A Gentle Introduction to Numerical Simulations with Python 3.6

Second Edition

Svein Linge
Fac of Tech, Natural Sci & Maritime Sci
University of South-Eastern Norway
Porsgrunn, Norway

Hans Petter Langtangen
Simula Research Laboratory BioComp
Lysaker, Norway

https://doi.org/10.1007/978-3-030-16877-3

Mathematics Subject Classification (2010): 26-01, 34A05, 34A30, 34A34, 39-01, 40-01, 65D15, 65D25, 65D30, 68-01, 68N01, 68N19, 68N30, 70-01, 92D25, 97-04, 97U50

This book is an open access publication.

*To My Family*
*Thanks to my dear wife, Katrin, and our lovely children, Stian, Mia, and Magnus, for their love, support, and patience. I am a very lucky man.*

*To Hans Petter*
*Dear friend and coauthor, it is so sad you are no longer among us.*[1] *Thank you for everything. I dedicate this second edition of our book to you.*

Porsgrunn, Norway
June 2018

Svein Linge

[1] Professor Hans Petter Langtangen (https://en.wikipedia.org/wiki/Hans_Petter_Langtangen) passed away with cancer on the 10th of October, 2016.

# Preface

Computing, in the sense of doing mathematical calculations, is a skill that mankind has developed over thousands of years. Programming, on the other hand, is in its infancy, with a history that spans a few decades only. Both topics are vastly comprehensive and usually taught as separate subjects in educational institutions around the world, especially at the undergraduate level. This book is about the *combination* of the two, because computing today becomes so much more powerful when combined with programming.

Most universities and colleges implicitly require students to specialize in computer science if they want to learn the craft of programming, since other student programs usually do not offer programming to an extent demanded for really mastering this craft. Common arguments claim that it is sufficient with a brief introduction, that there is not enough room for learning programming in addition to all other must-have subjects, and that there is so much software available that few really need to program themselves. A consequence is that engineering students often graduate with shallow knowledge about programming, unless they happened to choose the computer science direction.

We think this is an unfortunate situation. There is no doubt that practicing engineers and scientists need to know their pen-and-paper mathematics. They must also be able to run off-the-shelf software for important standard tasks and will certainly do that a lot. Nevertheless, the benefits of mastering programming are many.

**Why Learn Programming?**

1. Ready-made software is limited to handling certain standard problems. What do you do when the problem at hand is not covered by the software you bought? Fortunately, a lot of modern software systems are extensible via programming. In fact, many systems demand parts of the problem specification (e.g., material models) to be specified by computer code.
2. With programming skills, you may extend the flexibility of existing software packages by combining them. For example, you may integrate packages that do not speak to each other from the outset. This makes the work flow simpler, more efficient, and more reliable, and it puts you in a position to attack new problems.

3. It is easy to use excellent ready-made software the wrong way. The insight in programming and the mathematics behind is fundamental for understanding complex software, avoiding pitfalls, and becoming a safe user.
4. Bugs (errors in computer code) are present in most larger computer programs (also in the ones from the shop!). What do you do when your ready-made software gives unexpected results? Is it a bug, is it the wrong use, or is it the mathematically correct result? Experience with programming of mathematics gives you a good background for answering these questions. The one who can program can also make tailored code for a simplified problem setting and use that to verify the computations done with off-the-shelf software.
5. Lots of skilled people around the world solve computational problems by writing their own code and offering those for free on the Internet. To take advantage of this truly great source of software in a reliable way, one must normally be able to understand and possibly modify computer code offered by others.
6. It is recognized worldwide that students struggle with mathematics and physics. Too many find such subjects difficult and boring. With programming, we can execute the good old subjects in a brand new way! According to the authors' own experience, students find it much more motivating and enlightening when programming is made an integrated part of mathematics and physical science courses. In particular, the problem being solved can be much more realistic than when the mathematics is restricted to what you can do with pen and paper.
7. Finally, we launch our most important argument for learning computer programming: the *algorithmic thinking* that comes with the process of writing a program for a computational problem enforces a thorough understanding of both the problem and the solution method. We can simply quote the famous Norwegian computer scientist Kristen Nygaard: "Programming is understanding."

In the authors' experience, programming is an excellent pedagogical tool for understanding mathematics: "You think you know when you can learn, are more sure when you can write, even more when you can teach, but certain when you can program" (Alan Perlis, computer scientist, 1922–1990). Consider, for example, integration. A numerical method for integration has a much stronger focus on what the integral actually is and means compared to analytical methods, where much time and effort must be devoted to integration by parts, integration by substitution, etc. Moreover, when programming the numerical integration formula, it becomes evident that it works for "all" mathematical functions and that the implementation should be in terms of a *general* function applicable to "all" integrals. In this way, students learn to recognize a special problem as belonging to a class of problems (e.g., integration, differential equations, root finding), for which we have general numerical methods implemented in a widely applicable software. When they write this software, as we do in this book, they learn how to generalize and increase the abstraction level of the mathematical problem. When they use this software, they learn how a special case should be attacked by general methods and software for the class of problems that comprises the special case at hand. This is the power of mathematics in a nutshell, and it is paramount that students understand this way of thinking.

**Target Audience and Background Knowledge** This book was written for students, teachers, engineers, and scientists who know *nothing* about programming and numerical methods from before but who seek a *minimum* of the fundamental skills required to get started with programming as a tool for solving scientific and engineering problems. Some knowledge of one- and multivariable calculus is assumed. The basic programming concepts are presented in Chaps. 1–5 (about 150 pages), before practical applications of these concepts are demonstrated in important mathematical subjects addressed in the remaining parts of the book (Chaps. 6–9). Each chapter is followed by a set of exercises that covers a wide range of application areas, e.g., biology, geology, statistics, physics, and mathematics. The exercises were particularly designed to bring across important points from the text.

Learning the very basics of programming should not take long, but as with any other craft, mastering the skill requires continued and extensive practice. Some beginning practice is gained through Chaps. 6–9, but the authors strongly emphasize that this is only a start. Students should continue to practice programming in subsequent courses, while those who exercise self-study should keep up the learning process through continued application of the craft. The book is a good starting point when teaching computer programming as an integrated part of standard university courses in mathematics and natural science. In our experience, such an integration is doable and indeed rewarding.

**Numerical Methods** An overall goal with this book is to motivate computer programming as a very powerful tool for doing mathematics. All examples are related to mathematics and its use in engineering and science. However, to solve mathematical problems through computer programming, we need numerical methods. Explaining basic numerical methods is therefore an integral part of the book. Our choice of topics is governed by what is most needed in science and engineering, as well as in the teaching of applied natural science courses. Mathematical models are then central, with differential equations constituting the most frequent type of models. Consequently, the numerical focus in this book is on differential equations. As soft pedagogical starters for the programming of mathematics, we have chosen the topics of numerical integration and root finding. We remark that the book is deliberately brief on numerical methods. This is because our focus is on *implementing* numerical algorithms, and to develop reliable, working programs, the programmer must be confident about the basic ideas of the numerical approximations involved.

**The Computer Language: Python** We have chosen to use the programming language Python, because this language gives a very compact and readable code that closely resembles the mathematical recipe for solving the problem at hand. Python also has a gentle learning curve.

Other computer languages, like Fortran, C, and C++, have a strong position in science and engineering. During the last two decades, however, there has been a significant shift in popularity from these compiled languages to more high-level and easier-to-read languages, for instance, MATLAB, Python, R, Maple, Mathematica, and IDL. This latter class of languages is computationally less efficient but superior with respect to overall human problem-solving efficiency. This book emphasizes *how to think like a programmer*, rather than focusing on technical language details. Thus, the book should put the reader in a good position for learning other programming languages later, including the classic ones: Fortran, C, and C++.

**How This Book Is Different** There are numerous texts on computer programming and numerical methods, so how does the present one differ from the existing literature? Compared to standard books on numerical methods, our book has a much stronger emphasis on the craft of programming and on verification. We want to give students a thorough understanding of how to think about programming as a problem-solving method and how to provide convincing evidence for program correctness.

Even though there are lots of books on numerical methods where many algorithms have a corresponding computer implementation (see, e.g., [1, 3–6, 10, 15–17, 20, 23, 25, 27–31]—the latter two apply Python), it is often assumed that the reader "can program" beforehand. The present book teaches the craft of structured programming along with the fundamental ideas of numerical methods. In this book, unit testing and corresponding test functions are introduced early on. We also put much emphasis on coding algorithms as *functions*, as opposed to "flat programs," which often dominate in the literature and among practitioners. Functions are reusable because they utilize the general formulation of a mathematical algorithm such that it becomes applicable to a large class of problems.

There are also numerous books on computer programming, but not many that really emphasize how to *think* about programming in the context of numerical methods and scientific applications. One such book is [11], which gives a comprehensive introduction to Python programming and the thinking about programming as a computer scientist.

Sometimes, however, one needs a text like the present one. It does not go so deep into language-specific details, but rather targets the shortest path to reliable mathematical problem-solving through programming. With this attitude in mind, a lot of topics were left out of the present book, simply because they were not *strictly* needed in the mathematical problem-solving process. Examples of such topics are object-oriented programming and Python dictionaries (of which the latter omission is possibly subject to more debate). If you find the present book too shallow, [11] might be the right choice for you. That source should also work nicely as a more in-depth successor of the present text.

Whenever the need for a *structured introduction to programming* arises in science and engineering courses, the present book may be your option, either for self-study or for use in organized teaching. The thinking, habits, and practice covered herein will put readers in a firm position for utilizing and understanding the power of computers for problem-solving in science and engineering.

## Changes to the First Edition

1. All code is now in Python version 3.6 (the previous edition was based on Python version 2.7).
2. In the first edition, the introduction to programming was basically covered in 50 pages by Chap. 1 (*The First Few Steps*) and Chap. 2 (*Basic Constructions*). This *is* enough to get going, but many readers soon want more details. In this second edition, these two chapters have therefore been extended and split up into five

chapters. Explanations are now more complete, previous examples have been modified, new examples have been added, and more. In particular, the importing of code is now elaborated on in a greater detail, so is the making of modules. Also, Sect. 4.2 is new, illustrating the important stepwise strategy of code writing through a dedicated example. The five first chapters now cover about 150 pages that explain, in a brief and simple manner, all the code basics required to follow the remaining parts of the book.

3. The new Chap. 6 (*Computing Integrals and Testing Code*) and Chap. 7 (*Solving Nonlinear Algebraic Equations*) are seen as gentle first applications of programming to problem-solving in mathematics. Both these chapters now precede the mathematically more challenging Chaps. 8 and 9, which treat basic numerical solving of ODEs and PDEs, respectively (the chapter *Solving Nonlinear Algebraic Equations* was, in the first edition, the final chapter of the book, but it seems more appropriate to let it act as a "warm-up" chapter, together with the new Chap. 6, for the two final chapters on differential equation solving).
4. Section 8.1 (*Filling a Water Tank: Two Cases*) is new, particularly written for readers who lack experience with differential equations.
5. Section 8.5 (*Rate of Convergence*) is new, explaining convergence rate related to differential equations.
6. New exercises have been added, e.g., on Fibonacci numbers, the Leapfrog method, Adams-Bashforth methods, and more.
7. Errors and typos have been corrected, and many explanations have been reformulated throughout.

**Supplementary Materials** All program and data files referred to herein are available from the book's (2nd edition) primary web site:
https://github.com/slgit/prog4comp_2.

**Acknowledgments** We want to thank all students who attended the courses *FM1006 Modelling and simulation of dynamic systems*, *FM1115 Scientific Computing*, *FB1012 Mathematics*, and *FB2112 Physics* at the University of South-Eastern Norway over the last 5–10 years. They worked their way through early versions of this text and gave us constructive and positive feedback that helped us correct errors and improve the book in so many ways. Special acknowledgment goes to Guandong Kou, Edirisinghe V. P. J. Manjula, and Yapi Donatien Achou for their careful reading of the manuscript (first edition) and constructive suggestions for improvement. The constructive feedback and good suggestions received from Om Prakash Chapagain (second edition) is also highly appreciated. We thank all our good colleagues at the University of South-Eastern Norway, the University of Oslo, and Simula Research Laboratory for their continued support and interest, for the enlightening discussions, and for providing such an inspiring environment for teaching and science.

Special thanks go to Prof. Kent-Andre Mardal, the University of Oslo, for his insightful comments and suggestions.

The authors would also like to thank the Springer team with Dr. Martin Peters, Thanh-Ha Le Thi, and Leonie Kunz for the effective editorial and production process.

This text was written in the DocOnce[1] [12] markup language.

Lysaker, Norway — Hans Petter Langtangen
December 2015
Porsgrunn, Norway — Svein Linge
June 2018

[1] https://github.com/hplgit/doconce.

# Abstract

This second edition of the book presents computer programming as a key method for solving mathematical problems and represents a major revision: all code is now written in Python version 3.6 (the first edition was based on Python version 2.7). The first two chapters of the previous edition have been extended and split up into five new chapters, thus expanding the introduction to programming from 50 to 150 pages. Throughout, explanations are now more complete, previous examples have been modified, and new sections, examples, and exercises have been added. Also, errors and typos have been corrected. The book was inspired by the Springer book TCSE 6, *A Primer on Scientific Programming with Python* (by Langtangen), but the style is more accessible and concise in keeping with the needs of engineering students. The book outlines the shortest possible path from no previous experience with programming to a set of skills that allows the students to write simple programs for solving common mathematical problems with numerical methods in engineering and science courses. The emphasis is on generic algorithms, clean design of programs, use of functions, and automatic tests for verification.

# Contents

# List of Exercises

# The First Few Steps

# 1

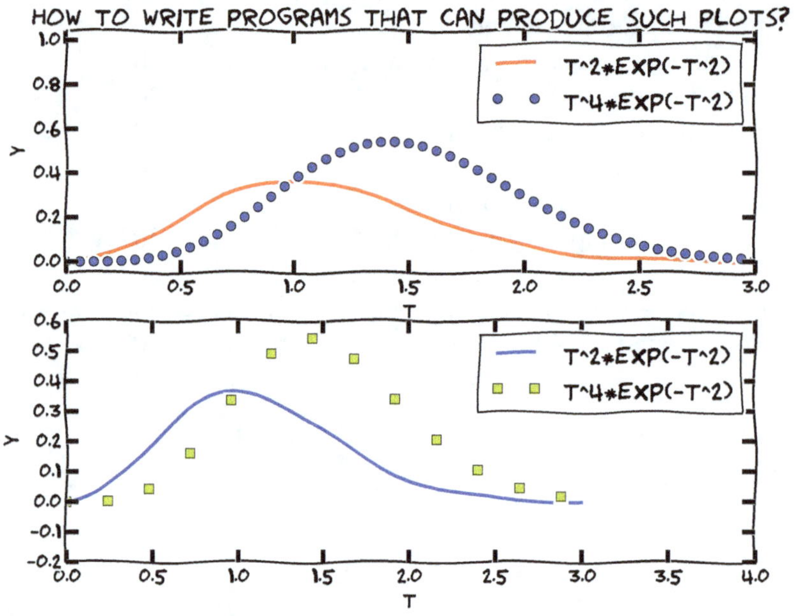


## 1.1 What Is a Program? And What Is Programming?

**Computer Programs** Today, most people are experienced with computer programs, typically programs such as Word, Excel, PowerPoint, Internet Explorer, and Photoshop. The interaction with such programs is usually quite simple and intuitive: you click on buttons, pull down menus and select operations, drag visual elements into locations, and so forth. The possible operations you can do in these programs can be combined in seemingly an infinite number of ways, only limited by your creativity and imagination.



S. Linge, H. P. Langtangen, *Programming for Computations - Python*,
Texts in Computational Science and Engineering 15,
https://doi.org/10.1007/978-3-030-16877-3_1

Nevertheless, programs often make us frustrated when they cannot do what we wish. One typical situation might be the following. Say you have some measurements from a device, and the data are stored in a file with a specific format. You may want to analyze these data in Excel and make some graphics out of it. However, assume there is no menu in Excel that allows you to import data in this specific format. Excel can work with many different data formats, but not this one. You start searching for alternatives to Excel that can do the same *and* read this type of data files. Maybe you cannot find any ready-made program directly applicable. You have reached the point where knowing how to write programs on your own would be of great help to you! With some programming skills, you may write your own little program which can translate one data format to another. With that little piece of tailored code, your data may be read and analyzed, perhaps in Excel, or perhaps by a new program tailored to the computations that the measurement data demand.

**Programming** The real power of computers can only be utilized if you can program them, i.e., write the programs yourself. With programming, *you* can tell the computer what *you* want it to do, which is great, since it frees you from possible limitations that come with programs written by others! Thus, with this skill, you get an important extra option for problem solving that goes beyond what ready-made programs offer.

A program that you write, will be a set of instructions that you store in a file. These instructions must be written (according to certain rules) in a very specialized language that has adopted words and expressions from English. Such languages are known as *programming* (or *computer*) *languages*. When you have written your instructions (your program), you may ask the programming language to read your program and carry out the instructions. The programming language will then (if there are no errors) translate the meaning of your instructions into real actions inside the computer.

To write a program that solves a computing problem, you need to have a thorough understanding of the given problem. That understanding may have to be *developed* along the way and will obviously guide the way you write your solution program. Typically, you need to write, test and re-write your program several times until you get it right. Thus, what starts out with a computing problem and ends with a sensible computer program for its solution, is a *process* that may take some time. By the term *programming*, we will mean the whole of this process.

The purpose of this book is to teach you how to develop computer programs dedicated to solve mathematical and engineering problems by fundamental numerical methods.

**Programming Languages** There are numerous computer languages for different purposes. Within the engineering area, the most widely used ones are Python, MATLAB, Octave, Fortran, C, C++, and to some extent, Maple and Mathematica. The rules for how to write the instructions (i.e. the *syntax*) differ between the languages. Let us use an analogy.

Assume you are an international kind of person, having friends abroad in England, Russia and China. They want to try your favorite cake. What can you do? Well, you may write down the recipe in those three languages and send them over. Now, if you have been able to think correctly when writing down the recipe, and you have written the explanations according to the rules in each language, each of your friends will produce the same cake. Your recipe is the "computer program", while English, Russian and Chinese represent the "computer languages" with their own rules of how to write things. The end product, though, is still the same cake. Note that you may unintentionally introduce errors in your "recipe". Depending on the error, this may cause "baking execution" to stop, or perhaps produce the wrong cake. In your computer program, the errors you introduce are called bugs (yes, small insects! ... for historical reasons), and the process of fixing them is called debugging. When you try to run your program that contains errors, you usually get warnings or error messages. However, the response you get depends on the error and the programming language. You may even get no response, but simply the wrong "cake". Note that the rules of a programming language have to be followed very strictly. This differs from languages like English etc., where the meaning might be understood even with spelling errors and "slang" included.

**We Use Python 3.6 in This Book** For good reasons, the programming language used in this book is Python (version 3.6). It is an excellent language for beginners (and experts!), with a simple and clear syntax. Some of Python's other strong properties are[1]: It has a huge and excellent *library* (i.e., ready-made pieces of code that you can utilize for certain tasks in your own programs), many global functions can be placed in only *one* file, functions are straightforwardly transferred as arguments to other functions, there is good support for interfacing C, C++ and Fortran code (i.e., a Python program may use code written in other languages), and functions explicitly written for scalar input often work fine, without modification, also with vector input. Another important thing, is that Python is available *for free*. It can be downloaded at no cost from the Internet and will run on most platforms.

**A Primer on Scientific Programming with Python**

Readers who want to expand their scientific programming skills beyond the introductory level of the present exposition, are encouraged to study *A Primer on Scientific Programming with Python* [11]. This comprehensive book is as suitable for beginners as for professional programmers, and teaches the art of programming through a huge collection of dedicated examples. This book is considered the primary reference, and a natural extension, of the programming matters in the present book. Note, however, that this reference [11] uses version 2.7 of Python, which means that, in a few cases, instructions will differ somewhat from what you find in the present book.

[1] Some of the words here will be new to you, but relax, they will all be explained as we move along.

**Some computer science terms**

Note that, quite often, the terms *script* and *scripting* are used as synonyms for program and programming, respectively.

The inventor of the Perl programming language, Larry Wall, tried to explain the difference between script and program in a humorous way (from perl.com[a]): *Suppose you went back to Ada Lovelace[b] and asked her the difference between a script and a program. She'd probably look at you funny, then say something like: Well, a script is what you give the actors, but a program is what you give the audience. That Ada was one sharp lady... Since her time, we seem to have gotten a bit more confused about what we mean when we say scripting. It confuses even me, and I'm supposed to be one of the experts.*

There are many other widely used computer science terms to pick up as well. For example, writing a program (or script or code) is often expressed as *implementing* the program. *Executing* a program means running the program. A *default value* is what will be used if nothing is specified. An *algorithm* is a recipe for how to construct a program. A *bug* is an error in a program, and the art of tracking down and removing bugs is called *debugging* (see, e.g., Wikipedia[c]). *Simulating* or *simulation* refers to using a program to mimic processes in the real world, often through solving differential equations that govern the physics of the processes. A *plot* is a graphical representation of a data set. For example, if you walk along a straight road, recording your position $y$ with time $t$, say every second, your data set will consist of pairs with corresponding $y$ and $t$ values. With two perpendicular axes in a plane (e.g., a computer screen or a sheet of paper), one "horizontal" axis for $t$ and one "vertical" axis for $y$, each pair of points could be marked in that plane. The axes and the points make up a plot, which represents the data set graphically. Usually, such plotting is done by a computer.

[a] http://www.perl.com/pub/2007/12/06/soto-11.html.
[b] http://en.wikipedia.org/wiki/Ada_Lovelace.
[c] http://en.wikipedia.org/wiki/Software_bug#Etymology.

### 1.1.1 Installing Python

To study this book, you need a Python installation that fits the purpose. The quickest way to get a useful Python installation on your Windows, Mac, or Linux computer, is to download and install Anaconda.[2] There are alternatives (as you can find on the internet), but we have had very good experiences with Anaconda for several years, so that is our first choice. No separate installation of Python or Spyder (our recommended environment for writing Python code) is then required, as they are both included in Anaconda.

[2] https://www.anaconda.com/distribution.

To download Anaconda, you must pick the Anaconda version suitable for your machine (Windows/Mac/Linux) and choose which version of Python you want (3.6 is used for this book). When the download has completed, proceed with the installation of Anaconda.

After installation, you may want to (search for and) start up Spyder to see what it looks like (see also Appendix A). Spyder is an excellent tool for developing Python code. So, unless you have good reasons to choose otherwise, we recommend Spyder to be your main "working" environment, meaning that to read, write and run code you start Spyder and do it there. Thus, it is a good idea to make Spyder easy accessible on your machine.

With Anaconda installed, the only additional package you need to install is Odespy.[3] Odespy is relevant for the solving of differential equations that we treat in Chaps. 8 and 9.

In Appendix A you will find more information on the installation and use of Python.

## 1.2 A Python Program with Variables

Our first example regards programming a *mathematical model* that predicts the height of a ball thrown straight up into the air. From Newton's 2nd law, and by assuming negligible air resistance, one can derive a mathematical model that predicts the vertical position $y$ of the ball at time $t$:

$$y = v_0 t - 0.5 g t^2 .$$

Here, $v_0$ is the initial upwards velocity and $g$ is the acceleration of gravity, for which $9.81\ \mathrm{ms}^{-2}$ is a reasonable value (even if it depends on things like location on the earth).

With this formula at hand, and when $v_0$ is known, you may plug in a value for time and get out the corresponding height.

### 1.2.1 The Program

Let us next look at a Python program for evaluating this simple formula. To do this, we need some values for $v_0$ and $t$, so we pick $v_0 = 5\,\mathrm{ms}^{-1}$ and $t = 0.6\,\mathrm{s}$ (other choices would of course have been just as good). Assume the program is contained as text in a file named `ball.py`, reading

```
# Program for computing the height of a ball in vertical motion

v0 = 5                   # Initial velocity
g = 9.81                 # Acceleration of gravity
```

[3] The original version of Odespy (https://github.com/hplgit/odespy) was written in Python 2.7 by H.P. Langtangen and L. Wang. However, since the sad loss of Prof. Langtangen in 2016, Odespy has been updated to Python 3.6 (https://github.com/thomasantony/odespy/tree/py36/odespy), thanks to Thomas Antony. This version is the one used herein.

```
t = 0.6               # Time

y = v0*t - 0.5*g*t**2          # Vertical position

print(y)
```

Let us now explain this program in full detail.

**Typesetting of Code** Computer programs, and parts of programs, are typeset with a blue background in this book. When a complete program is shown, the blue background has a slightly darker top and bottom bar (as for `ball.py` here). Without the bars, the code is just a *snippet* and will normally need additional lines to run properly.

We also use the blue background, without bars, for *interactive* sessions (Sect. 2.1).

### 1.2.2 Dissecting the Program

A computer program like `ball.py` contains instructions to the computer written as plain text. Humans can read the code and understand what the program is capable of doing, but the program itself does not trigger any actions on a computer before another program, the Python *interpreter*, reads the program text and translates this text into specific actions.

**You must learn to play the role of a computer**

Although Python is responsible for reading and understanding your program, it is of fundamental importance that you fully understand the program yourself. You have to know the implication of every instruction in the program and be able to figure out the consequences of the instructions. In other words, you must be able to play the role of a computer.

One important reason for this strong demand is that errors unavoidably, and quite often, will be committed in the program text, and to track down these errors, you have to simulate what the computer does with the program. Also, you will often need to understand code written by other people. If you are able to understand their code properly, you may modify and use it as it suits you.

When you run your program in Python, it will interpret the text in your file line by line, from the top, reading each line from left to right. The first line it reads is

```
# Program for computing the height of a ball in vertical motion.
```

This line is what we call a *comment*. That is, the line is not meant for Python to read and execute, but rather for a human that reads the code and tries to understand what is going on. Therefore, one rule in Python says that whenever Python encounters the sign # it takes the rest of the line as a comment. Python then simply skips reading the rest of the line and jumps to the next line. In the code, you see several such comments and probably realize that they make it easier for you to understand (or guess) what is meant with the code. In simple cases, comments are probably not much needed, but will soon be justified as the level of complexity steps up.

The next line read by Python is

```
v0 = 5  # Initial velocity
```

In Python, a statement like `v0 = 5` is known as an *assignment* statement. After this assignment, any appearance of `v0` in the code will "represent" the initial velocity, being 5 $\mathrm{ms}^{-1}$ in this case. This means that, whenever Python reads `v0`, it will *replace* `v0` by the integer value 5. One simple way to think of this, might be as follows. With the assignment `v0 = 5`, Python generates a "box" in computer memory with the name `v0` written on top. The number 5 is then put into that box. Whenever Python later meets the name `v0` in the code, it finds the box, opens it, takes out the number (here 5) and replaces the name `v0` with the number.

The next two lines

```
g = 9.81  # Acceleration of gravity
t = 0.6   # Time
```

are also assignment statements, giving two more "boxes" in computer memory. The box named `g` will contain the value 9.81, while the box named `t` contains 0.6. Similarly, when Python later reads `g` and `t` in the code, it plugs in the numerical values found in the corresponding boxes.

**The assignments in a bit more detail**

When Python interprets the assignment statement `v0 = 5`, the integer 5 becomes an *object* of *type int* and the variable name on the left-hand side becomes a named *reference* for that object. Similarly, when interpreting the assignment statements `g = 9.81` and `t = 0.6`, `g` and `t` become named references to objects created for the real numbers given. However, since we have real numbers, these objects will be of *type float* (in computer language, a real number is called a "floating point number").

Now, with these assignments in place, Python knows of three variables (`v0`, `g`, `t`) and their values. These variables are then used by Python when it reads the next line, the actual "formula",

```
y = v0*t - 0.5*g*t**2          # Vertical position
```

Again, according to its rules, Python interprets `*` as multiplication, `-` as minus and `**` as exponentiation (let us also add here that, not surprisingly, `+` and `/` would have been understood as addition and division, if such signs had been present in the expression). Having read the line, Python performs the mathematics on the right-hand side, and then assigns the result (in this case the number 1.2342) to the variable name `y`.

Finally, Python reads

```
print(y)
```

This is a `print` *function call*, which makes Python print the value of `y` on the screen.[4] Simply stated, the value of `y` is sent to a ready-made piece of code named `print` (being a *function*—see Chap. 4, here called with a single *argument* named `y`), which then takes care of the printing. Thus, when `ball.py` is run, the number 1.2342 appears on the screen.

**Readability and Coding Style** In the code above, you see several blank lines too. These are simply skipped by Python and you may use as many as you want to make a nice and readable layout of the code. Similarly, you notice that spaces are introduced to each side of − in the "formula" and to each side of = in the assignments. These spaces are not required, i.e., Python will understand perfectly well without them. However, they contribute to readability and it is *recommended* to use them[5] as part of good coding style.[6] Had there been a + sign in there, it too should have a space to each side. To the contrary, no extra spaces are recommended for /, * and **.

**Several Statements on One Line** Note that it's allowed to have several statements on the same line if they are separated by a semi-colon. So, with our program here, we could have written, e.g.,

```
# Program for computing the height of a ball in vertical motion

# v0 is the intial velocity, g is the acceleration of gravity, t is time
v0 = 5; g = 9.81; t = 0.6

y = v0*t - 0.5*g*t**2        # vertical position

print(y)
```

In general, however, readability is easily degraded this way, e.g., making commenting more difficult, so it should be done with care.

**Assignments like a=2*a**

Frequently, you will meet assignment statements in which the variable name on the left hand side (of =) *also* appears in the expression on the right hand side. Take, e.g., `a = 2*a`. Python would then, according to its rules, *first* compute the expression on the right hand side with the current value of `a` and *then* let the result become the updated value of `a` through the assignment (the updated value of `a` is placed in a new "box" in computer memory).

---

[4] In Python 2.7, this would have been a *print command* reading `print y`.

[5] Be aware that in certain situations programmers do skip such spaces, e.g., when listing arguments in function calls, as you will learn more about in Chap. 4.

[6] You might like to check out the style guide for Python coding at https://www.python.org/dev/peps/pep-0008/.

### 1.2.3 Why Use Variables?

But why do we introduce variables at all? Would it not be just as fine, or even simpler, to just use the numbers directly in the formula?

If we did, using the same numerical values, ball.py would become even shorter, reading

```
# Program for computing the height of a ball in vertical motion

y = 5*0.6 - 0.5*9.81*0.6**2          # vertical position

print(y)
```

What is wrong with this? After all, we do get the correct result when running the code!

**Coding and Mathematical Formulation** If you compare this coded formula with the corresponding mathematical formulation

$$y = v_0t - 0.5gt^2,$$

the equivalence between code and mathematics is *not* as clear now as in our original program ball.py, where the formula was coded as

```
y = v0*t - 0.5*g*t**2
```

In our little example here, this may not seem dramatic. Generally, however, you better believe that when, e.g., trying to find errors in code that lacks clear equivalence to the corresponding mathematical formulation, human code interpretation typically gets *much* harder and it might take you a while to track down those bugs!

**Changing Numerical Values** In addition, if we would like to redo the computation for another point in time, say $t = 0.9$ s, we would have to *change the code in two places* to arrive at the new code line

```
y = 5*0.9 - 0.5*9.81*0.9**2
```

You may think that this is not a problem, but imagine some other formula (and program) where the same number enters in a 100 places! Are you certain that you can do the right edit in all those places without any mistakes?[7] You should realize that by using a variable, you get away with *changing in one place* only! So, to change the point in time from 0.6 to 0.9 in our original program ball.py, we could simply change t = 0.6 into t = 0.9. That would be it! Quick and much safer than editing in many places.

[7] Using the editor to replace 0.6 in all places might seem like a quick fix, but you would have to be sure you did not change 0.6 in the wrong places. For example, another number in the code, e.g. 0.666, could easily be turned into 0.966, unless you were careful.

### 1.2.4 Mathematical Notation Versus Coding

Make sure you understand that, from the outset, we had a pure mathematical formulation of our formula

$$y = v_0 t - 0.5gt^2,$$

which does not contain any connection to programming at all. Remember, this formula was derived hundreds of years ago, long before computers entered the scene! When we next wrote a piece of code that applied this formula, that code had to *obey* the rules of the programming language, which in this case is Python. This means, for example, that multiplication *had to* be written with a star, simply because that is the way multiplication is coded in Python. In some other programming language, the multiplication could in principle have been coded otherwise, but the mathematical formulation would still read the same.

We have seen how the equals sign (=) is interpreted in Python code. This interpretation is very different from the interpretation in mathematics, as might be illustrated by the following little example. In mathematics, $x = 2 - x$ would imply that $2x = 2$, giving $x = 1$. In Python code, however, a code line like `x = 2 - x` would be interpreted, *not* as an equation, but rather as an assignment statement: compute the right hand side by subtracting the current value of `x` from 2 and let the result be the new value of `x`. In the code, the new value of `x` could thus be anything, all depending on the value `x` had above the assignment statement!

### 1.2.5 Write and Run Your First Program

Reading *only* does not teach you computer programming: you have to program yourself and practice heavily before you master mathematical problem solving via programming. In fact, this is very much like learning to swim. Nobody can do that by just reading about it! You simply have to practice real swimming to get good at it. Therefore, it is crucial at this stage that you start writing and running Python programs. We just went through the program `ball.py` above, so let us next write and run that code.

But first a warning: there are many things that must come together in the right way for `ball.py` to run correctly. There might be problems with your Python installation, with your writing of the program (it is very easy to introduce errors!), or with the location of the file, just to mention some of the most common difficulties for beginners. Fortunately, such problems are solvable, and if you do not understand how to fix the problem, ask somebody. Very often the guy next to you experienced the same problem and has already fixed it!

Start up Spyder and, in the editor (left pane), type in each line of the program `ball.py` shown earlier. Then you save the program (select `File` -> `save as`) where you prefer and finally run it (select `Run` -> `Run`, ... or press F5). With a bit of luck, you should now get the number 1.2342 out in the rightmost lower pane in the Spyder GUI. If so, congratulations, you have just executed your first self-written computer program in Python!

The documentation for Spyder[8] might be useful to you. Also, more information on writing and running Python programs is found in Appendix A.4 herein.

**Why not a pocket calculator instead?**

Certainly, finding the answer as with the program above could easily have been done with a pocket calculator. No objections to that and no programming would have been needed. However, what if you would like to have the position of the ball for every milli-second of the flight? All that punching on the calculator would have taken you something like 4 h!

If you know how to program, however, you could modify the code above slightly, using a minute or two of writing, and easily get all the positions computed in one go within a second.

An even stronger argument, however, is that mathematical models from real life are often complicated and comprehensive. The pocket calculator cannot cope with such problems, even not the programmable ones, because their computational power and their programming tools are far too weak compared to what a real computer can offer.

**Write programs with a text editor**

When Python interprets some code in a file, it is concerned with every character in the file, exactly as it was typed in. This makes it troublesome to write the code into a file with word processors like, e.g., Microsoft Word, since such a program will insert extra characters, invisible to us, with information on how to format the text (e.g., the font size and type).

Such extra information is necessary for the text to be nicely formatted for the human eye. Python, however, will be much annoyed by the extra characters in the file inserted by a word processor. Therefore, it is fundamental that you write your program in a *text editor* where what you type on the keyboard is *exactly* the characters that appear in the file and what Python will later read. There are many text editors around. Some are stand-alone programs like Emacs, Vim, Gedit, Notepad++, and TextWrangler. Others are integrated in graphical development environments for Python, such as Spyder.

[8] See, e.g., https://www.spyder-ide.org/.

**What about units?**

The observant reader has noticed that the handling of quantities in `ball.py` did not include *units*, even though velocity (`v0`), acceleration (`g`) and time (`t`) of course do have the units of $\text{ms}^{-1}$, $\text{ms}^{-2}$, and s, respectively. Even though there are tools[a] in Python to include units, it is usually considered out of scope in a beginner's book on programming. So also in this book.

[a] See, e.g., https://github.com/juhasch/PhysicalQuantities, https://github.com/hgrecco/pint and https://github.com/hplgit/parampool if you are curious.

## 1.3 A Python Program with a Library Function

Imagine you stand on a distance, say 10.0 m away, watching someone throwing a ball upwards. A straight line from you to the ball will then make an angle with the horizontal that increases and decreases as the ball goes up and down. Let us consider the ball at a particular moment in time, at which it has a height of 10.0 m. What is the angle of the line then?

Well, we do know (with, or without, a calculator) that the answer is 45°. However, when learning to code, it is generally a good idea to deal with *simple* problems with known answers. Simplicity ensures that the problem is well understood before writing any code. Also, knowing the answer allows an easy check on what your coding has produced when the program is run.

Before thinking of writing a program, one should always formulate the *algorithm*, i.e., the recipe for what kind of calculations that must be performed. Here, if the ball is $x$ m away and $y$ m up in the air, it makes an angle $\theta$ with the ground, where $\tan\theta = y/x$. The angle is then $\tan^{-1}(y/x)$.

**The Program** Let us make a Python program for doing these calculations. We introduce names `x` and `y` for the position data $x$ and $y$, and the descriptive name `angle` for the angle $\theta$. The program is stored in a file `ball_angle_first_try.py`:

```
x = 10.0                    # Horizontal position
y = 10.0                    # Vertical position

angle = atan(y/x)

print((angle/pi)*180)
```

Before we turn our attention to the running of this program, let us take a look at one new thing in the code. The line `angle = atan(y/x)`, illustrates how the *function* `atan`, corresponding to $\tan^{-1}$ in mathematics, is *called* with the ratio `y/x` as *argument*. The `atan` function takes one argument, and the computed value is *returned* from `atan`. This means that where we see `atan(y/x)`, a computation is performed ($\tan^{-1}(y/x)$) and the result "replaces" the text `atan(y/x)`. This is actually no more magic than if we had written just `y/x`: then the computation of y/x would take place, and the result of that division would replace the text y/x. Thereafter, the result is assigned to angle on the left-hand side of =.

Note that the trigonometric functions, such as atan, work with angles in radians. Thus, if we want the answer in degrees, the return value of atan must be converted accordingly. This conversion is performed by the computation (angle/pi)*180. Two things happen in the print command: first, the computation of (angle/pi)*180 is performed, resulting in a number, and second, print prints that number. Again, we may think that the arithmetic expression is replaced by its result and then print starts working with that result.

**Running the Program** If we next execute ball_angle_first_try.py, we get an error message on the screen saying

```
NameError: name 'atan' is not defined
WARNING: Failure executing file: <ball_angle_first_try.py>
```

We have definitely run into trouble, but why? We are told that

```
name 'atan' is not defined
```

so apparently Python does not recognize this part of the code as anything familiar. On a pocket calculator the inverse tangent function is straightforward to use in a similar way as we have written in the code. In Python, however, this function is one of many that must be *imported* before use. A lot of functionality[9] is immediately available to us (from the *Python standard library*) as we start a new programming session, but much more functionality exists in additional Python libraries. To activate functionality from these libraries, we must explicitly import it. In Python, the atan function is grouped together with many other mathematical functions in a library *module* called math. To get access to atan in our program, we may write an *import statement*:

```
from math import atan
```

Inserting this statement at the top of the program and rerunning it, leads to a new problem: pi is not defined. The constant pi, representing $\pi$, is also available in the math module, but it has to be imported too. We can achieve this by including both items atan and pi in the import statement,

```
from math import atan, pi
```

With this latter statement in place, we save the code as ball_angle.py:

```
from math import atan, pi

x = 10.0                # Horizontal position
y = 10.0                # Vertical position

angle = atan(y/x)

print((angle/pi)*180)
```

This script correctly produces 45.0 as output when executed.

[9] https://docs.python.org/3/library/functions.html.

Alternatively, we could use the import statement `import math`. This would require `atan` and `pi` to be *prefixed* with `math`, however, as shown in `ball_angle_prefix.py`:

```
import math

x = 10.0             # Horizontal position
y = 10.0             # Vertical position

angle = math.atan(y/x)

print (angle/math.pi)*180
```

The essential difference between the two import techniques shown here, is the prefix required by the latter. Both techniques are commonly used and represent the two basic ways of importing library code in Python. Importing code is an evident part of Python programming, so we better shed some more light on it.

## 1.4 Importing from Modules and Packages

At first, it may seem cumbersome to have code in different libraries, since it means you have to know (or find out) what resides in which library.[10] Also, there are many libraries around in addition to the Python standard library itself. To your comfort, you come a long way with just a few libraries, and for easy reference, the handful of libraries used in this book is listed below (Sect. 1.4.5). Having everything available at any time would be convenient, but this would also mean that computer memory would be filled with a lot of unused information, causing less memory to be available for computations on big data. Python has so many libraries, with so much functionality, that importing what is needed is indeed a very sensible strategy.

**Where to Place Import Statements?** The general recommendation is to place import statements at the top of a program, making them easy to spot.

### 1.4.1 Importing for Use *Without* Prefix

The need to prefix item names is avoided when import statements are on the form

```
from some_library import ...     # i.e., items will be used without prefix
```

as we saw in `ball_angle.py` above. Without prefixing, coded formulas often become easier to read, since code generally comes "closer" to mathematical writing. On the other hand, it is less evident where imported items "come from" and this may complicate matters, particularly when trying to understand more comprehensive code written by others.

[10] There is a built-in function called `dir`, which gives all the names defined in a library module. Another built-in function called `help` prints documentation. To see how they work, write (in Spyder, pane down to the right) `import math` followed by `dir(math)` or `help(math)`.

**Importing Individual Items** With ball_angle.py, we just learned that the import statement

```
from math import atan, pi
```

made the atan function and pi available to the program. To bring in even more functionality from math, the import statement could simply have been extended with the relevant items, say

```
from math import atan, pi, sin, cos, log
```

and so on.

**Having Several Import Statements** Very often, we need to import functionality from several libraries. This is straight forward, as we may show by combining imports from math with imports from the useful *Numerical Python* (or NumPy) library,[11] named numpy in Python:

```
from math import atan, pi, sin, cos, log
from numpy import zeros, linspace
```

Right now, do not worry what the functions zeros and linspace do, we will explain and use them soon.

**Importing All Items with "Import *"** The approach of importing individual items (atan, pi, etc.) might appear less attractive if you need many of them in your program. There is another way, though, but it should be used with care, for reasons to be explained. In fact, many programmers will advice you *not* to use it at all, unless you know very well what you are doing. With this import technique, the list of items in the import statement is exchanged with simply a star (i.e., *). The import statement then appears as

```
from some_library import *     # import all items from some_library
```

which with the math library reads

```
from math import *            # import all items from math
```

This will cause *all* items from math to be imported, however, also the ones you do *not* need! So, with this "lazy" import technique, Python has to deal with a lot of names that are not used. Like when importing individual items, items are used without prefix.

**Disadvantage: No Prefix Allows Name Conflicts!** When importing so that items are written without prefix, there is a potential problem with *name conflicts*. Let us illustrate the point with a simple example. Assume that, being new to Python, we want to write a little program for checking out some of the functions that the language has got to offer.

Our first candidate could be the exponential function and we might like to compute and print out $e^t$ for $t = 0, 1, 2$. A fellow student explains us how a function exp in the numpy library allows our calculations to be done with a single function

[11] The NumPy library (http://www.numpy.org/) is included in Anaconda. If you have not installed Anaconda, you may have to install NumPy separately.

call. This sounds good to us, so based on what we were told, we start writing our program as

```
from numpy import exp

x = exp([0, 1, 2])                # do all 3 calculations
print(x)                          # print all 3 results
```

The script runs without any problems and the printed numbers seem fine,

```
[ 1.          2.71828183  7.3890561 ]
```

Moving on, we want to test a number of functions from the `math` library (`cos`, `sin`, `tan`, etc.). Since we foresee testing quite many functions, we choose the "lazy" import technique and plan to extend the code with one function at a time.

Extending the program with a simple usage of the `cos` function, it reads

```
from numpy import exp
from math import *

x = exp([0, 1, 2])                # do all 3 calculations
print(x)                          # print all 3 results

y = cos(0)
print(y)
```

Running this version of the script, however, we get a longer printout (most of which is irrelevant at this point) ending with

```
TypeError: a float is required
```

Clearly, something has gone wrong! But why?

The explanation is the following. With the second import statement, i.e.,

```
from math import *
```

all items from `math` were imported, including a function from `math` that is *also* named `exp`. That is, there are two functions in play here that both go by the name `exp`! One `exp` function is found in the `numpy` library, while the other `exp` function is found in the `math` library, and the implementations of these two are *different*. This now becomes a problem, since the last imported `exp` function silently "takes the place" of the previous one, so that the name `exp` hereafter will be associated with the `exp` function from `math`! Thus, when Python interprets `x = exp([0, 1, 2])`, it tries to use `exp` from `math` for the calculations, but that version of `exp` can only take a single number (real or integer) as input argument, not several (as `exp` from `numpy` can). This mismatch then triggers the error message[12] and causes program execution to stop before reaching `y = cos(0)`.

Similar name conflicts may arise also with other functions than `exp`, since a lot of items appear with identical names in different libraries (e.g., also `cos`, `sin`, `tan`, and many more, exist with different implementations in both `numpy` and `math`). The fact that programmers may create, and share, their own libraries containing self

---

[12] It should be mentioned here, that error messages can not always be very accurate. With some experience, however, you will find them very helpful at many occasions. More about error messages later (Sect. 1.7).

chosen item names, makes it even more obvious that "name conflicts" is an issue that should be understood.

Several other coding alternatives would have helped the situation here. For example, instead of `from math import *`, we could switch the star (`*`) with a list of item names, i.e. as `from math import cos` for the present version. As long as we stay away from (by a mistake) importing `exp` also from `math`, no name conflict will occur and the program will run fine. Alternatively, we could simply have switched the order of the import statements (can you explain[13] why?), or, we could have moved the import statement `from math import *` down, so that it comes *after* the statement `x = exp([0, 1, 2])` and *before* the line `y = cos(0)`. Note that, in Python 3, import statements on the form `from module import *` are only allowed at module level, i.e., when placed inside functions, they give an error message.

Next, we will address the safer "standard" way of importing.

### 1.4.2 Importing for Use *with* Prefix

A safer implementation of our program would use the "standard" method of importing, which we saw a glimpse of in `ball_angle_prefix.py` above. With this import technique, the code would read

```
import numpy
import math

x = numpy.exp([0, 1, 2])                # do all 3 calculations
print(x)                                # print all 3 results

y = math.cos(0)
print(y)
```

We note that the import statements are on the form

```
import some_library       # i.e., items will be used with prefix
```

and that item names belonging to `some_library` are *prefixed* with `some_library` and a "dot". This means that, e.g., `numpy.exp([0, 1, 2])` refers to the (unique) `exp` function from the `numpy` library. When the import statements are on the "standard" form, the prefix is required. Leaving it out gives an error message. This version of the program runs fine, producing the expected output.

With the prefixing method, the order of imports does not matter, as there is no doubt where the functions (or items) come from. At the same time, though, it is clear that prefixing does *not* make it any easier for a human to read the "math meaning" out of the code. In mathematical writing, there would be no prefix, so a prefix will just complicate the job for a human interpreter, and more so the more comprehensive the expressions are.

---

[13] By switching the order, Python would first read `from math import *` and would import everything, including `exp`, from `math`. Then, it would read `from numpy import exp`, which would cause Python to import the `numpy` version of `exp`, which effectively means that the `math` version of `exp` is "overwritten" by the one from `numpy`. At any later point in the code then, Python will associate the word `exp` with the `numpy` function.

### 1.4.3 Imports with Name Change

Whether we import for use with or without prefix, we may *change names* of the imported items by minor adjustments of the import statements. Introducing such name changes in our program and saving this final version as `check_functions.py`, it reads

```
import numpy as np
import math as m

x = np.exp([0, 1, 2])                  # do all 3 calculations
print(x)                               # print all 3 results

y = m.cos(0)
print(y)
```

Effectively, the module names in this program now become `np` and `m` (by our own choice) instead of `numpy` and `math`, respectively. We still enjoy the safety of prefixing and notice that such name changes might bring computer coded expressions closer to mathematical writing and thus ease human interpretation.

When importing library items for use without prefix, name changes can be done, e.g., like

```
from math import cos as c, sin as s

print(c(0) + s(0))
```

### 1.4.4 Importing from Packages

Modules may be grouped into *packages*, often together with functions, variables, and more. We may import items (modules, functions, etc.) from such packages also, but the appearance of an import statement will then depend on the structure of the package in question. We leave out the details[14] and just exemplify with two packages often used in this book.

The `numpy` library used above *is*, in fact, a package and we saw how it could be used with different import statements, just as if it had been a module. Note that the import statement

```
import numpy as np              # standard way of importing numpy
```

is the standard way of importing `numpy`, i.e., also the "nickname" `np` is standard. This will be the standard import technique for `numpy` also in our book, meaning that we will generally use `numpy` items with the `np` prefix. We will deviate from this at times, typically during brief interactive sessions (see Sect. 2.1), in which case we will import items explicitly specified by name.

Another popular package you will meet often in this book, is the plotting library `matplotlib` (Sect. 1.5), used for generating and handling plots. The standard import statement, including the "nickname", is then

```
import matplotlib.pyplot as plt         # standard way of importing pyplot
```

[14] If you are curious, check for more details at https://docs.python.org/3.6/tutorial/modules.html.

Here, `pyplot` is a module in the `matplotlib` package[15] that is named `plt` when imported. Thus, when imported this way, all items from `pyplot` must have the prefix `plt`. We will stick to this import and naming standard for `pyplot` also in the present book, whenever plotting is on the agenda.

### 1.4.5 The Modules/Packages Used in This Book

Some readers might be curious to know which libraries are used in this book (apart from the modules we make ourselves). Well, here they are:

- `math`—see, e.g., `ball_angle.py`, Sect. 1.3.
- `numpy`—see, e.g., `check_functions.py` above.
- `matplotlib.pyplot`—see, e.g., `ball_plot.py`, Sect. 1.5.
- `random`—see, e.g., `throw_2_dice.py` in Sect. 2.4.
- `sympy`—see, e.g., Sect. 5.3.
- `timeit`—see, e.g., Sect. 5.6.
- `sys`—see, e.g., Sect. 7.2.2.

These libraries are all well known to Python programmers. The three first ones (`math`, `numpy` and `matplotlib.pyplot`) are used repeatedly throughout the text, while the remaining ones (`random`, `sympy`, `timeit` and `sys`) appear just occasionally.

Not listed, are two modules that are used just once each, the `keyword` module (Sect. 2.2) and the `os` module (Sect. 9.2.4). It should be mentioned that we also use a package called `odespy` (Sect. 8.4.6), previously developed by one of the authors (Langtangen).

## 1.5 A Python Program with Vectorization and Plotting

We return to the problem where a ball is thrown up in the air and we have a formula for the vertical position $y$ of the ball. Say we are interested in $y$ at every milli-second for the first second of the flight. This requires repeating the calculation of $y = v_0t - 0.5gt^2$ one thousand times. As we will see, the computed heights appear very informative when presented graphically with time, as opposed to a long printout of all the numbers.

**The Program** In Python, the calculations and the visualization of the curve may be done with the program `ball_plot.py`, reading

```
import numpy as np
import matplotlib.pyplot as plt

v0 = 5
g = 9.81
```

[15] The `matplotlib` package (https://matplotlib.org/) comes with Anaconda. If you have not installed Anaconda, you may have to install `matplotlib` separately.

```
t = np.linspace(0, 1, 1001)

y = v0*t - 0.5*g*t**2

plt.plot(t, y)          # plots all y coordinates vs. all t coordinates
plt.xlabel('t (s)')     # places the text t (s) on x-axis
plt.ylabel('y (m)')     # places the text y (m) on y-axis
plt.show()              # displays the figure
```

This program produces a plot of the vertical position with time, as seen in Fig. 1.1. As you notice, the code lines from the `ball.py` program in Sect. 1.2 have not changed much, but the height is now computed and plotted for a thousand points in time!

Let us take a closer look at this program. At the top, we recognize the import statements

```
import numpy as np
import matplotlib.pyplot as plt
```

As we know by now, these statements imply that items from `numpy` and `matplotlib.pyplot` must be prefixed with `np` and `plt`, respectively.

**The `linspace` Function** Next, there is a call to the function `linspace` from the `numpy` library. When `n` evenly spaced floating point numbers are sought on an interval $[a, b]$, `linspace` may generally be called like this:

```
np.linspace(a, b, n)
```

This means that the call

```
t = np.linspace(0, 1, 1001)
```

creates 1001 coordinates between 0 and 1, inclusive at both ends. The mathematically inclined reader might agree that 1001 coordinates correspond to 1000 equal-

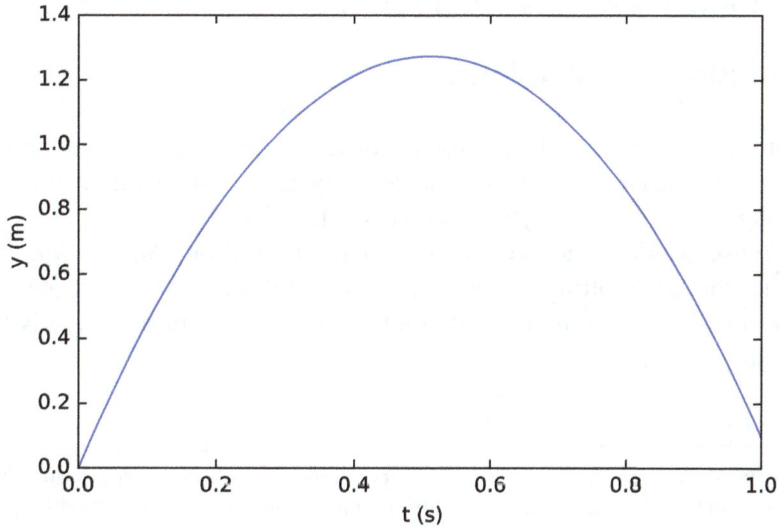


Fig. 1.1 Plot generated by the script `ball_plot.py` showing the vertical position of the ball (computed for a thousand points in time)

sized intervals in [0, 1] and that the coordinates are then given by $t_i = \frac{1-0}{1000}i = \frac{i}{1000}$, $i = 0, 1, \ldots, 1000$.

The object returned from `linspace` is an *array*, i.e., a certain collection of (in this case) numbers. Through the assignment, this array gets the name `t`. If we like, we may think of the array `t` as a collection of "boxes" in computer memory (each containing a number) that collectively go by the name `t` (later, we will demonstrate how these boxes are *numbered* consecutively from zero and upwards, so that each "box" may be identified and used individually).

**Vectorization** When we start computing with `t` in

```
y = v0*t - 0.5*g*t**2
```

the right hand side is computed for every number in `t` (i.e., every $t_i$ for $i = 0, 1, \ldots, 1000$), yielding a similar collection of 1001 numbers in the result `y`, which (automatically) also becomes an array!

This technique of computing all numbers "in one chunk" is referred to as *vectorization*. When it can be used, it is very handy, since both the amount of code and computation time is reduced compared to writing a corresponding loop[16] (Chap. 3) for doing the same thing.

**Plotting** The plotting commands are new, but simple:

```
plt.plot(t, y)          # plots all y coordinates vs. all t coordinates
plt.xlabel('t (s)')     # places the text t (s) on x-axis
plt.ylabel('y (m)')     # places the text y (m) on y-axis
plt.show()              # displays the figure
```

At this stage, you are encouraged to do Exercise 1.4. It builds on the example above, but is much simpler both with respect to the mathematics and the amount of numbers involved.

## 1.6 Plotting, Printing and Input Data

### 1.6.1 Plotting with Matplotlib

Often, computations and analyses produce data that are best illustrated graphically. Thus, programming languages usually have many good tools available for producing and working with plots, and Python is no exception.[17]

In this book, we shall stick to the excellent plotting library *Matplotlib*, which has become the standard plotting package in Python. Below, we demonstrate just a few of the possibilities that come with Matplotlib, much more information is found on the Matplotlib website.[18]

---

[16] It should be mentioned, though, that the computations are still done with loops "behind the scenes" (coded in C or Fortran). They generally run much quicker than the Python loops we write ourselves.

[17] In Sect. 9.2.4 we give a brief example of how plots may be turned into videos.

[18] https://matplotlib.org/index.html.

**A Single Curve** In Fig. 1.1, we saw a nice and smooth curve, showing how the height of a ball developed with time. The reader should realize that, even though the curve is continuous and *apparently* smooth, it is generated from a collection of points only. That is, *for the chosen points in time*, we have computed the height. For times in between, we have computed nothing! So, in principle, we actually do not know what the height is there. However, if only the time step between consecutive height computations is "small enough", the ball can not experience any significant change in its state of motion. Thus, inserting straight lines between two and two consecutive data points will be a good approximation. This is exactly what Python does, unless otherwise is specified. With "many" data points, as in Fig. 1.1, the curve appears smooth.

We saw previously, in `ball_plot.py`, how an array `y` (heights) could be plotted against another corresponding array `t` (points in time) with the statement

```
plt.plot(t, y)
```

A plot command like this is very typical and often just what we prefer, for example, in our case with the ball.

It is also possible, however, to plot an array without involving any second array at all. With reference to `ball_plot.py`, this means that `y` could have been plotted without any mention of `t`, and to do that, one could write the plot command rather like

```
plt.plot(y)
```

The curve would then have looked just like the one in Fig. 1.1, except that the x-axis would span the `y` array indices from 0 to 1000 instead of the corresponding points in time (check it and see for yourself).

**Quickly testing a (minor) code change**

Let us take the opportunity here, to mention how many programmers would go about to check the alternative plot command just mentioned. In `ball_plot.py`, one would typically just comment out the original lines and insert alternative code for these, i.e., as

```
#plt.plot(t, y)
#plt.xlabel('t (s)')
plt.plot(y)
plt.xlabel('Array indices')
```

One would then run the code and observe the impact of the change, which in this case is the modified plot described above.

After running the modified code, there are, generally, two alternatives. Should the original version be kept or should we make the change permanent? With the present ball example, most of us would prefer the original plot, so we would change the code back to its original form (remember to check that it works as before!).

When the code change to test is more comprehensive, it is much better to make a separate copy of the whole program, and then do the testing there.

The characteristics of a plotted line may also be changed in many ways with just minor modifications of the plot command. For example, a black line is achieved with

```
plt.plot(t, y, 'k')      # k - black, b - blue, r - red, g - green, ...
```

Other colors could be achieved by exchanging the `k` with certain other letters. For example, using `b`, you get a blue line, `r` gives a red line, while `g` makes the line green. In addition, the line style may be changed, either alone, or together with a color change. For example,

```
plt.plot(t, y, '--')      # default color, dashed line
```

```
plt.plot(t, y, 'r--')     # red and dashed line
```

```
plt.plot(t, y, 'g:')      # green and dotted line
```

Note that to avoid destroying a previously generated plot, you may precede your plot command by

```
plt.figure()
```

This causes a new figure to be created alongside any already present.

**Plotting Points Only** When there are not too many data points, it is sometimes desirable to plot each data point as a "point", rather than representing all the data points with a line. To illustrate, we may consider our case with the ball again, but this time computing the height each 0.1 s, rather than every millisecond. In `ball_plot.py`, we would then have to change our call to `linspace` into

```
t = np.linspace(0, 1, 11)    # 11 values give 10 intervals of 0.1
```

Note that we need to give 11 as the final argument here, since there will be 10 intervals of 0.1 s when 11 equally distributed values on [0, 1] are asked for. In addition, we would have to change the plot command to specify the plotting of data points as "points". To mark the points themselves, we may use one of many different alternatives, e.g., a circle (the lower case letter `o`) or a star (`*`). Using a star, for example, the plot command could read

```
plt.plot(t, y, '*')      # default color, points marked with *
```

With these changes, the plot from Fig. 1.1 would change as seen in Fig. 1.2.

Of course, not only can we choose between different kinds of point markers, but also their color may be specified. Some examples are:

```
plt.plot(t, y, 'r*')      # points marked with * in red
```

```
plt.plot(t, y, 'bo')      # points marked with o in blue
```

```
plt.plot(t, y, 'g+')      # points marked with + in green
```

When are the data points "too many" for plotting data points as points (and not as a line)? If plotting the data points with point markers and those markers *overlap* in the plot, the points will not appear as points, but rather as a very thick line. This is hardly what you want.

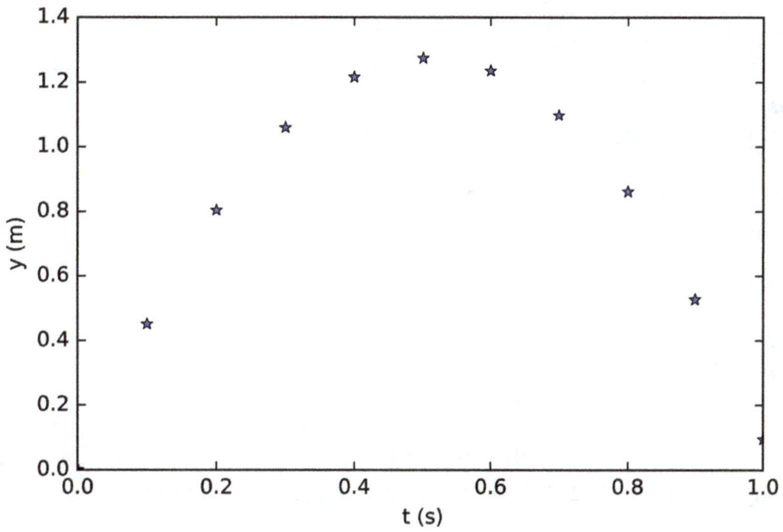


**Fig. 1.2** Vertical position of the ball computed and plotted for every 0.1 s

**Decorating a Plot** We have seen how the code lines `plt.xlabel('t (s)')` and `plt.ylabel('y (m)')` in `ball_plot.py` put labels `t (s)` and `y (m)` on the t- and y-axis, respectively. There are other ways to enrich a plot as well.

One thing, is to add a *legend* so that the curve itself gets labeled. With `ball_plot.py`, we could get the legend `v0*t - 0.5*g*t**2`, for example, by coding

```
plt.legend(['v0*t - 0.5*g*t**2'])
```

When there is more than a single curve, a legend is particularly important of course (see section below on "multiple curves" for a plot example).

Another thing, is to add a *grid*. This is useful when you want a more detailed impression of the curve and may be coded in this way,

```
plt.grid('on')
```

A plot may also get a title on top. To get a title like `This is a great title`, for example, we could write

```
plt.title('This is a great title')
```

Sometimes, the default ranges appearing on the axes are not what you want them to be. This may then be specified by a code line like

```
plt.axis([0, 1.2, -0.2, 1.5])    # x in [0, 1.2] and y in [-0.2, 1.5]
```

All statements just explained will be demonstrated in the next section, when we show how multiple curves may be plotted together in a single plot.

**Multiple Curves in the Same Plot** Assume we want to plot $f(t) = t^2$ and $g(t) = e^t$ in the same plot for $t$ on the interval $[-2, 2]$. The following script (`plot_multiple_curves.py`) will accomplish this task:

```
import numpy as np
import matplotlib.pyplot as plt
```

```
t = np.linspace(-2, 2, 100)    # choose 100 points in time interval

f_values = t**2
g_values = np.exp(t)

plt.plot(t, f_values, 'r', t, g_values, 'b--')
plt.xlabel('t')
plt.ylabel('f and g')
plt.legend(['t**2', 'e**t'])
plt.title('Plotting of two functions (t**2 and e**t)')
plt.grid('on')
plt.axis([-3, 3, -1, 10])
plt.show()
```

In this code, you recognize the commands explained just above. Their impact on the plot may be seen in Fig. 1.3, which is produced when the program is executed.

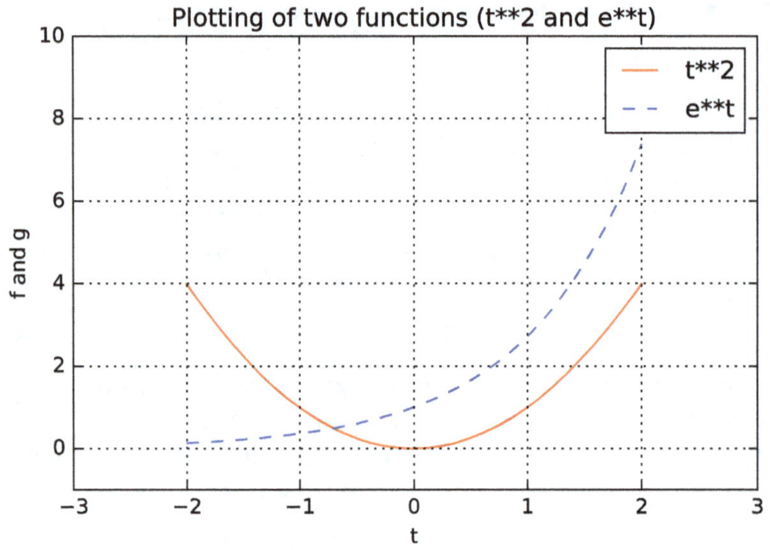


**Fig. 1.3** The functions $f(t) = t^2$ and $g(t) = e^t$

In addition, you see how

```
plt.plot(t, f_values, 'r', t, g_values, 'b--')
```

causes *both* curves to be seen in the same plot. Notice the structure here, within the parenthesis, we first describe plotting of the one curve with `t, f_values, 'r'`, before plotting of the second curve is specified by `t, g_values, 'b--'`. These two "plot specifications" are separated by a comma. Had there been more curves to plot in the same plot, we would simply extend the list in a similar way. For each curve, color and line style is specified independently of the other curve specifications in the plot command (no specification gives default appearance). Furthermore, you notice how

```
plt.legend(['t**2', 'e**t'])
```

creates the right labelling of the curves. Note that the order of curve specifications in the plot command must be the same as the order of legend specifications in the legend command. In the plot command above, we first specify the plotting of f_values and then g_values. In the legend command, t**2 should thus appear *before* e**t (as it does).

**Multiple Plots in One Figure** With the subplot command you may combine several plots into one. We may demonstrate this with the script two_plots_one_fig.py, which reproduces Figs. 1.2 and 1.3 as one:

```
import numpy as np
import matplotlib.pyplot as plt

plt.subplot(2, 1, 1)          # 2 rows, 1 column, plot number 1
v0 = 5
g = 9.81
t = np.linspace(0, 1, 11)
y = v0*t - 0.5*g*t**2
plt.plot(t, y, '*')
plt.xlabel('t (s)')
plt.ylabel('y (m)')
plt.title('Ball moving vertically')

plt.subplot(2, 1, 2)          # 2 rows, 1 column, plot number 2
t = np.linspace(-2, 2, 100)
f_values = t**2
g_values = np.exp(t)
plt.plot(t, f_values, 'r', t, g_values, 'b--')
plt.xlabel('t')
plt.ylabel('f and g')
plt.legend(['t**2', 'e**t'])
plt.title('Plotting of two functions (t**2 and e**t)')
plt.grid('on')
plt.axis([-3, 3, -1, 10])

plt.tight_layout()            # make subplots fit figure area
plt.show()
```

You observe that subplot appears in two places, first as plt.subplot(2, 1, 1), then as plt.subplot(2, 1, 2). This may be explained as follows. With a code line like

```
plt.subplot(r, c, n)
```

we tell Python that in an arrangement of r by c subplots, r being the number of rows and c being the number of columns, we address subplot number n, counted row-wise. So, in two_plots_one_fig.py, when we first write

```
plt.subplot(2, 1, 1)
```

Python understands that we want to plot in subplot number 1 in an arrangement with two rows and one column of subplots. Further down, Python interprets

```
plt.subplot(2, 1, 2)
```

and understands that plotting now is supposed to occur in subplot number 2 of the same arrangement.

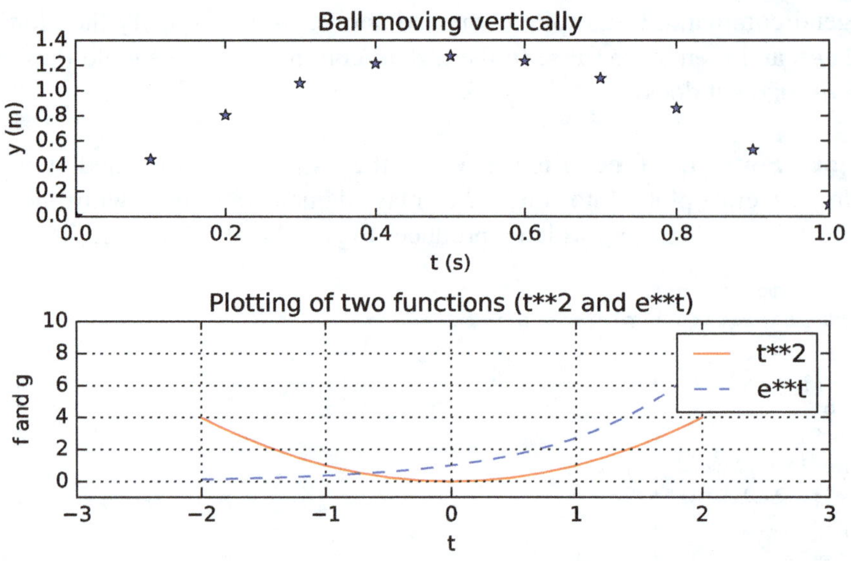


**Fig. 1.4** Ball trajectory and functions $f(t) = t^2$ and $g(t) = e^t$ as two plots in one figure

Note that, when dealing with subplots, some overlapping of subplots may occur. Usually, this is solved nicely by inserting the following line (as at the end of our code),

```
plt.tight_layout()
```

This will cause subplot parameters to be automatically adjusted, so that the subplots fit in to the figure area.

The plot generated by the code is shown in Fig. 1.4.

**Making a Hardcopy** Saving a figure to file is achieved by

```
plt.savefig('some_plot.png')    # PNG format
plt.savefig('some_plot.pdf')    # PDF format
plt.savefig('some_plot.jpg')    # JPG format
plt.savefig('some_plot.eps')    # Encanspulated PostScript format
```

### 1.6.2 Printing: The String Format Method

We have previously seen that

```
print(y)
```

will print the value of the variable y. In an equally simple way, the line

```
print('This is some text')
```

will print `This is some text` (note the enclosing single quotes in the call to `print`). Often, however, it is of interest to print variable values together with some descriptive text. As shown below, such printing can be done nicely and controlled in Python, since the language basically allows text and numbers to be mixed and formatted in any way you need.

**One Variable and Text Combined** Assume there is a variable v1 in your program, and that v1 has the value 10.0, for example. If you want your code to print the value of v1, so that the printout reads

```
v1 is 10.0
```

you can achieve that with the following line in your program:

```
print('v1 is {}'.format(v1))
```

This is a call to the function print with "an argument composed of two parts". The first part reads v1 is {} enclosed in single quotes (note the single quotes, they must be there!), while the second part is .format(v1). The single quotes of the first part means that it is a *string* (alternatively, double quotes may be used).[19] That string contains a pair of curly brackets {}, which acts as a *placeholder*. The brackets tell Python *where* to place the value of, in this case, v1, as specified in the second part .format(v1). So, the formatting creates the string v1 is 10.0, which then gets printed by print.

**Several Variables and Text Combined** Often, we have more variables to print, and with two variables v1 and v2, we could print them by

```
print('v1 is {}, v2 is {}'.format(v1, v2))
```

In this case, there are *two* placeholders {}, and—note the following: *the order* of v1 and v2 given in .format(v1, v2) will *dictate* the order in which values are filled into the preceding string. That is, reading the string from left to right, the value of v1 is placed where the first {} is found, while the value of v2 is placed where the second {} is located.

So, if v1 and v2 have values 10.0 and 20.0, respectively, the printout will read

```
v1 is 10.0, v2 is 20.0
```

When printing the values of several variables, it is often natural to use one line for each. This may be achieved by using \n as

```
print('v1 is {} \nv2 is {}'.format(v1, v2))    # \n gives new line
```

which will produce

```
v1 is 10.0
v2 is 20.0
```

We could print the values of more variables by a straight forward extension of what was shown here.

Note that, if we had accidentally switched the order of the variables as

```
print('v1 is {}, \nv2 is {}'.format(v2, v1))
```

where .format(v2, v1) is used instead of .format(v1, v2)), we would have got no error message, just an erroneous printout where the values are switched:

```
v1 is 20.0
v2 is 10.0
```

[19] Previously, we have met objects of type *int* and *float*. A string is an object of type *str*.

So, make sure the order of the arguments is correct. An alternative is to name the arguments.

**Naming the Arguments** If we name the arguments (`v1` and `v2` are arguments to `format`), we get the correct printout whether we call `print` as

```
print('v1 is {v1}, \nv2 is {v2}'.format(v1=v1, v2=v2))
```

or, switching the order,

```
print('v1 is {v1}, \nv2 is {v2}'.format(v2=v2, v1=v1))
```

Note that the names introduced do not have to be the same as the variable names, i.e., "any" names would do. Thus, if we (for the sake of demonstration) rather use the names `a` and `b`, any of the following calls to `print` would work just as fine (try it!):

```
print('v1 is {a}, \nv2 is {b}'.format(a=v1, b=v2))
```

or

```
print('v1 is {a}, \nv2 is {b}'.format(b=v2, a=v1))
```

Controlling the printout like we have demonstrated this far, may be sufficient in many cases. However, as we will see next, even more printing details can be controlled.

**Formatting More Details** Often, we want to control *how* numbers are formatted. For example, we may want to write 1/3 as `0.33` or `3.3333e-01` ($3.3333 \cdot 10^{-1}$), and as the following example will demonstrate, such details may indeed be specified in the argument to `print`. The essential new thing then, is that we supply the placeholders `{}` with some extra information in between the brackets.

Suppose we have a real number 12.89643, an integer 42, and a text `'some message'` that we want to write out in the following two different ways:

```
real=12.896, integer=42, string=some message
real=1.290e+01, integer=   42, string=some message
```

The real number is first to be written in *decimal notation* with three decimals, as `12.896`, but afterwards in *scientific notation* as `1.290e+01`. The integer should first be written as compactly as possible, while the second time, 42 should be placed in a five character wide text field.

The following program, `formatted_print.py`, produces the requested output:

```
r = 12.89643             # real number
i = 42                   # integer
s = 'some message'       # string    (equivalent: s = "some message")

print('real={:.3f}, integer={:d}, string={:s}'.format(r, i, s))
print('real={:9.3e}, integer={:5d}, string={:s}'.format(r, i, s))
```

Here, each placeholder carries a specification of what object *type* that will enter in the corresponding place, with `f` symbolizing a `float` (real number), `d` symbolizing an `int` (integer), and `s` symbolizing a `str` (string). Also, there is a specification of *how* each number is to be printed. Note the colon within the brackets, it must be there!

In the first call to `print`,

```
print('real={:.3f}, integer={:d}, string={:s}'.format(r, i, s))
```

`:.3f` tells Python that the floating point number `r` is to be written as compactly as possible in decimal notation with three decimals, `:d` tells Python that the integer `i` is to be written as compactly as possible, and `:s` tells Python to write the string `s`.

In the second call to `print`,

```
print('real={:9.3e}, integer={:5d}, string={:s}'.format(r, i, s))
```

the interpretation is the same, except that `r` and `i` now should be formatted according to `:9.3e` and `:5d`, respectively. For `r`, this means that its float value will be written in scientific notation (the `e`) with 3 decimals, in a field that has a width of 9 characters. As for `i`, its integer value will be written in a field of width 5 characters.

Other ways of formatting the numbers would also have been possible.[20] For example, specifying the printing of `r` rather as `:9.3f` (i.e., `f` instead of `e`), would give decimal notation, while with `:g`, Python itself would choose between scientific and decimal notation, automatically choosing the one resulting in the most compact output. Typically, scientific notation is appropriate for very small and very large numbers and decimal notation for the intermediate range.

**Printing with old string formatting**

There is another older string formatting that, when used with `print`, gives the same printout as the string format method. Since you will meet it frequently in Python programs found elsewhere, you better know about it. With this formatting, the calls to `print` in the previous example would rather read

```
print('real=%.3f, integer=%d, string=%s' % (r, i, s))
print('real=%9.3e, integer=%5d, string=%s' % (r, i, s))
```

As you might guess, the overall "structure" of the argument to `print` is the same as with the string format method, but, essentially, `%` is used instead of `{}` (with `:` inside) and `.format`.

**An Example: Printing Nicely Aligned Columns** A typical example of when formatted printing is required, arises when nicely aligned columns of numbers are to be printed. Suppose we want to print a column of $t$ values together with associated function values $g(t) = t \sin(t)$ in a second column.

We could achieve this in the following way (note that, repeating the same set of statements multiple times, like we do in the following code, is *not* good programming practice—one should use a `loop`. You will learn about loops in Chap. 3.)

```
from math import sin

t0 = 2
```

[20] https://docs.python.org/3/library/string.html#format-string-syntax.

```
dt = 0.55

t = t0 + 0*dt; g = t*sin(t)
print('{:6.2f} {:8.3f}'.format(t, g))

t = t0 + 1*dt; g = t*sin(t)
print('{:6.2f} {:8.3f}'.format(t, g))

t = t0 + 2*dt; g = t*sin(t)
print('{:6.2f} {:8.3f}'.format(t, g))
```

Running this program, we get the printout

```
  2.00     1.819
  2.55     1.422
  3.10     0.129
```

Observe that the columns are nicely aligned here. With the formatting, we effectively control the width of each column and also the number of decimals. The numbers in each column will then become nicely aligned under each other and written with the same precision.

To the contrary, if we had skipped the detailed formatting, and rather used a simpler call to `print` like

```
print(t, g)
```

the columns would be printed as

```
2.0 1.81859485365
2.55 1.42209347935
3.1 0.128900053543
```

Observe that the nice and easy-to-read structure of the printout now is gone.

### 1.6.3 Printing: The f-String

We should briefly also mention printing by use of *f-strings*. Above, we printed the values of variables `v1` and `v2`, being 10.0 and 20.0, respectively. One of the calls we used to `print` was (repeated here for easy reference)

```
print('v1 is {} \nv2 is {}'.format(v1, v2))    # \n gives new line
```

and it produced the output

```
v1 is 10.0
v2 is 20.0
```

However, if we rather skip `.format(v1, v2)`, and instead introduce an `f` in front of the string, we can produce the very same output by the following simpler call to `print`:

```
print(f'v1 is {v1} \nv2 is {v2}')
```

So, f-strings[21] are quite handy!

---

[21] Read more about f-strings at https://www.python.org/dev/peps/pep-0498.

**Printing Strings that Span Multiple Lines**

A handy way to print strings that run over several lines, is to use *triple double-quotes* (or, alternatively, *triple single-quotes*) like this:

```
print("""This is a long string that will run over several lines
         if we just manage to fill in
         enough words.""")
```

The output will then read

```
This is a long string that will run over several lines
         if we just manage to fill in
         enough words.
```

### 1.6.4 User Input

Computer programs need a set of input data and the purpose is to use these data to compute output (data), i.e., results. We have previously seen how input data can be provided simply by assigning values to variables directly in the code. However, to change values then, one must change them in the program.

There are more flexible ways of handling input, however. For example through some dialogue with the user (i.e., the person running the program). Here is one example where the program asks a question, and the user provides an answer by typing on the keyboard:

```
age = int(input('What is your age? '))
print('Ok, so you're half way to {}, wow!'.format(age*2))
```

In the first line, there are two function calls, first to `input` and then to `int`. The function call `input('What is your age? ')` will cause the question "What is your age?" to appear in the lower right pane. When the user has (after left-clicking the pane) typed in an integer for the age and pressed `enter`, that integer *will* be returned by `input` as a *string* (since `input` always returns a string[22]). Thus, that string must be converted to an integer by calling `int`, before the assignment to `age` takes place.

So, after having interpreted and run the first line, Python has established the variable `age` and assigned your input to it. The second line combines the calculation of twice the age with a message printed on the screen. Try these two lines in a little test program to see for yourself how it works.

It is possible to get more flexibility into user communication by building a string before `input` shows it to the user. Adding a bit to the previous dialogue may illustrate how it works:

```
# ...assume the variable "name" contains name of user

message = 'Hello {:s}! What is your age? '.format(name)

age = int(input(message))
print('Ok, so you're half way to {}, wow!'.format(age*2))
```

[22] The `input` function here in Python 3.6, corresponds to the `raw_input` function in Python 2.7.

Thus, if the user name was Paul, for example, he would get this question up on his screen

```
Hello Paul! What is your age?
```

He would type his age, press enter, and the code would proceed like before.

There are other ways of providing input to a program as well, e.g., via a graphical interface (as many readers will be used to) or at the command line (i.e., as parameters succeeding, on the same line, the command that starts the program). Reading data from a file is yet another way.

## 1.7 Error Messages and Warnings

All programmers experience error messages, and usually to a large extent during the early learning process. Sometimes error messages are understandable, sometimes they are not. Anyway, it is important to get used to them.

One idea is to start with a program that initially is working, and then deliberately introduce errors in it, one by one (but remember to take a copy of the original working code!). For each error, you try to run the program to see what Python's response is. Then you know what the problem is and understand what the error message is about. This will greatly help you when you get a similar error message or warning later.

**Debugging** Very often, you will experience that there are errors in the program you have written. This is normal, but frustrating in the beginning. You then have to find the problem, try to fix it, and then run the program again. Typically, you fix one error just to experience that another error is waiting around the corner. However, after some time you start to avoid the most common beginner's errors, and things run more smoothly. The process of finding and fixing errors, called *debugging*, is very important to learn. There are different ways of doing it too.

A special program (*debugger*) may be used to help you check (and do) different things in the program you need to fix. A simpler procedure, that often brings you a long way, is to print information to the screen from different places in the program. First of all, this is something you should do (several times) during program development anyway, so that things get checked as you go along. However, if the final program still ends up with error messages, you may save a copy of it, and do some testing on the copy. Useful testing may then be to remove, e.g., the latter half of the program (e.g., by inserting comment signs #), and insert print commands at clever places to see what is the case. When the first half looks ok, possibly after some corrections, insert parts of what was removed and repeat the process with the new code. Using simple numbers and doing this in parallel with hand calculations on a piece of paper (for comparison) is often a very good idea.

**Exception Handling** Python also offers means to detect and handle errors by the program itself! The programmer must then foresee (when writing the code) that there is a potential for error at some particular point. If, for example, a running program asks the user to give a number, things may go very wrong if the user inputs the word *five* in stead of the number 5. In Python, such cases may be handled elegantly in the code, since it is possible to (put simply) *try* some statements, and if they go wrong, rather run some other code lines! This way, an *exception* is handled, and an unintended program stop ("crash") is avoided. More about *exception handling* in Sect. 5.2.

**Testing Code** When a program finally runs without error messages, it might be tempting to think that *Ah..., I am finished!*. But no! Then comes program *testing*, you need to *verify* that the program does the computations as planned. This is almost an art and may take more time than to develop the program, but the program is useless unless you have much evidence showing that the computations are correct. Also, having a set of (automatic) tests saves huge amounts of time when you further develop the program.

**Verification Versus Validation**

Verification is important, but *validation* is equally important. It is great if your program can do the calculations according to the plan, *but* is it the right plan? Put otherwise, you need to check that the computations run correctly according to the *formula you have chosen/derived*. This is *verification*: doing the things right. Thereafter, you must also check whether the formula you have chosen/derived is *the right* formula for the case you are investigating. This is *validation*: doing the right things.

In the present book, it is beyond scope to question how well the mathematical models describe a given phenomenon in nature or engineering, as the answer usually involves extensive knowledge of the application area. We will therefore limit our testing to the verification part.

## 1.8 Concluding Remarks

### 1.8.1 Programming Demands You to Be Accurate!

In this chapter, you have seen some examples of how simple things may be done in Python. Hopefully, you have tried to do the examples on your own. If you have, most certainly you have discovered that what you write in the code has to be *very accurate*.

For example, in our program `ball_plot.py`, we called `linspace` in this way

```
t = np.linspace(0, 1, 1001)
```

If this had rather been written

```
t = np.linspace[0, 1, 1001)
```

we would have got an error message (`[` was used instead of (), even if you and I would understand the meaning perfectly well!

Remember that it is not a human that runs your code, it is a machine. Therefore, even if the meaning of your code looks fine to a human eye, it still has to comply in detail to the rules of the programming language. If not, you get warnings and error messages. This also goes for lower and upper case letters. If you (after importing from `math`) give the command `pi`, you get 3.1415.... However, if you write `Pi`, you get an error message. Pay attention to such details also when they are given in later chapters.

### 1.8.2 Write Readable Code

When you write a computer program, you have two very different kinds of readers. One is Python, which will interpret and run your program according to the rules. The other is some human, for example, yourself or a peer. It is very important to organize and comment the code so that you can go back to your own code after, e.g., a year and still understand what clever constructions you put in there. This is relevant when you need to change or extend your code (which usually happens often in reality). Organized coding and good commenting is even more critical if other people are supposed to understand code that you have written.

It might be instructive to see an example of code that is *not* very readable. If we use our very first problem, i.e. computing the height $y$ of a ball thrown up in the air, the mathematical formulation reads:

$$y = v_0 t - 0.5 g t^2 .$$

Now, instead of our previous program `ball.py`, we could write a working program (in *bad* style!) like:

```
# This is an example of bad style!
m=5;u=9.81;y=0.6
t=m*y-u*0.5*y**2;print(t)
```

Running this code, would give the correct answer printed out. However, upon comparison with the mathematical writing, it is not even clear that the two are related, unless you sit down and look carefully at it!

In this code,

- variable names do not correspond to the mathematical variables
- there are no (explaining) comments
- no blank lines
- no space to each side of = and -
- several statements appear on the same line with no space in between

When comparing this "bad style" code to the original code in `ball.py`, the point should be clear.

### 1.8.3 Fast Code or Slower and Readable Code?

In numerical computing, there is a strong tradition for paying much attention to *fast code*. Industrial applications of numerical computing often involve simulations that run for hours, days, and even weeks. Fast code is tremendously important in those cases.

The problem with a strong focus on fast code, unfortunately, is that sometimes clear and easily understandable constructions are replaced by fast (and possibly clever), but less readable code. For beginners, however, it is definitely most important to learn writing readable and correct code.

We will make some comments on constructions that are fast or slow, but the main focus of this book is to teach how to write correct programs, not the fastest possible programs.

### 1.8.4 Deleting Data No Longer in Use

Python has *automatic garbage collection*, meaning that there is no need to delete variables (or objects) that are no longer in use. Python takes care of this by itself. This is opposed to, e.g., Matlab, where explicit deleting sometimes may be required.

### 1.8.5 Code Lines That Are Too Long

If a code line in a program gets too long, it may be continued on the next line by inserting a back-slash at the end of the line before proceeding on the next line. However, *no blanks* must occur after the back-slash! A little demonstration could be the following,

```
my_sum = 1 + 2 + 3 + 4 + 5 + 6 + 7 + 8 + 9 + 10 + 11 + 12 + 13 +\
         14 + 15 + 16 + 17 + 18 + 19 + 20
```

So, the back-slash works as a *line continuation character* here.

### 1.8.6 Where to Find More Information?

We have already recommended Langtangen's book, *A Primer on Scientific Programming with Python* (Springer, 2016), as the main reference for the present book.

In addition, there is, of course, the official Python documentation website (http://docs.python.org/), which provides a Python tutorial, the *Python Library Reference*, a *Language Reference*, and more. Several other great books are also available, check out, e.g., http://wiki.python.org/moin/PythonBooks.

As you do know, search engines like Google are excellent for finding information quickly, so also with Python related questions! Finally, you will also find that the questions and answers at http://stackoverflow.com often cover exactly what you seek. If not, you may ask your own questions there.

## 1.9 Exercises

**Exercise 1.1: Error Messages**
Save a copy of the program `ball.py` and confirm that the copy runs as the original. You are now supposed to introduce errors in the code, one by one. For each error introduced, save and run the program, and comment how well Python's response corresponds to the actual error. When you are finished with one error, re-set the program to correct behavior (and check that it works!) before moving on to the next error.

a) Insert the word *hello* on the empty line above the assignment to `v0`.
b) Remove the # sign in front of the comment *initial velocity*.
c) Remove the = sign in the assignment to `v0`.
d) Change the reserved word `print` into `pint`.
e) Change the calculation of `y` to `y = v0*t`.
f) Change the line `print(y)` to `print(x)`.

Filename: `testing_ball.py`.

**Exercise 1.2: Volume of a Cube**
Write a program that computes the volume $V$ of a cube with sides of length $L = 4$ cm and prints the result to the screen. Both $V$ and $L$ should be defined as separate variables in the program. Run the program and confirm that the correct result is printed.

**Hint** See `ball.py` in the text.
Filename: `cube_volume.py`.

**Exercise 1.3: Area and Circumference of a Circle**
Write a program that computes both the circumference $C$ and the area $A$ of a circle with radius $r = 2$ cm. Let the results be printed to the screen on a single line with an appropriate text. The variables $C$, $A$ and $r$ should all be defined as separate variables in the program. Run the program and confirm that the correct results are printed.
Filename: `circumference_and_area.py`.

**Exercise 1.4: Volumes of Three Cubes**
We are interested in the volume $V$ of a cube with length $L$: $V = L^3$, computed for three different values of $L$.

a) In a program, use the `linspace` function to compute and print three values of $L$, equally spaced on the interval $[1, 3]$.
b) Carry out, by hand, the computation $V = L^3$ when $L$ is an array with three elements. That is, compute $V$ for each value of $L$.
c) Modify the program in a), so that it prints out the result `V` of `V = L**3` when `L` is an array with three elements as computed by `linspace`. Compare the resulting volumes with your hand calculations.
d) Make a plot of `V` versus `L`.

Filename: `volume3cubes.py`.

**Exercise 1.5: Average of Integers**
Write a program that stores the sum $1 + 2 + 3 + 4 + 5$ in one variable and then creates another variable with the average of these five numbers. Print the average to the screen and check that the result is correct.
Filename: `average_int.py`.

**Exercise 1.6: Formatted Print to Screen**
Write a program that defines two variables as `x = pi` and `y = 2`. Then let the program compute the product `z` of these two variables and print the result to the screen as

```
Multiplying 3.14159 and 2 gives 6.283
```

Filename: `formatted_print.py`.

# A Few More Steps

# 2

## 2.1 Using Python Interactively

### 2.1.1 The IPython Shell

Python can also be used interactively, in which case we do not first write a program, store it in a file and then execute it. Rather, we give statements and expressions directly to what is known as a Python *shell*. This means that we communicate with the Python interpreter via a particular interface. Interactive use of Python is a great way to quickly demonstrate different aspects of Python and we will use it repeatedly for this purpose. It is also very useful for testing out things like function behavior, syntax issues, etc., before finalizing related code in a program you are writing.

We recommend to use IPython as shell (because it is superior to alternative Python shells). With `Spyder`, `Ipython` is available at startup, appearing in the lower right pane (the *console*). An interactive session appears as a succession of pairwise corresponding input (to Python) and output (from Python). The user writes input commands after the IPython prompt[1] `In [p]:`, where $p = 1, 2, \ldots$, and gets the response back (if any) after `Out [p]:`. Thus, p serves as a counter for each pair of input and output (when there is no output, this "pair" will consist of only input). To exemplify, we may write:

```
In [1]: 2+2
Out[1]: 4

In [2]: 2*3
Out[2]: 6

In [3]: 10/2    # note: gives float
Out[3]: 5.0

In [4]: 2**3
Out[4]: 8
```

[1] A *prompt* means a "ready sign", i.e. the program allows you to enter a command, and different programs often have different looking prompts.



S. Linge, H. P. Langtangen, *Programming for Computations - Python*,
Texts in Computational Science and Engineering 15,
https://doi.org/10.1007/978-3-030-16877-3_2

Observe that, as in a program, certain items must be imported before use, e.g., pi, sin, cos, etc. For example, to interactively compute $sin(\frac{\pi}{2})$, you could write

```
In [1]: from math import sin, pi

In [2]: sin(pi/2)
Out[2]: 1.0
```

Observe that the import statement here, i.e. `from math import sin, pi`, is an example of input that does not produce any corresponding output.

You may also define variables and use formulas interactively as

```
In [1]: v0 = 5

In [2]: g = 9.81

In [3]: t = 0.6

In [4]: y = v0*t - 0.5*g*t**2

In [5]: print(y)
1.2342
```

### 2.1.2 Command History

IPython stores the dialogue, which allows you to easily repeat a previous command, with or without modifications. Using the up-arrow key, brings you "backwards" in command history. Pressing this one time gives you the previous command, pressing two times gives you the command before that, and so on. With the down-arrow key you can go "forward" again. When you have the relevant command at the prompt, you may edit it before pressing enter (which lets Python read it and take action).

### 2.1.3 TAB Completion

When typing in IPython, you may get assistance from the TAB key to finalize a variable name or command you are typing.

To illustrate, assume you have written

```
In [1]: import numpy as np

In [2]: x = np.lins                # before pressing TAB key
```

and *then* press the TAB key. IPython will then assume you intend to write `np.linspace` and therefore fill out the rest for you, so that you suddenly have

```
In [2]: x = np.linspace            # after pressing TAB key
```

You may then go on and fill out the rest, perhaps like

```
In [2]: x = np.linspace(0, 1, 11)        # after filling out the rest
```

Generally, if you press the TAB key "too early", IPython might have to give you a list of options, from which you may choose the intended word.

With longer words, or if you are a bit uncertain about the spelling, TAB completion is a handy tool.

## 2.2 Variables, Objects and Expressions

### 2.2.1 Choose Descriptive Variable Names

Names of variables should be chosen so that they are descriptive. If you are coding some formula that in mathematical writing contains $x$ and $y$, `x` and `y` ought to be the corresponding names for those variables in your code (unless there are special considerations for your case).

Some times it is difficult, or even impossible, to have a variable name in the code that is identical to the corresponding mathematical symbol. Some inventiveness is then called for, as, for example, when we used the variable name `v0` for the mathematical symbol $v_0$ in our first program `ball.py`. Similarly, if you need a variable for the counting of sheep, one appropriate name could be `no_of_sheep`, i.e., join well-chosen words by use of an underscore.[2] Such naming makes it much easier for a human to understand the written code, which in turn makes it easier to find errors or modify the code. Variable names may also contain any digit from 0 to 9, or underscores, but can not start with a digit. Letters may be lower or upper case, which to Python is different.

### 2.2.2 Reserved Words

Note that certain names in Python are *reserved*, meaning that you can not use these as names for variables. Interactively, we may get a complete list of the reserved words:

```
In [1]: import keyword

In [2]: keyword.kwlist
Out[2]:
['False', 'None', 'True', 'and', 'as', 'assert', 'break', 'class',
 'continue', 'def', 'del', 'elif', 'else', 'except', 'finally', 'for',
 'from', 'global', 'if', 'import', 'in', 'is', 'lambda', 'nonlocal',
 'not', 'or', 'pass', 'raise', 'return', 'try', 'while', 'with', 'yield']
```

As you can see, we have met some of these already, e.g., `from` and `import`. If you accidentally use a reserved word as a variable name you get an error message.

---

[2] Another common way of joining words into variable names, is to start each new word with a capital letter, e.g., like in `noOfSheep`. In this book, however, we stick to the convention with underscores.

### 2.2.3 Assignment

We have learned previously that, for example, `x = 2` is an assignment statement. Also, when discussing `ball.py` in Sect. 1.2, we learned that writing, e.g., `x = x + 4` causes the value of `x` to be increased by 4. Alternatively, this update could have been achieved (slightly faster) with `x += 4`. In a similar way, `x -= 4` reduces the value of `x` by 4, `x *= 4` multiplies `x` by 4, and `x /= 4` divides `x` by 4, updating the value of `x` accordingly.

The following also works as expected (but there is one point to make):

```
In [1]: x = 2

In [2]: y = x        # y gets the value 2

In [3]: y = y + 1    # y gets the value 3

In [4]: x        # x value not changed
Out[4]: 2
```

Observe that, after the assignment `y = x`, a change in `y` did not change the value of `x` (also, if rather `x` had been changed, `y` would have stayed unchanged). We would observe the same had `x` been the name of a `float` or a `string`, as you will realize if you try this yourself.[3] This probably seems obvious, but it is not the case for all kinds of objects.[4]

### 2.2.4 Object Type and Type Conversion

**The Type of an Object** By now, we know that an assignment like `x = 2` triggers the creation of an object by the name `x`. That object will be of *type* `int` and have the value 2. Similarly, the assignment `y = 2.0` will generate an object named `y`, with value 2.0 and type `float`, since real numbers like 2.0 are called *floating point numbers* in computer language (by the way, note that floats in Python are often written with just a trailing "dot", e.g., 2. in stead of 2.0). We have also learned that when Python interprets, e.g., `s = 'This is a string'`, it stores the text (in between the quotes) in an object of type `str` named `s`. These object types, i.e., `int`, `float` and `str`, are still just a few of the many built-in object types in Python.[5]

**The Type Function** There is a useful built-in function `type` that can be used to check the type of an object:

---

[3] To test the string, you may try (in the order given): `x = 'yes'; y = x; y = y + 'no'`, and then give the commands `y` and `x` to confirm that `y` has become `yesno` and `x` is still `yes`.

[4] In Python, there is an important distinction between *mutable* and *immutable* objects. Mutable objects *can* be changed after they have been created, whereas immutable objects can not. Here, the integer referred to by `x` is an immutable object, which is why the change in `y` does not change `x`. Among immutable objects we find integers, floats, strings and more, whereas arrays and lists (Sect. 5.1) are examples of mutable objects.

[5] https://docs.python.org/3/library/stdtypes.html.

```
In [1]: x = 2

In [2]: y = 4.0

In [3]: s = 'hello'

In [4]: type(x)          # ...object named x is an integer
Out[4]: int

In [5]: type(y)          # ...object named y is a float
Out[5]: float

In [6]: type(s)          # ...object named s is a string
Out[6]: str
```

**Type Conversion** Objects may be converted from one type to another if it makes sense. If, e.g., x is the name of an `int` object, writing

```
In [1]: x = 1

In [2]: y = float(x)

In [3]: y
Out[3]: 1.0
```

shows that y then becomes a floating point representation of x. Similarly, writing

```
In [1]: x = 1.0

In [2]: y = int(x)

In [3]: y
Out[3]: 1
```

illustrates that y becomes an integer representation of x. Note that the `int` function rounds down, e.g., `y = int(1.9)` also makes y become the integer 1. Type conversion may also occur automatically.

### 2.2.5 Automatic Type Conversion

What if we add a float object to an int object? We could, e.g., write

```
In [1]: x = 2

In [2]: x = x + 4.0

In [3]: x
Out[3]: 6.0
```

What happens here, is that *automatic type conversion* takes place, and the new x will have the value 6.0, i.e., refer to an object of type `float`.

**Python is Both Dynamically and Strongly Typed**

Python is a *dynamically typed language*, since a certain variable name may refer to objects of different types during the execution of a program. This means that writing

```
In [1]: z = 10                    # z refers to an integer

In [2]: z = 10.0                  # z refers to a float

In [3]: z = 'some string'         # z refers to a string
```

is perfectly fine and we get no error messages. In *statically typed languages* (e.g., C and Fortran), this would not be accepted, since a variable then would have to be of one particular type throughout.

Python is also a *strongly typed language*, since it is strict about how you can combine object types:

```
In [1]: 'yes' + 'no'              # add two strings
Out[1]: 'yesno'

In [2]: 'yes' + 10                # ...try adding string and integer
Traceback (most recent call last):

  File "<ipython-input-5-fdfd15f88bd0>", line 1, in <module>
    'yes' + 10

  TypeError: cannot concatenate 'str' and 'int' objects
```

Adding two strings is straight forward, but trying the same with a string and an integer gives an error message, since it is not well defined. In a *weakly typed language*, this could very well give `yes10` without any error message. If so, it would be based on a (vaguely) founded assumption that this is what the programmer intended (but perhaps it is just as likely an error?). For more details on these matters, see, e.g., https://en.wikipedia.org/wiki/Python_(programming_language).

### 2.2.6 Operator Precedence

When the arithmetic operators +, -, *, / and ** appear in an expression, Python gives them a certain precedence. Python interprets the expression from left to right, taking one term (part of expression between two successive + or −) at a time. Within each term, ** is done before * and /.

Consider the expression `x = 1*5**2 + 10*3 - 1.0/4`. There are three terms here and interpreting this, Python starts from the left. In the first term, `1*5**2`, it first does `5**2` which equals 25. This is then multiplied by 1 to give 25 again. The second term is `10*3`, i.e., 30. So the first two terms add up to 55. The last term gives 0.25, so the final result is 54.75 which becomes the value of `x`.

### 2.2.7 Division—Quotient and Remainder

It is sometimes desirable to pick out the quotient and remainder of a division $\frac{a}{b}$, for integer or floating point numbers $a$ and $b$. In Python, we can do this with the operators `//` (*integer division*)[6] and `%` (*modulo*), respectively. They have the same precedence as `*`, and their use may be exemplified by

```
In [1]: 11//2
Out[1]: 5

In [2]: 11%2
Out[2]: 1
```

Note that the sign of the remainder follows the sign of the denominator, i.e.,

```
In [1]: -11%2
Out[1]: 1

In [2]: 11%-2
Out[2]: -1
```

### 2.2.8 Using Parentheses

Note that parentheses are often very important to group parts of expressions together in the intended way. Let us consider some variable `x` with the value 4 and assume that you want to divide 1.0 by `x + 1`. We know the answer is 0.2, but the way we present the task to Python is critical, as shown by the following example.

```
In [1]: x = 4

In [2]: 1.0/x+1
Out[2]: 1.25

In [3]: 1.0/(x+1)
Out[3]: 0.2
```

In the first try, we see that 1.0 is divided by `x` (i.e., 4), giving 0.25, which is then added to 1. Python did not understand that our complete denominator was `x+1`. In our second try, we used parentheses to "group" the denominator, and we got what we wanted.

### 2.2.9 Round-Off Errors

Since most numbers can be represented only approximately on the computer, this gives rise to what is called *rounding* errors. We may illustrate this if we take a look

[6] Note that in Python 2.x, the operator / gives integer division, unless either the numerator and/or the denominator is a `float`.

at the previous calculation in more detail. Let us repeat the calculation, but this time print more decimals,

```
In [1]: x = 4

In [2]: y = 1.0/(x+1)

In [3]: print('The value of y is: {:.17f}'.format(y))
The value of y is: 0.20000000000000001
```

So, what should have been exactly 0.2, is really a slightly different value! The inexact number representation gave us a small error. Usually, such errors are so small compared to the other numbers of the calculation, that we do not need to bother with them. Still, keep it in mind, since you will encounter this issue from time to time. More details regarding number representations on a computer are given in Sect. 6.6.3.

### 2.2.10 Boolean Expressions

In programming, we often need to check whether something is true or not true, and then take action accordingly. This is handled by use of *logical* or *boolean expressions*, which evaluate to the *Boolean values* true or false (i.e., not true).[7] In Python, these values are written `True` and `False`, respectively (note capital letters T and F!).

The following session presents some examples of boolean expressions, while also explaining the operators involved:

```
In [1]: x = 4

In [2]: # The following is a series of boolean expressions:

In [3]: x > 5          # x greater than 5
Out[3]: False

In [4]: x >= 5         # x greater than, or equal to, 5
Out[4]: False

In [5]: x < 5          # x smaller than 5
Out[5]: True

In [6]: x <= 5         # x smaller than, or equal to, 5
Out[6]: True

In [7]: x == 4         # x equal to 4
Out[7]: True

In [8]: x != 4         # x not equal to 4
Out[8]: False
```

Boolean values may also be combined into longer expressions by use of `and` and `or`. Furthermore, preceding a boolean expression by `not`, will effectively switch

[7] https://en.wikipedia.org/wiki/Boolean_data_type.

True to False and vice versa. Continuing the preceding session with a few more examples will illustrate these points,

```
In [9]: x < 5 and x > 3      # x less than 5 AND x larger than 3
Out[9]: True

In [10]: x == 5 or x == 4    # x equal to 5 OR x equal to 4
Out[10]: True

In [11]: not x == 4          # not x equal to 4
Out[11]: False
```

The first of these compound expressions, i.e., `x < 5 and x > 3`, could alternatively be written `3 < x < 5`. It may also be added that the final boolean expression, i.e., `not x == 4` is equivalent to `x != 4` from above, which most of us find easier to read.

We will meet boolean expressions again soon, when we address `while` loops and branching in Chap. 3.

## 2.3 Numerical Python Arrays

We have seen simple use of arrays before, in `ball_plot.py` (Sect. 1.5), when the height of a ball was computed a thousand times. Corresponding heights and times were handled with arrays `y` and `t`, respectively. The kind of arrays used in `ball_plot.py` is the kind we will use in this book. They are not part of standard Python,[8] however, so we import what is needed from `numpy`. The arrays will be of *type* `numpy.ndarray`, referred to as N-dimensional arrays in NumPy.

Arrays are created and treated according to certain rules, and as a programmer, you may direct Python to compute and handle arrays as a whole, or as individual array *elements*. All array elements must be of the same type, e.g., all integers or all floating point numbers.

### 2.3.1 Array Creation and Array Elements

We saw previously how the `linspace` function from `numpy` could be used to generate an array of evenly distributed numbers from an interval $[a, b]$. As a quick reminder, we may interactively create an array `x` with three real numbers, evenly distributed on $[0, 2]$:

```
In [1]: from numpy import linspace

In [2]: x = linspace(0, 2, 3)

In [3]: x
Out[3]: array([ 0.,  1.,  2.])
```

[8] Standard Python *does* have an array object, but we will stick to `numpy` arrays, since they allow more efficient computations. Thus, whenever we write "array", it is understood to be a `numpy` array.

```
In [4]: type(x)              # check type of array as a whole
Out[4]: numpy.ndarray

In [5]: type(x[0])           # check type of array element
Out[5]: numpy.float64
```

The line `x = linspace(0, 2, 3)` makes Python reserve, or *allocate*, space in memory for the array produced by `linspace`. With the assignment, `x` becomes a reference to the array object from `linspace`, i.e. `x` becomes the "name of the array". The array will have three elements with names `x[0]`, `x[1]` and `x[2]`, where the bracketed numbers are referred to as *indices* (note that when *reading*, we say "x of zero" to `x[0]`, "x of one" to `x[1]`, and so on).

Observe that the indexing starts with 0, so that an array with `n` elements will have `n-1` as the last index. We say that Python has *zero based indexing*, which differs from *one based indexing* where array indexing starts with 1 (as, e.g., in Matlab). In `x`, the value of `x[0]` is 0.0, the value of `x[1]` is 1.0 and, finally, the value of `x[2]` is 2.0. These values are given by the printout `array([ 0., 1., 2.])` above.

With the command `type(x)`, we confirm that the array object named `x` has type `numpy.ndarray`. Note that, at the same time, the individual array elements refer to objects with another type. We see this from the very last command, `type(x[0])`, which makes Python respond with `numpy.float64` (being just a certain float data type in NumPy[9]).

If we continue the previous dialogue with a few lines, we can also demonstrate that use of individual array elements is straight forward:

```
In [4]: sum_elements = x[0] + x[1] + x[2]

In [5]: sum_elements
Out[5]: 3.0

In [6]: product_2_elements = x[1]*x[2]

In [7]: product_2_elements
Out[7]: 2.0

In [8]: x[0] = 5.0              # overwrite previous value

In [9]: x
Out[9]: array([ 5.,  1.,  2.])
```

**The Zeros Function** There are other common ways to generate arrays too. One way is to use another `numpy` function named `zeros`, which (as the name suggests) may be used to produce an array with zeros. These zeros can be either floating point numbers or integers, depending on the arguments provided when `zeros` is called.[10] Often, the zeros are overwritten in a second step to arrive at an array with the numbers actually wanted.

---

[9] You may check out the many numerical data types in NumPy at https://docs.scipy.org/doc/numpy-1.13.0/user/basics.types.html.

[10] https://docs.scipy.org/doc/numpy-1.13.0/reference/generated/numpy.zeros.html.

**The Built-In Len Function** It is appropriate here to also mention the built-in function `len`, which is useful when you need to find the length (i.e., the number of elements) of an array.[11]

A quick demonstration of `zeros` and `len` may go like this,

```
In [1]: from numpy import zeros

In [2]: x = zeros(3, int)          # get array with integer zeros

In [3]: x
Out[3]: array([ 0,  0,  0])

In [4]: y = zeros(3)               # get array with floating point zeros

In [5]: y
Out[5]: array([ 0.,  0.,  0.])

In [6]: y[0] = 0.0;   y[1] = 1.0;   y[2] = 2.0     # overwrite

In [7]: y
Out[7]: array([ 0.,  1.,  2.])

In [8]: len(y)
Out[8]: 3
```

Note that the line `x = zeros(3, int)` could, alternatively, have been written a bit more informative as `x = zeros(3, dtype=int)`, where `dtype` means data type. Just like with `linspace`, the line `y = zeros(3)` instructs Python to reserve, or *allocate*, space in memory for the array produced by `zeros`. As we see from the dialogue, the array gets the name `y` and will have three elements, all with a floating point zero value. Each element in `y` is next overwritten by "the numbers we actually wanted". Strictly speaking, the assignment `y[0] = 0.0` was redundant here, since the value of `y[0]` was known to be 0.0 from before. It should be mentioned, though, that programmers deliberately write such seemingly redundant statements from time to time, meaning to tell a human code interpreter that the value is not "accidental".

In our dialogue here, one explicit statement was written for each element value we changed, i.e. as `y[0] = 0.0; y[1] = 1.0; y[2] = 2.0`. For arrays with just a few elements, this is acceptable. However, with many elements, this is obviously not the way to go. Longer arrays are typically first generated by `zeros` (or otherwise), before individual array elements get new values in some loop arrangement (explained in Chap. 3).

**The Array Function** Another handy way of creating an array, is by using the function `array`, e.g., like this,

```
In [1]: from numpy import array

In [2]: x = array([0, 1, 2])          # get array with integers

In [3]: x
Out[3]: array([0, 1, 2])

In [4]: x = array([0., 1., 2.])       # get array with real numbers
```

[11] The `len` function may also be used with other objects, e.g., lists (Sect. 5.1).

```
In [5]: x
Out[5]: array([ 0.,  1.,  2.])
```

Note the use of "dots" to get floating point numbers and that we call `array` with bracketed[12] numbers, i.e., `[0, 1, 2]` and `[0., 1., 2.]`.

### 2.3.2 Indexing an Array from the End

By use of a minus sign, the elements of an array may be indexed from the end, rather from the beginning. That is, with our array `x` here, we could get hold of the very last element by writing `x[-1]`, the second last element by writing `x[-2]`, and so on. Continuing the previous interactive session, we may write

```
In [6]: x[-1]
Out[6]: 2.0

In [7]: x[-2]
Out[7]: 1.0

In [8]: x[-3]
Out[8]: 0.0
```

### 2.3.3 Index Out of Bounds

A typical error to make when working with arrays, is to accidentally use an illegal index. With the array `x` in our ongoing dialogue, we may illustrate this by

```
In [9]: x[3]
Traceback (most recent call last):

  File "<ipython-input-18-ed224ad0520d>", line 1, in <module>
    x[3]

IndexError: index 3 is out of bounds for axis 0 with size 3
```

Our index 3 is illegal and we get the error message shown. From the above, it should be clear that legal indices are 0, 1 and 2. Alternatively, if indexing from the end, legal indices are $-1$, $-2$ and $-3$. Note that counting is a bit "different" then, causing $-3$ to be a legal index (as we saw above), while 3 is not.

### 2.3.4 Copying an Array

Copying arrays requires some care, as can be seen next, when we try to make a copy of the `x` array from above:

```
In [10]: y = x

In [11]: y
Out[11]: array([ 0.,  1.,  2.])      # ...as expected
```

---

[12] The arguments to `array` are two examples of *lists*, which will be addressed in Sect. 5.1.

```
In [12]: y[0] = 10.0

In [13]: y
Out[13]: array([ 10.,   1.,   2.])     # ...as expected

In [14]: x
Out[14]: array([ 10.,    1.,    2.]) # ...x has changed too!
```

Intuitively, it may seem very strange that changing an element in y causes a similar change in x! The thing is, however, that our assignment y = x does *not* make a copy of the x array. Rather, Python creates another reference, named y, to the same array object that x refers to. That is, there is *one* array object with *two* names (x and y). Therefore, changing either x or y, simultaneously changes "the other" (note that this behavior differs from what we found in Sect. 2.2.3 for single integer, float or string objects).

To really get a copy that is decoupled from the original array, you may use the copy function from numpy,

```
In [15]: from numpy import copy

In [16]: x = linspace(0, 2, 3)          # x becomes array([ 0.,   1.,   2.])

In [17]: y = copy(x)

In [18]: y
Out[18]: array([ 0.,   1.,   2.])

In [19]: y[0] = 10.0

In [20]: y
Out[20]: array([ 10.,    1.,    2.]) # ...changed

In [21]: x
Out[21]: array([ 0.,   1.,   2.])      # ...unchanged
```

### 2.3.5 Slicing an Array

By use of a colon, you may work with a *slice* of an array. For example, by writing x[i:j], we address all elements from index i (inclusive) to j (exclusive) in an array x. An interactive session illustrates this,

```
In [1]: from numpy import linspace

In [2]: x = linspace(11, 16, 6)

In [3]: x
Out[3]: array([  11.,   12.,   13.,   14.,   15.,   16.])

In [4]: y = x[1:5]

In [5]: y
Out[5]: array([ 12.,   13.,   14.,   15.])
```

When copying a slice, the same logic applies as when copying the whole array. To demonstrate the problem, we continue the dialogue as

```
In [6]: y[0] = -1.0

In [7]: y
Out[7]: array([-1.,  13.,  14.,  15.])      # ...changed

In [8]: x
Out[8]: array([ 11.,  -1.,   13.,   14.,   15.,   16.])  # ...changed
```

As for the whole array, the function `copy` may be used (after importing: `from numpy import copy`) as `y = copy(x[1:5])` to give a "real" copy.

### 2.3.6 Two-Dimensional Arrays and Matrix Computations

For readers who are into linear algebra, it might be useful to see how matrices and vectors may be handled with NumPy arrays.[13] Above, we saw arrays where the individual elements could be addressed with a single index only. Such arrays are often called *vectors*.

To calculate with matrices, we need arrays with more than one "dimension". Such arrays may be generated in different ways, for example by use of the same `zeros` function that we have seen before, it just has to be called a bit differently. Let us illustrate by doing a simple matrix-vector multiplication with the numpy function `dot`:

```
In [1]: import numpy as np

In [2]: I = np.zeros((3, 3))      # create matrix (note parentheses!)

In [3]: I
Out[3]:
array([[ 0.,  0.,  0.],
       [ 0.,  0.,  0.],
       [ 0.,  0.,  0.]])

In [4]: type(I)                         # confirm that type is ndarray
Out[4]: numpy.ndarray

In [5]: I[0, 0] = 1.0;  I[1, 1] = 1.0;  I[2, 2] = 1.0  # identity matrix

In [6]: x = np.array([1.0, 2.0, 3.0])  # create vector

In [7]: y = np.dot(I, x)                # computes matrix-vector product

In [8]: y
Out[8]: array([ 1.,  2.,  3.])
```

[13] If you are not familiar with matrices and vectors, and such calculations are not on your agenda, you should consider skipping (or at least wait with) this section, as it is not required for understanding the remaining parts of the book.

Note how zeros must be called with double parentheses now. The accessing of individual matrix elements should be according to intuition. With some experience from matrix-vector algebra, it is clear that y is correctly computed here. Note that most programmers would use the NumPy function eye here, to generate the identity matrix directly. One would then call I = eye(3) and get I as a two dimensional array with ones on the diagonal.

If you are experienced with matrices and vectors in Matlab, there is another way to handle matrices and vectors with NumPy, which will appear more like you are used to. For example, a matrix-vector product is then coded as A*x and not by use of the dot function. To achieve this, we must use objects of another type, i.e., matrix objects (note that a matrix object will have *different properties* than an ndarray object!). If we do the same matrix-vector calculation as above, we can show how ndarray objects may be converted into matrix objects and how the calculations then can be fulfilled:

```
In [1]: import numpy as np

In [2]: I = np.eye(3)            # create identity matrix

In [3]: I
Out[3]:
array([[ 1.,  0.,  0.],
       [ 0.,  1.,  0.],
       [ 0.,  0.,  1.]])

In [4]: type(I)                       # confirm that type is ndarray
Out[4]: numpy.ndarray

In [5]: I = np.matrix(I)              # convert to matrix object

In [6]: type(I)                       # confirm that type is matrix
Out[6]: numpy.matrixlib.defmatrix.matrix

In [7]: x = np.array([1.0, 2.0, 3.0])   # create ndarray vector

In [8]: x = np.matrix(x)          # convert to matrix object (row vector)

In [9]: x = x.transpose()         # convert to column vector

In [10]: y = I*x                  # computes matrix-vector product

In [11]: y
Out[11]:
matrix([[ 1.],
        [ 2.],
        [ 3.]])
```

Note that np.matrix(x) turns x, with type ndarray, into a *row* vector by default (type matrix), so x must be transposed with x.transpose() before it can be multiplied with the matrix I.

## 2.4 Random Numbers

Programming languages usually offer ways to produce (apparently) random numbers, referred to as *pseudo-random numbers*. These numbers are not truly random, since they are produced in a predictable way once a "seed" has been set (the seed is a number, which generation depends on the current time).

**Drawing One Random Number at a Time** Pseudo-random numbers come in handy if your code is to deal with phenomena characterized by some randomness. For example, your code could simulate a throw of dice by generating pseudo-random integers between 1 and 6. A Python program (throw_2_dice.py) that mimics the throw of two dice could read

```
import random

a = 1; b = 6
r1 = random.randint(a, b)    # first die
r2 = random.randint(a, b)    # second die

print('The dice gave:  {:d} and {:d}'.format(r1, r2))
```

The function `randint` is available from the imported module `random`, which is part of the standard Python library, and returns a pseudo-random integer on the interval $[a, b]$, $a \leq b$. Each number on the interval has equal probability of being picked. It should be clear that, when numbers are generated pseudo-randomly, we can not tell in advance what numbers will be produced (unless we happen to have detailed knowledge about the number generation process). Also, running the code twice, generally gives different results, as you might confirm with `throw_2_dice.py`. Note that, since the seed depends on the current time, this applies even if you restart your computer in between the two runs.

When debugging programs that involve pseudo-random number generation, it is a great advantage to *fix the seed*, which ensures that the very same sequence of numbers will be generated each time the code is run. This simply means that you pick the seed yourself and tell Python what that seed should be. For our little program `throw_2_dice.py`, we could choose, e.g., 10 as our seed and insert the line

```
random.seed(10)
```

after the import statement (and before `randint` is called). Test this modification and confirm that it causes each run to print the same two numbers with every execution.

In fact, it is a good idea to fix the seed from the outset when you write the program. Later, when (you think) it works for a fixed seed, you change it so that the number generator sets its own seed, after which you proceed with further testing.

An alternative to `throw_2_dice.py`, could be to use Python interactively as

```
In [1]: import random

In [2]: random.randint(1, 6)
Out[2]: 6
```

```
In [3]: random.randint(1, 6)
Out[3]: 5
```

The `random` module contains also other useful functions, two of which are `random` (yes, same name as the module) and `uniform`. Both of these functions return a floating point number from an interval where each number has equal probability of being drawn. For `random`, the interval is always [0, 1) (i.e. 0 is included, but 1 is not), while `uniform` requires the programmer to specify the interval $[a, b]$ (where both $a$ and $b$ are included[14]). The functions are used similarly to `randint`, so, interactively, we may for example do:

```
In [1]: import random

In [2]: x = random.random()          # draw float from [0, 1), assign to x

In [3]: y = random.uniform(10, 20) # ...float from [10, 20], assign to y

In [4]: print('x = {:g}, y = {:g}'.format(x, y))
Out[5]: x = 0.714621 , y = 13.1233
```

**Drawing Many Random Numbers at a Time** You have now met three useful functions from the `random` module in Python's standard library and seen them in simple use. However, each of those functions provides only a single number with each function call. If you need many pseudo-random numbers, one option is to use such function calls inside a *loop* (Chap. 3). Another (faster) alternative, is to rather use functions that allow *vectorized drawing* of the numbers, so that a single function call provides all the numbers you need in one go. Such functionality is offered by another module, which also happens to be called `random`, but which resides in the `numpy` library. All three functions demonstrated above have their counterparts in `numpy` and we might show interactively how each of these can be used to generate, e.g., four numbers with one function call.

```
In [1]: import numpy as np

In [2]: np.random.randint(1, 6, 4)       # ...4 integers from [1, 6)
Out[2]: array([1, 3, 5, 3])

In [3]: np.random.random(4)              # ...4 floats from [0, 1)
Out[3]: array([ 0.79183276,  0.01398365,  0.04982849,  0.11630963])

In [4]: np.random.uniform(10, 20, 4)     # ...4 floats from [10, 20)
Out[4]: array([ 10.95846078,  17.3971301 ,  19.73964488,  18.14332234])
```

In each case, the size argument is here set to 4 and an array is returned. Of course, with the size argument, you may ask for thousands of numbers if you like. As is evident from the interval specifications in the code, none of these functions include the upper interval limit. However, if we wanted, e.g., `randint` to have 6 as the *inclusive* upper limit, we could simply give 7 as the second argument in stead.

[14] Strictly speaking, $b$ may or may not be included (http://docs.python.org/), depending on floating-point rounding in the equation `a + (b-a)*random()`.

One more handy function from numpy deserves mention. If you have an array[15] with numbers, you can shuffle those numbers in a randomized way with the shuffle function,

```
In [1]: import numpy as np

In [2]: a = np.array([1, 2, 3, 4])

In [3]: np.random.shuffle(a)

In [4]: a
Out[4]: array([1, 3, 4, 2])
```

Note that also numpy allows the seed to be set. For example, setting the seed to 10 (as above), could be done by

```
np.random.seed(10)
```

The fact that a module by the name random is found both in the standard Python library random and in numpy, calls for some alertness. With proper import statements (discussed in Sect. 1.4.1), however, there should be no problem.

For more details about the numpy functions for pseudo-random numbers, check out the documentation (https://docs.scipy.org/doc/).

## 2.5 Exercises

**Exercise 2.1: Interactive Computing of Volume**
Redo the task in Exercise 1.2 by using Python interactively. Compare with what you got previously from the written program.

**Exercise 2.2: Interactive Computing of Circumference and Area**
Redo the task in Exercise 1.3 by using Python interactively. Compare with what you got previously from the written program.

**Exercise 2.3: Update Variable at Command Prompt**
Invoke Python interactively and perform the following steps.

1. Initialize a variable `x` to 2.
2. Add 3 to `x`. Print out the result.
3. Print out the result of `x + 1*2` and `(x+1)*2`. (Observe how parentheses make a difference).
4. What object *type* does `x` refer to?

**Exercise 2.4: Multiple Statements on One Line**
a) The output produced by the following two lines has been removed. Can you tell, from just reading the input, what the output was in each case?

[15] Instead of an array, we can also use a *list*, see Sect. 5.1.

```
In [1]: x = 1; print(x + 1); x = x + 1; x += 1; x = x - 1; x -= 1

In [2]: print(x)
```

Then type it in and confirm that your predictions are correct.

b) Repeat the previous task, but this time without statements number 3 and 4 (counted from left) of the first input line. To confirm your prediction this time, use the command history facility to first bring up the previous command line, which you then edit appropriately before pressing enter.

**Remarks** With our statements here, it would clearly have been more readable to write them on separate lines (also making the semi-colon superfluous). Generally, this is also the case, although the possibility of writing several statements on a single line comes in handy from time to time.

**Exercise 2.5: Boolean Expression—Even or Odd Number?**
Let x be an integer. Use the modulo operator and suggest a boolean expression that can be used to check whether that integer is an even number (or odd, since if not even, the integer is odd). Then check your suggestion interactively, e.g., for x being 1, 2, 3 and 4.

**Exercise 2.6: Plotting Array Data**
Assume four members of a family with heights 1.60 m, 1.85 m, 1.75 m, and 1.80 m. Next door, there is another family, also with four members. Their heights are 0.50 m, 0.70 m, 1.90 m, and 1.75 m.

a) Write a program that creates a single plot with all the heights from both families. In your code, use the `zeros` function from `numpy` to generate three arrays, two for keeping the heights from each family and one for "numbering" of family members (e.g., as 1, 2, 3 and 4). Let the code overwrite the zeros in the arrays with the heights given, using appropriate assignment statements. Let the heights be presented as two continuous curves in red and blue (solid lines), respectively, when the heights of each family are plotted against family member number. Use also the `axis` function for the plot, so that the axis with family member numbers run from 0 to 5, while the axis with heights cover 0 to 2.
b) Suggest a minor modification of your code, so that only data points are plotted. Also, confirm that your suggestion works as planned.

Filename: `plot_heights.py`.

**Exercise 2.7: Switching Values**
In an interactive session, use `linspace` from `numpy` to generate an array `x` with the numbers 1.0, 2.0 and 3.0. Then, switch the content of `x[0]` and `x[1]`, before checking `x` to see that your switching worked as planned.
Filename: `switching_values.py`.

**Exercise 2.8: Drawing Random Numbers**
Write a program that prints four random numbers, from the interval [0, 10], to the screen. To generate the numbers, the program should use the `uniform` function from the `random` module of the standard Python library.
Filename: `drawing_random_numbers.py`.

# 3 Loops and Branching

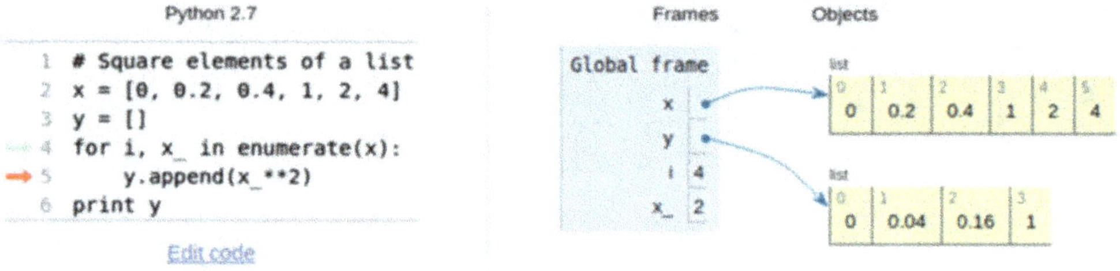


## 3.1 The for Loop

Many computations are repetitive by nature and programming languages have certain *loop structures* to deal with this. One such loop structure is the *for loop*.

### 3.1.1 Example: Printing the 5 Times Table

Assume the task is to print out the 5 times table. Before having learned about loop structures in programming, most of us would first think of coding this like:

```
# Naively printing the 5 times table
print('{:d}*5 = {:d}'.format(1, 1*5))
print('{:d}*5 = {:d}'.format(2, 2*5))
print('{:d}*5 = {:d}'.format(3, 3*5))
print('{:d}*5 = {:d}'.format(4, 4*5))
print('{:d}*5 = {:d}'.format(5, 5*5))
print('{:d}*5 = {:d}'.format(6, 6*5))
print('{:d}*5 = {:d}'.format(7, 7*5))
print('{:d}*5 = {:d}'.format(8, 8*5))
print('{:d}*5 = {:d}'.format(9, 9*5))
print('{:d}*5 = {:d}'.format(10, 10*5))
```



S. Linge, H. P. Langtangen, *Programming for Computations - Python*,
Texts in Computational Science and Engineering 15,
https://doi.org/10.1007/978-3-030-16877-3_3

When executed, the 10 results are printed quite nicely as

```
1*5  = 5
2*5  = 10
...
...
```

With a `for` loop, however, the very same printout may be produced by just two (!) lines of code:

```
for i in [1, 2, 3, 4, 5, 6, 7, 8, 9, 10]:        # Note... for, in and colon
    print('{:d}*5 = {:d}'.format(i, i*5))         # Note indent
```

With this construction, the *loop variable* `i` takes on each of the values 1 to 10, and for each value, the print function is called.

Since the numbers 1 to 10 appear in square brackets, they constitute a special structure called a *list*. The loop here would work equally well if the brackets had been dropped, but then the numbers would be a *tuple*:

```
for i in 1, 2, 3, 4, 5, 6, 7, 8, 9, 10:          # no brackets...
    print('{:d}*5 = {:d}'.format(i, i*5))
```

Both lists and tuples have certain properties, which we will come back to in Sect. 5.1.

### 3.1.2 Characteristics of a Typical for Loop

**Loop Structure** There are different ways to write `for` loops, but herein, they are typically structured as

```
for loop_variable in some_numbers:    # Loop header
    <code line 1>                         # 1st line in loop body
    <code line 2>                         # 2nd line in loop body
    ...
    ...                               # last line in loop body
# First line after the loop
```

where `loop_variable` runs through the numbers[1] given by `some_numbers`. In the very first line, called the *for loop header*, there are two reserved words, `for` and `in`. They are compulsory, as is the *colon* at the end. Also, the *block* of code lines inside a loop must be *indented*. These indented lines are referred to as the *loop body*. Once the indent is reversed, we are outside (and after) the loop (as commented with `# First line after the loop`, see code). One run-through of the loop body is called an *iteration*, i.e., in our example above with the 5 times table, the loop will do 10 iterations.

**Loop Variable** The name picked for the `loop_variable` is up to the programmer. In our times table example, the loop variable `i` appeared explicitly in the `print` command within the loop. Generally, however, the loop variable is not required to enter in any of the code lines within the loop, it is just *available* if you need it.

[1] In Python, the loop variable does not have to be a number. For example, a header like `for name in ['John', 'Paul', 'George', 'Ringo']:` is fine, causing the loop variable to be a name. If you place `print(name)` inside the loop and run it, you get each of the names printed. In this book, however, our focus will be loops with numbers.

This means that if we had, e.g., switched the print command inside our loop with `print('Hello!')` (i.e., so that `i` does not appear explicitly within the loop), `i` would still run through the numbers 1 to 10 as before, but `Hello!` would be printed 10 times instead.

The loop variable `i` takes on the values 1 to 10 *in the order listed*, and any order would be acceptable to Python. Thus, if we (for some reason) would like to reverse the order of the printouts, we could simply reverse the list of numbers, writing `[10, 9, 8, 7, 6, 5, 4, 3, 2, 1]` instead.

It should be noted that the loop variable is not restricted to run over integers. Our next example includes looping also over floating point values.

**Indentation and Nested Loops** In our simple times table example above, the print command inside the loop was indented 4 spaces, which is in accordance with the official style guide of Python.[2]

Strictly speaking, the style guide recommends an indent of *4 spaces per indentation level*. What this means, should become clear if we demonstrate how a `for` loop may appear within another `for` loop, i.e., if we show an arrangement with *nested loops*.

```
for i in [1, 2, 3]:
    # First indentation level (4 spaces)
    print('i = {:d}'.format(i))
    for j in [4.0, 5.0, 6.0]:
        # Second indentation level (4+4 spaces)
        print('      j = {:.1f}'.format(j))
    # First line AFTER loop over j
# First line AFTER loop over i
```

The meaning of indentation levels should be clear from the comments (see code), and it is straight forward to use more nested loops than shown here (see, e.g., Exercise 5.7). Note that, together with the colon, indenting is part of the syntax also for other basic programming constructions in Python (e.g., in `if-elif-else` constructions and functions).

When executing the nested loop construction, we get this printout:

```
i = 1
      j = 4.0
      j = 5.0
      j = 6.0
i = 2
      j = 4.0
      j = 5.0
      j = 6.0
i = 3
      j = 4.0
      j = 5.0
      j = 6.0
```

From the printout, we may infer how the execution proceeds. For *each* value of `i`, the loop over `j` runs through *all* its values before `i` is updated (or the loop is terminated). To test your understanding of nested loops, you are recommended to do Exercise 5.1.

[2] https://www.python.org/dev/peps/pep-0008/.

**Other `for` Loop Structures** In this book, you will occasionally meet `for` loops with a different structure, and as an example, take a look at this:

```
for i, j, k in (1, 2, 3), (4, 5, 6), (6, 7, 8):
    print(i, j, k)
```

Here, in the first iteration, the loop variables `i`, `j` and `k` will become 1, 2 and 3, respectively. In the second iteration, they will become 4, 5 and 6, respectively, and so on. Thus, the printout reads

```
1 2 3
4 5 6
6 7 8
```

As usual, each of `i`, `j` and `k` can be used in any desirable way within the loop.

### 3.1.3 Combining for Loop and Array

Often, loops are used in combination with arrays, so we should understand how that works. To reach this understanding, it is beneficial to do an example with just a small array.

Assume the case is to compute the average height of family members in a family of 5. We may choose to store all the heights in an array, which we then run through by use of a `for` loop to compute the average. The code (`average_height.py`) may look like this:

```
import numpy as np

N = 5
h = np.zeros(N)      # heights of family members (in meter)
h[0] = 1.60; h[1] = 1.85; h[2] = 1.75; h[3] = 1.80; h[4] = 0.50

sum = 0
for i in [0, 1, 2, 3, 4]:
    sum = sum + h[i]
average = sum/N

print('Average height: {:g} meter'.format(average))
```

When executed, the code gives 1.5 m as the average height, which compares favorably to a simple hand calculation. What happens here, is that we first sum up[3] all the heights being stored in the array `h`, before we divide by the number of family members `N` (i.e., just like we would do by hand). Observe how `sum` is initialized to 0 before entering the loop, and that with each iteration, a new height is added to `sum`. Note that the loop variable `i` takes on the integer index values of the array, which start with 0 and end with $N - 1$.

[3] Note this way of using a loop to compute a sum, it is a standard technique in programming.

**Running Through Code "by Hand"**

It is appropriate to stress that much understanding is often developed by first going through code "by hand", i.e. just read the code while doing calculations by hand, before comparing these hand calculations to what the code produces when run (often some print commands must be inserted in the code to enable detailed comparison).

Thus, to make sure you understand the important details in `average_height.py`, you are encouraged to go through that code by hand right now. Also, in a copy, insert a print command in the loop, so that you can compare the output from that program to your own calculations, iteration by iteration.

### 3.1.4 Using the `range` Function

At this point, the observant reader might argue: "Well, this `for` loop seems handy, but what if the loop must do a *really* large number of iterations? If the loop variable is to run through hundreds of numbers, we must spend all day typing those numbers into the loop header"!

**An Example** This is where the built-in `range` function enters the picture. When called, the `range` function will provide integers according to the arguments given in the function call. For example, we could have used `range` in `average_height.py` by just changing the header from

```
for i in [0, 1, 2, 3, 4]:          # original code line
```

to

```
for i in range(0, 5, 1):           # new code line
```

Here, `range(0, 5, 1)` is a function call, where the function `range` is told to provide the integers from 0 (inclusive) to 5 (exclusive!) in steps of 1. In this case, `range(0, 5, 1)` will provide exactly those numbers that we had in the original code, i.e., the loop variable `i` will run through the same values (0, 1, 2, 3 and 4) as before, and program computations stay the same.

With a little interactive test, we may confirm that the `range` function provides the promised numbers. However, since what is returned from the `range` function is an object of type `range`, the number sequence is not explicitly available.[4] Converting the range object to a list, however, does the trick.

```
In [1]: x = range(0, 5, 1)

In [2]: type(x)
Out[2]: range

In [3]: x
Out[3]: range(0, 5)
```

[4] In Python 2, the `range` function returned the requested numbers as a list.

```
In [4]: list(x)                 # convert to list
Out[4]: [0, 1, 2, 3, 4]
```

**A General Call to range** With a header like

```
for loop_variable in range(start, stop, step):
```

and a $step > 0$, `loop_variable` will run through the numbers `start, start + 1*step, start + 2*step, ...., start + n*step`, where $start+n*step < stop <= start + (n + 1) * step$. So, the final number is as close as we can get to the specified `stop` without equalling, or passing, it. For a negative step ($step < 0$, example given below), the same thing applies, meaning that the final number can not equal, or be more negative, than the argument `stop`. Note that an integer `step` different from 1 and $-1$ is perfectly legal.

**Different Ways of Calling range** The function `range` is most often used in `for` loops to produce a required sequence of integers, but the function is not restricted to `for` loops only, of course. It may be called in different ways, e.g., utilizing default values. Some examples are

```
In [1]: list(range(1, 11, 1))
Out[1]: [1, 2, 3, 4, 5, 6, 7, 8, 9, 10]

In [2]: list(range(1, 11))          # step not given, default 1
Out[2]: [1, 2, 3, 4, 5, 6, 7, 8, 9, 10]

In [3]: list(range(11))             # start not given either, default 0
Out[3]: [0, 1, 2, 3, 4, 5, 6, 7, 8, 9, 10]

In [4]: list(range(1, -11, -1))
Out[4]: [1, 0, -1, -2, -3, -4, -5, -6, -7, -8, -9, -10]
```

When calling `range`, there is no argument specifying how many numbers should be produced, like we saw with the `linspace` function of `numpy`. With `range`, this is implied by the function arguments `start`, `stop` and `step`.

**Computer Memory Considerations** Note that `range` does *not* return all the requested numbers at once. Rather, the call to `range` will cause the numbers to be provided *one by one* during loop execution, giving one number per iteration. This way, simultaneous storing of *all* (loop variable) numbers in computer memory is avoided, which may be very important when there is a large number of loop iterations to make.

### 3.1.5 Using `break` and `continue`

It is possible to break out of a loop, i.e., to jump directly to the first code line after the loop, by use of a `break` statement. This might be desirable, for example, if a certain condition is met during loop execution, which makes the remaining iterations redundant.

With loops, it may also become relevant to skip any remaining statements of an ongoing iteration, and rather proceed directly with the next iteration. That is, contrary to the "loop stop" caused by a `break` statement, the loop continues to run after a `continue` statement, unless the end of the loop has been reached.

An example of how to use break and continue can be found in Sect. 5.2 (times_tables_4.py).

The break and continue statements may also be used in while loops, to be treated next.

## 3.2 The while Loop

The other basic loop construction in Python is the *while loop*, which runs as long as a condition is True. Let us move directly to an example, and explain what happens there, before we consider the loop more generally.

### 3.2.1 Example: Finding the Time of Flight

To demonstrate a while loop in action, we will make a minor modification of the case handled with ball_plot.py in Sect. 1.5. Now, we choose to find the time of flight for the ball.

**The Case** Assume the ball is thrown with a slightly lower initial velocity, say 4.5 $ms^{-1}$, while everything else is kept unchanged. Since we still look at the first second of the flight, the heights at the end of the flight will then become negative. However, this only means that the ball has fallen below its initial starting position, i.e., the height where it left the hand, so there is nothing wrong with that. In an array y, we will then have a series of heights which towards the end of y become negative. As before, we will also have an array t with all the times for corresponding heights in y.

**The Program** In a program named ball_time.py, we may find the time of flight as the time when heights switch from positive to negative. The program could look like this

```
import numpy as np

v0 = 4.5                      # Initial velocity
g = 9.81                      # Acceleration of gravity
t = np.linspace(0, 1, 1000)   # 1000 points in time interval
y = v0*t - 0.5*g*t**2         # Generate all heights

# Find index where ball approximately has reached y=0
i = 0
while y[i] >= 0:
    i = i + 1

# Since y[i] is the height at time t[i], we do know the
# time as well when we have the index i...
print('Time of flight (in seconds): {:g}'.format(t[i]))

# We plot the path again just for comparison
import matplotlib.pyplot as plt
plt.plot(t, y)
plt.plot(t, 0*t, 'g--')
plt.xlabel('Time (s)')
plt.ylabel('Height (m)')
plt.show()
```

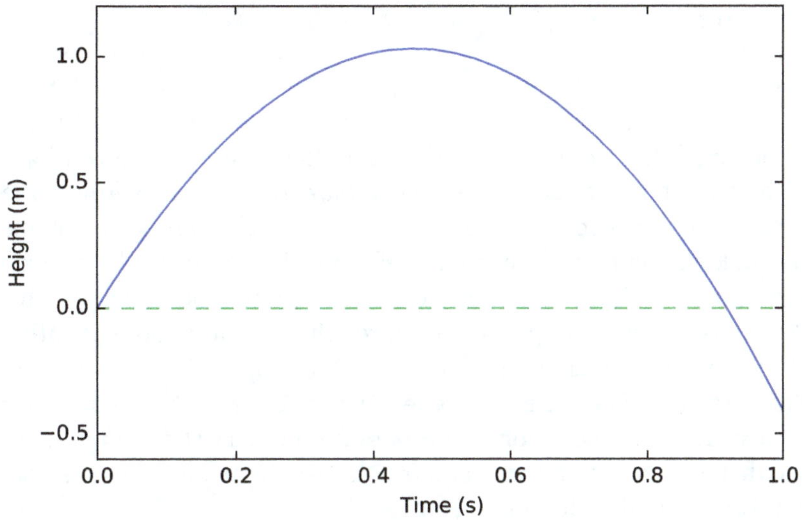


**Fig. 3.1** Vertical position of ball

The loop will run as long as the condition `y[i] >= 0` evaluates to `True`. Note that the programmer introduced a variable by the name `i`, initialized it (`i = 0`) before the loop, and updated it (`i = i + 1`) in the loop. So, each time the condition `y[i] >= 0` evaluates to `True`, `i` is *explicitly* increased by 1, allowing a check of successive elements in the array `y`.

When the condition `y[i] >= 0` evaluates to `False`, program execution proceeds with the code lines after the loop. This means that, after skipping the comments, the time of flight is printed, followed by a plotting of the heights (to allow an easy check of the time of flight).

**Reporting the Answer** Remember that the height is computed at chosen points in time only, so, most likely, we do not have the time for when the height is *exactly* zero. Thus, reporting `t[i]` as the time of flight is an approximation. Another alternative, could be to report `0.5*(t[i-1] + t[i])` as the answer, reasoning that since `y[i]` is negative (which is why the loop terminated), `t[i]` must be too large.

**Running the Program** If you run this program, you get the printout

```
Time of flight (in seconds): 0.917918
```

and the plot seen in Fig. 3.1. The printed time of flight seems consistent with what we can read off from the plot.

### 3.2.2 Characteristics of a Typical while Loop

**Loop Structure and Interpretation** The structure of a typical `while` loop may be put up as

```
while some_condition:   # Loop header
    <code line 1>           # 1st line in loop body
```

```
    <code line 2>           # 2nd line in loop body
    ...
    ...
# This is the first line after the loop
```

The first line here is the *while loop header*. It contains the reserved word `while` and ends with a colon, both are compulsory. The *indented* lines that follow the header (i.e., `<code line 1>`, `<code line 2>`, etc.) constitute a *block* of statements, the *loop body*. Indentation is done as with `for` loops, i.e., 4 spaces by convention. In our example above with the ball, there was only a single line in the loop body (i.e., `i = i + 1`). As with `for` loops, one run-through of the loop body is referred to as an *iteration*. Once the indentation is reversed, the loop body has ended. Here, the first line after the loop is `# This is the first line after the loop`.

Between `while` and the colon, there is `some_condition`, which is a boolean expression that evaluates to either `True` or `False`. The boolean expression may be a compound expression with `and`, `or`, etc.

When a `while` loop is encountered by the Python interpreter, it evaluates `some_condition` the first time. If `True`, one iteration of the *loop body* is carried out. After this first iteration, `some_condition` is evaluated once again (meaning that program execution goes back up to the top of the loop). If `True` again, there is another iteration, and so on, just like we saw above with `ball_time.py`. Once `some_condition` evaluates to `False`, the loop is finished and execution continues with the first line after the loop. Note that if `some_condition` evaluates to `False` the very first time, the statements inside the loop will *not* be executed at all, and execution simply continues immediately with the first line after the loop.

Compared to a `for` loop, the programmer does not have to specify the number of iterations when coding a `while` loop. It simply runs until the boolean expression becomes `False`. Remember that if you want to use a variable analogously to the loop variable of a `for` loop, you have to explicitly update that variable inside the `while` loop (as we did with `i` in `ball_time.py` above). This differs from the automatic update of a loop variable in `for` loops.

Just as in `for` loops, there might be (arbitrarily) many code lines in a `while` loop. Also, nested loops work just like nested `for` loops. Having `for` loops inside `while` loops, and vice versa, is straight forward. Any `for` loop may also be implemented as a `while` loop, but `while` loops are more flexible, so not all of them can be expressed as a `for` loop.

**Infinite Loops** It is possible to have a `while` loop in which the condition never evaluates to `False`, meaning that program execution can not escape the loop! This is referred to as an *infinite loop*. Sometimes, infinite loops are just what you need, for example, in surveillance camera systems. More often, however, they are unintentional, and when learning to code, it is quite common to unintentionally end up with an infinite loop (just wait and see!). If you accidentally enter an infinite loop and the program just hangs "forever", press `Ctrl+c` to stop the program.

To check that you have gained a basic understanding of the `while` loop construction, you are recommended to do Exercise 3.4.

## 3.3 Branching (if, elif and else)

Very often in life,[5] and in computer programs, the next action depends on the outcome of a question starting with "if". This gives the possibility of branching into different types of action depending on some criterion.

As an introduction to branching, let us "build up" a little program that evaluates a water temperature provided by the program user.

### 3.3.1 Example: Judging the Water Temperature

Assume we want to write a program that helps us decide, based on water temperature alone (in degrees Celcius), whether we should go swimming or not.

**One if-test** As a start, we code our program simply as

```
T = float(input('What is the water temperature? '))
if T > 24:
    print('Great, jump in!')
# First line after if part
```

Even if you have never seen an `if` test before, you are probably able to guess what will happen with this code. Python will first ask the user for the water temperature. Let us assume that 25 is entered, so that `T` becomes 25 through the assignment (note that, since the `input` returns a string, we convert it to a float before assigning to `T`). Next, the condition `T > 24` will evaluate to `True`, which implies that the print command gets executed and "Great, jump in!" appears on the screen.

To the contrary, if 24 (or lower) had been entered, the condition would have evaluated to `False` and the print command would *not* have been executed. Rather, execution would have proceeded directly to the line after the `if` part, i.e., to the line `# First line after if part`, and continued from there. This would mean, however, that our program would give us *no response* if we entered a water temperature of 24, or lower.

**Two if-tests** Immediately, we realize that this is not satisfactory, so (as a "first fix") we extend our code with a second `if` test, as

```
T = float(input('What is the water temperature? '))
if T > 24:                                      # testing condition 1
    print('Great, jump in!')
if T <= 24:                                     # testing condition 2
    print('Do not swim. Too cold!')
# First line after if-if construction
```

This will work, at least in the way that we get a planned printout ("Do not swim. Too cold!") also when the temperature is 24, or lower. However, something is not quite right here. If `T` is 24 (or lower), the first condition will evaluate to `False`, and

[5] Some readers may perhaps be puzzled by this sentence, bringing in such a huge thing as life itself. The truth is, that this sentence *is* as deep as it appears. My dear co-author Hans Petter Langtangen wrote this sentence well into his cancer treatment. Hans Petter passed away on October 10th, 2016, a few months after the 1st edition of this book was published.

Python will proceed immediately by *also* testing the second condition. However, this test is superfluous, since we *know beforehand* that it will evaluate to True! So, in this particular case, using two separate if tests is not suitable (generally, however, separate if tests may be just what you need. It all depends on the problem at hand).

**An if-else Construction** For our case, it is much better to use an else part, like this

```
T = float(input('What is the water temperature? '))
if T > 24:                                  # testing condition 1
    print('Great, jump in!')
else:
    print('Do not swim. Too cold!')
# First line after if-else construction
```

When the first condition evaluates to False in this code, execution proceeds directly with the print command in the else part, with no extra testing!

To students with little programming experience, this may seem like a very small thing to shout about. However, in addition to avoiding an unnecessary test with the if-else alternative, it also corresponds better to the actual logic: If the first condition is false, then the other condition has to be true, and vice versa. No further checking is needed.

**An if-elif-else Construction** Considering our "advisor program", we have to admit it is a bit crude, having only two categories. If the temperature is larger than 24 degrees, we are advised to swim, otherwise not. Some refinement seems to be the thing.

Let us say we allow some intermediate case, in which our program is less categoric for temperatures between 20 and 24 degrees, for example. There is a nice elif (short for else if) construction which then applies. Introducing that in our program (and saving it as swim_advisor.py), it reads

```
T = float(input('What is the water temperature? '))
if T > 24:                                        # testing condition 1
    print('Great, jump in!')
elif 20 <= T <= 24:                               # testing condition 2
    print('Not bad. Put your toe in first!')
else:
    print('Do not swim. Too cold!')
# First line after if-elif-else construction
```

You probably realize what will happen now. For temperatures above 24 and below 20, our "advisor" will respond just like in the previous version (i.e., the if-else version). However, for intermediate temperatures, the first condition will evaluate to False, which implies that the Python interpreter will continue with the elif line. Here, condition 2 will evaluate to True, which means that "Not bad. Put your toe in first!" will be printed. The else part is then skipped. As you might expect, more refinement would be straight forward to include by use of more elif parts.

**Programming as a Step-Wise Process** The reader should note that, besides demonstrating branching, the development of the previous program gave a (very) simple example of how code may be written by a step-wise approach. Starting out with the simplest version of the code, complexity is added step by step, before arriving at the final version. At each step, you make sure the code works as planned. Such a procedure is generally a good idea, and we will address it explicitly again, when we program a (slightly) more comprehensive case in Sect. 4.2.

### 3.3.2 The Characteristics of Branching

A more general form of an `if-elif-else` construction reads

```
if condition_1:              # testing condition 1
    <code line 1>
    <code line 2>
    ...
elif condition_2:            # testing condition 2
    <code line 1>
    <code line 2>
    ...
elif condition_3:            # testing condition 3
    <code line 1>
    <code line 2>
    ...
else:
    <code line 1>
    <code line 2>
    ...
# First line after if-elif-else construction
```

Here we see an `if` part, two `elif` parts and an `else` part. Note the compulsory *colon* and *indented* code lines (a *block* of statements) in each case. As with loops, indents are conventionally 4 spaces. In such an arrangement, there may be "any" number of `elif` parts (also none) and the `else` part may, or may not, be present.

When interpreting an arrangement like this, Python starts checking the conditions, one after the other, from the top. If a condition (here, either `condition_1`, `condition_2` or `condition_3`) evaluates to `True`, the corresponding code lines are executed, before proceeding *directly* to the first line after the whole arrangement (here, to the line `# First line after if-elif-else construction`). This means that any remaining tests, and the `else` part, are simply skipped! If none of the conditions evaluate to `True`, the `else` part (when present) is executed.

### 3.3.3 Example: Finding the Maximum Height

We have previously modified `ball_plot.py` from Sect. 1.5 to find the time of flight instead (see `ball_time.py`). Let us now change `ball_plot.py` in a slightly different way, so that the new program instead finds the maximum height achieved by the ball.

The solution illustrates a simple, and very common, search procedure, looping through an array by use of a `for` loop to find the maximum value. Our program `ball_max_height.py` reads

```
import numpy as np
import matplotlib.pyplot as plt

v0 = 5                        # Initial velocity
g = 9.81                      # Acceleration of gravity
t = np.linspace(0, 1, 1000)   # 1000 points in time interval
y = v0*t - 0.5*g*t**2         # Generate all heights

# At this point, the array y with all the heights is ready,
# and we need to find the largest value within y.

largest_height = y[0]         # Starting value for search
for i in range(1, len(y), 1):
    if y[i] > largest_height:
        largest_height = y[i]

print('The largest height achieved was {:g} m'.format(largest_height))

# We might also like to plot the path again just to compare
plt.plot(t,y)
plt.xlabel('Time (s)')
plt.ylabel('Height (m)')
plt.show()
```

We focus our attention on the new thing here, the search performed by the `for` loop. The value in `y[0]` is used as a starting value for `largest_height`. The very first check then, tests whether `y[1]` is larger than this height. If so, `y[1]` is stored as the largest height. The `for` loop then updates `i` to 2, and continues to check `y[2]`, and so on. Each time we find a larger number, we store it. When finished, `largest_height` will contain the largest number from the array `y`.

When you run the program, you get

```
The largest height achieved was 1.27421 m
```

which compares favorably to the plot that pops up (see Fig. 1.1).

The observant reader has already seen the similarity of finding the maximum height and finding the time of flight, as we addressed previously in Sect. 3.2.1. In fact, we could alternatively have solved the maximum height problem here by utilizing that `y[i+1] > y[i]` as the ball moves towards the top. Doing this, our search loop could have been written

```
i = 0
while y[i+1] > y[i]:
    i = i + 1
```

When the condition `y[i+1] > y[i]` becomes `False`, we could report `y[i+1]` as our approximation of the maximum height, for example.

> **Getting indices right**
>
> To implement the traversing of arrays with loops and indices, is often challenging to get right. You need to understand the start, stop and step length values for the loop variable, and also how the loop variable (possibly) enters expressions inside the loop. At the same time, however, it is something that programmers do often, so it is important to develop the right skills on these matters.
>
> You are encouraged to test your understanding of the search procedure in `ball_max_height.py` by doing Exercise 3.9. That exercise will ask you to compare what you get "by hand" to printouts from the code. It is of *fundamental importance* to get this procedure as an established habit of yours, so do the exercise right now!

### 3.3.4 Example: Random Walk in Two Dimensions

We will now turn to an example which represents the core of so-called *random walk* algorithms. These are used in many branches of science and engineering, including such different fields as materials manufacturing and brain research.

The procedure we will consider, is to walk a series of equally sized steps, and for each of those steps, there should be the same probability of going to the north (N), east (E), south (S), or west (W). No other directions are legal. How can we implement such an action in a computer program?

To prepare our minds for the coding, it might be useful to first reflect upon how this could be done for real. One way, is to use a deck of cards, letting the four suits correspond to the four directions: clubs to N, diamonds to E, hearts to S, and spades to W, for instance. We draw a card, perform the corresponding move, and repeat the process a large number of times. The resulting path mimics, e.g., a typical path followed by a diffusing molecule.

In a computer program, we can not draw cards, but we can draw random numbers. So, we may use a loop to repeatedly draw a random number, and depending on the number, we update the coordinates of our location. There are many ways to draw random numbers and "translate" them into our four directions, and the technical details will typically depend on the programming language. However, our technique here is universal: we draw a random number from the interval $[0, 1)$ and let $[0, 0.25)$ correspond to N, $[0.25, 0.5)$ to E, $[0.5, 0.75)$ to S, and $[0.75, 1)$ to W. We decide to simulate 1000 steps, each of length 1 (e.g., meter), starting from Origo in our coordinate system. To enable plotting our path, we use two arrays for storing the coordinate history, one for the x-coordinates and one for the corresponding y-coordinates.

The suggested code `random_walk_2D.py` then reads

```
import random
import numpy as np
import matplotlib.pyplot as plt

N = 1000                        # number of steps
```

```
d = 1                          # step length (e.g., in meter)
x = np.zeros(N+1)              # x coordinates
y = np.zeros(N+1)              # y coordinates
x[0] = 0;  y[0] = 0            # set initial position

for i in range(0, N, 1):
    r = random.random()            # random number in [0,1)
    if 0 <= r < 0.25:              # move north
        y[i+1] = y[i] + d
        x[i+1] = x[i]
    elif 0.25 <= r < 0.5:          # move east
        x[i+1] = x[i] + d
        y[i+1] = y[i]
    elif 0.5 <= r < 0.75:          # move south
        y[i+1] = y[i] - d
        x[i+1] = x[i]
    else:                          # move west
        x[i+1] = x[i] - d
        y[i+1] = y[i]

# plot path (mark start and stop with blue o and *, respectively)
plt.plot(x, y, 'r--', x[0], y[0], 'bo', x[-1], y[-1], 'b*')
plt.xlabel('x');  plt.ylabel('y')
plt.show()
```

Here, the initial position is explicitly set, even if `x[0]` and `y[0]` are known to be zero already. We do this, since the initial position is important, and by setting it explicitly, it is clearly not accidental what the starting position is. Note that if a step is taken in the x-direction, the y-coordinate is unchanged, and vice versa.

Executing the program produces the plot seen in Fig. 3.2, where the initial and final positions are marked in blue with a circle and a star, respectively. Remember that pseudo-random numbers are involved here, meaning that two consecutive runs will generally produce totally different paths.

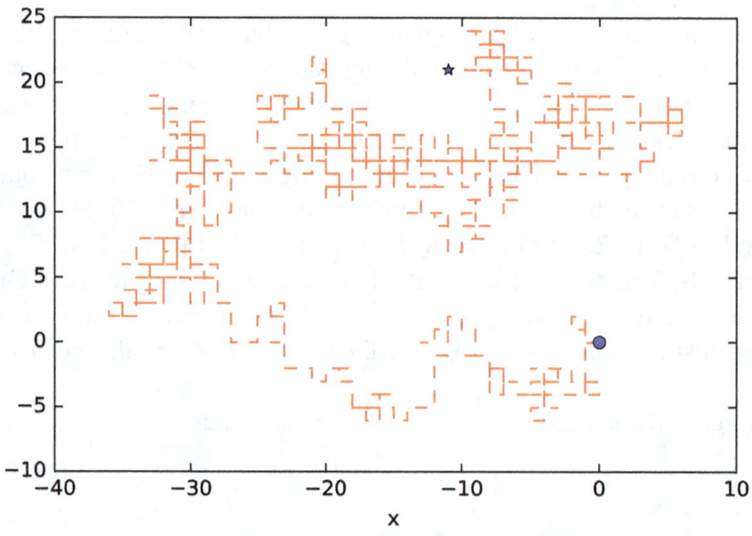


**Fig. 3.2** One realization of a random walk (N-E-S-W) with a 1000 steps. Initial and final positions are marked in blue with a circle and a star, respectively

## 3.4 Exercises

**Exercise 3.1: A `for` Loop with Errors**
Assume some program has been written for the task of adding all integers $i = 1, 2, \ldots, 10$ and printing the final result:

```
for i in [1, 2, 3, 4, 5, 6, 7, 8, 9, 10)
sum = Sum + x
print 'sum: ', sum
```

a) Identify the errors in the program by just reading the code.
b) Write a new version of the program with errors corrected. Run this program and confirm that it gives the correct output.

Filename: `for_loop_errors.py`.

**Exercise 3.2: The `range` Function**
Write a slightly different version of the program in Exercise 3.1. Now, the `range` function should be used in the `for` loop header, and only the even numbers from [2, 10] should be added. Also, the (only) statement within the loop should read `sum = sum + i`.
Filename: `range_function.py`.

**Exercise 3.3: A while Loop with Errors**
Assume some program has been written for the task of adding all integers $i = 1, 2, \ldots, 10$:

```
some_number = 0
i = 1
while i < 11
    some_number += 1
print some_number
```

a) Identify the errors in the program by just reading the code.
b) Write a new version of the program with errors corrected. Run this program and confirm that it gives the correct output.

Filename: `while_loop_errors.py`.

**Exercise 3.4: while Loop Instead of for Loop**
Rewrite `average_height.py` from Sect. 3.1.3, using a `while` loop instead.
Filename: `while_instead_of_for.py`.

**Exercise 3.5: Compare Integers a and b**
Explain briefly, in your own words, what the following program does.

```
a = int(input('Give an integer a: '))
b = int(input('Give an integer b: '))
```

```
if a < b:
    print('\na is the smallest of the two numbers')
elif a == b:
    print('\na and b are equal')
else:
    print('\na is the largest of the two numbers')
```

Proceed by writing the program, and then run it a few times with different values for a and b to confirm that it works as intended. In particular, choose combinations for a and b so that all three branches of the `if` construction get tested.
Filename: `compare_a_and_b.py`.

**Remarks** The program is not too robust, since it assumes the user types an integer as input (a real number gives trouble).

**Exercise 3.6: Area of Rectangle Versus Circle**
Consider one circle and one rectangle. The circle has a radius $r = 10.6$. The rectangle has sides $a$ and $b$, but only $a$ is known from the outset. Let $a = 1.3$ and write a program that uses a `while` loop to find the largest possible integer $b$ that gives a rectangle area smaller than, but as close as possible to, the area of the circle. Run the program and confirm that it gives the right answer (which is $b = 271$).
Filename: `area_rectangle_vs_circle.py`.

**Exercise 3.7: Frequency of Random Numbers**
Write a program that takes a positive integer $N$ as input and then draws $N$ random integers from the interval $[1, 6]$. In the program, count how many of the numbers, $M$, that equal 6 and print out the fraction $M/N$. Also, print all the random numbers to the screen so that you can check for yourself that the counting is correct. Run the program with a small value for `N` (e.g., `N = 10`) to confirm that it works as intended.

**Hint** Use `random.randint(1,6)` to draw a random integer between 1 and 6.

Filename: `count_random_numbers.py`.

**Remarks** For large $N$, this program computes the probability $M/N$ of getting six eyes when throwing a dice.

**Exercise 3.8: Game 21**
Consider some game where each participant draws a series of random integers evenly distributed between 0 and 10, with the aim of getting the sum as close as possible to 21, but *not larger* than 21. You are out of the game if the sum passes 21.

After each draw, you are told the number and your total sum, and are asked whether you want another draw or not. The one coming closest to 21 is the winner.

Implement this game in a program.

**Hint** Use `random.randint(0,10)` to draw random integers in [0, 10].
Filename: `game_21.py`.

**Exercise 3.9: Simple Search: Verification**
Check your understanding of the search procedure in `ball_max_height.py` from Sect. 3.3.3 by comparing what you get "by hand" to printouts from the code. Work on a copy of `ball_max_height.py`. Comment out what you do not need, and use an array `y` of just 4 elements (or so). Fill that array with integers, so that you place a maximum value in a certain location. Then, run through that code *by hand* for every iteration of the loop, writing down the numbers in `largest_height`. Finally, place a print command in the loop, so that `largest_height` gets printed with every iteration. Run the program and compare to what you found by hand.
Filename: `simple_search_verify.py`.

**Exercise 3.10: Sort Array with Numbers**
Write a script that uses the `uniform` function from the `random` module to generate an array of 6 random numbers between 0 and 10.

The program should then sort the array so that numbers appear in increasing order. Let the program make a formatted print of the array to screen both before and after sorting. Confirm that the array has been sorted correctly.
Filename: `sort_numbers.py`.

**Exercise 3.11: Compute $\pi$**
Up through history, great minds have developed different computational schemes for the number $\pi$. We will here consider two such schemes, one by Leibniz (1646–1716), and one by Euler (1707–1783).

The scheme by Leibniz may be written

$$\pi = 8\sum_{k=0}^{\infty}\frac{1}{(4k+1)(4k+3)},$$

while one form of the Euler scheme may appear as

$$\pi = \sqrt{6\sum_{k=1}^{\infty}\frac{1}{k^2}}.$$

If only the first $N$ terms of each sum are used as an approximation to $\pi$, each modified scheme will have computed $\pi$ with some error.

Write a program that takes $N$ as input from the user, and plots the error development with both schemes as the number of iterations approaches $N$. Your program should also print out the final error achieved with both schemes, i.e. when the number of terms is `N`. Run the program with $N = 100$ and explain briefly what the graphs show.
Filename: `compute_pi.py`.

# Functions and the Writing of Code

# 4

## 4.1 Functions: How to Write Them?

Until now, we have benefitted from *using* functions like, e.g., `zeros` and `linspace` from `numpy`. These have all been written by others for us to use. Now we will look at how to *write* such functions ourselves, an absolutely fundamental skill in programming.

In its simplest form, a function in a program is much like a mathematical function: some input number $x$ is transformed to some output number. One example is the $\tanh^{-1}(x)$ function, called `atan` in computer code: it takes one real number as input and returns another number. Functions in Python are more general and can take a series of values as input and return one or more results, or simply nothing. The purpose of functions is twofold:

1. to *group code lines* that naturally belong together (making such units of code is a strategy which may ease the problem solving process dramatically), and
2. to *parameterize* a set of code lines such that they can be written only once and easily be re-executed with variations.

Functions that we write ourselves are often referred to as *user-defined* functions. Throughout this book, we will present many examples, in various contexts, of how such functions may be written.

### 4.1.1 Example: Writing Our First Function

To grasp the first few essentials about function writing, we change `ball.py` from Sect. 1.2, so that the height `y` is rather computed by use of a *function* that we define ourselves. Also, to better demonstrate the use of our function, we compute `y` at two points in time (not only one, as in `ball.py`). The new program `ball_function.py` then appears as

```
def y(v0, t):
    g = 9.81                    # Acceleration of gravity
```



S. Linge, H. P. Langtangen, *Programming for Computations - Python*,
Texts in Computational Science and Engineering 15,
https://doi.org/10.1007/978-3-030-16877-3_4

```
    return v0*t - 0.5*g*t**2

v0 = 5                          # Initial velocity

time = 0.6                      # Just pick one point in time
print(y(v0, time))
time = 0.9                      # Pick another point in time
print(y(v0, time))
```

**The Function Definition** When Python reads this program from the top, it takes the code from the line with `def`, to the line with `return`, to be the *definition* of a function by the name `y`. Note that this function (or *any* function for that matter) is *not* executed until it is *called*. Here, that happens with the two calls (`y(v0, time)`) appearing in the print commands further down in the code. In other words, when Python reads the function definition for the first time, it just "stores the definition for later use" (and checks for syntax errors, see Exercise 4.8).

**Calling the Function** When the function is called the first time, the values of `v0` (5) and `time` (0.6) are transferred to the `y` function such that, in the function, `v0 = 5` and `t = 0.6`. Thereafter, Python executes the function line by line. In the final line `return v0*t - 0.5*g*t**2`, the expression `v0*t - 0.5*g*t**2` is computed, resulting in a number which is "returned" to replace `y(v0, time)` in the calling code. The function `print` is then called with this number as input argument and proceeds to print it (i.e., the height). Alternatively, the number returned from `y` could have been assigned to a variable, e.g., like `h = y(v0, time)`, before printing as `print(h)`.

Python then proceeds with the next line, setting `time` to 0.9, before a new function call is triggered in the following line, causing a second execution of the function `y` and printout of the new height.

**Variable Names in Function Calls** Observe that, when *calling* the function `y`, the time was contained in the variable `time`, whereas the corresponding input variable (called a *parameter*) in the function `y` had the name `t`. We should reveal already now, that in general, variable names in function calls *do not have to* be the same as the corresponding names in the function definition. However, with `v0` here, we see that variable names *can* be the same in the function call and the function definition (but technically, they are then two different variables with the same name, see Sect. 4.1.4). More rules about this will follow soon.

### 4.1.2 Characteristics of a Function Definition

**Function Structure** We may now write up a more general form of a Python function as

```
def function_name(p1, p2, p3, ...):      # function header
    """This is a docstring"""                    # ...in function body
    <code line>                                  # ...in function body
    <code line>                                  # ...in function body
```

```
    ...
    ...
    return result_1, result_2, ...          # last line in function body
# First line after function definition
```

A function definition must appear before the function is called, and usually, function definitions are placed one after the other at the top of a program, after import statements (if any).

**Function Header (Positional Parameters)** The first line, often called the *function header*, always starts with the reserved word `def`. This word is succeeded by the name of the function, followed by a listing of comma-separated names in parentheses, being the *parameters* of the function (here symbolized with `p1`, `p2`, `p3`,...). These parameters specify what input the function needs for execution. The header always ends with a colon. Function and parameter names must be decided by the programmer.

The function header may contain any number[1] of parameters, also none. When there are no parameters, the parentheses must still be there, i.e., like `def function_name():`.

When input parameters are listed on the form above, they are referred to as *positional parameters*. Below, in Sect. 4.1.5, we will see what freedom there is when calling functions defined with such parameters.

**Another Typical Function Header (Keyword Parameters)** Another kind of function header that you often will deal with, is one which allows default values to be given to some, or all, of the input parameters. We may write such a header on the following form[2] (it could replace the previous header that has only positional parameters):

```
def function_name(p1, p2, p3=default_3, p4=default_4, ...):
```

In this case, the two first parameters are positional, whereas `p3` and `p4` are known as *keyword parameters*. This means that, unless other values are specified for `p3` and `p4` when *calling* the function, they will get the default values `default_3` and `default_4`, respectively. This will soon (Sect. 4.1.7) be demonstrated and discussed in more detail through examples.

A function header may have only positional parameters, only keyword parameters, or some of each. However, positional parameters must always be listed *before* keyword parameters (as shown in the header above).

Note that there should be no space to each side of = when specifying keyword parameters.

**Function Body** All code lines inside a function must be *indented*, conventionally with 4 spaces, or more (if there are more indentation levels). In a function, these indented lines represent a *block* of statements, collectively referred to as the *function body*. Once the indent is reversed, we are outside (and after) the function.

[1] It is possible to have a variable number of input parameters (using `*args` and `**kwargs`). However, we do not pursue that any further here.

[2] Strictly speaking, this header also incorporates the previous header, but they were split just to clarify the presentation.

Here, the comment `# First line after function definition` is after the function.

The first line in the function body shown here, is an optional documentation string, a *docstring*. This string is meant for a human interpreter, so it should say something about the purpose with the function and explain input parameters and return values, unless obvious. By convention, a docstring is enclosed in triple double quotes (`"""`), which allows the string to run over several lines. When present, the docstring must appear immediately after the function header, as shown above.

The code lines of a function are executed only when the function is *called* (or *invoked*), as explained above with `ball_function.py`. Usually, a function ends with a *return statement*, starting with the reserved word `return`, which "returns" one or more results back to the place where the function was called. However, the explicit return statement may be dropped if not needed.[3] How to receive multiple return values from a function call will be exemplified in Sect. 4.1.6.

A function body can have loops, branching and calls to other functions, and may contain as many code lines as you need. Sometimes, a function body contains nothing more than a `return` statement of the form `return <some calculation>`, where some calculation is carried out before returning the result. Note that function input parameters are not required to be numbers. Any object will do, e.g., strings or other functions.

### 4.1.3 Functions and the Main Program

An expression you will often encounter in programming, is *main program*, or that some code is "in main". This is nothing particular to Python, and simply refers to that part of the program which is *outside* functions, taking function headers as part of the main program.

We may exemplify this with `ball_function.py` from above, using comments to tell which lines are *not* "in main".

```
def y(v0, t):
    g = 9.81                        # not in main
    return v0*t - 0.5*g*t**2        # not in main

v0 = 5

time = 0.6
print(y(v0, time))
time = 0.9
print(y(v0, time))
```

Thus, everything is in main except the two lines of the function body.

[3] In that case, something called `None` is returned, being a certain object that represents "nothing".

### 4.1.4 Local Versus Global Variables

In our program `ball_function.py`, we have defined the variable `g` *inside* the function `y`. This makes `g` a *local variable*, meaning that it is only known *inside* the function. Thus, if we had tried to use `g` outside of the function, we would have got an error message. To see this, we may insert `print(v0*t - 0.5*g*t**2)` as a new last line in main (i.e., after the last `print(y(v0, time))`) and try to run the code. Now, Python will not recognize `g`, even if Python just used it inside the function `y` (you should try this to see for yourself, but remember to remove the inserted code after the test!).

The variables `v0` and `time` are defined outside the function and are therefore *global variables*. They are known both outside and inside the function.[4]

Input parameters listed in a function header are by rule local variables inside the function. If you define one global and one local variable, both with the same name (as `v0` in `ball_function.py`), the function body only "sees" the local one, so the global variable is not affected by what happens to its local "name-brother".

If you want to change the value of a global variable inside a function, you need to declare the variable as global inside the function. That is, if some global variable was named `x`, we would need to write `global x` inside the function definition before we let the function change it. After function execution, `x` would then have a changed value.

### 4.1.5 Calling a Function Defined with Positional Parameters

We will here discuss alternative ways of *calling* the function `y` from `ballnrea_function.py`. This function has only got positional parameters, and throughout, the definition

```
def y(v0, t):
    g = 9.81
    return v0*t - 0.5*g*t**2
```

is kept unchanged.

**Parameter Versus Argument** As explained previously, the input variables specified in a function definition are called the *parameters* of the function. When we call that function, however, the values provided in the call are referred to as *arguments*.[5]

**Mixing the Position of Arguments** Assume now, like before, that we just want our main program to compute the height of the ball after 0.6 $s$, when the initial velocity

[4] The observant reader may then ask why not just define the function `y` without input parameters `v0` and `t`, and simply use `v0` and `time` directly inside the function (changing `t` to `time` in the return statement)? The answer is that this would have worked. However, there are several issues related to the use of global variables, so it is something that should be avoided in general.

[5] https://docs.python.org/3.3/faq/programming.html#faq-argument-vs-parameter.

is 5 $ms^{-1}$. In our main program, we could then try two alternative calls,

```
print(y(5, 0.6))          # works fine
print(y(0.6, 5))          # gives no error message, but the wrong result!
```

Here, y is called with *positional arguments* only (also termed *ordinary arguments*). The first alternative will do the job. Regarding the second alternative, it will print a result, but a wrong one, since arguments are in the wrong position when calling. With the second call to y (i.e., `y(0.6, 5)`), we get `v0 = 0.6` and `t = 5` in the function, which clearly is not what we intended. Note that Python has no way of knowing that this is wrong, so it will happily compute a height according to the function definition and print an answer.

Doing the same with variables, e.g., like

```
initial_velocity = 5
time = 0.6
print(y(initial_velocity, time))    # works fine
print(y(time, initial_velocity))    # No error message, but wrong result!
```

will of course not change anything. The first call will give the correct result, while the latter will print the wrong result (without any error message).

**Using Keywords in the Call** It is possible to use function input parameter names as *keywords* when calling the function (note, the function definition is still unchanged with only positional parameters!). This brings the advantage of making the function call more readable. Also, it allows the order of arguments to be switched, according to some rules. A few examples will illustrate how this works.

By use of the parameter names `v0` and `t` from the function definition, we may have the following statements in main:

```
print(y(v0=5, t=0.6))         # works fine
print(y(t=0.6, v0=5))         # order switched, works fine with keywords!
```

Here, y is called with *keyword arguments* only (also termed *named arguments*). Either of the two alternative calls will give the correct printout, since, irrespective of argument ordering, Python is explicitly told which function parameter should have which value. This generalizes: *as long as keywords are used for all arguments in a function call, any ordering of arguments can be used.*

It is allowed to have a mix of positional and keyword arguments in the call, however, but then we need to be a bit more careful. With the following lines in main,

```
v0 = 5
print(y(v0, t=0.6))          # works fine
print(y(t=0.6, v0))          # gives syntax error!
```

the first alternative is acceptable, while the second is not. The general rule is, that *when mixing positional and keyword arguments, all the positional arguments must precede the keyword arguments.* The positional arguments must also come in the very same order as the corresponding input parameters appear in the function definition, while the order of the keyword arguments may be changed.

Note that, if some function is defined with a "long" list of input parameters, when calling that function, you can not use a keyword for one of the arguments "in the middle", even if placed last in the list (make yourself an example with 3 parameters and test it!). This is because Python reads the listed arguments from left to right, and does not know that an argument is taken out of the list before it comes to the end (but then it is too late).

### 4.1.6 A Function with Two Return Values

Take a slight variation of our case with the ball, assuming that the ball is not thrown straight up, but at an angle, so that two coordinates are needed to specify its position at any time.

According to Newton's laws (when air resistance is negligible), the vertical position is given by $y(t) = v_{0y}t - 0.5gt^2$ and, simultaneously, the horizontal position by $x(t) = v_{0x}t$. We can include both these expressions in a new version of our program that finds the position of the ball at a given time:

```
def xy(v0x, v0y, t):
    """Compute horizontal and vertical positions at time t"""
    g = 9.81                                 # acceleration of gravity
    return v0x*t, v0y*t - 0.5*g*t**2

v_init_x = 2.0                               # initial velocity in x
v_init_y = 5.0                               # initial velocity in y
time = 0.6                                   # chosen point in time

x, y = xy(v_init_x, v_init_y, time)
print('Horizontal position: {:g} , Vertical position: {:g}'.format(x, y))
```

We note that in the return statement, the returned values (two here) are separated by a comma. Here, the x coordinate will be computed by `v0x*t`, while the y coordinate will be computed like before. These two calculations produce two numbers that are returned to variables x and y in main. Note that, the order of the results returned from the function must be the same as the order of the corresponding variables in the assignment statement. Note the use of a comma both in the return statement and the assignment statement.

### 4.1.7 Calling a Function Defined with Keyword Parameters

Let us adjust the previous program slightly, introducing keyword parameters in the definition. For example, if we use 0.6 as a default value for `t`, and aim to get the same printout as before, the program reads

```
def xy(v0x, v0y, t=0.6):
    """Compute horizontal and vertical positions at time t"""
    g = 9.81                                 # acceleration of gravity
    return v0x*t, v0y*t - 0.5*g*t**2

v_init_x = 2.0                               # initial velocity in x
v_init_y = 5.0                               # initial velocity in y

x, y = xy(v_init_x, v_init_y)
print('Horizontal position: {:g} , Vertical position: {:g}'.format(x, y))
```

Alternatively, with default values for all the parameters, and again aiming for the same printout, our program (`ball_position_xy.py`) appears as

```
def xy(v0x=2.0, v0y=5.0, t=0.6):
    """Computes horizontal and vertical positions at time t"""
    g = 9.81                                # acceleration of gravity
    return v0x*t, v0y*t - 0.5*g*t**2

x, y = xy()
print('Horizontal position: {:g} , Vertical position: {:g}'.format(x, y))
```

Running the code, we get the printout

```
Horizontal position: 1.2 , Vertical position: 1.2342
```

Some, or all, of the default values may also be overridden, e.g., like

```
x, y = xy(v0y=6.0)      # override default value for v0y only
```

which means that `xy` will run with default values for `v0x` and `t`, while `v0y` will have the value 6.0, as specified in the function call. The output then, becomes

```
Horizontal position: 1.2 , Vertical position: 1.8342
```

which is reasonable, since the initial velocity for the vertical direction was higher than in the previous case.

### 4.1.8 A Function with Another Function as Input Argument

Functions are straightforwardly passed as arguments to other functions. This is illustrated by the following script `function_as_argument.py`, where a function sums up function values of another function:

```
def f(x):
    return x

def g(x):
    return x**2

def sum_function_values(f, start, stop):
    """Sum up function values for integer arguments as
    f(start) + f(start+1) + f(start+2) + ... + f(stop)"""
    S = 0
    for i in range(start, stop+1, 1):
        S = S + f(i)
    return S

print('Sum with f becomes {:g}'.format(sum_function_values(f, 1, 3)))
print('Sum with g becomes {:g}'.format(sum_function_values(g, 1, 3)))
```

We note that the function `sum_function_values` takes a function as its first argument and repeatedly calls that function without (of course) knowing what that function does, it just gets the function values back and sums them up!

Remember that the argument `f` in the function header `sum_funcion_values (f, start, stop)` and the function defined by the name `f`, is *not* the same. The function argument `f` in `sum_funcion_values(f, start, stop)` will act as the local "nick-name" (inside the function `sum_funcion_values`) for any function that is used as first argument when calling `sum_funcion_values`.

Executing the program, gives the expected printout as

```
Sum with f becomes 6
Sum with g becomes 14
```

### 4.1.9 Lambda Functions

A one-line function may be defined in a compact way, as a so-called *lambda function*. This may be illustrated as

```
g = lambda x: x**2

# ...which is equivalent to:
def g(x):
    return x**2
```

Lambda functions are particularly convenient as function arguments, as seen next, when calling `sum_function_values` from above with lambda functions replacing the functions `f` and `g`:

```
print(sum_function_values(lambda x: x, 1, 3))
print(sum_function_values(lambda x: x**2, 1, 3))
```

This gives the same output as we got above. In this way, the lambda function is defined "in" the function call, so we avoid having to define the function separately prior to the (function) call.

A lambda function may take several comma-separated arguments. A more general form of a lambda function is thus

```
function_name = lambda arg1, arg2, ... : <some_expression>

# ...which is equivalent to:
def function_name(arg1, arg2, ...):
    return <some_expression>
```

The general syntax consists of the reserved word `lambda`, followed by a series of parameters, then a colon, and, finally, some Python expression resulting in an object to be returned from the function.

### 4.1.10 A Function with Several Return Statements

It is possible to have several `return` statements in a function, as illustrated here:

```
def check_sign(x):
    if x > 0:
        return 'x is positive'
    elif x < 0:
        return 'x is negative'
    else:
        return 'x is zero'
```

Remember that only one of the branches is executed for a single call to `check_sign`, so depending on the number `x`, the return may take place from any of the three return alternatives.

**To Return at the End or Not**

Programmers disagree whether it is a good idea to use `return` inside a function, or if there should be just a single `return` statement *at the end of the function*. The authors of this book emphasize readable code and think that `return` can be useful in branches as in the example above when the function is short. For longer or more complicated functions, it might be better to have one single `return` statement at the end.

**Nested Functions**

Functions may also be defined *within* other functions. In that case, they become *local functions*, or *nested functions*, known only to the function inside which they are defined.

Functions defined in main are referred to as *global functions*. A nested function has full access to all variables in the *parent function*, i.e. the function within which it is defined.

**Overhead of Function Calls**

Function calls have the downside of slowing down program execution. Usually, it is a good thing to split a program into functions, but in very computing intensive parts, e.g., inside long loops, one must balance the convenience of calling a function and the computational efficiency of avoiding function calls. It is a good rule to develop a program using plenty of functions and then in a later optimization stage, when everything computes correctly, remove function calls that are quantified to slow down the code. Let it be clear, however, that newcomers to programming should focus on writing readable code, not fast code!

In Sect. 5.6, we investigate (for a particular case) the impact that function calls have on CPU time.

## 4.2 Programming as a Step-Wise Strategy

When students start out with programming, they usually pick up the basic ideas quite fast and learn to *read* simpler code rather swiftly. However, when it comes to the *writing* of code, many find it hard to even get started.

In this chapter, we will use an example to present a typical code writing process in detail. Our focus will be on a *step-wise approach* that is so often required, unless the programmer is experienced and the programming task is "small".

Often, such a step-wise approach starts out with a *very* simple version of the final program you have in mind. You test and modify that simple version until it runs like you want. Then you include some more code, test and modify that version until it works fine. Then you include more code, test and modify, and so on. Each of these steps then brings you closer to your final target program. In some cases, all the steps are clear in advance, but often, new insight develops along the way, making it necessary to modify the plan. The step-wise approach is good also in that it allows you to get started with a step or two (that you see are needed), even if you do not know how to proceed from there, at least yet.

How to break up a programming task into a series of steps is not unique. It will also depend on the problem, as well as on the programmer. More experienced programmers can save time by writing the final version of some program in one go (or at least with few steps). Beginners, however, may greatly benefit from a step-wise procedure with the sufficient number of steps. The following example should illustrate the idea.

### 4.2.1 Making a Times Tables Test

**The Programming Task** Write a program that tests the user's knowledge of the times tables from 1 to 10.

**Breaking up the Task** There are many possible ways to do such a times tables testing, but our reasoning goes as follows. In this test, there will be 10 different questions for the 1 times table, 10 different questions for the 2 times table, and so on, giving a 100 different questions in total. We decide to ask each of those questions one time only. There are quite many questions, so we also allow the user to quit with `Ctrl-c` (i.e., hold the `Ctrl` key down while typing `c`) before reaching the end.

To code this, the first idea that possibly comes to mind, is to use a double `for` loop on a form like:

```
for a in [1, 2, ..., 10]:
    for b in [1, 2, ..., 10]:
        < ask user: a*b = ? >
        < check answer, give points >
```

With a construction like this, we see that for each value of `a`, the second factor `b` will run over all values 1 to 10. The questions will then appear in a predictable and systematic way. First we get the 1 times table (`1*1, 1*2, ..., 1*10`), then the 2 times table (`2*1, 2*2, ..., 2*10`), and so on. Clearly, this would be an acceptable approach. However, some would still argue that it might be better if the 100 questions were randomized, depriving the user any benefit from just remembering a sequence of answers.

Based on these reflections, we choose to break up the programming task into three steps:

- 1st version—has no dialogue with the user. It contains the double loop construction and two functions, `ask_user` and `points`. The function `ask_user` will (in later versions) ask the user for an answer to `a*b`, while `points` (in later versions) will check that answer, inform the user (correct or not), and give a score (1 point if correct). To simplify, the function bodies of these two functions will deliberately *not* be coded for this version of the program. Rather, we simply insert a print command in each, essentially printing the arguments provided in the call, to confirm that the function calls work as planned.
- 2nd version—asking and checking done systematically with predictable questions (first the 1 times table, then the 2 times table, etc.).
- 3rd version—asking and checking done with randomized questions. How to implement this randomization, will be kept as an open question till we get there.

(We do reveal, however, that something "unforeseen" will be experienced with the 3rd version, which will motivate us also for a 4th version of the program.)

### 4.2.2 The 1st Version of Our Code

Our very first version of the code (`times_tables_1.py`) may be written like this:

```
def ask_user(a, b):                                    # preliminary
    """get answer from user: a*b = ?"""
    print('{:d}*{:d} = '.format(a, b))
    return a*b

def points(a, b, answer_given):                        # preliminary
    """Check answer. Correct: 1 point, else 0"""
    print('{:d}*{:d} = {:d}'.format(a, b, a*b))
    return 1

print('\n*** Welcome to the times tables test! ***\
       \n           (To stop: ctrl-c)')

# Ask user for a*b, ... a, b are in [1, N]
N = 2
score = 0
for i in range(1, N+1, 1):
    for j in range(1, N+1, 1):
        user_answer = ask_user(i, j)
        score = score + points(i, j, user_answer)
        print('Your score is now: {:d}'.format(score))

print('\nFinished! \nYour final score: {:d}   (max: {:d})'\
      .format(score, N*N))
```

In this implementation, the function `ask_user` will, by choice, not ask the user about anything. It will simply return the correct answer. Regarding `points`, it will return 1 without actually testing anything. In this way, we will be able to run the program, while still having unfinished parts in there.

We have introduced N as a variable here to allow easy adjustment of "problem size" (the total number of questions will be N*N). We know N must be 10, but that requirement applies to the *final* version only. Thus, we are free to do our steps with a smaller N, and that makes life much easier for us when assessing code behavior. If you have not already done so, go through the code by hand to confirm that you understand what happens, in what order.

When executed, the program simply prints:

```
*** Welcome to the times tables test! ***
           (To stop: ctrl-c)
1*1 =
1*1 = 1
Your score is now:  1
1*2 =
1*2 = 2
Your score is now:  2
2*1 =
2*1 = 2
Your score is now:  3
2*2 =
2*2 = 4
Your score is now:  4

Finished!
Your final score: 4   (max: 4)
```

From the printout, we see that the two functions seem to get the right arguments in each call. We are thus ready for the next step, i.e., to implement the function bodies of the two functions.

### 4.2.3 The 2nd Version of Our Code

After implementing the remaining parts of the code, we have a version (times_tables_2.py) of our program that actually does the testing that was asked for. The code reads

```
def ask_user(a, b):
    """get answer from user: a*b = ?"""
    question = '{:d} * {:d} = '.format(a, b)
    answer = int(input(question))
    return answer

def points(a, b, answer_given):
    """Check answer. Correct: 1 point, else 0"""
    true_answer = a*b
    if answer_given == true_answer:
        print('Correct!')
        return 1
    else:
        print('Sorry! Correct answer was: {:d}'.format(true_answer))
        return 0
```

```
print('\n*** Welcome to the times tables test! ***\
      \n          (To stop: ctrl-c)')

# Ask user for a*b, ... a, b are in [1, N]
N = 2
score = 0
for i in range(1, N+1, 1):
    for j in range(1, N+1, 1):
        user_answer = ask_user(i, j)
        score = score + points(i, j, user_answer)
        print('Your score is now: {:d}'.format(score))

print('\nFinished! \nYour final score: {:d}   (max: {:d})'\
      .format(score, N*N))
```

Running the program, the dialogue could, for example, proceed like

```
*** Welcome to the times tables test! ***
            (To stop: ctrl-c)

1 * 1 = 1
Correct!
Your score is now:  1

1 * 2 = 2
Correct!
Your score is now:  2

2 * 1 = 3
Sorry! Correct answer was:  2
Your score is now:  2

2 * 2 = 4
Correct!
Your score is now:  3

Finished!
Your final score: 3   (max: 4)
```

We see that the behavior is as expected. Again, it is important that you read the code and confirm that your understanding is in line with the output shown.

**Testing for Equality with ==**

In our code, we compare two integers in the `if` test

```
if user_answer == true_answer:
```

Testing for equality with == works fine for the integers we have here. In general, however, such tests need to account for the inexact number representation that we have on computers. More about this in Sect. 6.6.3.

Note that the new code implemented when updating from `times_tables_1.py` to `times_tables_2.py`, included the function bodies in both functions `ask_user` and `points`. Often, however, it is a good idea to finalize one function at a time, particularly with larger and/or more complicated functions.

The reader should take a moment to reflect on the use of functions in general (`ask_user` and `points` here). They represent "logical units", each dedicated to a special task. Structuring code this way, may greatly ease human code interpretation, which in turn makes debugging and future code changes much simpler. "Seen" from the main program, `ask_user`, for example, is given the factors of `a*b` and returns the answer. The inner workings of `ask_user` is neither known, nor of any concern, to the main program. It just calls the function and waits for the returned value. Moreover, the inner workings of `ask_user` may be changed in any way, without affecting the code elsewhere in the program, as long as function input and output stays the same.

By setting `N = 10` in `times_tables_2.py`, and confirming that the dialogue runs correctly, we have a program that carries out the required test. However, we have yet another step to make, which means we have to figure out how the questions can be randomized. Let us see what we can make out of it.

### 4.2.4 The 3rd Version of Our Code

How can we randomize the 100 questions, while keeping to the plan of asking each question only once? Based on our previous version(s) of the code, it would be natural to first think of something like

```
<loop arrangement with 100 iterations>
    i = <draw random number from 1 to 10>
    j = <draw random number from 1 to 10>
    user_answer = ask_user(i, j)                    # ...NOT what we want!

    <check answer, inform user>
```

However, it is immediately realized that some products `a*b` then will come several times, whereas others, are likely to not appear at all. Clearly, this is not what we want. Some more reasoning is required.

One solution, the one presented here, is based on two key observations. The first observation, is that the integers 0 to 99 can be used to uniquely represent each of our 100 products. We might demonstrate this by the following little piece of code:

```
for i in range(0, 100, 1):
    a = i//10 + 1                  # integer division
    b = i%10 + 1                   # modulo

    print('i = {:d},  {:d}*{:d} = '.format(i, a, b))
```

When executed, we get a printout like

```
i = 0 :   1*1 =
i = 1 :   1*2 =
i = 2 :   1*3 =
i = 3 :   1*4 =
i = 4 :   1*5 =
i = 5 :   1*6 =
i = 6 :   1*7 =
```

```
i = 7 :   1*8 =
i = 8 :   1*9 =
i = 9 :   1*10 =
i = 10 :   2*1 =
i = 11 :   2*2 =

...
...  < longer printout... author's comment >
...

i = 97 :   10*8 =
i = 98 :   10*9 =
i = 99 :   10*10 =
```

Thus, from the 100 values of $i$, we can uniquely derive the two factors in all the 100 products (!), as the printout confirms. With the sequence of $i$ values just shown, however, we get the systematic ordering of the questions used in our 2nd version of the program. So, to get the questions in random order, we need something more.

The second observation, is that the function `shuffle` (Sect. 2.4) from `numpy` can be used to randomize the numbers 0 to 99, and thereby give us a randomized ordering of the products.

Now, based on these two observations, we are ready to write down the 3rd version of our program (`times_tables_3.py`), in which the functions `ask_user` and `points` are unchanged compared to the 2nd version:

```
import numpy as np

def ask_user(a, b):
    """get answer from user: a*b = ?"""
    question = '{:d} * {:d} = '.format(a, b)
    answer = int(input(question))
    return answer

def points(a, b, answer_given):
    """Check answer. Correct: 1 point, else 0"""
    true_answer = a*b
    if answer_given == true_answer:
        print('Correct!')
        return 1
    else:
        print('Sorry! Correct answer was: {:d}'.format(true_answer))
        return 0

print('\n*** Welcome to the times tables test! ***\
       \n           (To stop: ctrl-c)')

N = 10
NN = N*N
score = 0
index = list(range(0, NN, 1))
np.random.shuffle(index)        # randomize order of integers in index
for i in range(0, NN, 1):
    a = (index[i]//N) + 1
    b = index[i]%N + 1
    user_answer = ask_user(a, b)
```

```
    score = score + points(a, b, user_answer)
    print('Your score is now: {:d}'.format(score))

print('\nFinished! \nYour final score: {:d}   (max: {:d})'\
      .format(score, N*N))
```

Running this code, the order of the questions will be generated anew with each execution (because of the randomization), but the dialogue may, for example, appear like:

```
*** Welcome to the times tables test! ***
            (To stop: ctrl-c)

5 * 5 = 25
Correct!
Your score is now:  1

5 * 3 = 15
Correct!
Your score is now:  2

9 * 9 = 81
Correct!
Your score is now:  3

...
...      <longer printout... author's comment>
...

Finished!
Your final score: 95   (max: 100)
```

Great! Our code seems to run smoothly, so what can possibly go wrong now? This will go wrong:

```
*** Welcome to the times tables test! ***
            (To stop: ctrl-c)

3 * 2 = six
Traceback (most recent call last):
...
...     < longer printout... author's comment >
...

ValueError: invalid literal for int() with base 10: 'six'
```

If a user gives some unexpected input that the code is not prepared to handle, things can go very wrong! In this case, we get an error message (referring to some `ValueError`), since our program does not understand that "six" actually means the number 6.

It would not be very professional to leave our program with this potential problem, so it should be fixed, but how? The good news is that modern programming languages, Python inclusive, do have the right tools to deal with such cases. For now, we will leave our code as it is, but we hereby add yet another step to our program development plan, and will solve the problem when we turn to *exception handling* in Sect. 5.2. That will also bring us to the fourth version of our program, which also will be regarded as the final version (in general, however, programs are typically changed and improved again and again, making it hard to reach *the* "final" version!).

**Developing a Computational Plan**

To write a program, you need to *plan* what that program should do, and a good plan requires a thorough *understanding* of the addressed problem. One fundamentally important thing with the step-wise strategy, is that it invites you to *think through* your computational problem very carefully: What bits and pieces, or "sub-problems", make up the whole task? Should the "sub-problems" be solved in any particular order, i.e., do parts of the problem depend on results from other parts? What is the best way to compute each of the "sub-problems"?

This kind of thinking, which combines favorably with discussions among students/colleagues, often pays off in terms of a much deeper understanding of the problem at hand. Good solutions often require such an understanding.

**Compound Statements**

The constructions met in this chapter, and the previous chapter, are characterized by a grouping of statements that generally span several lines (although it is possible to write simpler cases on a single line, when statements are separated with a semi-colon). Such constructions are often referred to as *compound statements*, having headers (ending with a colon) and bodies (with indented statements).[a]

Interactive handling of compound statements is straight forward. For example, a `for` loop may be written (and executed) like

```
In [1]: for i in [1, 2, 3]:        # write header, press enter
   ...:     print(i)               # indent comes automatically
   ...:                            # press only enter, i.e., finished
1
2
3
```

When the header has been typed in and we press enter, we are automatically given the indent on the next line. We can then proceed directly by writing `print(i)` and press enter again. We then want to finish our loop, which is understood when we simply press enter, writing nothing else.

[a] https://docs.python.org/3/reference/compound_stmts.html.

## 4.3 Exercises

**Exercise 4.1: Errors with Colon, Indent, etc.**
Write the program `ball_function.py` as given in the text and confirm that the program runs correctly. Then save a copy of the program and use that program during the following error testing.

You are supposed to introduce errors in the code, one by one. For each error introduced, save and run the program, and comment how well Python's response corresponds to the actual error. When you are finished with one error, re-set the program to correct behavior (and check that it works!) before moving on to the next error.

a) Change the first line from `def y(v0, t):` to `def y(v0, t)`, i.e., remove the colon.
b) Remove the indent in front of the statement `g = 9.81` inside the function `y`, i.e., shift the text four spaces to the left.
c) Now let the statement `g = 9.81` inside the function `y` have an indent of three spaces (while the remaining two lines of the function have four).
d) Remove the left parenthesis in the first statement `def y(v0, t):`
e) Change the first line of the function definition from `def y(v0, t):` to `def y(v0):`, i.e., remove the parameter `t` (and the comma).
f) Change the first occurrence of the command `print(y(v0, time))` to `print(y(v0))`.

Filename: `errors_colon_indent_etc.py`.

**Exercise 4.2: Reading Code 1**
a) Read the following code and predict the printout produced when the program is executed.

```
def f(x):
    return x**2
def g(x):
    return 2*x

for x in [1, 5, 6, 9]:
    if x < 5:
        # case 1
        print(f(x))
    elif x == 5:
        # case 2
        print(2*f(x))
    elif x > 5 and x < 8:
        # case 3
        print(f(x+4) + g(x*2) - g(2))
    else:
        # case 4
        y = x + 2
        print(g(y))
```

b) Type in the code and run the program to confirm that your predictions are correct.

Filename: `read_code_1.py`.

**Exercise 4.3: Reading Code 2**

a) Read the following code and predict the printout produced when the program is executed.

```
def f(x):
    if x < 2:
        return 0
    else:
        return 2*x

x = 0
for i in range(0, 4, 1):
    x += i
    print(x)

for i in range(0, 4, 1):
    x += i*i
print(x)

for i in range(0, 4, 1):
    print(f(3*i-1))
```

b) Type in the code and run the program to confirm that your predictions are correct.

Filename: `read_code_2.py`.

**Exercise 4.4: Functions for Circumference and Area of a Circle**

Write a program that takes a circle radius `r` as input from the user and then computes the circumference `C` and area `A` of the circle. Implement the computations of `C` and `A` as two separate functions that each takes `r` as input parameter. Print `C` and `A` to the screen along with an appropriate text. Run the program with $r = 1$ and confirm that you get the right answer.
Filename: `functions_circumference_area.py`.

**Exercise 4.5: Function for Adding Vectors**

Write a function `add_vectors` that takes 2 vectors (arrays with one index are often called *vectors*) `a` and `b` as input arguments and returns the vector `c`, where $c = a+b$. Place the function in a little program that calls the function and prints the result. The function should check that `a` and `b` have the same length. If not, `None` should be returned. Confirm that your function works by comparing to hand calculations (i.e., just choose some arrays and test).
Filename: `add_vectors.py`.

**Exercise 4.6: Function for Area of a Rectangle**
Write a program that computes the area $A = bc$ of a rectangle. The values of $b$ and $c$ should be user input to the program. Also, write the area computation as a function that takes $b$ and $c$ as input parameters and returns the computed area. Let the program print the result to screen along with an appropriate text. Run the program with $b = 2$ and $c = 3$ to confirm correct program behavior.
Filename: `function_area_rectangle.py`.

**Exercise 4.7: Average of Integers**
Write a program that gets an integer $N > 1$ from the user and computes the average of all integers $i = 1, \ldots, N$. The computation should be done in a function that takes $N$ as input parameter. Print the result to the screen with an appropriate text. Run the program with $N = 5$ and confirm that you get the correct answer.
Filename: `average_1_to_N.py`.

**Exercise 4.8: When Does Python Check Function Syntax?**
You are told that, when Python reads a function definition for the first time, it does not execute the function, but still checks the syntax.

Now, you come up with some code lines to confirm that this is the case.

**Hint** You may, for example, use a print command and a deliberate syntax error in a modification of `ball_function.py` (note that the modified code is one of those quick "one-time" tests you might make for yourself, meant to be deleted once you have the answer).
Filename: `when_check_function_syntax.py`.

**Exercise 4.9: Find Crossing Points of Two Graphs**
Consider two functions $f(x) = x$ and $g(x) = x^2$ on the interval $[-4, 4]$.

Write a program that, by trial and error, finds approximately for which values of $x$ the two graphs cross, i.e., $f(x) = g(x)$. Do this by considering $N$ equally distributed points on the interval, at each point checking whether $|f(x) - g(x)| < \epsilon$, where $\epsilon$ is some small number. Let $N$ and $\epsilon$ be user input to the program and let the result be printed to screen. Run your program with $N = 400$ and $\epsilon = 0.01$. Explain the output from the program. Finally, try also other values of $N$, keeping the value of $\epsilon$ fixed. Explain your observations.
Filename: `crossing_2_graphs.py`.

**Exercise 4.10: Linear Interpolation**
Some measurements $y_i$, $i = 0, 1, \ldots, N$, of a quantity $y$ have been collected regularly, once every minute, at times $t_i = i$, $i = 0, 1, \ldots, N$. We want to find the value $y$ *in between* the measurements, e.g., at $t = 3.2$ min. Computing such $y$ values is called *interpolation*.

Let your program use *linear interpolation* to compute $y$ between two consecutive measurements:

1. Find $i$ such that $t_i \leq t \leq t_{i+1}$.

2. Find a mathematical expression for the straight line that goes through the points $(i, y_i)$ and $(i + 1, y_{i+1})$.
3. Compute the $y$ value by inserting the user's time value in the expression for the straight line.

a) Implement the linear interpolation technique in a function `interpolate` that takes as input an array with the $y_i$ measurements, the time between them $\Delta t$, and some time $t$, for which the interpolated value is requested. The function should return the interpolated $y$ value at time $t$.
b) Write another function `find_y` that finds and prints an interpolated $y$ value at times requested by the user. Let `find_y` use a loop in which the user is asked for a time on the interval $[0, N]$. The loop can terminate when the user gives a negative time.
c) Use the following measurements: $4.4, 2.0, 11.0, 21.5, 7.5$, corresponding to times $0, 1, \ldots, 4$ (min), and compute interpolated values at $t = 2.5$ and $t = 3.1$ min. Perform separate hand calculations to check that the output from the program is correct.

Filename: `linear_interpolation.py`.

**Exercise 4.11: Test Straight Line Requirement**
Assume the straight line function $f(x) = 4x + 1$. Write a script that tests the "point-slope" form for this line as follows. Within a chosen interval on the $x$-axis (for example, for $x$ between 0 and 10), randomly pick 100 points on the line and check if the following requirement is fulfilled for each point:

$$\frac{f(x_i) - f(c)}{x_i - c} = a, \qquad i = 1, 2, \ldots, 100,$$

where $a$ is the slope of the line and $c$ defines a fixed point $(c, f(c))$ on the line. Let $c = 2$ here.
Filename: `test_straight_line.py`.

**Exercise 4.12: Fit Straight Line to Data**
Assume some measurements $y_i, i = 1, 2, \ldots, 5$ have been collected, once every second. Your task is to write a program that fits a straight line to those data.

a) Make a function that, for given measurements and parameter values $a$ and $b$, computes the error between the straight line $f(x) = ax + b$ and the measurements:
$$e = \sum_{i=1}^{5} (ax_i + b - y_i)^2 .$$
b) Make a function that, in a loop, asks the user to give $a$ and $b$ for the line. The corresponding value of $e$ should then be computed and printed to screen, and a plot of the straight line $f(x) = ax + b$, together with the discrete measurements, should be produced.

c) Given the measurements $0.5, 2.0, 1.0, 1.5, 7.5$, at times $0, 1, 2, 3, 4$, use the function in b) to interactively search for $a$ and $b$ such that $e$ is minimized.

Filename: `fit_straight_line.py`.

**Remarks** Fitting a straight line to measured data points is a very common task. The manual search procedure in c) can be automated by using a mathematical method called the *method of least squares*.

**Exercise 4.13: Fit Sines to Straight Line**
A lot of technology, especially most types of digital audio devices for processing sound, is based on representing a signal of time as a sum of sine functions. Say the signal is some function $f(t)$ on the interval $[-\pi, \pi]$ (a more general interval $[a, b]$ can easily be treated, but leads to slightly more complicated formulas). Instead of working with $f(t)$ directly, we approximate $f$ by the sum

$$S_N(t) = \sum_{n=1}^{N} b_n \sin(nt), \tag{4.1}$$

where the coefficients $b_n$ must be adjusted such that $S_N(t)$ is a good approximation to $f(t)$. We shall in this exercise adjust $b_n$ by a trial-and-error process.

a) Make a function `sinesum(t, b)` that returns $S_N(t)$, given the coefficients $b_n$ in an array `b` and time coordinates in an array `t`. Note that if `t` is an array, the return value is also an array.
b) Write a function `test_sinesum()` that calls `sinesum(t, b)` in a) and determines if the function computes a test case correctly. As test case, let `t` be an array with values $-\pi/2$ and $\pi/4$, choose $N = 2$, and $b_1 = 4$ and $b_2 = -3$. Compute $S_N(t)$ by hand to get reference values.
c) Make a function `plot_compare(f, N, M)` that plots the original function $f(t)$ together with the sum of sines $S_N(t)$, so that the quality of the approximation $S_N(t)$ can be examined visually. The argument `f` is a Python function implementing $f(t)$, `N` is the number of terms in the sum $S_N(t)$, and `M` is the number of uniformly distributed $t$ coordinates used to plot $f$ and $S_N$.
d) Write a function `error(b, f, M)` that returns a mathematical measure of the error in $S_N(t)$ as an approximation to $f(t)$:

$$E = \sqrt{\sum_i (f(t_i) - S_N(t_i))^2},$$

where the $t_i$ values are $M$ uniformly distributed coordinates on $[-\pi, \pi]$. The array `b` holds the coefficients in $S_N$ and `f` is a Python function implementing the mathematical function $f(t)$.
e) Make a function `trial(f, N)` for interactively giving $b_n$ values and getting a plot on the screen where the resulting $S_N(t)$ is plotted together with $f(t)$. The error in the approximation should also be computed as indicated in d). The

argument `f` is a Python function for $f(t)$ and `N` is the number of terms $N$ in the sum $S_N(t)$. The `trial` function can run a loop where the user is asked for the $b_n$ values in each pass of the loop and the corresponding plot is shown. You must find a way to terminate the loop when the experiments are over. Use `M=500` in the calls to `plot_compare` and `error`.

f) Choose $f(t)$ to be a straight line $f(t) = \frac{1}{\pi}t$ on $[-\pi, \pi]$. Call `trial(f, 3)` and try to find through experimentation some values $b_1$, $b_2$, and $b_3$ such that the sum of sines $S_N(t)$ is a good approximation to the straight line.

g) Now we shall try to automate the procedure in f). Write a function that has three nested loops over values of $b_1$, $b_2$, and $b_3$. Let each loop cover the interval $[-1, 1]$ in steps of 0.1. For each combination of $b_1$, $b_2$, and $b_3$, the error in the approximation $S_N$ should be computed. Use this to find, and print, the smallest error and the corresponding values of $b_1$, $b_2$, and $b_3$. Let the program also plot $f$ and the approximation $S_N$ corresponding to the smallest error.

Filename: `fit_sines.py`.

### Remarks

1. The function $S_N(x)$ is a special case of what is called a *Fourier series*. At the beginning of the nineteenth century, Joseph Fourier (1768–1830) showed that any function can be approximated analytically by a sum of cosines and sines. The approximation improves as the number of terms ($N$) is increased. Fourier series are very important throughout science and engineering today.
   (a) Finding the coefficients $b_n$ is solved much more accurately in Exercise 6.12, by a procedure that also requires much less human and computer work!
   (b) In real applications, $f(t)$ is not known as a continuous function, but function values of $f(t)$ are provided. For example, in digital sound applications, music in a CD-quality WAV file is a signal with 44,100 samples of the corresponding analog signal $f(t)$ per second.

# 5 Some More Python Essentials

## 5.1 Lists and Tuples: Alternatives to Arrays

We have seen that a group of numbers may be stored in an array that we may treat as a whole, or element by element. In Python, there is another way of organizing data that actually is much used, at least in non-numerical contexts, and that is a construction called *list*.

**Some Properties of Lists** A list is quite similar to an array in many ways, but there are pros and cons to consider. For example, the number of elements in a list is allowed to change, whereas arrays have a fixed length that must be known at the time of memory allocation. Elements in a list can be of different type, so you may mix, e.g., integers, floats and strings, whereas elements in an array must be of the same type. In general, lists provide more flexibility than do arrays. On the other hand, arrays give faster computations than lists, making arrays our prime choice unless the flexibility of lists is needed. Arrays also require less memory use and there is a lot of ready-made code for various mathematical operations. Vectorization requires arrays to be used.

A list has elements that we may use for computations, just like we can with array elements. As with an array, we may find the number of elements in a list with the function `len` (i.e., we find the "length" of the list), and with the `array` function from `numpy`, we may create an array from an existing list:

```
In [1]: x = list(range(6, 11, 1))

In [2]: x
Out[2]: [6, 7, 8, 9, 10]

In [3]: x[0]
Out[3]: 6

In [4]: x[4]
Out[4]: 10

In [5]: x[0] + x[1]
Out[5]: 13
```



S. Linge, H. P. Langtangen, *Programming for Computations - Python*,
Texts in Computational Science and Engineering 15,
https://doi.org/10.1007/978-3-030-16877-3_5

```
In [6]: import numpy as np

In [7]: y = np.array(x)                         # create array y

In [8]: y
Out[8]: array([ 6,  7,  8,  9, 10])

In [9]: x[0] = -1

In [10]: x
Out[10]: [-1, 7, 8, 9, 10]                     # x is changed

In [11]: y
Out[11]: array([ 6,  7,  8,  9, 10])           # y is not changed

In [12]: len(x)
Out[12]: 5

In [13]: len(y)
Out[13]: 5
```

A list may also be created by simply writing, e.g.,

```
x = ['hello', 4, 3.14, 6]
```

giving a list where `x[0]` contains the string `hello`, `x[1]` contains the integer 4, etc.

We may add and delete elements anywhere in a list:

```
x = ['hello', 4, 3.14, 6]
x.insert(0, -2)            # x then becomes [-2, 'hello', 4, 3.14, 6]
del x[3]                   # x then becomes [-2, 'hello', 4, 6]
x.append(3.14)             # x then becomes [-2, 'hello', 4, 6, 3.14]
```

Note the ways of writing the different operations here. Using `append()` will always increase the list at the end. If you like, you may create an empty list as `x = []` before you enter a loop which appends element by element. Note that there are many more operations on lists possible than shown here.

**List and `for` Loops** Previously, we saw how a `for` loop may run over array elements. When we want to do the same with a list in Python, we may do it simply like:

```
x = ['hello', 4, 3.14, 6]
print('The elements of the list x:\n')
for e in x:
    print(e)
```

We observe that `e` runs over the elements of `x` directly, avoiding the need for indexing. Be aware, however, that when loops are written like this, you can not change any element in `x` by "changing" `e`. That is, writing `e += 2` will not change anything in `x`, since `e` can only be used to read (as opposed to overwrite) the list elements. Running the code gives the output

```
The elements of the list x:

hello
4
3.14
6
```

**List Comprehension** There is a special construct in Python that allows you to run through all elements of a list, do the same operation on each, and store the new elements in another list. It is referred to as *list comprehension* and may be demonstrated as follows:

```
In [1]: L1 = [1, 2, 3, 4]

In [2]: L2 = [e*10 for e in L1]

In [3]: L2
Out[3]: [10, 20, 30, 40]
```

So, we get a new list by the name `L2`, with the elements `10`, `20`, `30` and `40`, in that order. Notice the syntax within the brackets for `L2`, `e*10 for e in L1` signals that `e` is to successively be each of the list elements in `L1`, and for each `e`, create the next element in `L2` by doing `e*10`. More generally, the syntax may be written as

```
L2 = [E(e) for e in L1]
```

where `E(e)` means some expression involving `e`.

In some cases, it is required to run through 2 (or more) lists at the same time. Python has a handy function called `zip` for this purpose. An example of how to use `zip` is provided in Sect. 5.5 (`file_handling.py`).

**Some Properties of Tuples** We should also briefly mention about *tuples*, which are very much like lists, the main difference being that tuples cannot be changed. To a freshman, it may seem strange that such "constant lists" could ever be preferable over lists. However, the property of being constant is a good safeguard against unintentional changes. Also, it is quicker for Python to handle data in a tuple than in a list, which contributes to faster code. With the data from above, we may create a tuple and print the content by writing

```
x = ('hello', 4, 3.14, 6)
print('The elements of the tuple x:\n')
for e in x:
    print(e)
```

Trying `insert` or `append` for the tuple gives an error message (because it cannot be changed), stating that the tuple object has no such attribute.

## 5.2 Exception Handling

An *exception*, is an error that is detected during program execution. We experienced such an error previously with our times tables program in Sect. 4.2.4. When we were asked about `3*2`, and replied with the word `six` in stead of the *number* 6, we caused the program to stop and report about some `ValueError`. The program would have responded in the same way, for example, if we had rather given 6.0 (i.e., a float) as input, or just pressed enter (without typing anything else).

Our code could only handle "expected" input from the user, i.e., an integer as an answer to `a*b`. It would have been much better, however, if it could account also for "unexpected" input. If possible, we would prefer our program not to stop (or "crash") unexpectedly for some kind of input, it should just handle it, get back on track, and keep on running. Can this be done in Python? Yes! Python has excellent constructions for dealing with exceptions in general, and we will show, in particular, how such *exception handling* will bring us to the fourth version of our times table program.

To get the basic idea with exception handling, we will first explain the very simplest `try-except` construction, and also see how it could be used in the times tables program. It will only partly solve our problem, so we will immediately move on to a more refined `try-except` construction that will be just what we need.

Generally, a simple `try-except` construction may be put up as

```
try:
    <block of statements>          # ...in try block
except:
    <block of statements>          # ...in except block

# indent reversed, i.e., first line after 'try-except' construction.
```

When executed, Python recognizes the reserved words `try` and `except` (note *colon* and subsequent *indent*), and will do the following. First, Python will *try* to execute the statements in the *try block*. In the case when these statements execute without trouble, the *except block* is skipped (like the else block in an `if-else` construction). However, if something goes wrong in the try block, an *exception* is raised by Python, and execution jumps immediately to the except block without executing remaining statements of the try block.

It is up to the programmer what statements to have in the except block (as in the try block, of course), and that makes the programmer free to choose what will happen when an exception occurs! Sometimes, e.g., a program stop is desirable, sometimes not.

### 5.2.1 The Fourth Version of Our Times Tables Program

**Simple Use of try-except** Let us now make use of this simple `try-except` construction in the main program of `times_tables_3.py`, as a first attempt to improve the program. Doing so, the code may appear as (we give the whole program for easy reference):

```
import numpy as np

def ask_user(a, b):
    """get answer from user: a*b = ?"""
    question = '{:d} * {:d} = '.format(a, b)
    answer = int(input(question))
    return answer

def points(a, b, answer_given):
    """Check answer. Correct: 1 point, else 0"""
    true_answer = a*b
    if answer_given == true_answer:
        print('Correct!')
        return 1
    else:
        print('Sorry! Correct answer was: {:d}'.format(true_answer))
        return 0

print('\n*** Welcome to the times tables test! ***\
       \n           (To stop: ctrl-c)')

N = 10
NN = N*N
score = 0
index = list(range(0, NN, 1))
np.random.shuffle(index)       # randomize order of integers in index
for i in range(0, NN, 1):
    a = index[i]//N + 1
    b = index[i]%N + 1
    try:
        user_answer = ask_user(a, b)
    except:
        print('You must give a valid number!')
        continue                # jump to next loop iteration

    score = score + points(a, b, user_answer)
    print('Your score is now: {:d}'.format(score))

print('\nFinished! \nYour final score: {:d}   (max: {:d})'\
      .format(score, N*N))
```

What will happen here? During execution, Python will first *try* to execute `user_answer = ask_user(a, b)` in the try block. If it executes without trouble, the except block is skipped, and execution continues with the line `score = score + points(a, b, user_answer)`. However, if an exception is raised, execution proceeds immediately with `print` and `continue` in the except block. If so, the assignment to `user_answer` does not take place. The `continue` statement makes us move to the next question, since it immediately brings execution to the next loop iteration, i.e., `score` is neither updated, nor printed, before "leaving" that iteration.

This solution is a step forward for our program, since we avoid an unintentional stop if someone accidentally hits the wrong key. However, the except block here will handle *all* kinds of exceptions, and, in particular, trying to stop the program with `Ctrl-c` will no longer work (in stead, you may choose `Consoles` and `Restart kernel` from the `Spyder` menu)! It would be better programming to differentiate between different kinds of exceptions, coding a dedicated response in each case. That can be done in Python,[1] and it will also allow us to get back the `Ctrl-c` functionality that we had in the earlier versions.

**A More Detailed Use of try-except** We let the final version of our code (`times_tables_4.py`) serve as an example of a more refined `try-except` construction. It is still simple, but has what we need. We present this final version in its completeness, before explaining the details. All code changes are still confined to the main part of the program:

```
import numpy as np

def ask_user(a, b):
    """Get answer from user: a*b = ?"""
    question = '{:d} * {:d} = '.format(a, b)
    answer = int(input(question))
    return answer

def points(a, b, answer_given):
    """Check answer. Correct answer gives 1 point, else zero"""
    true_answer = a*b
    if answer_given == true_answer:
        print('Correct!')
        return 1
    else:
        print('Sorry! Correct answer was: {:d}'.format(true_answer))
        return 0

print('\n*** Welcome to the times tables test! ***\
      \n           (To stop: ctrl-c)')

N = 10
NN = N*N
score = 0
index = list(range(0, NN, 1))
np.random.shuffle(index)      # randomize order of integers in index
for i in range(0, NN, 1):
    a = index[i]//N + 1
    b = index[i]%N + 1
    try:
        user_answer = ask_user(a, b)
    except KeyboardInterrupt:
        print('\nOk, you want to stop!')
        break
    except ValueError:
        print('You must give a valid number!')
        continue                             # jump to next loop iteration

    score = score + points(a, b, user_answer)
    print('Your score is now: {:d}'.format(score))

print('\nFinished! \nYour final score: {:d}   (max: {:d})'\
      .format(score, N*N))
```

[1] https://docs.python.org/3/tutorial/errors.html.

Python has many different exception types, and we use two of them here, `KeyboardInterrupt` and `ValueError` (some more examples will be given soon). Unless the user answers with a valid integer, one of these exceptions is raised. A `KeyboardInterrupt` is raised if we type `Ctrl-c` to stop execution, whereas a `ValueError` is raised otherwise. We note that in each case an appropriate printout is given first. Furthermore, when a `ValueError` is raised, execution proceeds directly with the next question (after the printout). When a `KeyboardInterrupt` is raised, the printout is succeeded by execution of the `break` statement. This implies that execution breaks out of the `for` loop and the program stops after printing the final score.

One dialogue with the program could then be, for example:

```
*** Welcome to the times tables test! ***
            (To stop: ctrl-c)

6 * 8 = 48
Correct!
Your score is now:  1

5 * 8 = u                  (accidentally hit wrong key - author's comment)
You must give a valid number!

3 * 10 =                             (only press enter - author's comment)
You must give a valid number!

5 * 6 = 30
Correct!
Your score is now:  2

7 * 6 =                                   (type ctrl-c - author's comment)
Ok, you want to stop!

Finished!
Your final score: 2   (max: 100)
```

With our final version, we see that some typical error situations are handled according to plan, and also that `Ctrl-c` now works as previously. For the present problem, we found that only two different types of exceptions (`KeyboardInterrupt` and `ValueError`) were required. Had more exceptions been needed, we could just have extended the structure straight forwardly, with

```
except exception_type:
    <statements>
```

for each of them. Note that it is possible to have a unified response to several exceptions, by just collecting the exception types in a parentheses and separating them with a comma. For example, with two such exceptions, they would appear on the form

```
except (exception_type_1, exception_type_2):
    <statements>
```

Before ending this chapter on exception handling, it is appropriate to briefly exemplify a few more of the many built-in exceptions in Python.

If we try to use an uninitialized variable, a `NameError` exception is raised:

```
In [1]: print(x)                        # x is uninitialized
...
...
NameError: name 'x' is not defined
```

When division by zero is attempted, it results in a `ZeroDivisionError` exception:

```
In [2]: 1.0/0
...
...
ZeroDivisionError: float division by zero
```

Using illegal indices causes Python to raise an `IndexError` exception.:

```
In [3]: x = [7, 8, 9]

In [4]: x[2]
Out[4]: 9

In [5]: x[3]                           # legal indices are 0, 1 and 2
...
...
IndexError: list index out of range
```

Wrong Python grammar, or wrong typing of reserved words, gives a `SyntaxError` exception:

```
In [6]: impor numpy as np              # typo... missing t in import
...
    impor numpy as np
              ^
SyntaxError: invalid syntax
```

If object types do not match, Python raises a `TypeError` exception:

```
In [7]: 'a string' + 1         # attempt to add string and integer
...
...
TypeError: must be str, not int
```

(We might add that, in the last example here, two strings could have been straight forwardly concatenated with +.)

**Abort Execution with `sys.exit`**

In some cases, it is desirable to stop execution there and then. This may be done effectively by use of the `exit` function in the `sys` module[a] (a module with functions and parameters that are specific to the system). For an application of `sys.exit`, see Sect. 7.2.2.

[a] https://docs.python.org/3/library/sys.html.

We have been careful to check code behavior in a step-wise fashion while developing our program. Still, testing should be done also with (what, for now, is regarded as) the "final" version. To test our times tables program, we should check that all the 100 questions actually get asked, and also that points are given correctly. The simplicity of the present program allows this to be done while running it. Experienced programmers, however, usually write dedicated code for such testing. How to do this for implementations of numerical methods, will be presented later (see Chap. 6).

Note that, even if some error handling can be implemented by use of `if-elif-else` constructions, exception handling allows better programming, and is the preferred and modern way of handling errors. The recommendation to novice programmers is therefore to develop the habit of using `try-except` constructions.

## 5.3 Symbolic Computations

Even though the main focus in this book is programming of *numerical* methods, there are occasions where *symbolic* (also called *exact* or *analytical*) operations are useful.

### 5.3.1 Numerical Versus Symbolic Computations

Doing symbolic computations means, as the name suggests, that we do computations with the symbols themselves rather than with the numerical values they could represent. Let us illustrate the difference between symbolic and numerical computations with a little example. A numerical computation could be

```
x = 2
y = 3
z = x*y
print(z)
```

which will make the number 6 appear on the screen.

A symbolic counterpart of this code could be written by use of the *SymPy* package[2] (named `sympy` in Python):

```
import sympy as sym

x, y = sym.symbols('x y')  # define x and y as a mathematical symbols
z = x*y
print(z)
```

which causes the *symbolic* result `x*y` to appear on the screen. Note that no numerical value was assigned to any of the variables in the symbolic computation. Only the symbols were used, as when you do symbolic mathematics by hand on a piece of paper. Note also how symbol names must be declared by using `symbols`.

[2] SymPy (http://docs.sympy.org/latest/index.html) is included in Anaconda. In case you have not installed Anaconda, you may have to install SymPy separately.

### 5.3.2 SymPy: Some Basic Functionality

The following script example_symbolic.py gives a quick demonstration of some of the basic symbolic operations that are supported in Python.

```
import sympy as sym

x, y = sym.symbols('x y')

print(2*x + 3*x - y)                          # Algebraic computation
print(sym.diff(x**2, x))                      # Differentiates x**2 wrt. x
print(sym.integrate(sym.cos(x), x))           # Integrates cos(x) wrt. x
print(sym.simplify((x**2 + x**3)/x**2))       # Simplifies expression
print(sym.limit(sym.sin(x)/x, x, 0))          # lim of sin(x)/x as x->0
print(sym.solve(5*x - 15, x))                 # Solves 5*x = 15
```

Another useful possibility with sympy, is that sympy expressions may be converted to lambda functions, which then may be used as "normal" Python functions for numerical calculations. An example will illustrate.

Let us use sympy to analytically find the derivative of the function $f(x) = 5x^3 + 2x^2 - 1$, and then make both f and its derivative into Python functions:

```
import sympy as sym

x = sym.symbols('x')
f_expr = 5*x**3 + 2*x**2 - 1         # symbolic expression for f(x)
dfdx_expr = sym.diff(f_expr, x)      # compute f'(x) symbolically

# turn symbolic expressions into functions
f    = sym.lambdify([x], f_expr)       # f = lambda x: 5*x**3 + 2*x**2 - 1
dfdx = sym.lambdify([x], dfdx_expr)    # dfdx = lambda x: 15*x**2 + 4*x

print(f(1), dfdx(1))        # call and print, x = 1
```

Note the arguments to lambdify. The first argument [x] specifies the argument that the generated function f (and the function dfdx) is supposed to take, while the second argument f_expr (and dfdx_expr) specifies the expression to be evaluated. When executed, the program prints 6 and 19, corresponding to f(1) and dfdx(1), respectively.

Other symbolic calculations for, e.g., Taylor series[3] expansion, linear algebra (with matrix and vector operations), and (some) differential equation solving are also possible.

### 5.3.3 Symbolic Calculations with Some Other Tools

Symbolic computations are also readily accessible through the (partly) free online tool WolframAlpha,[4] which applies the very advanced Mathematica[5] package as symbolic engine. The disadvantage with WolframAlpha compared to the SymPy

[3] See, e.g., https://en.wikipedia.org/wiki/Taylor_series.

[4] http://www.wolframalpha.com.

[5] http://en.wikipedia.org/wiki/Mathematica.

package is that the results cannot automatically be imported into your code and used for further analysis. On the other hand, WolframAlpha has the advantage that it displays many additional mathematical results related to the given problem. For example, if we type `2x + 3x - y` in WolframAlpha, it not only simplifies the expression to `5x - y`, but it also makes plots of the function $f(x, y) = 5x - y$, solves the equation $5x - y = 0$, and calculates the integral $\int\int(5x + y)dxdy$. The commercial Pro version also offers a step-by-step demonstration of the analytical computations that solve the problem. You are encouraged to try out these commands in WolframAlpha:

- `diff(x^2, x)` or `diff(x**2, x)`
- `integrate(cos(x), x)`
- `simplify((x**2 + x**3)/x**2)`
- `limit(sin(x)/x, x, 0)`
- `solve(5*x - 15, x)`

WolframAlpha is very flexible with respect to syntax. In fact, WolframAlpha will use your input to *guess* what you want it to do! Depending on what you write, it may be more or less easy to do that guess, of course. However, in WolframAlpha's response, you are also told how your input was interpreted, so that you may adjust your input in a second try.

Another impressive tool for symbolic computations is Sage,[6] which is a very comprehensive package with the aim of "creating a viable free open source alternative to Magma, Maple, Mathematica and Matlab". Sage is implemented in Python. Projects with extensive symbolic computations will certainly benefit from exploring Sage.

## 5.4 Making Our Own Module

As we know by now, Python has a huge collection of useful modules and packages written by clever people. This far, we have experienced how these libraries (`math`, `numpy`, `matplotlib`, etc.) could simplify our own programming, making ready and professional code available through simple import statements. This is very good, but it gets even better, since it is straight forward (whether we are programming newbies or not) to also create modules containing our own code.

What *is* a module then, really? The truth is, that we may regard any of the Python scripts we have presented in this book as a module! In fact, any text file with extension `.py` that contains Python code written with a text editor, is a module. If the file name is `my_module.py`, then the module name is `my_module`. Up until now, we have written `.py` files for execution as programs. To design and use such files as module files, however, there are a few things we better get conscious about.

To bring across the essential points, we will develop our own little demonstration module for vertical motion, named `vertical_motion` (surprising!). The motion is of the kind we have addressed also previously in this book, i.e., a special case of projectile motion, in which an object starts out with some vertical velocity, and

[6] http://sagemath.org/.

moves without any air resistance.[7] As with built-in modules, we will see that functionality may be imported in the usual ways, e.g., as `import vertical_motion`, which allows easy reuse of module functions.

### 5.4.1 A Naive Import

Before turning to the making of our vertical motion module, we will do some "warm-up" testing with a previous script of ours, just to enlighten ourselves a bit.

Let us pick `ball_function.py` from Sect. 4.1.1 (which addresses vertical motion), and argue that, if this script *is* a module, we should be able to "import it" as `import ball_function`, right? This sounds like a reasonable expectation, so without too deep reasoning, let us just start there.

First, however, we better take another look at that code (after all, it has been a while). For easy reference, we just repeat the few code lines of `ball_function.py` here:

```
def y(v0, t):
    g = 9.81                        # Acceleration of gravity
    return v0*t - 0.5*g*t**2

v0 = 5                          # Initial velocity

time = 0.6                      # Just pick one point in time
print(y(v0, time))
time = 0.9                      # Pick another point in time
print(y(v0, time))
```

We recognize the function definition of `y` and the two applications of that function, involving a function call and a printout for each of the chosen points in time.

Now, we previously thought of this code as a program, executed it, and got the printouts. What will happen now, when we rather consider it a module and import it?

Here is what happens:

```
In [1]: import ball_function
1.2342
0.52695
```

What? Printing of numbers? We asked for an import,[8] not something that looks like program execution!

The thing is, that when any module is imported, Python *does* actually execute the module code (!), i.e., function definitions are read and statements (outside functions) executed. This is Python's way of bringing module content "to life", so that, e.g.,

---

[7] The reader who is into physics, will know that the computations done here, work equally well if the object has some simultaneous horizontal motion. In that case, our computations apply to the vertical component of the motion only, not the motion as a whole.

[8] Doing the import differently, e.g., like `from vertical_motion import y`, would still give the printouts! Also if the import were done in a script.

functions defined in that module get ready for use. To see that the function y now *is* ready for use, we may proceed our interactive session as:

```
In [2]: ball_function.y(v0=5, t=0.6)      # remember to prefix y
Out[2]: 1.2342
```

Thus, apart from the undesirable printouts, the import seems to work!

To realize how inappropriate those printouts are, we might consider the following situation. A friend of yours wants to use your function y. You provide the file `ball_function.py`, your friend imports `ball_function`, and gets two numbers printed on the screen. Your friend did not ask for those numbers, and would probably end up reading your code to see what they were all about. It should not be like that.

Our main observation here, is that those undesirable printouts came from statements placed *outside of functions*. Thus, the lesson learned, is seemingly that when preparing modules for import, there should be no statements outside functions. Or, could there be a way to treat such statements, so that undesirable printouts are avoided? We will see.

These thoughts will be in the back of our minds as we now proceed to design the vertical motion module.

**Multiple Imports of the Same Module**

Note that, when executing a program (or during an interactive session), Python *does* keep track of which modules that already have been imported. Thus, if another import is tried for a certain module, Python avoids the time consuming and unnecessary task of executing the module file once again (all module functionality is already in place, ready for use). You can check this out if you like, by doing a second `import ball_function`. This time, there are no printouts! Doing the import differently (i.e., with our example, as `from ball_function import y` or `from ball_function import *`), would not make any difference.

### 5.4.2 A Module for Vertical Motion

One simple way to avoid undesirable printouts during import, is to let the module file contain only function definitions. This is how we will arrange the first version of our vertical motion module.

We proceed to make ourselves a preliminary version[9] of our new module file `vertical_motion.py`. In this file, we place three function definitions only (which should suffice for our demonstration). One of these, is the y function from

[9] Note that only the final version, presented in Sect. 5.4.3, is found on the book's website.

ball_function.py, while the other two, time_of_flight and max_height, compute the time of flight and maximum height attained, respectively (consult any introductory book on mechanics regarding the implemented formulas).

In line with good programming practice, we also equip our module file with a doc string on top. Generally, that doc string should give the purpose of the module and explain how the module is used. More comprehensive doc strings are often required for larger and more "complicated" modules (here, our doc string is very simple, but professional programmers write their doc strings with great care[10]). The module file reads:

```
"""
Module for computing vertical motion
characteristics for a projectile.
"""
def y(v0, t):
    """
    Compute vertical position at time t, given the initial vertical
    velocity v0. Assume negligible air resistance.
    """
    g = 9.81
    return v0*t - 0.5*g*t**2

def time_of_flight(v0):
    """
    Compute time in the air, given the initial vertical
    velocity v0. Assume negligible air resistance.
    """
    g = 9.81
    return 2*v0/g

def max_height(v0):
    """
    Compute maximum height reached, given the initial vertical
    velocity v0. Assume negligible air resistance.
    """
    g = 9.81
    return v0**2/(2*g)

# Other function definitions could be added here...
```

As with built-in modules, the built-in help function can be used to retrieve documentation from user-defined modules:

```
In [1]: import vertical_motion

In [2]: help(vertical_motion)
Help on module vertical_motion:

NAME
    vertical_motion

FILE
    /.../.../.../vertical_motion.py
```

[10] https://www.python.org/dev/peps/pep-0257/.

```
DESCRIPTION
    Module for computing vertical motion
    characteristics for a projectile.

FUNCTIONS
    max_height(v0)
        Compute maximum height reached, given the initial vertical
        velocity v0. Assume negligible air resistance.

    time_of_flight(v0)
        Compute time in the air, given the initial vertical
        velocity v0. Assume negligible air resistance.

    y(v0, t)
        Compute vertical position at time t, given the initial vertical
        velocity v0. Assume negligible air resistance.
```

We recognize the doc strings in the printout and should realize that it is a good idea to keep those doc strings informative.

With the following interactive session, comparing the answers to hand calculations (using the formulas and a calculator), we confirm that the module now seems to work as intended,

```
In [1]: import vertical_motion as vm

In [2]: vm.y(v0=5, t=0.6)
Out[2]: 1.2342

In [3]: vm.time_of_flight(v0=5)
Out[3]: 1.019367991845056

In [4]: vm.max_height(v0=5)
Out[4]: 1.27420998980632
```

We now have a useful version of our own vertical motion module, from which imports work just like from built-in modules. Still, there is room for useful modifications, as we will turn to next.

**Where to Place a Module File?**

For a module import to be successful, a first requirement is that Python can *find* the module file. A simple way to make this happen, is to place the module file in the *same folder* as the program (that tries to import the module).[a] There are other alternatives, but then you should know how Python looks for module files.

When Python proceeds to import a module, it looks for the module file within the folders contained in the `sys.path` list. To see the folders in `sys.path`, we may do:

```
In [1]: import sys

In [2]: sys.path
Out[2]:
['',
 '/.../.../site-packages/spyder/utils/site',
  ...
  ...          < longer printout... author's comment >
  ...
 '/.../.../site-packages/IPython/extensions',
 '/.../.../.ipython']
```

Placing your module in one of the folders listed, assures that Python will find it. If, for some reason, you want to place your module in a folder that is not listed in `sys.path`, you may insert that folder name in `sys.path`. With our `sys.path` here, we could insert the folder name `my_folder`, for example, by continuing our session as

```
In [3]: sys.path.insert(0, 'my_folder')  # 0 - location in sys.path

In [2]: sys.path
Out[2]:
['my_folder',
 '',
 '/.../.../site-packages/spyder/utils/site',
  ...
  ...
  ...
 '/.../.../site-packages/IPython/extensions',
 '/.../.../.ipython']
```

The first argument to `insert` gives the location in the `sys.path` list where you want the folder name to be inserted (0 gives first place, 1 gives second, and so on).

You may also use the PYTHONPATH variable (https://docs.python.org/3/using/cmdline.html#envvar-PYTHONPATH), but the above should suffice for a beginner.

If you want to run your module file also as a program, the location of the file might require that you first update the PATH environment variable (see, e.g., http://hplgit.github.io/primer.html/doc/pub/input/._input-readable009.html).

[a] In this book, we keep to this simple way.***

### 5.4.3 Module or Program?

We know how a `.py` file can be executed as a program, and we have seen how functions may be collected in a `.py` file, so that imports do not trigger any undesirable printouts. However, we have already realized that Python does not force a `.py` file to be *either* a program, or a module. No, it can be both, and thanks to a clever construction, Python allows a very flexible switch between the two ways of using a `.py` file.

This clever construction is based on an `if` test, which tests whether the file should be run as a program, or act as a module only. This is doable by use of the variable `__name__`, which (behind the scenes) Python sets to `'__main__'` only if the file is executed as a program (note the compulsory two underscores to each side of `name` and `main` here). We may put up a rather general form of the construction, that we place in the `.py` file, as

```
< function definitions >

if __name__ == '__main__':        # note double underscores (and colon)
    < statement 1 >
    < statement 2 >
        ...
        ...
```

So, if the file is run as a program, Python immediately sets `__name__` to `'__main__'`. When reaching the `if` test, it will thus evaluate to `True`, which in turn causes the corresponding (indented) statements, i.e., the statements of the so-called *test block*, to be executed. To the contrary, if the file is used for imports only, `__name__` will *not* be set to `'__main__'`, the `if` test will consequently evaluate to `False`, and the corresponding statements are not executed.

Often, the statements in the test block are best placed in one or several functions (then defined above the `if` test, together with the other function definitions), so that when the `if` test evaluates to `True`, one or more function calls will follow. This is particularly important when different tasks are handled, so that each function contains statements that logically belong together.

As a simple illustration, when one function is natural (e.g., named `application`), the construction may be reformulated as

```
< function definitions >

def application():
    < statement 1 >
    < statement 2 >
        ...
        ...

if __name__ == '__main__':
    application()
```

**Our `.py` File as Both Module and Program** We will now incorporate this construction in `vertical_motion.py`. This allows us to use the functions from `vertical_motion.py` also in a program (our `application`) that asks the user for an object's initial vertical velocity, and then computes height (as it develops with time), maximum height and flight duration.

The more flexible version of `vertical_motion.py` then reads,

```
"""
Module for computing vertical motion
characteristics for a projectile.
"""
def y(v0, t):
    """
    Compute vertical position at time t, given the initial vertical
    velocity v0. Assume negligible air resistance.
    """
    g = 9.81
    return v0*t - 0.5*g*t**2

def time_of_flight(v0):
    """
    Compute time in the air, given the initial vertical
    velocity v0. Assume negligible air resistance.
    """
    g = 9.81
    return 2*v0/g

def max_height(v0):
    """
    Compute maximum height reached, given the initial vertical
    velocity v0. Assume negligible air resistance.
    """
    g = 9.81
    return v0**2/(2*g)

def application():
    import numpy as np
    import matplotlib.pyplot as plt
    import sys

    print("""This program computes vertical motion characteristics for a
    projectile. Given the intial vertical velocity, it computes height
    (as it develops with time), maximum height reached, as well as time
    of flight.""")

    try:
        v_initial = float(input('Give the initial velocity: '))
    except:
        print('You must give a valid number!')
        sys.exit(1)

    H = max_height(v_initial)
    T = time_of_flight(v_initial)
    print('Maximum height: {:g} m, \nTime of flight: {:g} s'.format(H, T))

    # compute and plot position as function of time
    dt = 0.001                           # just pick a "small" time step
    N = int(T/dt)                        # number of time steps
    t = np.linspace(0, N*dt, N+1)
```

```
    position = y(v_initial, t)          # compute all positions (over T)
    plt.plot(t, position, 'b--')
    plt.xlabel('Time (s)')
    plt.ylabel('Vertical position (m)')
    plt.show()
    return

if __name__ == '__main__':
    application()
```

The code in `application` represents the main program and should be understandable from what we have learned previously. Note that, like we have done here, it is usually a good idea to print some information about how the program works.

**Testing** As a simple test of the code in `vertical_motion.py`, we might compare the output to hand calculations, as we did before. In Chap. 6, however, we will learn how testing ought to be done via dedicated *test functions*. These test functions may be run in different ways. One alternative, however, is to include an option within the test block, which allows the user to run through the test functions whenever wanted, but more about that later.

**Placing Import Statements in Our Module**

Note that if we have import statements in our module, it is possible to run into trouble if we do not place them at the top of the file (which is according to the general recommendation).

With the following sketchy example module, it will work fine to import `some_function` in another program and use it (since, when importing `some_function`, the import of numpy is done).

```
import numpy as np

def some_function(n):
    a = np.zeros(n)
    ...
    return r

def application():
    ....
    n = 10
    r = some_function(n)
    ...
    return

if __name__ == '__main__':
    application()
```

One choice that would *not* work in the same way, however, would be to instead have the import statement `import numpy as np` after `if __name__ == '__main__':` . Then, this import statement would not be run if `some_function` is imported for use in another program.

## 5.5 Files: Read and Write

Input data for a program often come from files and the results of the computations are often written to file. To illustrate basic file handling, we consider an example where we read $x$ and $y$ coordinates from two columns in a file, apply a function $f$ to the $y$ coordinates, and write the results to a new two-column data file. The first line of the input file is a heading that we can just skip:

```
# x and y coordinates
1.0  3.44
2.0  4.8
3.5  6.61
4.0  5.0
```

The relevant Python lines for reading the numbers and writing out a similar file are given in the file `file_handling.py`

```
filename = 'tmp.dat'
infile = open(filename, 'r')  # Open file for reading
line = infile.readline()      # Read first line
# Read x and y coordinates from the file and store in lists
x = []
y = []
for line in infile:           # Read one line at a time
    words = line.split()      # Split line into words
    x.append(float(words[0]))
    y.append(float(words[1]))
infile.close()

# Transform y coordinates
from math import log

def f(y):
    return log(y)

for i in range(len(y)):
    y[i] = f(y[i])

# Write out x and y to a two-column file
filename = 'tmp_out.dat'
outfile = open(filename, 'w')  # Open file for writing
outfile.write('# x and y coordinates\n')
for xi, yi in zip(x, y):
    outfile.write('{:10.5f} {:10.5f}\n'.format(xi, yi))
outfile.close()
```

If you have problems understanding the details here, make your own copy and insert printouts of `line` and the `word` elements in the (first) loop.

With `zip`, in the first iteration, `xi` and `yi` will represent the first element of `x` and `y`, respectively. In the second iteration, `xi` and `yi` will represent the second element of `x` and `y`, and so on.[11]

---

[11] Generally, `zip` allows running over multiple lists at the same time, ending when the shortest list is finished.

## 5.6 Measuring Execution Time

Even though computational speed should have low priority among beginners to programming, it might be useful, at least, to have seen how execution time can be found for some code snippet. This is relevant for more experienced programmers, when it is required to find a particularly fast code alternative.

The measuring of execution time is complicated by the fact that a number of background processes (virus scans, check for new mail, check for software updates, etc.) will affect the timing. To some extent, it is possible to turn off such background processes, but that strategy soon gets too complicated for most of us. Fortunately, simpler and safer tools are available. To find the execution time of small code snippets, a good alternative is to use the `timeit` module[12] from the Python standard library.

### 5.6.1 The `timeit` Module

To demonstrate how this module may be used, we will investigate how function calls affect execution time. Our brief "investigation" is confined to the filling of an array with integers, done with and without a particular function call. The details are best explained with reference to the following code (no timing yet!):

```
import numpy as np

def add(a, b):
    return a + b

x = np.zeros(1000)
y = np.zeros(1000)

for i in range(len(x)):
    x[i] = add(i, i+1)        # use function call to fill array

for i in range(len(x)):
    y[i] = i + (i+1)          # ...no function call
```

So, the sum of two integers is assigned to each array element. The arrays x and y will contain exactly the same numbers when the second loop is finished, but to fill x, we use a call to the function add. Thus, the time to fill x is expected to take longer than filling y, which just adds the numbers directly. Our question is, how much longer does it take to use the function call?

To answer this question by use of `timeit`, we may write the script `timing_function_call.py`:

```
import timeit
import numpy as np

def add(a, b):
    return a + b

x = np.zeros(1000)
```

[12] https://docs.python.org/3/library/timeit.html.

```
y = np.zeros(1000)

# ...use the function add
t = timeit.Timer('for i in range(len(x)): x[i] = add(i, i+1)', \
                 setup='from __main__ import add, x')
x_time = t.timeit(10000)      # Time 10000 runs of the whole loop
print('Time, function call: {:g} seconds'.format(x_time))

# ...no use of function add
t = timeit.Timer('for i in range(len(y)): y[i] = i + (i+1)', \
                 setup='from __main__ import y')
y_time = t.timeit(10000)      # Time 10000 runs of the whole loop
print('Time: {:g} seconds'.format(y_time))
```

What will happen here? Well, first of all, note that there are two calls to `timeit.Timer`, one for each of the two loops from above. If we look at the first call to `timeit.Timer`, i.e.,

```
t = timeit.Timer('for i in range(len(x)): x[i] = add(i, i+1)', \
                 setup='from __main__ import add, x')
```

we notice that two arguments are provided. You may recognize the first argument, `for i in range(len(x)): x[i] = add(i, i+1)`, as a one-line version of the first loop from above, i.e. the loop over `x` (usually, we prefer to write such loops *not* on a single line. However, when used as an argument in a function call like here, the one-line version is handy). This first argument, given as a string, is what we want the timing of. The second argument, `setup='from __main__ import add, x'`, is required for initialization, i.e., what the timer needs to do prior to timing of the loop. If you look carefully at the string-part of this second argument, you notice an import statement for `add` and `x`. You may wonder *why* you have to do that when they are defined in your code above, but stay relaxed about that, it is simply the way this timer function works. What is required for the timer function to execute the code given in the first argument, must be provided in the `setup` argument, even if it is defined in the code above.

The following line,

```
x_time = t.timeit(10000)      # Time 10000 runs of the whole loop
```

will cause the whole loop to actually be executed, not a single time, but 10000 times! There will be *one* recorded time, the time required to run the loop 10000 times. Thus, if an average time for a single run-through of the loop is desired, we must divide the recorded time by (in this case) 10000. Often, however, the total time is fine for comparison between alternatives. The `print` command brings the recorded time to the screen, before the next loop is timed in an equivalent way.

Why is the loop run 10000 times? To get reliable timings, the execution times must be on the order of seconds, that is why. How many times the requested code snippet needs to be run, will of course depend on the code snippet in question. Sometimes, a single execution is enough. Other times, many more executions than 10000 are required. Some trial and error is usually required to find an appropriate number.

Executing the program produces the following result,

```
Time, function call: 2.22121 seconds
Time: 1.4738 seconds
```

So, using the function add to fill the array, takes 50% longer time!

## 5.7 Exercises

**Exercise 5.1: Nested `for` Loops and Lists**
The code below has `for` loops that traverse lists of different kinds. One is with integers, one with real numbers and one with strings. Read the code and write down the printout you would have got if the program had been run (i.e., you are *not* supposed to actually run the program, just read it!).

```
for i in [1, 2]:
    # First indentation level (4 spaces)
    print('i: {:d}'.format(i))
    for j in [3.0, 4.0]:
        # Second indentation level (4+4 spaces)
        print('      j: {:.1f}'.format(j))
        for w in ['yes', 'no']:
            # Third indentation level (4+4+4 spaces)
            print('                  w: {:s}'.format(w))
    # First indentation level
    for k in [5.0, 6.0]:
        # Second indentation level (4+4 spaces)
        print('      k: {:.1f}'.format(k))
```

Filename: `read_nested_for_loops.py`.

**Exercise 5.2: Exception Handling: Divisions in a Loop**
Write a program that N times will ask the user for two real numbers `a` and `b` and print the result of `a/b`. Any exceptions should be handled properly (for example, just give an informative printout and let the program proceed with the next division, if any). The user should also be allowed to stop execution with Ctrl-c.

Set `N = 4` in the code (for simplicity) and demonstrate that it handles different types of user input (i.e., floats, integers, text, just pressing enter, etc.) in a sensible way.
Filename: `compute_division.py`.

**Exercise 5.3: Taylor Series, `sympy` and Documentation**
In this exercise, you are supposed to develop a Python function that approximates $sin(x)$ when x is near zero. To do this, write a program that utilizes `sympy` to develop a Taylor series for $sin(x)$ around $x = 0$, keeping only 5 terms from the resulting expression. Then, use `sympy` to turn the expression into a function. Let the program also plot $sin(x)$ and the developed function together for x in $[-\pi, \pi]$.
Filename: `symbolic_Taylor.py`.

*Remarks* Part of your task here, is to *find* and *understand* the required documentation. Most likely, this means that you have to seek more information than found in our book. You might have to read about the Taylor series (perhaps use Wikipedia or

Google), and you probably have to look into more details about how Taylor series are handled with `sympy`.

To your comfort, this is a *very* typical situation for engineers and scientists. They need to solve a problem, but do not (yet!) have the required knowledge for all parts of the problem. Being able to find and understand the required information is then very important.

**Exercise 5.4: Fibonacci Numbers**

The Fibonacci numbers[13] is a sequence of integers in which each number (except the two first ones) is given as a sum of the two preceding numbers:

$$F_n = F_{n-1} + F_{n-2}, \qquad F_0 = 1, F_1 = 1, \qquad n = 2, 3, \ldots$$

Thus, the sequence starts out as

$$1, 1, 2, 3, 5, 8, 13, 21, 34, \ldots$$

a) Write a function `make_Fibonacci` that generates, and returns, the $N$ first Fibonacci numbers, when $N$ is an input parameter to the function. Place the function in a module named `fibonacci` (i.e., a file named `fibonacci.py`). The module should have a test block, so that if run as a program, e.g., the 20 first Fibonacci numbers are printed to screen. Check that the program behaves as intended.
b) The famous Johannes Kepler[14] found that the ratio of consecutive Fibonacci numbers converges to the *golden ratio*, i.e.

$$\lim_{n\to\infty} \frac{F_{n+1}}{F_n} = \frac{1+\sqrt{5}}{2}.$$

Extend your module by defining a function `converging_ratio`, which takes an array (or a list) `F` with (e.g., 20) Fibonacci numbers as input and then checks (you decide *how*) whether Kepler's understanding seems correct. Place a call to the function in the test block and run the program. Was Kepler right?
c) With the iterative procedure of the previous question, the ratios converged to the golden ratio at a certain *rate*. This brings in the concept of *convergence rate*, which we have not yet addressed (see, e.g., Sect. 7.5, or elsewhere). However, if you are motivated, you may get a head start right now.

In brief, if we define the difference (in absolute value) between $\frac{F_{n+1}}{F_n}$ and the golden ratio as the error $e_n$ at iteration $n$, this error (when small enough) will develop as $e_{n+1} = Ce_n^q$, where $C$ is some constant and $q$ is the *convergence rate* (in fact, this error model is typical for iterative methods). That is, we have a relation that predicts how the error changes from one iteration to the next. We note that the

13 Read more about the Fibonacci numbers, e.g., on Wikipedia (https://en.wikipedia. org/wiki/Fibonacci_number).

14 https://en.wikipedia.org/wiki/Johannes_Kepler.

larger the $q$, the quicker the error goes to zero as the number of iterations ($n$) grows (when $e_n < 1$). With the given error model, we may compute the convergence rate from

$$q = \frac{\ln(e_{n+1}/e_n)}{\ln(e_n/e_{n-1})} .$$

This is derived by considering the error model for three consecutive iterations, dividing one equation by the other and solving for $q$. If then a series of iterations is run, we can compute a sequence of values for $q$ as the iteration counter $n$ increases. As $n$ increases, the computed $q$ values are expected to approach the convergence rate that characterizes the particular iterative method. For the ratio we are looking at here, the convergence ratio is 1.

Extend your module with a function `compute_rates`, which takes an array (or a list) `F` with (e.g., 20) Fibonacci numbers as input and computes (and prints) the corresponding values for $q$. Call the function from the test block and run the program. Do the convergence rates approach the expected value?

Later, in Sect. 6.6.2, you will learn that convergence rates are very useful when testing (verifying) software.
Filename: `Fibonacci_numbers.py`.

**Exercise 5.5: Read File: Total Volume of Boxes**
A file `box_data.dat` contains volume data for a collection of rectangular boxes. These boxes all have the same bottom surface area, but (typically) differ in height. The file could, for example, read:

```
Volume data for rectangular boxes
10.0 3.0
4.0
2.0
3.0
5.0
```

Apart from the header, each line represents one box. However, since they all have the same bottom surface area, that area (10.0) is only given for the first box. For that first box, also the height (3.0) is given, as it is for each of the following boxes.

a) Write down a formula for computing the total volume of all boxes represented in the file. That formula should be written such that a minimum of multiplications and additions is used.
b) Write a program that reads the file `box_data.dat`, computes the total volume of all boxes represented in the file, and prints that volume to the screen. In the calculations, apply the formula just derived.

   (Note that, as a first step, you may read the file and just print (to screen) what is read. Comparing this printout with file content (use some editor) is then a good idea.)
c) In the file `box_data.dat`, after the last line (containing the height of the "last" box), insert a couple of empty lines, i.e. just press enter a few times. Then, save the file and run the program anew. What happens? Explain briefly.

Filename: `total_volume_boxes.py`.

**Exercise 5.6: Area of a Polygon**
One of the most important mathematical problems through all times has been to find the area of a polygon, especially because real estate areas often had the shape of polygons, and it was necessary to pay tax for the area. We have a polygon as depicted below.

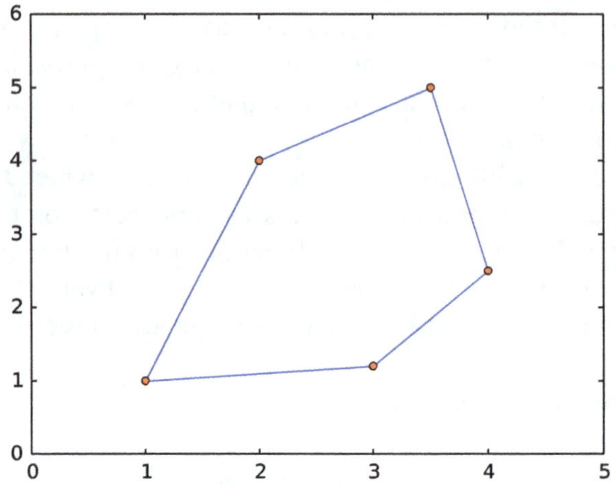


The vertices ("corners") of the polygon have coordinates $(x_1, y_1)$, $(x_2, y_2)$, ..., $(x_n, y_n)$, numbered either in a clockwise or counter clockwise fashion. The area $A$ of the polygon can amazingly be computed by just knowing the boundary coordinates:

$$A = \frac{1}{2}\left|(x_1y_2 + x_2y_3 + \cdots + x_{n-1}y_n + x_ny_1) - (y_1x_2 + y_2x_3 + \cdots + y_{n-1}x_n + y_nx_1)\right| .$$

Write a function `polyarea(x, y)` that takes two coordinate arrays with the vertices as arguments and returns the area.

Test the function on a triangle, a quadrilateral, and a pentagon where you can calculate the area by alternative methods for comparison.

*Hint* Since Python lists and arrays have 0 as their first index, it is wise to rewrite the mathematical formula in terms of vertex coordinates numbered as $x_0, x_1, \ldots, x_{n-1}$ and $y_0, y_1, \ldots, y_{n-1}$.
Filename: `polyarea.py`.

**Exercise 5.7: Count Occurrences of a String in a String**
In the analysis of genes one encounters many problem settings involving searching for certain combinations of letters in a long string. For example, we may have a string like

```
gene = 'AGTCAATGGAATAGGCCAAGCGAATATTTGGGCTACCA'
```

We may traverse this string, letter by letter, by the for loop `for letter in gene`. The length of the string is given by `len(gene)`, so an alternative traversal over an index `i` is `for i in range(len(gene))`. Letter number `i` is reached through `gene[i]`, and a substring from index `i` up to, but not including `j`, is created by `gene[i:j]`.

a) Write a function `freq(letter, text)` that returns the frequency of the letter `letter` in the string `text`, i.e., the number of occurrences of `letter` divided by the length of `text`. Call the function to determine the frequency of `C` and `G` in the `gene` string above. Compute the frequency by hand too.
b) Write a function `pairs(letter, text)` that counts how many times a pair of the letter `letter` (e.g., `GG`) occurs within the string `text`. Use the function to determine how many times the pair `AA` appears in the string `gene` above. Perform a manual counting too to check the answer.
c) Write a function `mystruct(text)` that counts the number of a certain structure in the string `text`. The structure is defined as `G` followed by `A` or `T` until a double `GG`. Perform a manual search for the structure too to control the computations by `mystruct`.

Filename: `count_substrings.py`.

*Remarks* You are supposed to solve the tasks using simple programming with loops and variables. While a) and b) are quite straightforward, c) quickly involves demanding logic. However, there are powerful tools available in Python that can solve the tasks efficiently in very compact code: a) `text.count(letter)/len(text)`; b) `text.count(letter*2)`; c) `len(re.findall('G[AT]+?GG', text))`. That is, there is rich functionality for analysis of text in Python and this is particularly useful in analysis of gene sequences.

**Exercise 5.8: Compute Combinations of Sets**

Consider an ID number consisting of two letters and three digits, e.g., RE198. How many different numbers can we have, and how can a program generate all these combinations?

If a collection of $n$ things can have $m_1$ variations of the first thing, $m_2$ of the second and so on, the total number of variations of the collection equals $m_1 m_2 \cdots m_n$. In particular, the ID number exemplified above can have $26 \cdot 26 \cdot 10 \cdot 10 \cdot 10 = 676,000$ variations. To generate all the combinations, we must have five nested for loops. The first two run over all letters A, B, and so on to Z, while the next three run over all digits $0, 1, \ldots, 9$.

To convince yourself about this result, start out with an ID number on the form A3 where the first part can vary among A, B, and C, and the digit can be among 1, 2, or 3. We must start with A and combine it with 1, 2, and 3, then continue with B, combined with 1, 2, and 3, and finally combine C with 1, 2, and 3. A double for loop does the work.

a) In a deck of cards, each card is a combination of a rank and a suit. There are 13 ranks: ace (A), 2, 3, 4, 5, 6, 7, 8, 9, 10, jack (J), queen (Q), king (K), and four suits: clubs (C), diamonds (D), hearts (H), and spades (S). A typical card may be D3. Write statements that generate a deck of cards, i.e., all the combinations `CA`, `C2`, `C3`, and so on to `SK`.

b) A vehicle registration number is on the form `DE562`, where the letters vary from A to Z and the digits from 0 to 9. Write statements that compute all the possible registration numbers and stores them in a list.
c) Generate all the combinations of throwing two dice (the number of eyes can vary from 1 to 6). Count how many combinations where the sum of the eyes equals 7.

Filename: `combine_sets.py`.

# 6 Computing Integrals and Testing Code

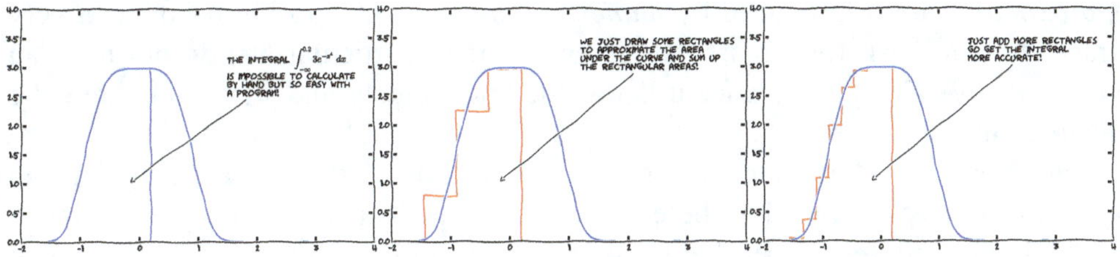


We now turn our prime attention to the solving of mathematical problems through computer programming. A fundamentally important part of programming, is to check that the written code works as intended. That is, the code must be *tested*. This far, we have checked our coding in rather simple ways, e.g., by comparing to hand calculations. Now, we will look at more powerful test strategies, while addressing numerical computation of integrals.

There are many reasons to choose integration as our first application. Integration is well known already from high school mathematics. Most integrals are not tractable by pen and paper, and a computerized solution approach is both very much simpler and much more powerful—you can essentially treat all integrals $\int_a^b f(x)dx$ in 10 lines of computer code!

Integration also demonstrates the difference between exact mathematics by pen and paper and *numerical mathematics* on a computer. The latter approaches the result of the former without any worries about rounding errors due to finite precision arithmetics in computers (in contrast to differentiation, where such errors prevent us from getting a result as accurate as we desire).

Finally, integration is thought of as a somewhat difficult mathematical concept to grasp, and programming integration should greatly improve the understanding of what integration really *is* and how it works.

Not only shall we understand how to use the computer to integrate, but we shall also learn a series of good habits to ensure your computer work is of the highest scientific quality. In particular, we will have a strong focus on how to write Python code that is free of programming mistakes.



S. Linge, H. P. Langtangen, *Programming for Computations - Python*,
Texts in Computational Science and Engineering 15,
https://doi.org/10.1007/978-3-030-16877-3_6

Calculating an integral is traditionally done by

$$\int_a^b f(x)\,dx = F(b) - F(a), \tag{6.1}$$

where

$$f(x) = \frac{dF}{dx}\,.$$

The major problem with this procedure is that we need to find an *anti-derivative* $F(x)$ corresponding to a given $f(x)$. For some relatively simple integrands $f(x)$, finding $F(x)$ is a doable task. Often, however, it is really challenging, and sometimes even impossible!

The method (6.1) provides an *exact* or *analytical* value of the integral. If we relax the requirement of computing an exact value for the integral, and instead look for *approximate* values, produced by *numerical methods*, integration becomes a very straightforward task for almost any given $f(x)$! In particular, we do not need an anti-derivative $F(x)$ at all, since it is just the known integrand $f(x)$ that enters the calculations.

The (apparent) downside of a numerical method is that it can only find an approximate answer. Leaving the exact for the approximate is a mental barrier in the beginning, but remember that most real applications of integration will involve an $f(x)$ function that contains physical parameters, which are measured with some error. That is, $f(x)$ is very seldom exact, and it does not make sense trying to compute the integral with a smaller error than the one already present in $f(x)$.

Another advantage of numerical methods is that we can easily integrate a function $f(x)$ that is only known as *samples*, i.e., discrete values at some $x$ points, and not as a continuous function of $x$ expressed through a formula. This is highly relevant when $f$ is measured in a physical experiment.

## 6.1 Basic Ideas of Numerical Integration

We consider the integral

$$\int_a^b f(x)dx\,. \tag{6.2}$$

Most numerical methods for computing this integral split up the original integral into a sum of several integrals, each covering a smaller part of the original integration interval $[a, b]$. This re-writing of the integral is based on a selection of *integration points* $x_i$, $i = 0, 1, \ldots, n$ that are distributed on the interval $[a, b]$. Integration points may, or may not, be evenly distributed. An even distribution simplifies expressions and is often sufficient, so we will mostly restrict ourselves to that choice. The integration points are then computed as

$$x_i = a + ih, \quad i = 0, 1, \ldots, n, \tag{6.3}$$

where

$$h = \frac{b-a}{n}. \tag{6.4}$$

That is, we get $n$ sub-intervals of the same size $h$. Given the integration points, the original integral is re-written as a sum of integrals, each integral being computed over the sub-interval between two consecutive integration points. The integral in (6.2) is thus expressed as

$$\int_a^b f(x)dx = \int_{x_0}^{x_1} f(x)dx + \int_{x_1}^{x_2} f(x)dx + \ldots + \int_{x_{n-1}}^{x_n} f(x)dx. \tag{6.5}$$

Note that $x_0 = a$ and $x_n = b$.

Proceeding from (6.5), the different integration methods will differ in the way they approximate each integral on the right hand side. The fundamental idea is that each term is an integral over a small interval $[x_i, x_{i+1}]$, and over this small interval, it makes sense to approximate $f$ by a simple shape, say a constant, a straight line, or a parabola, that can be easily integrated. The details will become clear in the coming examples.

**Computational Example** To understand and compare the numerical integration methods, it is advantageous to use a specific integral for computations and graphical illustrations. In particular, we want to use an integral that we can calculate by hand such that the accuracy of the approximation methods can easily be assessed.

Our specific integral is taken from basic physics. Assume that you speed up your car from rest, on a straight road, and wonder how far you go in $T$ seconds. The displacement is given by the integral $\int_0^T v(t)dt$, where $v(t)$ is the velocity as a function of time. A rapidly increasing velocity function might be

$$v(t) = 3t^2 e^{t^3}. \tag{6.6}$$

The distance traveled in 1 s is then

$$\int_0^1 v(t)dt, \tag{6.7}$$

which is the integral we aim to compute by numerical methods.

By hand, we get

$$\int_0^1 3t^2 e^{t^3} dt = \left[e^{t^3}\right]_0^1 \approx 1.718, \tag{6.8}$$

which is rounded to 3 decimals for convenience.

## 6.2 The Composite Trapezoidal Rule

The integral $\int_a^b f(x)dx$ may be interpreted as the area between the $x$ axis and the graph $y = f(x)$ of the integrand. Figure 6.1 illustrates this area for the case in (6.7). Computing the integral $\int_0^1 v(t)dt$ amounts to computing the area of the hatched region.

If we *replace* the true graph in Fig. 6.1 by a set of straight line segments, we may view the area rather as composed of trapezoids, the areas of which are easy to compute. This is illustrated in Fig. 6.2, where four straight line segments give rise to four trapezoids, covering the time intervals [0, 0.2), [0.2, 0.6), [0.6, 0.8) and [0.8, 1.0]. Note that we have taken the opportunity here to demonstrate the computations with time intervals that differ in size.

The areas of the four trapezoids shown in Fig. 6.2 now constitute our approximation to the integral (6.7):

$$\int_0^1 v(t)dt \approx h_1(\frac{v(0)+v(0.2)}{2}) + h_2(\frac{v(0.2)+v(0.6)}{2}) + h_3(\frac{v(0.6)+v(0.8)}{2}) + h_4(\frac{v(0.8)+v(1.0)}{2}), \tag{6.9}$$

where

$$h_1 = (0.2 - 0.0), \tag{6.10}$$

$$h_2 = (0.6 - 0.2), \tag{6.11}$$

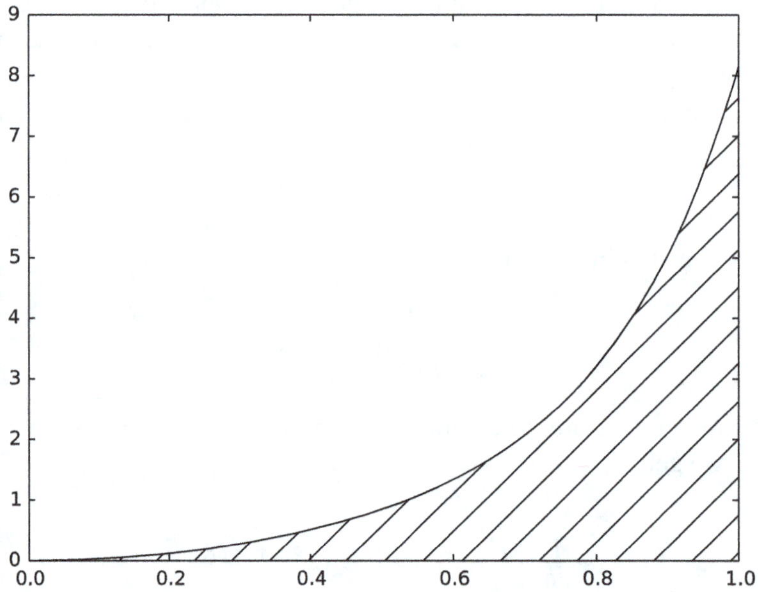


**Fig. 6.1** The integral of $v(t)$ interpreted as the area under the graph of $v$

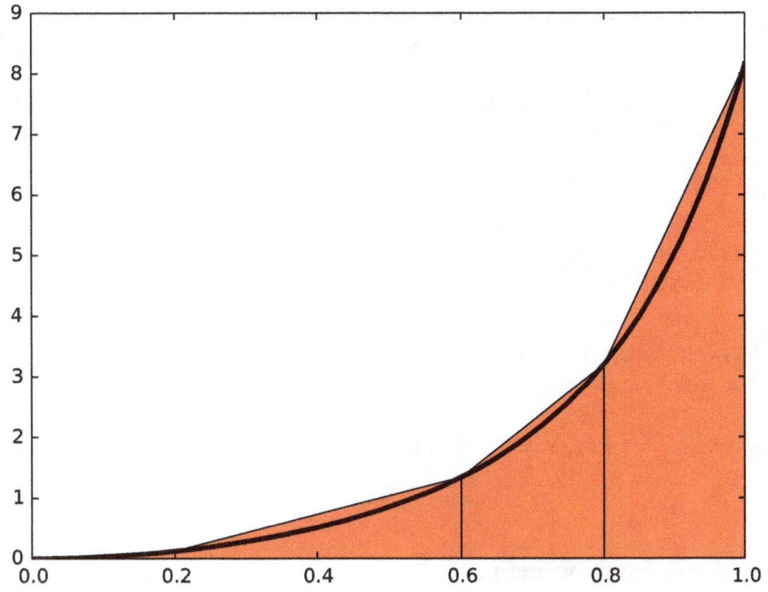


**Fig. 6.2** Computing approximately the integral of a function as the sum of the areas of the trapezoids

$$h_3 = (0.8 - 0.6), \tag{6.12}$$

$$h_4 = (1.0 - 0.8) \tag{6.13}$$

With $v(t) = 3t^2e^{t^3}$, each term in (6.9) is readily computed and our approximate computation gives

$$\int_0^1 v(t)dt \approx 1.895\,. \tag{6.14}$$

Compared to the true answer of 1.718, this is off by about 10%. However, note that we used just four trapezoids to approximate the area. With more trapezoids, the approximation would have become better, since the straight line segments at the upper trapezoid side then would follow the graph more closely. Doing another hand calculation with more trapezoids is not too tempting for a lazy human, though, but it is a perfect job for a computer! Let us therefore derive the expressions for approximating the integral by an arbitrary number of trapezoids.

### 6.2.1 The General Formula

For a given function $f(x)$, we want to approximate the integral $\int_a^b f(x)dx$ by $n$ trapezoids (of equal width). We start out with (6.5) and approximate each integral on the right hand side with a single trapezoid. In detail,

$$\begin{aligned}\int_a^b f(x)\,dx &= \int_{x_0}^{x_1} f(x)dx + \int_{x_1}^{x_2} f(x)dx + \ldots + \int_{x_{n-1}}^{x_n} f(x)dx,\\ &\approx h\frac{f(x_0)+f(x_1)}{2} + h\frac{f(x_1)+f(x_2)}{2} + \ldots +\\ &\quad h\frac{f(x_{n-1})+f(x_n)}{2}\end{aligned} \tag{6.15}$$

By simplifying the right hand side of (6.15) we get

$$\int_a^b f(x)\,dx \approx \frac{h}{2}\left[f(x_0) + 2f(x_1) + 2f(x_2) + \ldots + 2f(x_{n-1}) + f(x_n)\right] \tag{6.16}$$

which is more compactly written as

$$\int_a^b f(x)\,dx \approx h\left[\frac{1}{2}f(x_0) + \sum_{i=1}^{n-1} f(x_i) + \frac{1}{2}f(x_n)\right]. \tag{6.17}$$

**Composite Integration Rules**

The word *composite* is often used when a numerical integration method is applied with more than one sub-interval. Strictly speaking then, writing, e.g., “the trapezoidal method”, should imply the use of only a single trapezoid, while “the composite trapezoidal method” is the most correct name when several trapezoids are used. However, this naming convention is not always followed, so saying just “the trapezoidal method” may point to a single trapezoid as well as the composite rule with many trapezoids.

### 6.2.2 A General Implementation

**Specific or General Implementation?** Suppose we want to compute the specific integral $\int_0^1 v(t)dt$, where $v(t) = 3t^2e^{t^3}$, using the (composite) trapezoidal method in (6.17). Although simple in principle, the practical steps are often confusing to many, because the notation in the abstract formulation in (6.17) differs from the notation in our special problem. Clearly, the $f$, $x$, and $h$ in (6.17) correspond to $v$, $t$, and perhaps $\Delta t$ for the trapezoid width in our special problem.

**The Programmer's Dilemma**

1. **Specific implementation**: Should we write a special program for the particular integral, using the ideas from the general rule (6.17), but replacing $f$ by $v$, $x$ by $t$, and $h$ by $\Delta t$?
2. **General implementation**: Should we implement the general method (6.17), as written, in a general function `trapezoidal(f, a, b, n)` and solve the particular integral by a specialized call to this function?

**A general implementation is always the best choice, not only for integrals, but when programming in general!**

The first alternative in the box above sounds less abstract and therefore more attractive to many. Nevertheless, as we hope will be evident from the following, the second alternative is actually the simplest *and* most reliable from both a mathematical and a programming point of view.

These authors will claim that the second alternative is the essence of the power of mathematics, while the first alternative is the source of much confusion about mathematics!

**General Implementation** For the integral $\int_a^b f(x)dx$, computed by the formula (6.17), we want a corresponding Python function `trapezoidal` to take any $f$, $a$, $b$, and $n$ as input and return the approximation to the integral.

We write `trapezoidal` as close as possible to the formula (6.17), making sure variable names correspond to the mathematical notation:

```
def trapezoidal(f, a, b, n):
    h = (b-a)/n
    f_sum = 0
    for i in range(1, n, 1):
        x = a + i*h
        f_sum = f_sum + f(x)
    return h*(0.5*f(a) + f_sum + 0.5*f(b))
```

Observe how the `for` loop takes care of (only) the sum over $f(x_i)$, and that the $x$ values start with $x = a + h$ (when $i$ is 1), increases with $h$ for each iteration, before ending with $x = a + (n - 1)h$. This is consistent with the $x$ values of the sum in (6.17). After the loop, we finalize the computation and return the result. This will be our implementation of choice for the `trapezoidal` function, even though, typically for programming, it could have been implemented in different ways. Which implementation to choose, is sometimes just a matter of personal taste.

One alternative version could be:

```
def trapezoidal(f, a, b, n):
    h = (b-a)/n
    result = 0.5*f(a) + 0.5*f(b)
    for i in range(1, n):
        result += f(a + i*h)
    result *= h
    return result
```

where `0.5*f(a) + 0.5*f(b)` is used in an initialization of `result`, before adding all the function evaluations $f(x_i)$ in the loop. After the loop, the only remaining thing, is to multiply by `h`. In this second alternative, there are also a few other differences to note. The `range` function is called with two parameters only, giving the (default) step of 1. In the loop, instead of computing `x = a + i*h` prior to calling `f(x)`, we combine this into `f(a + i*h)`, which first computes `a + i*h` and then makes the call to `f`. Also, the compact operators `+=` and `*=` have been used.

**Using the General Implementation in a Session** Having the `trapezoidal` function as the only content of a file `trapezoidal.py` automatically makes that file a module that we can import and test in an interactive session:

```
In [1]: from trapezoidal import trapezoidal

In [2]: from math import exp

In [3]: v = lambda t: 3*(t**2)*exp(t**3)

In [4]: n = 4

In [5]: numerical = trapezoidal(v, 0, 1, n)

In [6]: numerical
Out[6]: 1.9227167504675762
```

Let us compute the exact expression and the error in the approximation. Using $V$ for the anti-derivative, we get:

```
In [7]: V = lambda t: exp(t**3)

In [8]: exact = V(1) - V(0)

In [9]: abs(exact - numerical)    # absolute value of error
Out[9]: 0.20443492200853108
```

Since the sign of the error is irrelevant, we find the absolute value of the error. So, is this error convincing? We can try a larger $n$:

```
In [10]: numerical = trapezoidal(v, 0, 1, n=400)

In [11]: abs(exact - numerical)
Out[11]: 2.1236490512777095e-05
```

Fortunately, many more trapezoids give a much smaller error.

**Using the General Implementation in a Program** Instead of computing our integral in an interactive session, we can do it in a program. In that program, we need the (general) function definition of `trapezoidal`, and we need some code that specifies our particular integrand, as well as the other arguments required for calling `trapezoidal`. This code might be placed in a main program. However, it could also be placed in a function that is called from the main program. This is what we will do. A chunk of code doing a particular thing is always best isolated as a function, even if we do not see any future reason to call the function several times, and even if we have no need for arguments to parameterize what goes on inside the function. Thus, in the present case, we put the statements (otherwise placed a main program) inside a function named `application`.

To achieve flexibility, we proceed to modify `trapezoidal.py`, so that it has a test block and function definitions of `trapezoidal` and `application`:

```
def trapezoidal(f, a, b, n):
    h = (b-a)/n
    f_sum = 0
    for i in range(1, n, 1):
        x = a + i*h
        f_sum = f_sum + f(x)
    return h*(0.5*f(a) + f_sum + 0.5*f(b))

def application():
    from math import exp
    v = lambda t: 3*(t**2)*exp(t**3)
    n = int(input('n: '))
    numerical = trapezoidal(v, 0, 1, n)

    # Compare with exact result
    V = lambda t: exp(t**3)
    exact = V(1) - V(0)
    error = abs(exact - numerical)
    print('n={:d}: {:.16f}, error: {:g}'.format(n, numerical, error))

if __name__ == '__main__':
    application()
```

With our newly gained knowledge about the making of modules, we understand that the `if` test becomes true when the module file, `trapezoidal.py`, is run as a program, and false when the module (or part of it) is imported in another program. Consequently, with an import like `from trapezoidal import trapezoidal`, the test fails and `application()` is not called. On the other hand, if we run `trapezoidal.py` as a program, the test condition is positive and `application()` is called. A call to `application` implies that our special problem gets computed. The main program now gets very small, being just a single function call to `application`.

Running the program, e.g., with $n = 4$ gives the output

```
n=4: 1.9227167504675762, error: 0.204435
```

Clearly, with a module like the one shown here, the `trapezoidal` function alone (i.e., without `application`) can easily be imported by other programs to compute other integrals.

### 6.2.3 A Specific Implementation: What's the Problem?

Let us illustrate the implementation implied by alternative 1 in the *Programmer's dilemma* box in Sect. 6.2.2. That is, we make a special-purpose code, where we adapt the general formula (6.17) to the specific problem $\int_0^1 3t^2e^{t^3}dt$, in which the integrand is a velocity function $v(t)$.

**Implementation Without Function Definitions** Basically, we use a `for` loop to compute the sum. Each term with $f(x)$ in the formula (6.17) is replaced by $3t^2e^{t^3}$, $x$ by $t$, and $h$ by $\Delta t$.[1] A first version of this special implementation, without any function definition, could read

```
from math import exp

a = 0.0;  b = 1.0
n = int(input('n: '))
dt = (b - a)/n

# Integral by the trapezoidal method
v_sum = 0
for i in range(1, n, 1):
    t = a + i*dt
    v_sum = v_sum + 3*(t**2)*exp(t**3)

numerical = dt*(0.5*3*(a**2)*exp(a**3) +
                v_sum +
                0.5*3*(b**2)*exp(b**3))

exact_value = exp(1**3) - exp(0**3)
error = abs(exact_value - numerical)
rel_error = (error/exact_value)*100
print('n={:d}: {:.16f}, error: {:g}'.format(n, numerical, error))
```

The problem with the above strategy is at least three-fold:

1. To write the code, we had to reformulate (6.17) for our special problem with a different notation. Errors come easy then.
2. To write the code, we had to insert the integrand $3t^2e^{t^3}$ several places in the code, which quickly leads to errors.
3. If we later want to compute a different integral, the code must be edited in several places. Such edits are likely to introduce errors.

The potential errors related to point 2 serve to illustrate how important it is to define and use appropriate functions.

**Implementation with Function Definitions** An improved second version of the special implementation, now with functions for the integrand `v` and the anti-derivative `V`, might then read

```
from math import exp

v = lambda t: 3*(t**2)*exp(t**3)        # Define integrand
a = 0.0;  b = 1.0
n = int(input('n: '))
dt = (b - a)/n

# Integral by the trapezoidal method
```

[1] Replacing $h$ by $\Delta t$ is not strictly required as many use $h$ as interval also along the time axis. Nevertheless, $\Delta t$ is an even more popular notation for a small time interval, so we use that here.

```
v_sum = 0
for i in range(1, n, 1):
    t = a + i*dt
    v_sum = v_sum + v(t)
numerical = dt*(0.5*v(a) + v_sum + 0.5*v(b))

V = lambda t: exp(t**3)
exact_value = V(b) - V(a)
error = abs(exact_value - numerical)
rel_error = (error/exact_value)*100
print('n={:d}: {:.16f}, error: {:g}'.format(n, numerical, error))
```

Unfortunately, the two other problems (1. and 3.) remain, and they are fundamental.

**Computing Another Integral** Suppose you next want to compute another integral, say $\int_{-1}^{1.1} e^{-x^2} dx$, using the previous specific implementation as your "starting point". What changes are required in the code then?

First of all, an anti-derivative can not (easily) be found[2,3] for this new integrand, so we drop computing the integration error, and must remove the corresponding code lines. In addition,

- the notation should be changed to fit the new problem. Thus, `t` and `dt` should be replaced by `x` and `h`. Also, the integrand is (most likely) not a velocity any more, so the name `v` should be changed with, e.g., `f`. Similarly, `v_sum` should rather be `f_sum` then.
- the formula for `v` (or `f`) must be replaced by a new formula
- the limits `a` and `b` must be changed

These changes are straightforward to implement, but *they are scattered around in the program*, a fact that requires us to be very careful so we do not introduce new programming errors while we modify the code. It is also very easy to forget one or two of the required changes.

For the sake of comparison, we might see how easy it is to rather use our *general implementation* in `trapezoidal.py` for the task. With the following interactive session, it should be clear that this implementation allows us to compute the new integral $\int_{-1}^{1.1} e^{-x^2} dx$ *without touching the implemented mathematical algorithm*! We can simply do:

```
In [1]: from trapezoidal import trapezoidal  # ...general implementation

In [2]: from math import exp

In [3]: trapezoidal(lambda x: exp(-x**2), -1, 1.1, 400)
Out[3]: 1.5268823686123285
```

---

[2] You cannot integrate $e^{-x^2}$ by hand, but this particular integral is appearing so often in so many contexts that the integral is a special function, called the Error function and written $\text{erf}(x)$. In a code, you can call `erf(x)`. The `erf` function is found in the `math` module.

[3] http://en.wikipedia.org/wiki/Error_function.

Looking back on the two different solutions, the specific implementation and the general implementation, you should realize that *implementing a general mathematical algorithm in a general function* requires somewhat more abstract thinking, but the resulting code can be used over and over again! Essentially, if you apply the special-purpose style, you have to retest the implementation of the algorithm after every change of the program.

The present integral problems result in short code. In more challenging engineering problems, the code quickly grows to hundreds and thousands of lines. Without abstractions, in terms of general algorithms in general reusable functions, the complexity of the program grows so fast that it will be extremely difficult to make sure that the program works properly.

Another advantage of packaging mathematical algorithms in functions, is that a function can be reused by anyone to solve a problem by just calling the function with a proper set of arguments. Understanding the function's inner details is strictly not necessary to compute a new integral. Similarly, you can find libraries of functions on the Internet and use these functions to solve your problems without specific knowledge of every mathematical detail in the functions.

This desirable feature has its downside, of course: the user of a function may misuse it, and the function may contain programming errors and lead to wrong answers. Testing the output of downloaded functions is therefore extremely important before relying on the results.

## 6.3 The Composite Midpoint Method

**The Idea** Rather than approximating the area under a curve by trapezoids, we can use plain rectangles. It may sound less accurate to use horizontal lines and not skew lines following the function to be integrated, but an integration method based on rectangles (the *midpoint method*) is in fact slightly more accurate than the one based on trapezoids! In the midpoint method, we construct a rectangle for every sub-interval where the height equals the integrand $f$ at the midpoint of the sub-interval.

For the sake of comparison, we may repeat the hand calculation of $\int_0^1 v(t)dt$ in (6.7), but this time with the midpoint method. With four rectangles (Fig. 6.3) and the same sub-intervals that we used with the trapezoidal method, [0, 0.2), [0.2, 0.6), [0.6, 0.8), and [0.8, 1.0], we get

$$\int_0^1 v(t)dt \approx h_1 v\left(\frac{0+0.2}{2}\right) + h_2 v\left(\frac{0.2+0.6}{2}\right) + h_3 v\left(\frac{0.6+0.8}{2}\right) + h_4 v\left(\frac{0.8+1.0}{2}\right), \tag{6.18}$$

where $h_1$, $h_2$, $h_3$, and $h_4$ are the widths of the sub-intervals, used previously with the trapezoidal method and defined in (6.10)–(6.13).

With $v(t) = 3t^2 e^{t^3}$, the approximation becomes 1.632. Compared with the true answer (1.718), this is about 5% too small, but it is better than what we got with

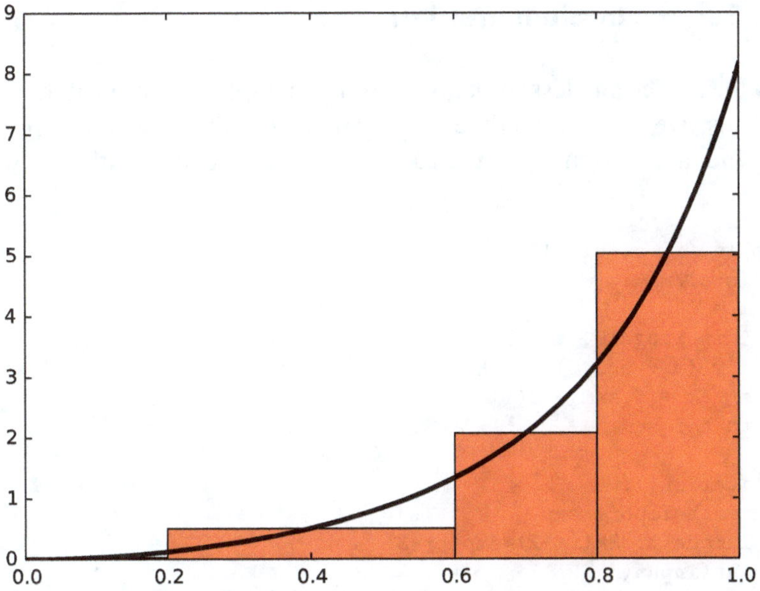


**Fig. 6.3** Computing approximately the integral of a function as the sum of the areas of the rectangles

the trapezoidal method (10%) with the same sub-intervals. More rectangles give a better approximation.

### 6.3.1 The General Formula

Let us derive a formula for the midpoint method based on $n$ rectangles of equal width:

$$\begin{aligned}\int_a^b f(x)\,dx &= \int_{x_0}^{x_1} f(x)dx + \int_{x_1}^{x_2} f(x)dx + \ldots + \int_{x_{n-1}}^{x_n} f(x)dx,\\ &\approx hf\left(\frac{x_0+x_1}{2}\right) + hf\left(\frac{x_1+x_2}{2}\right) + \ldots + hf\left(\frac{x_{n-1}+x_n}{2}\right),\\ &\approx h\left(f\left(\frac{x_0+x_1}{2}\right) + f\left(\frac{x_1+x_2}{2}\right) + \ldots + f\left(\frac{x_{n-1}+x_n}{2}\right)\right).\end{aligned} \tag{6.19}$$

This sum may be written more compactly as

$$\int_a^b f(x)dx \approx h\sum_{i=0}^{n-1} f(x_i), \tag{6.20}$$

where $x_i = \left(a + \frac{h}{2}\right) + ih$.

### 6.3.2 A General Implementation

We follow the advice and lessons learned from the implementation of the trapezoidal method. Thus, we make a module `midpoint.py` with a general implementation of (6.20) and a function `application`, just like we did with the trapezoidal function:

```
def midpoint(f, a, b, n):
    h = (b-a)/n
    f_sum = 0
    for i in range(0, n, 1):
        x = (a + h/2.0) + i*h
        f_sum = f_sum + f(x)
    return h*f_sum

def application():
    from math import exp
    v = lambda t: 3*(t**2)*exp(t**3)
    n = int(input('n: '))
    numerical = midpoint(v, 0, 1, n)

    # Compare with exact result
    V = lambda t: exp(t**3)
    exact = V(1) - V(0)
    error = abs(exact - numerical)
    print('n={:d}: {:.16f}, error: {:g}'.format(n, numerical, error))

if __name__ == '__main__':
    application()
```

In `midpoint`, observe how the $x$ values in the loop start out at $x = a + \frac{h}{2}$ (when $i$ is 0), which is in the middle of the first rectangle. The $x$ values then increase by $h$ for each iteration, meaning that we repeatedly "jump" to the midpoint of the next rectangle as $i$ increases. This is consistent with the formula in (6.20), as is the final $x$ value of $x = a + \frac{h}{2} + (n-1)h$. To convince yourself that the first, intermediate and final $x$ values are correct, look at a case with only three rectangles, for example.

When `application` is called, the particular problem $\int_0^1 3t^2 e^{t^3} dt$ is computed, i.e., the same integral that we handled with the trapezoidal method. Running the program with `n = 4` gives the output

```
n=4: 1.6189751378083810, error: 0.0993067
```

The magnitude of this error is now about 0.1 in contrast to 0.2, which we got with the trapezoidal rule. This is in fact not accidental: one can show mathematically that the error of the midpoint method is a bit smaller than for the trapezoidal method. The differences are seldom of any practical importance, and on a laptop we can easily use $n = 10^6$ and get the answer with an error of about $10^{-12}$ in a couple of seconds.

### 6.3.3 Comparing the Trapezoidal and the Midpoint Methods

The next example shows how easy it is to combine the `trapezoidal` and `midpoint` functions to make a comparison of the two methods. The coding is given in `compare_integration_methods.py`:

```
from trapezoidal import trapezoidal
from midpoint import midpoint
from math import exp

g = lambda y: exp(-y**2)
a = 0
b = 2
print('    n        midpoint          trapezoidal')
for i in range(1, 21):
    n = 2**i
    m = midpoint(g, a, b, n)
    t = trapezoidal(g, a, b, n)
    print('{:7d} {:.16f} {:.16f}'.format(n, m, t))
```

Note the efforts put into nice formatting—the output becomes

```
      n        midpoint          trapezoidal
      2 0.8842000076332692 0.8770372606158094
      4 0.8827889485397279 0.8806186341245393
      8 0.8822686991994210 0.8817037913321336
     16 0.8821288703366458 0.8819862452657772
     32 0.8820933014203766 0.8820575578012112
     64 0.8820843709743319 0.8820754296107942
    128 0.8820821359746071 0.8820799002925637
    256 0.8820815770754198 0.8820810181335849
    512 0.8820814373412922 0.8820812976045025
   1024 0.8820814024071774 0.8820813674728968
   2048 0.8820813936736116 0.8820813849400392
   4096 0.8820813914902204 0.8820813893068272
   8192 0.8820813909443684 0.8820813903985197
  16384 0.8820813908079066 0.8820813906714446
  32768 0.8820813907737911 0.8820813907396778
  65536 0.8820813907652575 0.8820813907567422
 131072 0.8820813907631487 0.8820813907610036
 262144 0.8820813907625702 0.8820813907620528
 524288 0.8820813907624605 0.8820813907623183
1048576 0.8820813907624268 0.8820813907623890
```

A visual inspection of the numbers shows how fast the digits stabilize in both methods. It appears that 13 digits have stabilized in the last two rows.

**Remark**

The trapezoidal and midpoint methods are just two examples in a jungle of numerical integration rules. Other famous methods are Simpson's rule and Gauss quadrature. They all work in the same way:

$$\int_a^b f(x)dx \approx \sum_{i=0}^{n-1} w_i f(x_i)\,.$$

That is, the integral is approximated by a sum of function evaluations, where each evaluation $f(x_i)$ is given a weight $w_i$. The different methods differ in the way they construct the evaluation points $x_i$ and the weights $w_i$. Higher accuracy can be obtained by optimizing the location of $x_i$.

## 6.4 Vectorizing the Functions

The functions `midpoint` and `trapezoidal` usually run fast in Python and compute an integral to satisfactory precision within a fraction of a second. However, long loops in Python may run slowly in more complicated implementations. To increase speed, the loops can be replaced by vectorized code. The integration functions offer simple and good examples on how to vectorize loops.

We have already seen simple examples on vectorization in Sect. 1.5, when we evaluated a mathematical function $f(x)$ for a large number of $x$ values stored in an array. Basically, we can write

```
def f(x):
    return exp(-x)*sin(x) + 5*x

from numpy import exp, sin, linspace
x = linspace(0, 4, 101)  # coordinates from 100 intervals on [0, 4]
y = f(x)                 # all points evaluated at once
```

The result `y` is an array that, alternatively, could have been computed by running a `for` loop over the individual `x` values and called `f` for each value. Vectorization essentially eliminates this explicit loop in Python (i.e., the looping over `x` and application of `f` to each `x` value are instead performed in a library with fast, compiled code).

### 6.4.1 Vectorizing the Midpoint Rule

We start by vectorizing the `midpoint` function, since `trapezoidal` is not equally straightforward to vectorize. In both cases, our vectorization will remove the explicit loop. The fundamental ideas of the vectorized algorithm are to

1. compute and store all the evaluation points in one array `x`
2. call `f(x)` to produce an array of corresponding function values
3. use the `sum` function to sum up the `f(x)` values

The evaluation points in the midpoint method are $x_i = a + \frac{h}{2} + ih, i = 0, \ldots, n-1$. That is, $n$ uniformly distributed coordinates between $a + h/2$ and $b - h/2$. Such coordinates can be calculated by `x = linspace(a+h/2, b-h/2, n)`. Given that the Python implementation `f` of the mathematical function $f$ works with an array argument, which is very often the case in Python, `f(x)` will produce all the function values in an array. The array elements are then summed up by `sum`, when calling `sum(f(x))`. The resulting sum is to be multiplied by the rectangle width $h$ to produce the integral value. The complete function is listed below.

```
from numpy import linspace, sum

def midpoint(f, a, b, n):
    h = (b-a)/n
    x = linspace(a + h/2, b - h/2, n)
    return h*sum(f(x))
```

The code is found in the file `integration_methods_vec.py`.

Let us test the code interactively in a Python shell by computing $\int_0^1 3t^2 e^{t^3} dt$. The file with the code above has the name `integration_methods_vec.py` and is a valid module from which we can import the vectorized function:

```
In [1]: from integration_methods_vec import midpoint

In [2]: from numpy import exp

In [3]: v = lambda t: 3*t**2*exp(t**3)

In [4]: midpoint(v, 0, 1, 10)
Out[4]: 1.7014827690091872
```

Note the necessity to use `exp` from `numpy`: our `v` function will be called with `x` as an array, and the `exp` function must be capable of working with an array.

The vectorized code performs all loops very efficiently in compiled code, resulting in much faster execution. Moreover, many readers of the code will also say that the algorithm looks clearer than in the loop-based implementation.

### 6.4.2 Vectorizing the Trapezoidal Rule

We can use the same approach to vectorize the `trapezoidal` function. However, the trapezoidal rule performs a sum where the end points have different weight. If we do `sum(f(x))`, we get the end points `f(a)` and `f(b)` with a weight of unity instead of one half. A remedy is to subtract the error from `sum(f(x))`: `sum(f(x)) - 0.5*f(a) - 0.5*f(b)`. The vectorized version of the trapezoidal method then becomes (the code is found in `integration_methods_vec.py`)

```
def trapezoidal(f, a, b, n):
    h = (b-a)/n
    x = linspace(a, b, n+1)
    s = sum(f(x)) - 0.5*f(a) - 0.5*f(b)
    return h*s
```

### 6.4.3 Speed up Gained with Vectorization

Now that we have created faster, vectorized versions of the functions, it is of interest to measure how much faster they are. Restricting ourselves to the midpoint method, we might proceed as:

```
import timeit
from integration_methods_vec import midpoint as midpoint_vec
from midpoint import midpoint
from numpy import exp

v = lambda t: 3*t**2*exp(t**3)

t = timeit.Timer('midpoint(v, 0, 1, 1000000)', \
                 setup='from __main__ import midpoint, v')
time_midpoint = t.timeit(10)
print('Time, midpoint: {:g} seconds'.format(time_midpoint))

# Vectorized version
t = timeit.Timer('midpoint_vec(v, 0, 1, 1000000)', \
                 setup='from __main__ import midpoint_vec, v')
time_midpoint_vec = t.timeit(10)
print('Time, midpoint vec: {:g} seconds'.format(time_midpoint_vec))

print('Efficiency factor: {:g}'.format(time_midpoint/time_midpoint_vec))
```

Running the program gives

```
Time, midpoint: 19.6083 seconds
Time, midpoint vec: 0.868379 seconds
Efficiency factor: 22.5804
```

We see that the vectorized version is about 20 times faster. The results for the trapezoidal method are very similar, and the factor of about 20 is independent of the number of intervals.

## 6.5 Rate of Convergence

We have seen that the numerical integration error drops when the number of sub-intervals $n$ is increased (causing each sub-interval to become smaller). This is fine and in line with our expectations, but some important details should be added.

**Asymptotic Behavior of the Integration Error** It is known that, if only the size $h$ of the sub-intervals is small enough, numerical integration methods typically give an error

$$E = Kh^r\,, \tag{6.21}$$

where $K$ is an unknown constant, while the *convergence rate* $r$ is a known constant that depends on the method. When a method has convergence rate $r$, it is known as an $r$-th order method. A large $r$ is beneficial, since $E$ then drops quicker when $h \to 0$.

Clearly, when

$$h = \frac{b-a}{n},$$

($n$ sub-intervals of equal size $h$ for an integration interval $[a, b]$), an alternative expression for $E$ follows from

$$E = Kh^r, \tag{6.22}$$

$$= K\left(\frac{b-a}{n}\right)^r, \tag{6.23}$$

$$= K\,(b-a)^r\left(\frac{1}{n}\right)^r, \tag{6.24}$$

which, by introducing another constant $C = K\,(b-a)^r$, gives

$$E = Cn^{-r}. \tag{6.25}$$

**Convergence Rate for the Trapezoidal and Midpoint Methods** Using, for example, the trapezoidal method, we may carry out some experimental runs with our test problem $\int_0^1 3t^2e^{t^3}dt$, doubling $n$ for each run: $n = 4, 8, 16$. The corresponding errors are then 12%, 3% and 0.78%, respectively. These numbers indicate that the error is reduced by roughly a factor 4 when doubling $n$. Thus, it seems that the error converges to zero as $n^{-2}$, which suggests a convergence rate $r = 2$. In fact, it can be shown mathematically that the trapezoidal and the midpoint method both have a convergence rate $r = 2$, i.e., they are both second-order methods. Soon, we will see how this fact (and more) can be exploited in the testing of code.

**Remark on the Definition of Convergence Rate**

When we later address numerical solution methods for ordinary differential equations (Chap. 8), convergence rate is essentially defined like in (6.21), we just switch (not required) the symbol $h$ with $\Delta t$ (i.e., the spacing between computed solution values).

However, with iterative methods for the solving of nonlinear algebraic equations (Chap. 7), convergence rate is defined differently. In that case, one usually relates the *error* at an iteration to the *error* at the previous iteration, and the convergence rate appears as a parameter in that relation.

## 6.6 Testing Code

### 6.6.1 Problems with Brief Testing Procedures

Previously in this book, our programs have been tested in very simple ways, usually by comparing to hand calculations. For numerical integration, in particular, testing has so far employed two strategies. When the exact solution *was* available, we computed the error and saw that an increase of $n$ gave a decrease in the error. When the exact solution *was not* available, we could (as in the comparison example of the previous section) look at the integral values and see that they stabilized as $n$ grew.

Unfortunately, these are very weak test procedures and not at all satisfactory for claiming that the software we have produced is correctly implemented.

**A Deliberate Bug** To see this, we can introduce a bug in the `application` function that calls `trapezoidal`: instead of integrating $3t^2e^{t^3}$, we write "accidentally" $3t^3e^{t^3}$, but keep the same anti-derivative $x(t) = e^{t^3}$ for computing the error. With the bug and $n = 4$, the error is 0.1, but without the bug the error is 0.2! It is of course completely impossible to tell if 0.1 is the right value of the error. Fortunately, in this case, increasing $n$ shows that the error stays about 0.3 in the program with the bug, so the test procedure with increasing $n$ (and checking that the error then decreases) points to a problem in the code.

**Another Deliberate Bug** Let us look at another bug, this time in the mathematical algorithm: instead of computing $\frac{1}{2}(f(a) + f(b))$ as we should, we "forget" the second $\frac{1}{2}$ and write `0.5*f(a) + f(b)`. The error for $n = 440, 400$ when computing $\int_{1.1}^{1.9} 3t^2e^{t^3}dt$ goes like 1400, 107, 10, respectively, which looks promising. The problem is that the right errors should be 369, 4.08, and 0.04. That is, the error should be reduced faster in the correct than in the buggy code. The problem, however, is that it is reduced in both codes, and we may stop further testing and believe everything is correctly implemented.

**Unit Testing**

A good habit is to test small pieces of a larger code individually, one at a time. This is known as *unit testing*: A (small) unit of the code is identified, so that a separate test for this unit can be made. The unit test should be "stand-alone" in the sense that it can be run without the outcome of other tests. Typically, one algorithm in scientific programs is considered a unit. The challenge with unit tests in numerical computing, is to deal with numerical approximation errors. A fortunate side effect of unit testing is that the programmer is forced to use functions to modularize the code into smaller, logical pieces.

### 6.6.2 Proper Test Procedures

There are three serious ways to test the implementation of numerical methods via unit tests:

1. *Comparing with hand-computed results.* Relevant for problems with few arithmetic operations, i.e., small $n$.
2. *Solving a problem without numerical errors.* We know, for example, that the trapezoidal rule must be exact for linear integrand functions. The error produced by the program must then be zero (to machine precision).
3. *Demonstrating correct convergence rates.* When exact errors can be computed, a strong test is to let $n$ grow and see if the error approaches zero as fast as theory predicts. As stated previously, for the trapezoidal and midpoint rules it is known that the error depends on $n$ as $n^{-2}$ when $n \to \infty$.

**Remark**

When testing code, we usually choose computational problems for which the exact solution *is* known. This is obviously a good idea, since it allows the quality of approximate numerical answers to be judged. Do not forget, however, that the exact solution is available because we *deliberately* chose a problem with known exact solution. When we have finished testing (and probably fixing) the code, our belief is that the code will work also for problems with unknown exact solutions. Our strategy then, is to trust the approximate answer from our code.

**Hand-Computed Results** Let us use two trapezoids and compute the integral $\int_0^1 v(t)dt$, where $v(t) = 3t^2 e^{t^3}$:

$$h\frac{(v(0) + v(0.5))}{2} + h\frac{(v(0.5) + v(1))}{2} = 2.463642041244344,$$

when $h = 0.5$ is the width of each trapezoid. Running the program gives exactly the same result.

Note that the exact solution is not involved here. We simply carry out the numerical algorithm by hand, "independent" from the code. We should of course get agreement between these hand calculations and program output when the same $n$ is used. However, assuming we do get agreement, that numerical answer may still differ substantially from the exact solution to the problem. That is of no concern in this test, as the aim is *not* to get as good an answer as possible (potentially achieved with a large $n$), but rather to check in a simple manner whether the algorithm "seems to be" correctly implemented.

**Solving a Problem Without Numerical Errors** The best unit tests for numerical algorithms involve mathematical problems where we know the numerical result beforehand. For these unit tests, we choose problems that fulfill two criteria. One criterion is that the exact solution is known. The other criterion is that the numerical algorithm should produce the exact solution, within machine precision, for any chosen $n$.

The second criterion may seem strange at first, but take the trapezoidal method, for example, and consider an integral like $\int_a^b (6x - 4)dx$. The integrand is here a straight line, and if you sketch it in a coordinate system along with some relevant trapezoids, you realize that the topmost side of each trapezoid comes exactly on the straight line. This is the case for whatever number $n$ of trapezoids you may choose to use. Thus, the trapezoidal method should solve that problem without any numerical error.[4] We can therefore pick some linear function and construct a test function that checks for equality between the exact solution and the numerical approximation produced by our implementation of the trapezoidal method.

Note that, when testing, numbers should not just be taken out of the air. For example, a specific test case can be $\int_{1.2}^{4.4} (6x - 4)dx$. This integral involves an "arbitrary" interval $[1.2, 4.4]$ and an "arbitrary" linear function $f(x) = 6x - 4$. By "arbitrary", we mean expressions where the special numbers 0 and 1 are avoided, since these have special properties in arithmetic operations (e.g., forgetting to multiply is equivalent to multiplying by 1, and forgetting to add is equivalent to adding 0).

**Demonstrating Correct Convergence Rates** Also for these unit tests we choose problems for which the exact solution is known. However, contrary to the previous test procedure, we now work with problems for which the numerical algorithm does *not* give zero approximation error. Normally, unit tests must be based on that kind of problems. Thus, the answer we get from our code will contain an approximation error, and since we know the exact solution, we may compute the size of this error. Unfortunately, this is not too helpful, since we have little chance telling if this error is what we *should* have got for the particular $n$ used!

Now the convergence rate comes in handy. If we know (or have reason to assume) that the numerical error has a certain *asymptotic* behavior when $n \to \infty$, we know at what *rate* the numerical error should be reduced. The idea of a corresponding unit test is then to run the algorithm for some $n$ values, compute the error (the absolute value of the difference between the exact solution and the one produced by the numerical method), and check that the error has *approximately* correct asymptotic behavior. For the trapezoidal and midpoint methods in particular, this means that the error should become proportional to $n^{-2}$ when $n \to \infty$.

Let us develop a more precise method for such unit tests based on convergence rates. Consider a set of $q + 1$ experiments with various $n$: $n_0, n_1, n_2, \ldots, n_q$. We compute the corresponding errors $E_0, \ldots, E_q$. For two consecutive experiments, number $i$ and $i - 1$, we have the error model

$$E_i = Cn_i^{-r}, \tag{6.26}$$

$$E_{i-1} = Cn_{i-1}^{-r}. \tag{6.27}$$

[4] In fact, so would the midpoint method! This is because, for each rectangle, the error to each side of the midpoint is equally large with opposite signs, meaning that they cancel each other.

These are two equations for two unknowns $C$ and $r$. We can easily eliminate $C$ by dividing, e.g., (6.26) by (6.27). Doing so, and proceeding to solve for $r$, followed by also introducing a subscript $i-1$ for $r$, gives

$$r_{i-1} = -\frac{\ln(E_i/E_{i-1})}{\ln(n_i/n_{i-1})}\,. \tag{6.28}$$

The subscript is introduced, since the estimated value for $r$ will vary with $i$. Hopefully, $r_{i-1}$ approaches the correct convergence rate as the number of intervals increases and $i \rightarrow q$.

### 6.6.3 Finite Precision of Floating-Point Numbers

The test procedures above lead to comparison of numbers for checking that calculations were correct. Such comparison is more complicated than what a newcomer might think. Suppose we have a calculation `a + b` and want to check that the result is what we expect.

**Adding Integers** We start with 1 + 2:

```
In [1]: a = 1; b = 2; expected = 3

In [2]: a + b == expected
Out[2]: True
```

**Adding Real Numbers** Then we proceed with 0.1 + 0.2:

```
In [3]: a = 0.1; b = 0.2; expected = 0.3

In [4]: a + b == expected
Out[4]: False
```

**Approximate Representation of Real Numbers on a Computer** So why is $0.1 + 0.2 \neq 0.3$? The reason is that, generally, real numbers cannot be represented exactly on a computer. They must instead be approximated by a floating-point number[5] that can only store a finite amount of information, usually about 17 digits of a real number. Let us print 0.1, 0.2, 0.1 + 0.2, and 0.3 with 17 decimals:

```
In [5]: print('{:.17f}\n{:.17f}\n{:.17f}\n{:.17f}'\
              .format(0.1, 0.2, 0.1 + 0.2, 0.3))
0.10000000000000001
0.20000000000000001
0.30000000000000004
0.29999999999999999
```

We see that all of the numbers have an inaccurate digit in the 17th decimal place. Because 0.1 + 0.2 evaluates to 0.30000000000000004 and 0.3 is represented as 0.29999999999999999, these two numbers are not equal. In general, real numbers in Python have (at most) 16 correct decimals.

[5] `https://en.wikipedia.org/wiki/Floating_point`.

**Rounding Errors** When we compute with real numbers, these numbers are inaccurately represented on the computer, and arithmetic operations with inaccurate numbers lead to small rounding errors in the final results. Depending on the type of numerical algorithm, the rounding errors may or may not accumulate.

**Testing with a Tolerance** If we cannot make tests like `0.1 + 0.2 == 0.3`, what should we then do? The answer is that we must accept some small inaccuracy and make a test with a *tolerance*. Here is the recipe:

```
In [1]: a = 0.1; b = 0.2; expected = 0.3

In [2]: computed = a + b

In [3]: diff = abs(expected - computed)

In [4]: tol = 1E-15

In [5]: diff < tol
Out[5]: True
```

Here we have set the tolerance for comparison to $10^{-15}$, but calculating `0.3 - (0.1 + 0.2)` shows that it equals `-5.55e-17`, so a lower tolerance could be used in this particular example. However, in other calculations we have little idea about how accurate the answer is (there could be accumulation of rounding errors in more complicated algorithms), so $10^{-15}$ or $10^{-14}$ are robust values. As we demonstrate below, these tolerances depend on the magnitude of the numbers in the calculations.

**Absolute and Relative Differences** Doing an experiment with $10^k + 0.3 - (10^k + 0.1 + 0.2)$ for $k = 1, \ldots, 10$ shows that the answer (which should be zero) is around $10^{16-k}$. This means that the tolerance must be larger if we compute with larger numbers. Setting a proper tolerance therefore requires some experiments to see what level of accuracy one can expect. A way out of this difficulty is to work with *relative* instead of *absolute* differences. In a relative difference we divide by one of the operands, e.g.,

$$a = 10^k + 0.3, \quad b = (10^k + 0.1 + 0.2), \quad c = \frac{a - b}{a}.$$

Computing this $c$ for various $k$ shows a value around $10^{-16}$. A safer procedure is thus to use *relative differences*.

We may exemplify this in a quick session, using $k = 10$,

```
In [1]: a = 10**10 + 0.3

In [2]: b = 10**10 + 0.1 + 0.2

In [3]: diff = a-b

In [4]: diff
Out[4]: -1.9073486328125e-06

In [5]: rel_diff = (a-b)/a
```

```
In [6]: rel_diff
Out[6]: -1.9073486327552798e-16
```

Clearly, `diff` here would certainly not be smaller than a tolerance of $1E - 15$ (as we used above). So, to check whether $a$ and $b$ are equal, we should rather proceed as

```
In [7]: tol = 1E-15

In [8]: rel_diff < tol
Out[8]: True
```

### 6.6.4 Constructing Unit Tests and Writing Test Functions

Python has several frameworks for automatic testing of software. By just one command, you can get Python to run through a (potentially) very large number of tests for various parts of your software. This is an extremely useful feature during program development: whenever you have done some changes to one or more files, launch the test command and make sure nothing is broken because of your edits.

The test frameworks `nose` and `py.test` are particularly attractive, since they are very easy to use. Tests are placed in special *test functions* that the frameworks can recognize and run for you. The requirements to a test function are simple:

- the name must start with `test_`
- the test function cannot have any arguments
- the tests inside test functions must be boolean expressions
- a boolean expression `b` must be tested in an *assert statement* of the form `assert b, msg`. When `b` is true, nothing happens. However, if `b` is false, `msg` is written out, where `msg` is an optional object (string or number).

Suppose we have written a function

```
def add(a, b):
    return a + b
```

A corresponding test function can then be

```
def test_add():
    expected = 2
    computed = add(1, 1)
    assert computed == expected, '1+1={:g}'.format(computed)
```

Test functions can be in any program file or in separate files, typically with names starting with `test`. You can also collect tests in subdirectories: running `py.test -s -v` will actually run all tests in all `test*.py` files in all subdirectories, while `nosetests -s -v` restricts the attention to subdirectories whose names start with `test` or end with `_test` or `_tests`.

As long as we add integers, the equality test in the `test_add` function is appropriate, but if we try to call `add(0.1, 0.2)` instead, we will face the rounding error problems explained in Sect. 6.6.3, and we must use a test with tolerance instead:

```
def test_add():
    expected = 0.3
    computed = add(0.1, 0.2)
    tol = 1E-14
    diff = abs(expected - computed)
    assert diff < tol, 'diff={:g}'.format(diff)
```

Below we shall write test functions for each of the three test procedures we suggested: comparison with hand calculations, checking problems that can be exactly solved, and checking convergence rates. We stick to testing the trapezoidal integration code and collect all test functions in one common file by the name `test_trapezoidal.py`.

**Hand-Computed Numerical Results** Our previous hand calculations for two trapezoids can be utilized in a test function like this:

```
from trapezoidal import trapezoidal

def test_trapezoidal_one_exact_result():
    """Compare one hand-computed result."""
    from math import exp
    v = lambda t: 3*(t**2)*exp(t**3)
    n = 2
    computed = trapezoidal(v, 0, 1, n)
    expected = 2.463642041244344
    error = abs(expected - computed)
    tol = 1E-14
    success = error < tol
    msg = 'error={:g} > tol={:g}'.format(error, tol)
    assert success, msg
```

Note the importance of checking `computed` against `expected` with a tolerance: rounding errors from the arithmetics inside `trapezoidal` will not make the result exactly like the hand-computed one.

**Solving a Problem Without Numerical Errors** We know that the trapezoidal rule is exact for linear integrands. Choosing the integral $\int_{1.2}^{4.4}(6x-4)dx$ as a test case, the corresponding test function could, for example, check with three different $n$ values, and may look like

```
def test_trapezoidal_linear():
    """Check that linear functions are integrated exactly."""
    f = lambda x: 6*x - 4
    F = lambda x: 3*x**2 - 4*x # Anti-derivative
    a = 1.2; b = 4.4
    expected = F(b) - F(a)
    tol = 1E-14
    for n in 2, 20, 21:
        computed = trapezoidal(f, a, b, n)
        error = abs(expected - computed)
        success = error < tol
        msg = 'n={:d}, err={:g}'.format(n, error)
        assert success, msg
```

**Demonstrating Correct Convergence Rates** Computing convergence rates requires somewhat more tedious programming than for the previous tests, but it can be applied to more general integrands. The algorithm typically goes like

- for $i = 0, 1, 2, \ldots, q$
  - $n_i = 2^{i+1}$
  - Compute integral with $n_i$ intervals
  - Compute the error $E_i$
  - Estimate $r_i$ from (6.28) if $i > 0$

The corresponding code may look like

```
def convergence_rates(f, F, a, b, num_experiments=14):
    from math import log
    from numpy import zeros
    expected = F(b) - F(a)
    n = zeros(num_experiments, dtype=int)
    E = zeros(num_experiments)
    r = zeros(num_experiments-1)
    for i in range(num_experiments):
        n[i] = 2**(i+1)
        computed = trapezoidal(f, a, b, n[i])
        E[i] = abs(expected - computed)
        if i > 0:
            r_im1 = -log(E[i]/E[i-1])/log(n[i]/n[i-1])
            # Truncate to two decimals:
            r[i-1] = float('{:.2f}'.format(r_im1))
    return r
```

Making a test function is a matter of choosing f, F, a, and b, and then checking the value of $r_i$ for the largest $i$:

```
def test_trapezoidal_conv_rate():
    """Check empirical convergence rates against the expected value 2."""
    from math import exp
    v = lambda t: 3*(t**2)*exp(t**3)
    V = lambda t: exp(t**3)
    a = 1.1; b = 1.9
    r = convergence_rates(v, V, a, b, 14)
    print(r)
    tol = 0.01
    msg = str(r[-4:])  # show last 4 estimated rates
    assert (abs(r[-1]) - 2) < tol, msg
```

Running the test shows that all $r_i$, except the first one, equal the target limit 2 within two decimals. This observation suggests a tolerance of $10^{-2}$.

## 6.7 Double and Triple Integrals

### 6.7.1 The Midpoint Rule for a Double Integral

Given a double integral over a rectangular domain $[a, b] \times [c, d]$,

$$\int_a^b \int_c^d f(x, y) dy dx,$$

how can we approximate this integral by numerical methods?

**Derivation via One-Dimensional Integrals** Since we know how to deal with integrals in one variable, a fruitful approach is to view the double integral as two integrals, each in one variable, which can be approximated numerically by previous one-dimensional formulas. To this end, we introduce a help function $g(x)$ and write

$$\int_a^b \int_c^d f(x, y)dydx = \int_a^b g(x)dx, \quad g(x) = \int_c^d f(x, y)dy\,.$$

Each of the integrals

$$\int_a^b g(x)dx, \quad g(x) = \int_c^d f(x, y)dy$$

can be discretized by any numerical integration rule for an integral in one variable. Let us use the midpoint method (6.20) and start with $g(x) = \int_c^d f(x, y)dy$. We introduce $n_y$ intervals on $[c, d]$ with length $h_y$. The midpoint rule for this integral then becomes

$$g(x) = \int_c^d f(x, y)dy \approx h_y \sum_{j=0}^{n_y-1} f(x, y_j), \quad y_j = c + \frac{1}{2}h_y + jh_y\,.$$

The expression looks somewhat different from (6.20), but that is because of the notation: since we integrate in the $y$ direction and will have to work with both $x$ and $y$ as coordinates, we must use $n_y$ for $n$, $h_y$ for $h$, and the counter $i$ is more naturally called $j$ when integrating in $y$. Integrals in the $x$ direction will use $h_x$ and $n_x$ for $h$ and $n$, and $i$ as counter.

The double integral is $\int_a^b g(x)dx$, which can be approximated by the midpoint method:

$$\int_a^b g(x)dx \approx h_x \sum_{i=0}^{n_x-1} g(x_i), \quad x_i = a + \frac{1}{2}h_x + ih_x\,.$$

Putting the formulas together, we arrive at the *composite midpoint method for a double integral*:

$$\begin{aligned}\int_a^b \int_c^d f(x, y)dydx &\approx h_x \sum_{i=0}^{n_x-1} h_y \sum_{j=0}^{n_y-1} f(x_i, y_j)\\ &= h_x h_y \sum_{i=0}^{n_x-1}\sum_{j=0}^{n_y-1} f(a + \frac{h_x}{2} + ih_x, c + \frac{h_y}{2} + jh_y)\,.\end{aligned} \tag{6.29}$$

**Direct Derivation** The formula (6.29) can also be derived directly in the two-dimensional case by applying the idea of the midpoint method. We divide the rectangle $[a, b] \times [c, d]$ into $n_x \times n_y$ equal-sized parts called *cells*. The idea of the midpoint method is to approximate $f$ by a constant over each cell, and evaluate the constant at the midpoint. Cell $(i, j)$ occupies the area

$$[a + ih_x, a + (i + 1)h_x] \times [c + jh_y, c + (j + 1)h_y],$$

and the midpoint is $(x_i, y_j)$ with

$$x_i = a + ih_x + \frac{1}{2}h_x, \quad y_j = c + jh_y + \frac{1}{2}h_y .$$

The integral over the cell is therefore $h_x h_y f(x_i, y_j)$, and the total double integral is the sum over all cells, which is nothing but formula (6.29).

**Programming a Double Sum** The formula (6.29) involves a double sum, which is normally implemented as a double for loop. A Python function implementing (6.29) may look like

```
def midpoint_double1(f, a, b, c, d, nx, ny):
    hx = (b - a)/nx
    hy = (d - c)/ny
    I = 0
    for i in range(nx):
        for j in range(ny):
            xi = a + hx/2 + i*hx
            yj = c + hy/2 + j*hy
            I = I + hx*hy*f(xi, yj)
    return I
```

If this function is stored in a module file `midpoint_double.py`, we can compute some integral, e.g., $\int_2^3 \int_0^2 (2x + y)dxdy = 9$ in an interactive shell and demonstrate that the function computes the right number:

```
In [1]: from midpoint_double import midpoint_double1

In [2]: def f(x, y):
   ...:     return 2*x + y
   ...:

In [3]: midpoint_double1(f, 0, 2, 2, 3, 5, 5)
Out[3]: 9.000000000000005
```

**Reusing Code for One-Dimensional Integrals** It is very natural to write a two-dimensional midpoint method as we did in function `midpoint_double1` when we have the formula (6.29). However, we could alternatively ask, much as we did in the mathematics, can we reuse a well-tested implementation for one-dimensional integrals to compute double integrals? That is, can we use function `midpoint`

```
def midpoint(f, a, b, n):
    h = (b-a)/n
    f_sum = 0
```

```
    for i in range(0, n, 1):
        x = (a + h/2.0) + i*h
        f_sum = f_sum + f(x)
    return h*f_sum
```

from Sect. 6.3.2 "twice"? The answer is yes, if we think as we did in the mathematics: compute the double integral as a midpoint rule for integrating $g(x)$ and define $g(x_i)$ in terms of a midpoint rule over $f$ in the $y$ coordinate. The corresponding function has very short code:

```
def midpoint_double2(f, a, b, c, d, nx, ny):
    def g(x):
        return midpoint(lambda y: f(x, y), c, d, ny)

    return midpoint(g, a, b, nx)
```

The important advantage of this implementation is that we reuse a well-tested function for the standard one-dimensional midpoint rule and that we apply the one-dimensional rule exactly as in the mathematics.

**Verification via Test Functions** How can we test that our functions for the double integral work? The best unit test is to find a problem where the numerical approximation error vanishes because then we know exactly what the numerical answer should be. The midpoint rule is exact for linear functions, regardless of how many subinterval we use. Also, any linear two-dimensional function $f(x, y) = px + qy + r$ will be integrated exactly by the two-dimensional midpoint rule. We may pick $f(x, y) = 2x + y$ and create a proper *test function* that can automatically verify our two alternative implementations of the two-dimensional midpoint rule. To compute the integral of $f(x, y)$ we take advantage of SymPy to eliminate the possibility of errors in hand calculations. The test function becomes

```
def test_midpoint_double():
    """Test that a linear function is integrated exactly."""
    def f(x, y):
        return 2*x + y

    a = 0;  b = 2;  c = 2;  d = 3
    import sympy
    x, y = sympy.symbols('x  y')
    I_expected = sympy.integrate(f(x, y), (x, a, b), (y, c, d))
    # Test three cases: nx < ny, nx = ny, nx > ny
    for nx, ny in (3, 5), (4, 4), (5, 3):
        I_computed1 = midpoint_double1(f, a, b, c, d, nx, ny)
        I_computed2 = midpoint_double2(f, a, b, c, d, nx, ny)
        tol = 1E-14
        #print I_expected, I_computed1, I_computed2
        assert abs(I_computed1 - I_expected) < tol
        assert abs(I_computed2 - I_expected) < tol
```

**Let Test Functions Speak Up?**

If we call the above `test_midpoint_double` function and nothing happens, our implementations are correct. However, it is somewhat annoying to have a function that is completely silent when it works—are we sure all things are properly computed? During development it is therefore highly recommended to insert a print command such that we can monitor the calculations and be convinced that the test function does what we want. Since a test function should not have any print command, we simply comment it out as we have done in the function listed above.

The trapezoidal method can be used as alternative for the midpoint method. The derivation of a formula for the double integral and the implementations follow exactly the same ideas as we explained with the midpoint method, but there are more terms to write in the formulas. Exercise 6.13 asks you to carry out the details. That exercise is a very good test on your understanding of the mathematical and programming ideas in the present section.

### 6.7.2 The Midpoint Rule for a Triple Integral

**Theory** Once a method that works for a one-dimensional problem is generalized to two dimensions, it is usually quite straightforward to extend the method to three dimensions. This will now be demonstrated for integrals. We have the triple integral

$$\int_a^b \int_c^d \int_e^f g(x, y, z) dz dy dx$$

and want to approximate the integral by a midpoint rule. Following the ideas for the double integral, we split this integral into one-dimensional integrals:

$$p(x, y) = \int_e^f g(x, y, z) dz$$

$$q(x) = \int_c^d p(x, y) dy$$

$$\int_a^b \int_c^d \int_e^f g(x, y, z) dz dy dx = \int_a^b q(x) dx$$

For each of these one-dimensional integrals we apply the midpoint rule:

$$p(x, y) = \int_e^f g(x, y, z)dz \approx \sum_{k=0}^{n_z-1} g(x, y, z_k),$$

$$q(x) = \int_c^d p(x, y)dy \approx \sum_{j=0}^{n_y-1} p(x, y_j),$$

$$\int_a^b \int_c^d \int_e^f g(x, y, z)dzdydx = \int_a^b q(x)dx \approx \sum_{i=0}^{n_x-1} q(x_i),$$

where

$$z_k = e + \frac{1}{2}h_z + kh_z, \quad y_j = c + \frac{1}{2}h_y + jh_y \quad x_i = a + \frac{1}{2}h_x + ih_x\,.$$

Starting with the formula for $\int_a^b \int_c^d \int_e^f g(x, y, z)dzdydx$ and inserting the two previous formulas gives

$$\int_a^b \int_c^d \int_e^f g(x, y, z)\, dzdydx \approx$$
$$h_x h_y h_z \sum_{i=0}^{n_x-1} \sum_{j=0}^{n_y-1} \sum_{k=0}^{n_z-1} g(a + \frac{1}{2}h_x + ih_x, c + \frac{1}{2}h_y + jh_y, e + \frac{1}{2}h_z + kh_z)\,. \tag{6.30}$$

Note that we may apply the ideas under *Direct derivation* at the end of Sect. 6.7.1 to arrive at (6.30) directly: divide the domain into $n_x \times n_y \times n_z$ cells of volumes $h_x h_y h_z$; approximate $g$ by a constant, evaluated at the midpoint $(x_i, y_j, z_k)$, in each cell; and sum the cell integrals $h_x h_y h_z g(x_i, y_j, z_k)$.

**Implementation** We follow the ideas for the implementations of the midpoint rule for a double integral. The corresponding functions are shown below and found in the file midpoint_triple.py.

```
def midpoint_triple1(g, a, b, c, d, e, f, nx, ny, nz):
    hx = (b - a)/nx
    hy = (d - c)/ny
    hz = (f - e)/nz
    I = 0
    for i in range(nx):
        for j in range(ny):
            for k in range(nz):
                xi = a + hx/2 + i*hx
                yj = c + hy/2 + j*hy
                zk = e + hz/2 + k*hz
                I = I + hx*hy*hz*g(xi, yj, zk)
    return I
```

```
def midpoint(f, a, b, n):
    h = (b-a)/n
    f_sum = 0
    for i in range(0, n, 1):
        x = (a + h/2.0) + i*h
        f_sum = f_sum + f(x)
    return h*f_sum

def midpoint_triple2(g, a, b, c, d, e, f, nx, ny, nz):
    def p(x, y):
        return midpoint(lambda z: g(x, y, z), e, f, nz)

    def q(x):
        return midpoint(lambda y: p(x, y), c, d, ny)

    return midpoint(q, a, b, nx)

def test_midpoint_triple():
    """Test that a linear function is integrated exactly."""
    def g(x, y, z):
        return 2*x + y - 4*z

    a = 0;  b = 2;  c = 2;  d = 3;  e = -1;  f = 2
    import sympy
    x, y, z = sympy.symbols('x y z')
    I_expected = sympy.integrate(
        g(x, y, z), (x, a, b), (y, c, d), (z, e, f))
    for nx, ny, nz in (3, 5, 2), (4, 4, 4), (5, 3, 6):
        I_computed1 = midpoint_triple1(
            g, a, b, c, d, e, f, nx, ny, nz)
        I_computed2 = midpoint_triple2(
            g, a, b, c, d, e, f, nx, ny, nz)
        tol = 1E-14
        print(I_expected, I_computed1, I_computed2)
        assert abs(I_computed1 - I_expected) < tol
        assert abs(I_computed2 - I_expected) < tol

if __name__ == '__main__':
    test_midpoint_triple()
```

### 6.7.3 Monte Carlo Integration for Complex-Shaped Domains

Repeated use of one-dimensional integration rules to handle double and triple integrals constitute a working strategy only if the integration domain is a rectangle or box. For any other shape of domain, completely different methods must be used. A common approach for two- and three-dimensional domains is to divide the domain into many small triangles or tetrahedra and use numerical integration methods for each triangle or tetrahedron. The overall algorithm and implementation is too complicated to be addressed in this book. Instead, we shall employ an alternative, very simple and general method, called Monte Carlo integration. It can be implemented in half a page of code, but requires orders of magnitude more function evaluations in double integrals compared to the midpoint rule.

Monte Carlo integration, however, is much more computationally efficient than the midpoint rule when computing higher-dimensional integrals in more than three variables over hypercube domains. Our ideas for double and triple integrals can easily be generalized to handle an integral in $m$ variables. A midpoint formula then involves $m$ sums. With $n$ cells in each coordinate direction, the formula requires $n^m$ function evaluations. That is, the computational work explodes as an exponential function of the number of space dimensions. Monte Carlo integration, on the other hand, does not suffer from this explosion of computational work and is the preferred method for computing higher-dimensional integrals. So, it makes sense in a chapter on numerical integration to address Monte Carlo methods, both for handling complex domains and for handling integrals with many variables.

**The Monte Carlo Integration Algorithm** The idea of Monte Carlo integration of $\int_a^b f(x)dx$ is to use the mean-value theorem from calculus, which states that the integral $\int_a^b f(x)dx$ equals the length of the integration domain, here $b - a$, times the *average* value of $f$, $\bar{f}$, in $[a, b]$. The average value can be computed by sampling $f$ at a set of *random* points inside the domain and take the mean of the function values. In higher dimensions, an integral is estimated as the area/volume of the domain times the average value, and again one can evaluate the integrand at a set of random points in the domain and compute the mean value of those evaluations.

Let us introduce some quantities to help us make the specification of the integration algorithm more precise. Suppose we have some two-dimensional integral

$$\int_\Omega f(x, y)dxdx,$$

where $\Omega$ is a two-dimensional domain defined via a help function $g(x, y)$:

$$\Omega = \{(x, y) \mid g(x, y) \geq 0\}$$

That is, points $(x, y)$ for which $g(x, y) \geq 0$ lie inside $\Omega$, and points for which $g(x, y) < \Omega$ are outside $\Omega$. The boundary of the domain $\partial\Omega$ is given by the implicit curve $g(x, y) = 0$. Such formulations of geometries have been very common during the last couple of decades, and one refers to $g$ as a *level-set function* and the boundary $g = 0$ as the zero-level contour of the level-set function. For simple geometries one can easily construct $g$ by hand, while in more complicated industrial applications one must resort to mathematical models for constructing $g$.

Let $A(\Omega)$ be the area of a domain $\Omega$. We can estimate the integral by this Monte Carlo integration method:

1. embed the geometry $\Omega$ in a rectangular area $R$
2. draw a large number of *random* points $(x, y)$ in $R$

3. count the fraction $q$ of points that are inside $\Omega$
4. approximate $A(\Omega)/A(R)$ by $q$, i.e., set $A(\Omega) = qA(R)$
5. evaluate the mean of $f$, $\bar{f}$, at the points inside $\Omega$
6. estimate the integral as $A(\Omega)\bar{f}$

Note that $A(R)$ is trivial to compute since $R$ is a rectangle, while $A(\Omega)$ is unknown. However, if we assume that the fraction of $A(R)$ occupied by $A(\Omega)$ is the same as the fraction of random points inside $\Omega$, we get a simple estimate for $A(\Omega)$.

To get an idea of the method, consider a circular domain $\Omega$ embedded in a rectangle as shown below. A collection of random points is illustrated by black dots.

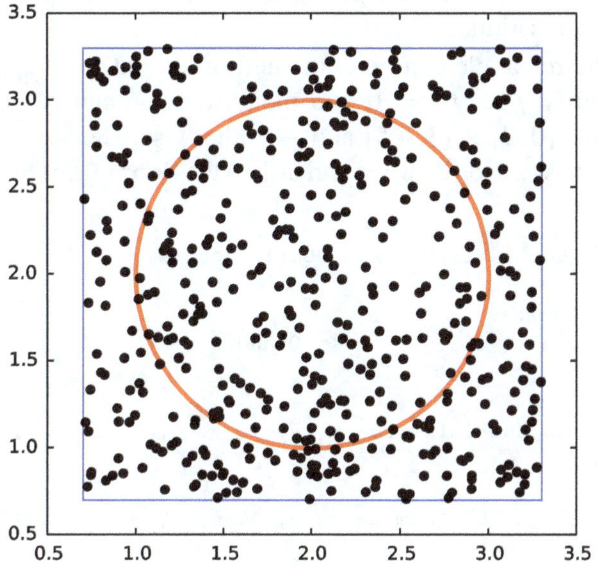


**Implementation** A Python function implementing $\int_\Omega f(x, y)dxdy$ can be written like this:

```
import numpy as np

def MonteCarlo_double(f, g, x0, x1, y0, y1, n):
    """
    Monte Carlo integration of f over a domain g>=0, embedded
    in a rectangle [x0,x1]x[y0,y1]. n^2 is the number of
    random points.
    """
    # Draw n**2 random points in the rectangle
    x = np.random.uniform(x0, x1, n)
    y = np.random.uniform(y0, y1, n)
    # Compute sum of f values inside the integration domain
    f_mean = 0
    num_inside = 0   # number of x,y points inside domain (g>=0)
    for i in range(len(x)):
        for j in range(len(y)):
            if g(x[i], y[j]) >= 0:
                num_inside = num_inside + 1
```

```
                f_mean = f_mean + f(x[i], y[j])
    f_mean = f_mean/num_inside
    area = num_inside/(n**2)*(x1 - x0)*(y1 - y0)
    return area*f_mean
```

(See the file MC_double.py.)

**Verification** A simple test case is to check the area of a rectangle $[0, 2] \times [3, 4.5]$ embedded in a rectangle $[0, 3] \times [2, 5]$. The right answer is 3, but Monte Carlo integration is, unfortunately, never exact so it is impossible to predict the output of the algorithm. All we know is that the estimated integral should approach 3 as the number of random points goes to infinity. Also, for a fixed number of points, we can run the algorithm several times and get different numbers that fluctuate around the exact value, since different sample points are used in different calls to the Monte Carlo integration algorithm.

The area of the rectangle can be computed by the integral $\int_0^2 \int_3^{4.5} dydx$, so in this case we identify $f(x, y) = 1$, and the $g$ function can be specified as (e.g.) 1 if $(x, y)$ is inside $[0, 2] \times [3, 4.5]$ and $-1$ otherwise. Here is an example, using samples of different sizes, on how we can utilize the MonteCarlo_double function to compute the area:

```
In [1]: from MC_double import MonteCarlo_double

In [2]: def g(x, y):
   ...:     return (1 if (0 <= x <= 2 and 3 <= y <= 4.5) else -1)
   ...:

In [3]: MonteCarlo_double(lambda x, y: 1, g, 0, 3, 2, 5, 100)
Out[3]: 2.9484

In [4]: MonteCarlo_double(lambda x, y: 1, g, 0, 3, 2, 5, 1000)
Out[4]: 2.947032

In [5]: MonteCarlo_double(lambda x, y: 1, g, 0, 3, 2, 5, 1000)
Out[5]: 3.0234600000000005

In [6]: MonteCarlo_double(lambda x, y: 1, g, 0, 3, 2, 5, 2000)
Out[6]: 2.9984580000000003

In [7]: MonteCarlo_double(lambda x, y: 1, g, 0, 3, 2, 5, 2000)
Out[7]: 3.1903469999999996

In [8]: MonteCarlo_double(lambda x, y: 1, g, 0, 3, 2, 5, 5000)
Out[8]: 2.986515
```

Note the compact if-else construction in the definition of g. It is a one-line alternative to, for example,

```
if (0 <= x <= 2) and (3 <= y <= 4.5):
    return 1
else:
    return -1
```

From the output, we see that the values fluctuate around 3, a fact that supports a correct implementation, but in principle, bugs could be hidden behind the inaccurate answers.

It is mathematically known that the standard deviation of the Monte Carlo estimate of an integral converges as $n^{-1/2}$, where $n$ is the number of samples. This kind of convergence rate estimate could be used to verify the implementation, but the topic is beyond the scope of this book.

**Test Function for Function with Random Numbers** To make a test function, we need a unit test that has identical behavior each time we run the test. Thus, since the algorithm generates pseudo-random numbers, we apply the standard technique of fixing the seed (of the random number generator), so that the sequence of numbers generated is the same every time we run the algorithm. Assuming that the `MonteCarlo_double` function works, we fix the seed, observe a certain result, and take this result as the correct result. Provided the test function always uses this seed, we should get exactly this result every time the `MonteCarlo_double` function is called. Of course, this procedure does not test whether the `MonteCarlo_double` function works right now (but we hope our assumption of correctness is well founded!). Still, it is nevertheless useful when future changes are made, since at any time we can confirm that `MonteCarlo_double` gives the same answer as before. The test function can be written as shown below.

```
def test_MonteCarlo_double_rectangle_area():
    """Check the area of a rectangle."""
    def g(x, y):
        return (1 if (0 <= x <= 2 and 3 <= y <= 4.5) else -1)

    x0 = 0;  x1 = 3;  y0 = 2;  y1 = 5  # embedded rectangle
    n = 1000
    np.random.seed(8)       # must fix the seed!
    I_expected = 3.121092  # computed with this seed
    I_computed = MonteCarlo_double(
        lambda x, y: 1, g, x0, x1, y0, y1, n)
    assert abs(I_expected - I_computed) < 1E-14
```

(See the file `MC_double.py`.)

**Integral Over a Circle** The test above involves a trivial function $f(x, y) = 1$. We should also test a non-constant $f$ function and a more complicated domain. Let $\Omega$ be a circle at the origin with radius 2, and let $f = \sqrt{x^2 + y^2}$. This choice makes it possible to compute an exact result: in polar coordinates, $\int_\Omega f(x, y)dxdy$ simplifies to $2\pi \int_0^2 r^2dr = 16\pi/3$. We must be prepared for quite crude approximations that fluctuate around this exact result. As in the test case above, we experience better results with larger number of points. When we have such evidence for a working implementation, we can turn the test into a proper test function. Here is an example:

```
def test_MonteCarlo_double_circle_r():
    """Check the integral of r over a circle with radius 2."""
    def g(x, y):
        xc, yc = 0, 0  # center
        R = 2          # radius
        return  R**2 - ((x-xc)**2 + (y-yc)**2)

    # Exact: integral of r*r*dr over circle with radius R becomes
    # 2*pi*1/3*R**3
    import sympy
```

```
r = sympy.symbols('r')
I_exact = sympy.integrate(2*sympy.pi*r*r, (r, 0, 2))
print('Exact integral: {:g}'.format(I_exact.evalf()))
x0 = -2;  x1 = 2;  y0 = -2;  y1 = 2
n = 1000
np.random.seed(6)
I_expected = 16.7970837117376384  # Computed with this seed
I_computed = MonteCarlo_double(
    lambda x, y: np.sqrt(x**2 + y**2),
    g, x0, x1, y0, y1, n)
print('MC approximation, {:d} samples: {:.16f}'\
      .format(n**2, I_computed))
assert abs(I_expected - I_computed) < 1E-15
```

(See the file MC_double.py.)

**Remark About Version Control of Files**

Having a suite of test functions for automatically checking that your software works is considered as a fundamental requirement for reliable computing. Equally important is a system that can keep track of different versions of the files and the tests, known as a *version control system*. Today's most popular version control system is Git,[a] which the authors strongly recommend the reader to use for programming and writing reports. The combination of Git and cloud storage such as GitHub is a very common way of organizing scientific or engineering work. We have a quick intro[b] to Git and GitHub that gets you up and running within minutes.

The typical workflow with Git goes as follows.

1. Before you start working with files, make sure you have the latest version of them by running `git pull`.
2. Edit files, remove or create files (new files must be registered by `git add`).
3. When a natural piece of work is done, *commit* your changes by the `git commit` command.
4. Implement your changes also in the cloud by doing `git push`.

A nice feature of Git is that people can edit the same file at the same time and very often Git will be able to automatically merge the changes (!). Therefore, version control is crucial when you work with others or when you do your work on different types of computers. Another key feature is that anyone can at any time view the history of a file, see who did what when, and roll back the entire file collection to a previous commit. This feature is, of course, fundamental for reliable work.

[a] https://en.wikipedia.org/wiki/Git_(software).
[b] http://hplgit.github.io/teamods/bitgit/Langtangen_bitgit-bootstrap.html.

## 6.8 Exercises

**Exercise 6.1: Hand Calculations for the Trapezoidal Method**
Compute by hand the area composed of two trapezoids (of equal width) that approximates the integral $\int_1^3 2x^3 dx$. Make a test function that calls the `trapezoidal` function in `trapezoidal.py` and compares the return value with the hand-calculated value.
Filename: `trapezoidal_test_func.py`.

**Exercise 6.2: Hand Calculations for the Midpoint Method**
Compute by hand the area composed of two rectangles (of equal width) that approximates the integral $\int_1^3 2x^3 dx$. Make a test function that calls the `midpoint` function in `midpoint.py` and compares the return value with the hand-calculated value.
Filename: `midpoint_test_func.py`.

**Exercise 6.3: Compute a Simple Integral**
Apply the `trapezoidal` and `midpoint` functions to compute the integral $\int_2^6 x(x-1)dx$ with 2 and 100 subintervals. Compute the error too.
Filename: `integrate_parabola.py`.

**Exercise 6.4: Hand-Calculations with Sine Integrals**
We consider integrating the sine function: $\int_0^b \sin(x)dx$.

a) Let $b = \pi$ and use two intervals in the trapezoidal and midpoint method. Compute the integral by hand and illustrate how the two numerical methods approximate the integral. Compare with the exact value.
b) Do a) when $b = 2\pi$.

Filename: `integrate_sine.py`.

**Exercise 6.5: Make Test Functions for the Midpoint Method**
Modify the file `test_trapezoidal.py` such that the three tests are applied to the function `midpoint` implementing the midpoint method for integration.
Filename: `test_midpoint.py`.

**Exercise 6.6: Explore Rounding Errors with Large Numbers**
The trapezoidal method integrates linear functions exactly, and this property was used in the test function `test_trapezoidal_linear` in the file `test_trapezoidal.py`. Change the function used in Sect. 6.6.2 to $f(x) = 6 \cdot 10^8 x - 4 \cdot 10^6$ and rerun the test. What happens? How must you change the test to make it useful? How does the convergence rate test behave? Any need for adjustment?
Filename: `test_trapezoidal2.py`.

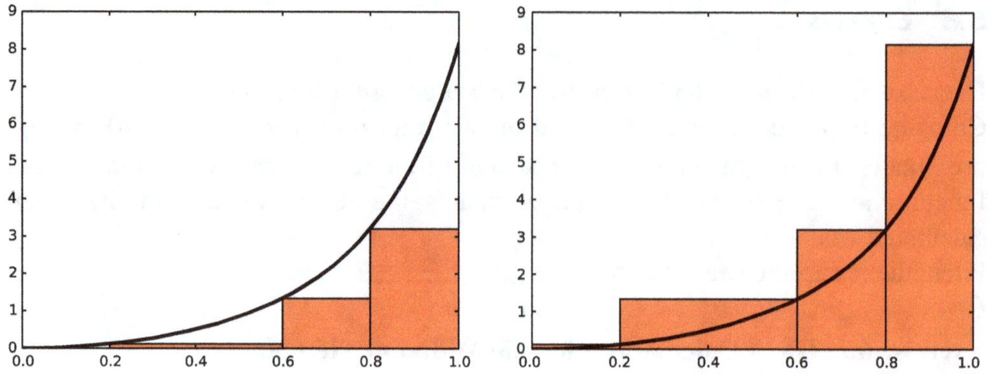


Fig. 6.4 Illustration of the rectangle method with evaluating the rectangle height by either the left or right point

**Exercise 6.7: Write Test Functions for $\int_0^4 \sqrt{x}dx$**

We want to test how the `trapezoidal` function works for the integral $\int_0^4 \sqrt{x}dx$. Two of the tests in `test_trapezoidal.py` are meaningful for this integral. Compute by hand the result of using two or three trapezoids and modify the `test_trapezoidal_one_exact_result` function accordingly. Then modify `test_trapezoidal_conv_rate` to handle the square root integral.
Filename: `test_trapezoidal3.py`.

**Remarks** The convergence rate test fails. Printing out `r` shows that the actual convergence rate for this integral is 1.5 and not 2. The reason is that the error in the trapezoidal method[6] is $-(b-a)^3 n^{-2} f''(\xi)$ for some (unknown) $\xi \in [a, b]$. With $f(x) = \sqrt{x}$, $f''(\xi) \to -\infty$ as $\xi \to 0$, pointing to a potential problem in the size of the error. Running a test with $a > 0$, say $\int_{0.1}^4 \sqrt{x}dx$ shows that the convergence rate is indeed restored to 2.

**Exercise 6.8: Rectangle Methods**

The midpoint method divides the interval of integration into equal-sized subintervals and approximates the integral in each subinterval by a rectangle whose height equals the function value at the midpoint of the subinterval. Instead, one might use either the left or right end of the subinterval as illustrated in Fig. 6.4. This defines a *rectangle method* of integration. The height of the rectangle can be based on the left or right end or the midpoint.

a) Write a function `rectangle(f, a, b, n, height='left')` for computing an integral $\int_a^b f(x)dx$ by the rectangle method with height computed based on the value of `height`, which is either `left`, `right`, or `mid`.
b) Write three test functions for the three unit test procedures described in Sect. 6.6.2. Make sure you test for `height` equal to `left`, `right`, and `mid`. You may call the `midpoint` function for checking the result when `height=mid`.

6 http://en.wikipedia.org/wiki/Trapezoidal_rule#Error_analysis.

**Hint** Edit `test_trapezoidal.py`.
Filename: `rectangle_methods.py`.

**Exercise 6.9: Adaptive Integration**
Suppose we want to use the trapezoidal or midpoint method to compute an integral $\int_a^b f(x)dx$ with an error less than a prescribed tolerance $\epsilon$. What is the appropriate size of $n$?

To answer this question, we may enter an iterative procedure where we compare the results produced by $n$ and $2n$ intervals, and if the difference is smaller than $\epsilon$, the value corresponding to $2n$ is returned. Otherwise, we halve $n$ and repeat the procedure.

**Hint** It may be a good idea to organize your code so that the function `adaptive_integration` can be used easily in future programs you write.

a) Write a function

```
adaptive_integration(f, a, b, eps, method=midpoint)
```

that implements the idea above (`eps` corresponds to the tolerance $\epsilon$, and `method` can be `midpoint` or `trapezoidal`).

b) Test the method on $\int_0^2 x^2dx$ and $\int_0^2 \sqrt{x}dx$ for $\epsilon = 10^{-1}, 10^{-10}$ and write out the exact error.
c) Make a plot of $n$ versus $\epsilon \in [10^{-1}, 10^{-10}]$ for $\int_0^2 \sqrt{x}dx$. Use logarithmic scale for $\epsilon$.

Filename: `adaptive_integration.py`.

**Remarks** The type of method explored in this exercise is called *adaptive*, because it tries to adapt the value of $n$ to meet a given error criterion. The true error can very seldom be computed (since we do not know the exact answer to the computational problem), so one has to find other indicators of the error, such as the one here where the changes in the integral value, as the number of intervals is doubled, is taken to reflect the error.

**Exercise 6.10: Integrating x Raised to x**
Consider the integral

$$I = \int_0^4 x^x \, dx\,.$$

The integrand $x^x$ does not have an anti-derivative that can be expressed in terms of standard functions (visit http://wolframalpha.com and type `integral(x**x,x)` to convince yourself that our claim is right. Note that Wolfram alpha does give you an answer, but that answer is an approximation, it is *not* exact. This is because Wolfram alpha too uses numerical methods to arrive at the answer, just as you will in this exercise). Therefore, we are forced to compute the integral by numerical methods. Compute a result that is right to four digits.

**Hint** Use ideas from Exercise 6.9.
Filename: `integrate_x2x.py`.

**Exercise 6.11: Integrate Products of Sine Functions**
In this exercise we shall integrate

$$I_{j,k} = \int_{-\pi}^{\pi} \sin(jx)\sin(kx)dx,$$

where $j$ and $k$ are integers.

a) Plot $\sin(x)\sin(2x)$ and $\sin(2x)\sin(3x)$ for $x \in [-\pi, \pi]$ in separate plots. Explain why you expect $\int_{-\pi}^{\pi} \sin x \sin 2x\, dx = 0$ and $\int_{-\pi}^{\pi} \sin 2x \sin 3x\, dx = 0$.
b) Use the trapezoidal rule to compute $I_{j,k}$ for $j = 1, \ldots, 10$ and $k = 1, \ldots, 10$.

Filename: `products_sines.py`.

**Exercise 6.12: Revisit Fit of Sines to a Function**
This is a continuation of Exercise 4.13. The task is to approximate a given function $f(t)$ on $[-\pi, \pi]$ by a sum of sines,

$$S_N(t) = \sum_{n=1}^{N} b_n \sin(nt)\,. \tag{6.31}$$

We are now interested in computing the unknown coefficients $b_n$ such that $S_N(t)$ is in some sense the *best approximation* to $f(t)$. One common way of doing this is to first set up a general expression for the *approximation error*, measured by "summing up" the squared deviation of $S_N$ from $f$:

$$E = \int_{-\pi}^{\pi} (S_N(t) - f(t))^2 dt\,.$$

We may view $E$ as a function of $b_1, \ldots, b_N$. Minimizing $E$ with respect to $b_1, \ldots, b_N$ will give us a *best approximation*, in the sense that we adjust $b_1, \ldots, b_N$ such that $S_N$ deviates as little as possible from $f$.

Minimization of a function of $N$ variables, $E(b_1, \ldots, b_N)$ is mathematically performed by requiring all the partial derivatives to be zero:

$$\frac{\partial E}{\partial b_1} = 0,$$
$$\frac{\partial E}{\partial b_2} = 0,$$
$$\vdots$$
$$\frac{\partial E}{\partial b_N} = 0\,.$$

a) Compute the partial derivative $\partial E/\partial b_1$ and generalize to the arbitrary case $\partial E/\partial b_n$, $1 \leq n \leq N$.
b) Show that

$$b_n = \frac{1}{\pi}\int_{-\pi}^{\pi} f(t)\sin(nt)\,dt\,.$$

c) Write a function `integrate_coeffs(f, N, M)` that computes $b_1, \ldots, b_N$ by numerical integration, using $M$ intervals in the trapezoidal rule.
d) A remarkable property of the trapezoidal rule is that it is exact for integrals $\int_{-\pi}^{\pi} \sin nt\,dt$ (when subintervals are of equal size). Use this property to create a function `test_integrate_coeff` to verify the implementation of `integrate_coeffs`.
e) Implement the choice $f(t) = \frac{1}{\pi}t$ as a Python function `f(t)` and call `integrate_coeffs(f, 3, 100)` to see what the optimal choice of $b_1, b_2, b_3$ is.
f) Make a function `plot_approx(f, N, M, filename)` where you plot `f(t)` together with the best approximation $S_N$ as computed above, using $M$ intervals for numerical integration. Save the plot to a file with name `filename`.
g) Run `plot_approx(f, N, M, filename)` for $f(t) = \frac{1}{\pi}t$ for $N = 3, 6, 12, 24$. Observe how the approximation improves.
h) Run `plot_approx` for $f(t) = e^{-(t-\pi)}$ and $N = 100$. Observe a fundamental problem: regardless of $N$, $S_N(-\pi) = 0$, not $e^{2\pi} \approx 535$. (There are ways to fix this issue.)

Filename: `autofit_sines.py`.

**Exercise 6.13: Derive the Trapezoidal Rule for a Double Integral**
Use ideas in Sect. 6.7.1 to derive a formula for computing a double integral $\int_a^b \int_c^d f(x, y)dydx$ by the trapezoidal rule. Implement and test this rule.
Filename: `trapezoidal_double.py`.

**Exercise 6.14: Compute the Area of a Triangle by Monte Carlo Integration**
Use the Monte Carlo method from Sect. 6.7.3 to compute the area of a triangle with vertices at $(-1, 0)$, $(1, 0)$, and $(3, 0)$.
Filename: `MC_triangle.py`.

# 7 Solving Nonlinear Algebraic Equations

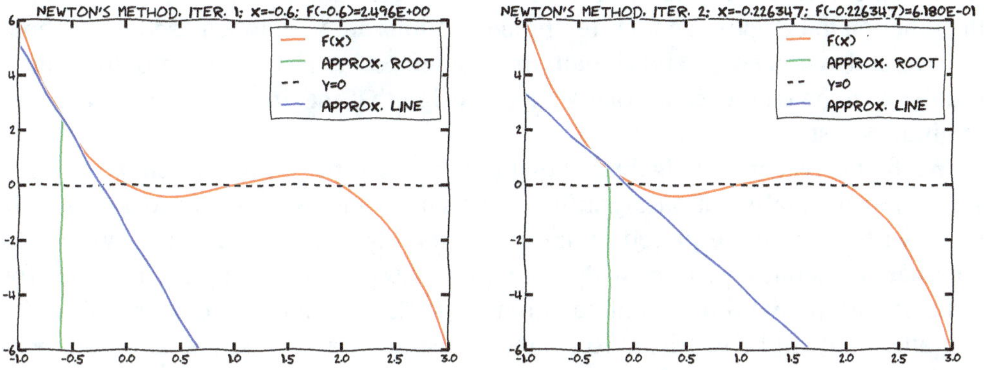


As a reader of this book, you might be well into mathematics and often "accused" of being particularly good at solving equations (a typical comment at family dinners!). How true is it, however, that you can solve *many* types of equations with pen and paper alone? Restricting our attention to *algebraic equations in one unknown* $x$, you can certainly do linear equations: $ax + b = 0$, and quadratic ones: $ax^2 + bx + c = 0$. You may also know that there are formulas for the roots of cubic and quartic equations too. Maybe you can do the special trigonometric equation $\sin x + \cos x = 1$ as well, but there it (probably?) stops. Equations that are not reducible to one of those mentioned, cannot be solved by general analytical techniques, which means that most algebraic equations arising in applications cannot be treated with pen and paper!

If we exchange the traditional idea of finding *exact* solutions to equations with the idea of rather finding *approximate* solutions, a whole new world of possibilities opens up. With such an approach, we can in principle solve *any* algebraic equation.

Let us start by introducing a common generic form for any algebraic equation:

$$f(x) = 0\,.$$



S. Linge, H. P. Langtangen, *Programming for Computations - Python*,
Texts in Computational Science and Engineering 15,
https://doi.org/10.1007/978-3-030-16877-3_7

Here, $f(x)$ is some prescribed formula involving $x$. For example, the equation

$$e^{-x}\sin x = \cos x$$

has

$$f(x) = e^{-x}\sin x - \cos x\,.$$

Just move all terms to the left-hand side and then the formula to the left of the equality sign is $f(x)$.

So, when do we really need to solve algebraic equations beyond the simplest types we can treat with pen and paper? There are two major application areas. One is when using *implicit* numerical methods for ordinary differential equations. These give rise to one or a system of algebraic equations. The other major application type is optimization, i.e., finding the maxima or minima of a function. These maxima and minima are normally found by solving the algebraic equation $F'(x) = 0$ if $F(x)$ is the function to be optimized. Differential equations are very much used throughout science and engineering, and actually most engineering problems are optimization problems in the end, because one wants a design that maximizes performance and minimizes cost.

We first consider one algebraic equation in one variable, for which we present some fundamental solution algorithms that any reader should get to know. Our focus will, as usual, be placed on the programming of the algorithms. *Systems* of nonlinear algebraic equations with *many variables* arise from implicit methods for ordinary and partial differential equations as well as in multivariate optimization. Our attention will be restricted to Newton's method for such systems of nonlinear algebraic equations.

**Root Finding**

When solving algebraic equations $f(x) = 0$, we often say that the solution $x$ is a *root* of the equation. The solution process itself is thus often called *root finding*.

## 7.1 Brute Force Methods

The representation of a mathematical function $f(x)$ on a computer takes two forms. One is a Python function returning the function value given the argument, while the other is a collection of points $(x, f(x))$ along the function curve. The latter is the representation we use for plotting, together with an assumption of linear variation between the points. This representation is also very well suited for equation solving: we simply go through all points and see if the function crosses the $x$ axis, or for optimization: we test for local maximum or minimum points. Because there is a lot of work to examine a huge number of points, and also because the idea is extremely simple, such approaches are often referred to as *brute force* methods.

### 7.1.1 Brute Force Root Finding

Assume that we have a set of points along the curve of a continuous function $f(x)$:

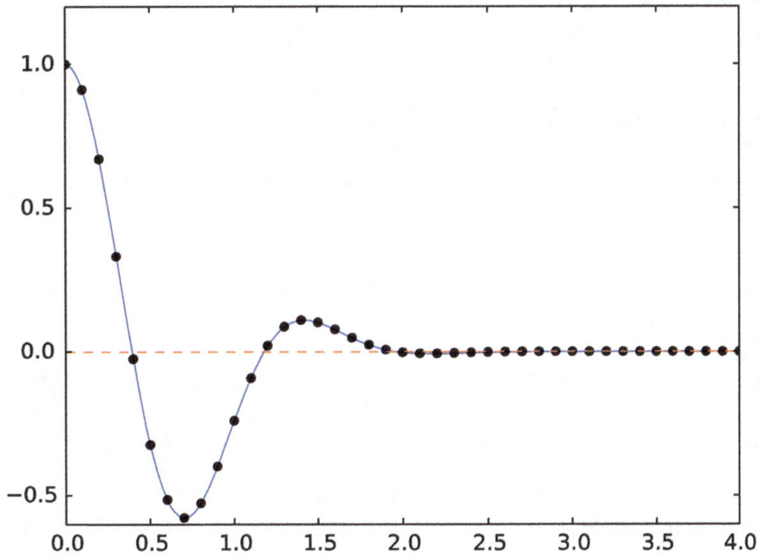


We want to solve $f(x) = 0$, i.e., find the points $x$ where $f$ crosses the $x$ axis. A brute force algorithm is to run through all points on the curve and check if one point is below the $x$ axis and if the next point is above the $x$ axis, or the other way around. If this is found to be the case, we know that, when $f$ is continuous, it has to cross the $x$ axis at least once between these two $x$ values. In other words, $f$ is zero at least once on that sub-interval.

Note that, in the following algorithm, we refer to "the" root on a sub-interval, even if there may be more than one root in principle. Whether there are more than one root on a sub-interval will of course depend on the function, as well as on the size and location of the sub-interval. For simplicity, we will just assume there is at most one root on a sub-interval (or that it is sufficiently precise to talk about one root, even if there could be more).

**Numerical Algorithm** More precisely, we have a set of $n + 1$ points $(x_i, y_i)$, $y_i = f(x_i)$, $i = 0, \ldots, n$, where $x_0 < \ldots < x_n$. We check if $y_i < 0$ and $y_{i+1} > 0$ (or the other way around). A compact expression for this check is to perform the test $y_i y_{i+1} < 0$. If so, the root of $f(x) = 0$ is in $[x_i, x_{i+1}]$.

Assuming a linear variation of $f$ between $x_i$ and $x_{i+1}$, we have the approximation

$$f(x) \approx \frac{f(x_{i+1}) - f(x_i)}{x_{i+1} - x_i}(x - x_i) + f(x_i) = \frac{y_{i+1} - y_i}{x_{i+1} - x_i}(x - x_i) + y_i,$$

which, when set equal to zero, gives the root

$$x = x_i - \frac{x_{i+1} - x_i}{y_{i+1} - y_i} y_i .$$

**Implementation** Given some Python implementation `f(x)` of our mathematical function, a straightforward implementation of the above algorithm that quits after finding one root, looks like

```
x = linspace(0, 4, 10001)
y = f(x)

root = None  # Initialization
for i in range(len(x)-1):
    if y[i]*y[i+1] < 0:
        root = x[i] - (x[i+1] - x[i])/(y[i+1] - y[i])*y[i]
        break  # Jump out of loop
    elif y[i] == 0:
        root = x[i]
        break  # Jump out of loop

if root is None:
    print('Could not find any root in [{:g}, {:g}]'.format(x[0], x[-1]))
else:
    print('Find (the first) root as x={:.17f}'.format(root))
```

(See the file `brute_force_root_finder_flat.py`.)

Note the nice use of setting `root` to `None`: we can simply test `if root is None` to see if we found a root and overwrote the `None` value, or if we did not find any root among the tested points.

Running this program with some function, say $f(x) = e^{-x^2}\cos(4x)$ (which has a solution at $x = \frac{\pi}{8}$), gives the root 0.39269910538048097, which has an error of $2.4 \times 10^{-8}$. Increasing the number of points with a factor of ten gives a root with an error of $2.9 \times 10^{-10}$.

After such a quick "flat" implementation of an algorithm, we should always try to offer the algorithm as a Python function, applicable to as wide a problem domain as possible. The function should take $f$ and an associated interval $[a, b]$ as input, as well as a number of points $(n)$, and return a list of all the roots in $[a, b]$. Here is our candidate for a good implementation of the brute force root finding algorithm:

```
def brute_force_root_finder(f, a, b, n):
    from numpy import linspace
    x = linspace(a, b, n)
    y = f(x)
    roots = []
    for i in range(n-1):
        if y[i]*y[i+1] < 0:
            root = x[i] - (x[i+1] - x[i])/(y[i+1] - y[i])*y[i]
            roots.append(root)
        elif y[i] == 0:
            root = x[i]
            roots.append(root)
    return roots
```

(See the file `brute_force_root_finder_function.py`.)

This time we use another elegant technique to indicate if roots were found or not: `roots` is an empty list if the root finding was unsuccessful, otherwise it contains all the roots. Application of the function to the previous example can be coded as

```
def demo():
    from numpy import exp, cos
    roots = brute_force_root_finder(
        lambda x: exp(-x**2)*cos(4*x), 0, 4, 1001)
    if roots:
        print(roots)
    else:
        print('Could not find any roots')
```

Note that `if roots` evaluates to `True` if `roots` is non-empty. This is a general test in Python: `if X` evaluates to `True` if `X` is non-empty or has a nonzero value.

Running the program gives the output

```
[0.39270091800495166, 1.1781066425246509, 1.9635022750438742,
 2.7489089483136029, 3.534319340895673]
```

### 7.1.2 Brute Force Optimization

**Numerical Algorithm** We realize that $x_i$ corresponds to a maximum point if $y_{i-1} < y_i > y_{i+1}$. Similarly, $x_i$ corresponds to a minimum if $y_{i-1} > y_i < y_{i+1}$. We can do this test for all "inner" points $i = 1, \ldots, n-1$ to find all local minima and maxima. In addition, we need to add an end point, $i = 0$ or $i = n$, if the corresponding $y_i$ is a global maximum or minimum.

**Implementation** The algorithm above can be translated to the following Python function (file brute_force_optimizer.py):

```
def brute_force_optimizer(f, a, b, n):
    from numpy import linspace
    x = linspace(a, b, n)
    y = f(x)
    # Let maxima and minima hold the indices corresponding
    # to (local) maxima and minima points
    minima = []
    maxima = []
    for i in range(1, n-1):
        if y[i-1] < y[i] > y[i+1]:
            maxima.append(i)
        if y[i-1] > y[i] < y[i+1]:
            minima.append(i)

    # What about the end points?
    y_max_inner = max([y[i] for i in maxima])
    y_min_inner = min([y[i] for i in minima])
    if y[0] > y_max_inner:
        maxima.append(0)
    if y[len(x)-1] > y_max_inner:
        maxima.append(len(x)-1)
    if y[0] < y_min_inner:
        minima.append(0)
    if y[len(x)-1] < y_min_inner:
        minima.append(len(x)-1)
```

```
    # Return x and y values
    return [(x[i], y[i]) for i in minima], \
           [(x[i], y[i]) for i in maxima]
```

The `max` and `min` functions are standard Python functions for finding the maximum and minimum element of a list or an object that one can iterate over with a for loop.

An application to $f(x) = e^{-x^2}\cos(4x)$ looks like

```
def demo():
    from numpy import exp, cos
    minima, maxima = brute_force_optimizer(
        lambda x: exp(-x**2)*cos(4*x), 0, 4, 1001)
    print('Minima:\n', minima)
    print('Maxima:\n', maxima)
```

Running the program gives

```
Minima:
 [(0.70000000000000007, -0.5772302750838405), (2.1520000000000001,
-0.0066704807422565023), (3.6600000000000001, -7.3338267339366542e-07)]
Maxima:
 [(1.4159999999999999, 0.10965467991643564), (2.8999999999999999,
0.00012651823896373234), (0.0, 1.0)]
```

### 7.1.3 Model Problem for Algebraic Equations

We shall consider the very simple problem of finding the square root of 9. That is, we want to solve $x^2 = 9$, but will (for simplicity) seek only the positive solution. Knowing the solution beforehand, allows us to easily investigate how the numerical method (and the implementation of it) performs in the search for a solution. The $f(x)$ function that corresponds to the equation $x^2 = 9$ is

$$f(x) = x^2 - 9 .$$

Our interval of interest for solutions will be [0, 1000] (the upper limit here is chosen somewhat arbitrarily).

In the following, we will present several efficient and accurate methods for solving nonlinear algebraic equations, both single equation and systems of equations. The methods all have in common that they search for *approximate* solutions. The methods differ, however, in the way they perform the search for solutions. The idea for the search influences the efficiency of the search and the reliability of actually finding a solution. For example, Newton's method is very fast, but not reliable, while the bisection method is the slowest, but absolutely reliable. No method is best at all problems, so we need different methods for different problems.

**What Is the Difference Between Linear and Nonlinear Equations?**

You know how to solve linear equations $ax + b = 0$: $x = -b/a$. All other types of equations $f(x) = 0$, i.e., when $f(x)$ is not a linear function of $x$, are called nonlinear. A typical way of recognizing a nonlinear equation is to observe that $x$ is "not alone" as in $ax$, but involved in a product with itself, such as in $x^3 + 2x^2 - 9 = 0$. We say that $x^3$ and $2x^2$ are nonlinear terms. An equation like $\sin x + e^x \cos x = 0$ is also nonlinear although $x$ is not explicitly multiplied by itself, but the Taylor series of $\sin x$, $e^x$, and $\cos x$ all involve polynomials of $x$ where $x$ is multiplied by itself.

## 7.2 Newton's Method

*Newton's method*, also known as *Newton-Raphson's method*, is a very famous and widely used method for solving nonlinear algebraic equations.[1] Compared to the other methods presented in this chapter, i.e., secant and bisection, it is generally the fastest one (although computational speed rarely is an issue with a single equation on modern laptops). However, it does not guarantee that an existing solution will be found.

A fundamental idea of numerical methods for nonlinear equations is to construct a series of linear equations (since we know how to solve linear equations) and hope that the solutions of these linear equations bring us closer and closer to the solution of the nonlinear equation. The idea will be clearer when we present Newton's method and the secant method.

### 7.2.1 Deriving and Implementing Newton's Method

Figure 7.1 shows the $f(x)$ function in our model equation $x^2 - 9 = 0$. Numerical methods for algebraic equations require us to guess at a solution first. Here, this guess is called $x_0$. The fundamental idea of Newton's method is to approximate the original function $f(x)$ by a straight line, i.e., a linear function, since it is straightforward to solve linear equations. There are infinitely many choices of how to approximate $f(x)$ by a straight line. Newton's method applies the tangent of $f(x)$ at $x_0$, see the rightmost tangent in Fig. 7.1. This linear tangent function crosses the $x$ axis at a point we call $x_1$. This is (hopefully) a better approximation to the solution of $f(x) = 0$ than $x_0$. The next fundamental idea is to repeat this process. We find the tangent of $f$ at $x_1$, compute where it crosses the $x$ axis, at a point called $x_2$, and repeat the process again. Figure 7.1 shows that the process brings us closer and closer to the left. It remains, however, to see if we hit $x = 3$ or come sufficiently close to this solution.

[1] Read more about Newton's method, e.g., on https://en.wikipedia.org/wiki/Newton%27s_method.

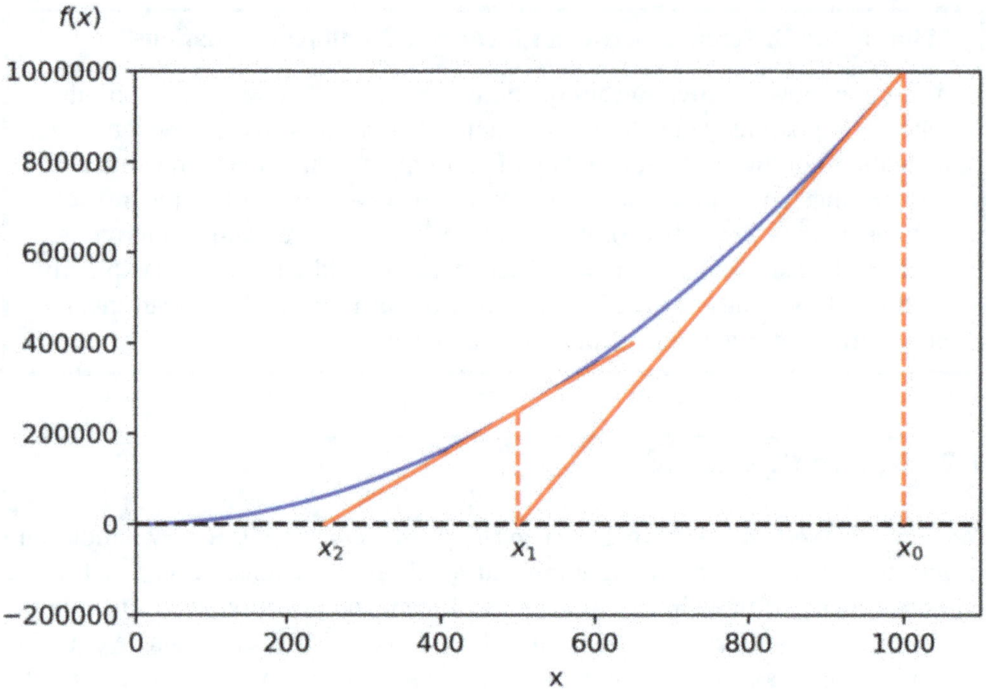


**Fig. 7.1** Illustrates the idea of Newton's method with $f(x) = x^2 - 9$, repeatedly solving for crossing of tangent lines with the $x$ axis

How do we compute the tangent of a function $f(x)$ at a point $x_0$? The tangent function, here called $\tilde{f}(x)$, is linear and has two properties:

1. the slope equals to $f'(x_0)$
2. the tangent touches the $f(x)$ curve at $x_0$

So, if we write the tangent function as $\tilde{f}(x) = ax + b$, we must require $\tilde{f}'(x_0) = f'(x_0)$ and $\tilde{f}(x_0) = f(x_0)$, resulting in

$$\tilde{f}(x) = f(x_0) + f'(x_0)(x - x_0)\,.$$

The key step in Newton's method is to find where the tangent crosses the $x$ axis, which means solving $\tilde{f}(x) = 0$:

$$\tilde{f}(x) = 0 \quad \Rightarrow \quad x = x_0 - \frac{f(x_0)}{f'(x_0)}\,.$$

This is our new candidate point, which we call $x_1$:

$$x_1 = x_0 - \frac{f(x_0)}{f'(x_0)}\,.$$

With $x_0 = 1000$, we get $x_1 \approx 500$, which is in accordance with the graph in Fig. 7.1. Repeating the process, we get

$$x_2 = x_1 - \frac{f(x_1)}{f'(x_1)} \approx 250\,.$$

The general scheme[2] of Newton's method may be written as

$$x_{n+1} = x_n - \frac{f(x_n)}{f'(x_n)}, \qquad n = 0, 1, 2, \ldots \tag{7.1}$$

The computation in (7.1) is repeated until $f(x_n)$ is close enough to zero. More precisely, we test if $|f(x_n)| < \epsilon$, with $\epsilon$ being a small number.

We moved from 1000 to 250 in two iterations, so it is exciting to see how fast we can approach the solution $x = 3$. A computer program can automate the calculations. Our first try at implementing Newton's method is in a function `naive_Newton` (found in `naive_Newton.py`):

```
def naive_Newton(f, dfdx, x, eps):
    while abs(f(x)) > eps:
        x = x - (f(x))/dfdx(x)
    return x
```

The argument `x` is the starting value, called $x_0$ in our previous mathematical description.

To solve the problem $x^2 = 9$ we also need to implement

```
def f(x):
    return x**2 - 9

def dfdx(x):
    return 2*x

print(naive_Newton(f, dfdx, 1000, 0.001))
```

which in `naive_Newton.py` is included by use of an extra function and a test block.

[2] The term *scheme* is often used as a synonym for method or computational recipe.

**Why Not Use an Array for the $x$ Approximations?**

Newton's method is normally formulated with an *iteration index n*,

$$x_{n+1} = x_n - \frac{f(x_n)}{f'(x_n)} .$$

Seeing such an index, many would implement this as

```
x[n+1] = x[n] - f(x[n])/dfdx(x[n])
```

Such an array is fine, but requires storage of all the approximations. In large industrial applications, where Newton's method solves millions of equations at once, one cannot afford to store all the intermediate approximations in memory, so then it is important to understand that the algorithm in Newton's method has no more need for $x_n$ when $x_{n+1}$ is computed. Therefore, we can work with one variable x and overwrite the previous value:

```
x = x - f(x)/dfdx(x)
```

Running `naive_Newton(f, dfdx, 1000, eps=0.001)` results in the approximate solution 3.000027639. A smaller value of `eps` will produce a more accurate solution. Unfortunately, the plain `naive_Newton` function does not return how many iterations it used, nor does it print out all the approximations $x_0, x_1, x_2, \ldots$, which would indeed be a nice feature. If we insert such a printout (`print(x)` in the `while` loop), a rerun results in

```
500.0045
250.011249919
125.02362415
62.5478052723
31.3458476066
15.816483488
8.1927550496
4.64564330569
3.2914711388
3.01290538807
3.00002763928
```

We clearly see that the iterations approach the solution quickly. This speed of the search for the solution is the primary strength of Newton's method compared to other methods.

### 7.2.2 Making a More Efficient and Robust Implementation

The `naive_Newton` function works fine for the example we are considering here. However, for more general use, there are some pitfalls that should be fixed in an improved version of the code. An example may illustrate what the problem is.

Let us use `naive_Newton` to solve $\tanh(x) = 0$, which has solution $x = 0$ (interactively, you may define $f(x) = tanh(x)$ and $f'(x) = 1-tanh^2(x)$ as Python functions and import the `naive_Newton` function from `naive_Newton.py`). With $|x_0| \leq 1.08$ everything works fine. For example, $x_0 = 1.08$ leads to six iterations if $\epsilon = 0.001$:

```
-1.05895313436
0.989404207298
-0.784566773086
0.36399816111
-0.0330146961372
2.3995252668e-05
```

Adjusting $x_0$ slightly to 1.09 gives division by zero! The approximations computed by Newton's method become

```
-1.09331618202
1.10490354324
-1.14615550788
1.30303261823
-2.06492300238
13.4731428006
-1.26055913647e+11
```

The division by zero is caused by $x_7 = -1.26055913647 \times 10^{11}$, because $\tanh(x_7)$ is 1.0 to machine precision, and then $f'(x) = 1 - \tanh(x)^2$ becomes zero in the denominator in Newton's method.

The underlying problem, leading to the division by zero in the above example, is that Newton's method *diverges*: the approximations move further and further away from $x = 0$. If it had not been for the division by zero, the condition in the `while` loop would always be true and the loop would run forever. Divergence of Newton's method occasionally happens, and the remedy is to abort the method when a maximum number of iterations is reached.

Another disadvantage of the `naive_Newton` function is that it calls the $f(x)$ function twice as many times as necessary. This extra work is of no concern when $f(x)$ is fast to evaluate, but in large-scale industrial software, one call to $f(x)$ might take hours or days, and then removing unnecessary calls is important. The solution in our function is to store the call `f(x)` in a variable (`f_value`) and reuse the value instead of making a new call `f(x)`.

To summarize, we want to write an improved function for implementing Newton's method where we

- handle division by zero properly
- allow a maximum number of iterations
- avoid the extra evaluation of $f(x)$

A more robust and efficient version of the function, inserted in a complete program (`Newtons_method.py`) for solving $x^2 - 9 = 0$, is listed below.

```
import sys

def Newton(f, dfdx, x, eps):
    f_value = f(x)
```

```
    iteration_counter = 0
    while abs(f_value) > eps and iteration_counter < 100:
        try:
            x = x - f_value/dfdx(x)
        except ZeroDivisionError:
            print('Error! - derivative zero for x = ', x)
            sys.exit(1)     # Abort with error

        f_value = f(x)
        iteration_counter = iteration_counter + 1

    # Here, either a solution is found, or too many iterations
    if abs(f_value) > eps:
        iteration_counter = -1
    return x, iteration_counter

if __name__ == '__main__':
    def f(x):
        return x**2 - 9

    def dfdx(x):
        return 2*x

    solution, no_iterations = Newton(f, dfdx, x=1000, eps=1.0e-6)

    if no_iterations > 0:    # Solution found
        print('Number of function calls: {:d}'.format(1+2*no_iterations))
        print('A solution is: {:f}'.format(solution))
    else:
        print('Solution not found!')
```

Handling of the potential division by zero is done by a `try-except` construction.[3]

The division by zero will always be detected and the program will be stopped. The main purpose of our way of treating the division by zero is to give the user a more informative error message and stop the program in a gentler way.

Calling `sys.exit` with an argument different from zero (here `1`) signifies that the program stopped because of an error. It is a good habit to supply the value `1`, because tools in the operating system can then be used by other programs to detect that our program failed.

To prevent an infinite loop because of divergent iterations, we have introduced the integer variable `iteration_counter` to count the number of iterations in Newton's method. With `iteration_counter` we can easily extend the condition in the `while` loop such that no more iterations take place when the number of iterations reaches 100. We could easily let this limit be an argument to the function rather than a fixed constant.

The `Newton` function returns the approximate solution and the number of iterations. The latter equals $-1$ if the convergence criterion $|f(x)| < \epsilon$ was not reached within the maximum number of iterations. In the calling code, we print out

[3] Professional programmers would avoid calling `sys.exit` inside a function. Instead, they would raise a new exception with an informative error message, and let the calling code have another `try-except` construction to stop the program.

the solution and the number of function calls. The main cost of a method for solving $f(x) = 0$ equations is usually the evaluation of $f(x)$ and $f'(x)$, so the total number of calls to these functions is an interesting measure of the computational work. Note that in function `Newton` there is an initial call to $f(x)$ and then one call to $f$ and one to $f'$ in each iteration.

Running `Newtons_method.py`, we get the following printout on the screen:

```
Number of function calls: 25
A solution is: 3.000000
```

The Newton scheme will work better if the starting value is close to the solution. A good starting value may often make the difference as to whether the code actually *finds* a solution or not. Because of its speed (and when speed matters), Newton's method is often the method of first choice for solving nonlinear algebraic equations, even if the scheme is not guaranteed to work. In cases where the initial guess may be far from the solution, a good strategy is to run a few iterations with the bisection method (see Sect. 7.4) to narrow down the region where $f$ is close to zero and then switch to Newton's method for fast convergence to the solution.

**Using `sympy` to Find the Derivative** Newton's method requires the analytical expression for the derivative $f'(x)$. Derivation of $f'(x)$ is not always a reliable process by hand if $f(x)$ is a complicated function. However, Python has the symbolic package SymPy, which we may use to create the required `dfdx` function. With our sample problem, we get:

```
import sympy as sym

x = sym.symbols('x')
f_expr = x**2 - 9                 # symbolic expression for f(x)
dfdx_expr = sym.diff(f_expr, x)  # compute f'(x) symbolically

# turn f_expr and dfdx_expr into plain Python functions
f = sym.lambdify([x],         # argument to f
            f_expr)           # symbolic expression to be evaluated

dfdx = sym.lambdify([x], dfdx_expr)

print(f(3), dfdx(3))               # will print 0 and 6
```

The nice feature of this code snippet is that `dfdx_expr` is the exact analytical expression for the derivative, `2*x` (seen if you print it out). This is a symbolic expression, so we cannot do numerical computing with it. However, with `lambdify`, such symbolic expression are turned into callable Python functions, as seen here with `f` and `dfdx`.

The next method is the secant method, which is usually slower than Newton's method, but it does not require an expression for $f'(x)$, and it has only one function call per iteration.

## 7.3 The Secant Method

When finding the derivative $f'(x)$ in Newton's method is problematic, or when function evaluations take too long; we may adjust the method slightly. Instead of using tangent lines to the graph we may use secants.[4] The approach is referred to as the *secant method*, and the idea is illustrated graphically in Fig. 7.2 for our example problem $x^2 - 9 = 0$.

The idea of the secant method is to think as in Newton's method, but instead of using $f'(x_n)$, we approximate this derivative by a finite difference or the *secant*, i.e., the slope of the straight line that goes through the points $(x_n, f(x_n))$ and $(x_{n-1}, f(x_{n-1}))$ on the graph, given by the two most recent approximations $x_n$ and $x_{n-1}$. This slope reads

$$\frac{f(x_n) - f(x_{n-1})}{x_n - x_{n-1}} . \tag{7.2}$$

Inserting this expression for $f'(x_n)$ in Newton's method simply gives us the secant method:

$$x_{n+1} = x_n - \frac{f(x_n)}{\frac{f(x_n)-f(x_{n-1})}{x_n - x_{n-1}}},$$

or

$$x_{n+1} = x_n - f(x_n)\frac{x_n - x_{n-1}}{f(x_n) - f(x_{n-1})} . \tag{7.3}$$

Comparing (7.3) to the graph in Fig. 7.2, we see how *two* chosen starting points ($x_0$ = 1000, $x_1$ = 700, and corresponding function values) are used to compute $x_2$. Once we have $x_2$, we similarly use $x_1$ and $x_2$ to compute $x_3$. As with Newton's method, the procedure is repeated until $f(x_n)$ is below some chosen limit value, or some limit on the number of iterations has been reached. We use an iteration counter here too, based on the same thinking as in the implementation of Newton's method.

We can store the approximations $x_n$ in an array, but as in Newton's method, we notice that the computation of $x_{n+1}$ only needs knowledge of $x_n$ and $x_{n-1}$, not "older" approximations. Therefore, we can make use of only three variables: `x` for $x_{n+1}$, `x1` for $x_n$, and `x0` for $x_{n-1}$. Note that `x0` and `x1` must be given (guessed) for the algorithm to start.

A program `secant_method.py` that solves our example problem may be written as:

```
import sys

def secant(f, x0, x1, eps):
    f_x0 = f(x0)
    f_x1 = f(x1)
```

[4] https://en.wikipedia.org/wiki/Secant_line.

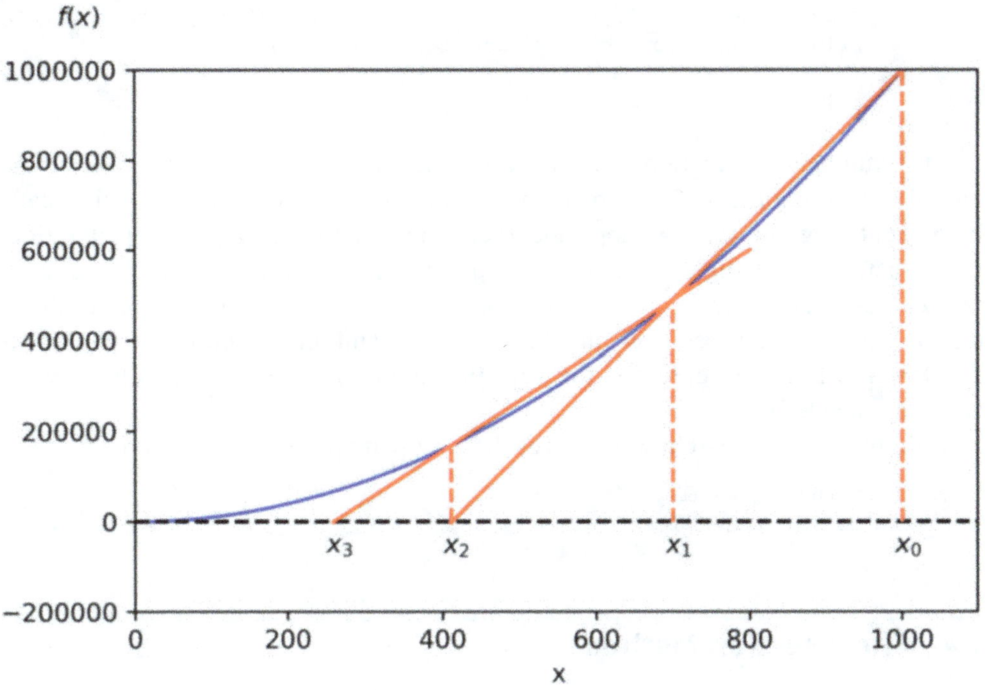


**Fig. 7.2** Illustrates the use of secants in the secant method when solving $x^2-9=0$, $x \in [0, 1000]$. From two chosen starting values, $x_0 = 1000$ and $x_1 = 700$ the crossing $x_2$ of the corresponding secant with the $x$ axis is computed, followed by a similar computation of $x_3$ from $x_1$ and $x_2$

```
    iteration_counter = 0
    while abs(f_x1) > eps and iteration_counter < 100:
        try:
            denominator = (f_x1 - f_x0)/(x1 - x0)
            x = x1 - f_x1/denominator
        except ZeroDivisionError:
            print('Error! - denominator zero for x = ', x)
            sys.exit(1)     # Abort with error
        x0 = x1
        x1 = x
        f_x0 = f_x1
        f_x1 = f(x1)
        iteration_counter = iteration_counter + 1
    # Here, either a solution is found, or too many iterations
    if abs(f_x1) > eps:
        iteration_counter = -1
    return x, iteration_counter

if __name__ == '__main__':
    def f(x):
        return x**2 - 9

    x0 = 1000;   x1 = x0 - 1

    solution, no_iterations = secant(f, x0, x1, eps=1.0e-6)

    if no_iterations > 0:    # Solution found
```

```
    print('Number of function calls: {:d}'.format(2+no_iterations))
    print('A solution is: {:f}'.format(solution))
else:
    print('Solution not found!')
```

The number of function calls is now related to `no_iterations`, i.e., the number of iterations, as `2 + no_iterations`, since we need two function calls before entering the `while` loop, and then one function call per loop iteration. Note that, even though we need two points on the graph to compute each updated estimate, only a *single* function call (`f(x1)`) is required in each iteration since `f(x0)` becomes the "old" `f(x1)` and may simply be copied as `f_x0 = f_x1` (the exception is the very first iteration where two function evaluations are needed).

Running `secant_method.py`, gives the following printout on the screen:

```
Number of function calls: 19
A solution is: 3.000000
```

## 7.4 The Bisection Method

Neither Newton's method nor the secant method can guarantee that an existing solution will be found (see Exercises 7.1 and 7.2). The bisection method, however, does that. However, if there are several solutions present, it finds only one of them, just as Newton's method and the secant method. The bisection method is slower than the other two methods, so reliability comes with a cost of speed (but, again, for a single equation that is rarely an issue with laptops of today).

To solve $x^2 - 9 = 0$, $x \in [0, 1000]$, with the bisection method, we reason as follows. The first key idea is that if $f(x) = x^2 - 9$ is *continuous* on the interval and the function values for the interval endpoints ($x_L = 0$, $x_R = 1000$) have *opposite signs*, $f(x)$ *must* cross the $x$ axis at least once on the interval. That is, we know there is at least one solution.

The second key idea comes from dividing the interval in two equal parts, one to the left and one to the right of the midpoint $x_M = 500$. By evaluating the sign of $f(x_M)$, we will immediately know whether a solution must exist to the left or right of $x_M$. This is so, since if $f(x_M) \geq 0$, we know that $f(x)$ has to cross the $x$ axis between $x_L$ and $x_M$ at least once (using the same argument as for the original interval). Likewise, if instead $f(x_M) \leq 0$, we know that $f(x)$ has to cross the $x$ axis between $x_M$ and $x_R$ at least once.

In any case, we may proceed with half the interval only. The exception is if $f(x_M) \approx 0$, in which case a solution is found. Such interval halving can be continued until a solution is found. A "solution" in this case, is when $|f(x_M)|$ is sufficiently close to zero, more precisely (as before): $|f(x_M)| < \epsilon$, where $\epsilon$ is a small number specified by the user.

The sketched strategy seems reasonable, so let us write a reusable function that can solve a general algebraic equation $f(x) = 0$ (bisection_method.py):

```
import sys

def bisection(f, x_L, x_R, eps):
    f_L = f(x_L)
    if f_L*f(x_R) > 0:
        print('Error! Function does not have opposite \
                 signs at interval endpoints!')
        sys.exit(1)
    x_M = (x_L + x_R)/2.0
    f_M = f(x_M)
    iteration_counter = 1

    while abs(f_M) > eps:
        if f_L*f_M > 0:   # i.e. same sign
            x_L = x_M
            f_L = f_M
        else:
            x_R = x_M
        x_M = (x_L + x_R)/2
        f_M = f(x_M)
        iteration_counter = iteration_counter + 1
    return x_M, iteration_counter

if __name__ == '__main__':
    def f(x):
        return x**2 - 9

    a = 0;   b = 1000

    solution, no_iterations = bisection(f, a, b, eps=1.0e-6)

    print('Number of function calls: {:d}'.format(1 + 2*no_iterations))
    print('A solution is: {:f}'.format(solution))
```

Note that we first check if $f$ changes sign in $[a, b]$, because that is a requirement for the algorithm to work. The algorithm also relies on a continuous $f(x)$ function, but this is very challenging for a computer code to check.

We get the following printout to the screen when bisection_method.py is run:

```
Number of function calls: 63
A solution is: 3.000000
```

We notice that the number of function calls is much higher than with the previous methods.

**Required Work in the Bisection Method**

If the starting interval of the bisection method is bounded by $a$ and $b$, and the solution at step $n$ is taken to be the middle value, the error is bounded as

$$\frac{|b-a|}{2^n}, \tag{7.4}$$

because the initial interval has been halved $n$ times. Therefore, to meet a tolerance $\epsilon$, we need $n$ iterations such that the length of the current interval equals $\epsilon$:

$$\frac{|b-a|}{2^n} = \epsilon \quad \Rightarrow \quad n = \frac{\ln((b-a)/\epsilon)}{\ln 2}.$$

This is a great advantage of the bisection method: we know beforehand how many iterations $n$ it takes to meet a certain accuracy $\epsilon$ in the solution.

## 7.5 Rate of Convergence

With the methods above, we noticed that the number of iterations or function calls could differ quite substantially. The number of iterations needed to find a solution is closely related to the *rate of convergence*, which dictates the speed of error reduction as we approach the root. More precisely, we introduce the error in iteration $n$ as $e_n = |x - x_n|$, and define the *convergence rate* $q$ as

$$e_{n+1} = Ce_n^q, \tag{7.5}$$

where $C$ is a constant. The exponent $q$ measures how fast the error is reduced from one iteration to the next. The larger $q$ is, the faster the error goes to zero (when $e_n < 1$), and the fewer iterations we need to meet the stopping criterion $|f(x)| < \epsilon$.

**Convergence Rate and Iterations**

When we previously addressed numerical integration (Chap. 6), the approximation error $E$ was related to the size $h$ of the sub-intervals and the convergence rate $r$ as $E = Kh^r$, $K$ being some constant.

Observe that (7.5) gives a *different* definition of convergence rate. This makes sense, since numerical integration is based on a partitioning of the original integration interval into $n$ sub-intervals, which is very different from the iterative procedures used here for solving nonlinear algebraic equations.

A single $q$ in (7.5) is defined in the limit $n \to \infty$. For finite $n$, and especially smaller $n$, $q$ will vary with $n$. To estimate $q$, we can compute all the errors $e_n$ and set up (7.5) for three consecutive experiments $n-1$, $n$, and $n+1$:

$$e_n = Ce_{n-1}^q,$$
$$e_{n+1} = Ce_n^q.$$

Dividing, e.g., the latter equation by the former, and solving with respect to $q$, we get that

$$q = \frac{\ln(e_{n+1}/e_n)}{\ln(e_n/e_{n-1})}.$$

Since this $q$ will vary somewhat with $n$, we call it $q_n$. As $n$ grows, we expect $q_n$ to approach a limit ($q_n \to q$).

**Modifying Our Functions to Return All Approximations** To compute all the $q_n$ values, we need *all* the $x_n$ approximations. However, our previous implementations of Newton's method, the secant method, and the bisection method returned just the final approximation.

Therefore, we have modified our solvers[5] accordingly, and placed them in `nonlinear_solvers.py`. A user can choose whether the final value or the whole history of solutions is to be returned. Each of the extended implementations now takes an extra parameter `return_x_list`. This parameter is a boolean, set to `True` if the function is supposed to return all the root approximations, or `False`, if the function should only return the final approximation.

As an example, let us take a closer look at `Newton`:

```
def Newton(f, dfdx, x, eps, return_x_list=False):
    f_value = f(x)
    iteration_counter = 0
    if return_x_list:
        x_list = []

    while abs(f_value) > eps and iteration_counter < 100:
        try:
            x = x - float(f_value)/dfdx(x)
        except ZeroDivisionError:
            print('Error! - derivative zero for x = {:g}'.format(x))
            sys.exit(1)     # Abort with error

        f_value = f(x)
        iteration_counter += 1
        if return_x_list:
            x_list.append(x)

    # Here, either a solution is found, or too many iterations
    if abs(f_value) > eps:
        iteration_counter = -1  # i.e., lack of convergence
```

[5] An implemented numerical solution algorithm is often called a *solver*.

```
    if return_x_list:
        return x_list, iteration_counter
    else:
        return x, iteration_counter
```

We can now make a call

```
x, iter = Newton(f, dfdx, x=1000, eps=1e-6, return_x_list=True)
```

and get a list x returned. With knowledge of the exact solution $x$ of $f(x) = 0$ we can compute all the errors $e_n$ and all the associated $q_n$ values with the compact function (also found in nonlinear_solvers.py)

```
def rate(x, x_exact):
    e = [abs(x_ - x_exact) for x_ in x]
    q = [log(e[n+1]/e[n])/log(e[n]/e[n-1])
         for n in range(1, len(e)-1, 1)]
    return q
```

The error model (7.5) works well for Newton's method and the secant method. For the bisection method, however, it works well in the beginning, but not when the solution is approached.

We can compute the rates $q_n$ and print them nicely (print_rates.py),

```
def print_rates(method, x, x_exact):
    q = ['{:.2f}'.format(q_) for q_ in rate(x, x_exact)]
    print(method + ':')
    for q_ in q:
        print(q_, " ", end="")     # end="" suppresses newline
```

The result for print_rates('Newton', x, 3) is

```
Newton:
1.01 1.02 1.03 1.07 1.14 1.27 1.51 1.80 1.97 2.00
```

indicating that $q = 2$ is the rate for Newton's method. A similar computation using the secant method, gives the rates

```
secant:
1.26 0.93 1.05 1.01 1.04 1.05 1.08 1.13 1.20 1.30 1.43
1.54 1.60 1.62 1.62
```

Here it seems that $q \approx 1.6$ is the limit.

**Remark** If we in the bisection method think of the length of the current interval containing the solution as the error $e_n$, then (7.5) works perfectly since $e_{n+1} = \frac{1}{2}e_n$, i.e., $q = 1$ and $C = \frac{1}{2}$, but if $e_n$ is the true error $|x - x_n|$, it is easily seen from a sketch that this error can oscillate between the current interval length and a potentially very small value as we approach the exact solution. The corresponding rates $q_n$ fluctuate widely and are of no interest.

## 7.6 Solving Multiple Nonlinear Algebraic Equations

So far in this chapter, we have considered a single nonlinear algebraic equation. However, *systems* of such equations arise in a number of applications, foremost nonlinear ordinary and partial differential equations. Of the previous algorithms, only Newton's method is suitable for extension to systems of nonlinear equations.

### 7.6.1 Abstract Notation

Suppose we have $n$ nonlinear equations, written in the following abstract form:

$$F_0(x_0, x_1, \ldots, x_n) = 0, \tag{7.6}$$

$$F_1(x_0, x_1, \ldots, x_n) = 0, \tag{7.7}$$

$$\vdots = \vdots \tag{7.8}$$

$$F_n(x_0, x_1, \ldots, x_n) = 0\,. \tag{7.9}$$

It will be convenient to introduce a *vector notation*

$$\boldsymbol{F} = (F_0, \ldots, F_1), \quad \boldsymbol{x} = (x_0, \ldots, x_n)\,.$$

The system can now be written as $\boldsymbol{F}(\boldsymbol{x}) = \boldsymbol{0}$.

As a specific example on the notation above, the system

$$x^2 = y - x\cos(\pi x) \tag{7.10}$$

$$yx + e^{-y} = x^{-1} \tag{7.11}$$

can be written in our abstract form by introducing $x_0 = x$ and $x_1 = y$. Then

$$F_0(x_0, x_1) = x^2 - y + x\cos(\pi x) = 0,$$

$$F_1(x_0, x_1) = yx + e^{-y} - x^{-1} = 0\,.$$

### 7.6.2 Taylor Expansions for Multi-Variable Functions

We follow the ideas of Newton's method for one equation in one variable: approximate the nonlinear $f$ by a linear function and find the root of that function. When $n$ variables are involved, we need to approximate a *vector function* $\boldsymbol{F}(\boldsymbol{x})$ by some linear function $\tilde{\boldsymbol{F}} = \boldsymbol{J}\boldsymbol{x} + \boldsymbol{c}$, where $\boldsymbol{J}$ is an $n \times n$ matrix and $\boldsymbol{c}$ is some vector of length $n$.

The technique for approximating $\boldsymbol{F}$ by a linear function is to use the first two terms in a Taylor series expansion. Given the value of $\boldsymbol{F}$ and its partial derivatives with respect to $\boldsymbol{x}$ at some point $\boldsymbol{x}_i$, we can approximate the value at some point $\boldsymbol{x}_{i+1}$

by the two first term in a Taylor series expansion around $\boldsymbol{x}_i$:

$$\boldsymbol{F}(\boldsymbol{x}_{i+1}) \approx \boldsymbol{F}(\boldsymbol{x}_i) + \nabla \boldsymbol{F}(\boldsymbol{x}_i)(\boldsymbol{x}_{i+1} - \boldsymbol{x}_i) .$$

The next terms in the expansions are omitted here and of size $||\boldsymbol{x}_{i+1} - \boldsymbol{x}_i||^2$, which are assumed to be small compared with the two terms above.

The expression $\nabla \boldsymbol{F}$ is the matrix of all the partial derivatives of $\boldsymbol{F}$. Component $(i, j)$ in $\nabla \boldsymbol{F}$ is

$$\frac{\partial F_i}{\partial x_j} .$$

For example, in our 2 × 2 system (7.10) and (7.11) we can use SymPy to compute the Jacobian:

```
In [1]: from sympy import *

In [2]: x0, x1 = symbols('x0 x1')

In [3]: F0 = x0**2 - x1 + x0*cos(pi*x0)

In [4]: F1 = x0*x1 + exp(-x1) - x0**(-1)

In [5]: diff(F0, x0)
Out[5]: -pi*x0*sin(pi*x0) + 2*x0 + cos(pi*x0)

In [6]: diff(F0, x1)
Out[6]: -1

In [7]: diff(F1, x0)
Out[7]: x1 + x0**(-2)

In [8]: diff(F1, x1)
Out[8]: x0 - exp(-x1)
```

We can then write

$$\nabla \boldsymbol{F} = \begin{pmatrix} \frac{\partial F_0}{\partial x_0} & \frac{\partial F_0}{\partial x_1} \\ \frac{\partial F_1}{\partial x_0} & \frac{\partial F_1}{\partial x_1} \end{pmatrix} = \begin{pmatrix} 2x_0 + \cos(\pi x_0) - \pi x_0 \sin(\pi x_0) & -1 \\ x_1 + x_0^{-2} & x_0 - e^{-x_1} \end{pmatrix}$$

The matrix $\nabla \boldsymbol{F}$ is called the *Jacobian* of $\boldsymbol{F}$ and often denoted by $\boldsymbol{J}$.

### 7.6.3 Newton's Method

The idea of Newton's method is that we have some approximation $\boldsymbol{x}_i$ to the root and seek a new (and hopefully better) approximation $\boldsymbol{x}_{i+1}$ by approximating $\boldsymbol{F}(\boldsymbol{x}_{i+1})$ by a linear function and solve the corresponding linear system of algebraic equations. We approximate the nonlinear problem $\boldsymbol{F}(\boldsymbol{x}_{i+1}) = 0$ by the linear problem

$$\boldsymbol{F}(\boldsymbol{x}_i) + \boldsymbol{J}(\boldsymbol{x}_i)(\boldsymbol{x}_{i+1} - \boldsymbol{x}_i) = \boldsymbol{0}, \tag{7.12}$$

where $\boldsymbol{J}(\boldsymbol{x}_i)$ is just another notation for $\nabla \boldsymbol{F}(\boldsymbol{x}_i)$. The Eq. (7.12) is a linear system with coefficient matrix $\boldsymbol{J}$ and right-hand side vector $\boldsymbol{F}(\boldsymbol{x}_i)$. We therefore write this system in the more familiar form

$$\boldsymbol{J}(\boldsymbol{x}_i)\boldsymbol{\delta} = -\boldsymbol{F}(\boldsymbol{x}_i),$$

where we have introduced a symbol $\boldsymbol{\delta}$ for the unknown vector $\boldsymbol{x}_{i+1} - \boldsymbol{x}_i$ that multiplies the Jacobian $\boldsymbol{J}$.

The $i$-th iteration of Newton's method for systems of algebraic equations consists of two steps:

1. Solve the linear system $\boldsymbol{J}(\boldsymbol{x}_i)\boldsymbol{\delta} = -\boldsymbol{F}(\boldsymbol{x}_i)$ with respect to $\boldsymbol{\delta}$.
2. Set $\boldsymbol{x}_{i+1} = \boldsymbol{x}_i + \boldsymbol{\delta}$.

Solving systems of linear equations must make use of appropriate software. Gaussian elimination is the most common, and in general the most robust, method for this purpose. Python's `numpy` package has a module `linalg` that interfaces the well-known LAPACK package with high-quality and very well tested subroutines for linear algebra. The statement `x = numpy.linalg.solve(A, b)` solves a system $Ax = b$ with a LAPACK method based on Gaussian elimination.

When nonlinear systems of algebraic equations arise from discretization of partial differential equations, the Jacobian is very often sparse, i.e., most of its elements are zero. In such cases it is important to use algorithms that can take advantage of the many zeros. Gaussian elimination is then a slow method, and (much) faster methods are based on iterative techniques.

### 7.6.4 Implementation

Here is a very simple implementation of Newton's method for systems of nonlinear algebraic equations:

```
import numpy as np

def Newton_system(F, J, x, eps):
    """
    Solve nonlinear system F=0 by Newton's method.
    J is the Jacobian of F. Both F and J must be functions of x.
    At input, x holds the start value. The iteration continues
    until ||F|| < eps.
    """
    F_value = F(x)
    F_norm = np.linalg.norm(F_value, ord=2)     # l2 norm of vector
    iteration_counter = 0
    while abs(F_norm) > eps and iteration_counter < 100:
        delta = np.linalg.solve(J(x), -F_value)
        x = x + delta
        F_value = F(x)
        F_norm = np.linalg.norm(F_value, ord=2)
        iteration_counter = iteration_counter + 1
```

```
    # Here, either a solution is found, or too many iterations
    if abs(F_norm) > eps:
        iteration_counter = -1
    return x, iteration_counter
```

We can test the function `Newton_system` with the $2 \times 2$ system (7.10) and (7.11):

```
def test_Newton_system1():
    from numpy import cos, sin, pi, exp

    def F(x):
        return np.array(
            [x[0]**2 - x[1] + x[0]*cos(pi*x[0]),
             x[0]*x[1] + exp(-x[1]) - x[0]**(-1.)])

    def J(x):
        return np.array(
            [[2*x[0] + cos(pi*x[0]) - pi*x[0]*sin(pi*x[0]), -1],
             [x[1] + x[0]**(-2.), x[0] - exp(-x[1])]])

    expected = np.array([1, 0])
    tol = 1e-4
    x, n = Newton_system(F, J, x=np.array([2, -1]), eps=0.0001)
    print(n, x)
    error_norm = np.linalg.norm(expected - x, ord=2)
    assert error_norm < tol, 'norm of error ={:g}'.format(error_norm)
    print('norm of error ={:g}'.format(error_norm))
```

Here, the testing is based on the L2 norm[6] of the error vector. Alternatively, we could test against the values of `x` that the algorithm finds, with appropriate tolerances. For example, as chosen for the error norm, if `eps=0.0001`, a tolerance of $10^{-4}$ can be used for `x[0]` and `x[1]`.

## 7.7 Exercises

**Exercise 7.1: Understand Why Newton's Method Can Fail**

The purpose of this exercise is to understand when Newton's method works and fails. To this end, solve $\tanh x = 0$ by Newton's method and study the intermediate details of the algorithm. Start with $x_0 = 1.08$. Plot the tangent in each iteration of Newton's method. Then repeat the calculations and the plotting when $x_0 = 1.09$. Explain what you observe.

Filename: `Newton_failure.*`.

**Exercise 7.2: See If the Secant Method Fails**

Does the secant method behave better than Newton's method in the problem described in Exercise 7.1? Try the initial guesses

1. $x_0 = 1.08$ and $x_1 = 1.09$
2. $x_0 = 1.09$ and $x_1 = 1.1$

[6] https://en.wikipedia.org/wiki/Norm_(mathematics)#Euclidean_norm.

3. $x_0 = 1$ and $x_1 = 2.3$
4. $x_0 = 1$ and $x_1 = 2.4$

Filename: `secant_failure.*`.

**Exercise 7.3: Understand Why the Bisection Method Cannot Fail**
Solve the same problem as in Exercise 7.1, using the bisection method, but let the initial interval be $[-5, 3]$. Report how the interval containing the solution evolves during the iterations.
Filename: `bisection_nonfailure.*`.

**Exercise 7.4: Combine the Bisection Method with Newton's Method**
An attractive idea is to combine the reliability of the bisection method with the speed of Newton's method. Such a combination is implemented by running the bisection method until we have a narrow interval, and then switch to Newton's method for speed.

Write a function that implements this idea. Start with an interval $[a, b]$ and switch to Newton's method when the current interval in the bisection method is a fraction $s$ of the initial interval (i.e., when the interval has length $s(b-a)$). Potential divergence of Newton's method is still an issue, so if the approximate root jumps out of the narrowed interval (where the solution is known to lie), one can switch back to the bisection method. The value of $s$ must be given as an argument to the function, but it may have a default value of 0.1.

Try the new method on $\tanh(x) = 0$ with an initial interval $[-10, 15]$.
Filename: `bisection_Newton.py`.

**Exercise 7.5: Write a Test Function for Newton's Method**
The purpose of this function is to verify the implementation of Newton's method in the `Newton` function in the file `nonlinear_solvers.py`. Construct an algebraic equation and perform two iterations of Newton's method by hand or with the aid of SymPy. Find the corresponding size of $|f(x)|$ and use this as value for `eps` when calling `Newton`. The function should then also perform two iterations and return the same approximation to the root as you calculated manually. Implement this idea for a unit test as a test function `test_Newton()`.
Filename: `test_Newton.py`.

**Exercise 7.6: Halley's Method and the Decimal Module**
A nonlinear algebraic equation $f(x) = 0$ may also be solved by Halley's method,[7] given as:

$$x_{n+1} = x_n - \frac{2f(x_n)f'(x_n)}{2f'(x_n)^2 - f(x_n)f''(x_n)}, \qquad n = 0, 1, \ldots,$$

with some starting value $x_0$.

[7] http://mathworld.wolfram.com/HalleysMethod.html.

a) Implement Halley's method as a function `Halley`. Place the function in a module that has a test block, and test the function by solving $x^2 - 9 = 0$, using $x_0 = 1000$ as your initial guess.
b) Compared to Newton's method, more computations per iteration are needed with Halley's method, but a convergence rate of 3 may be achieved close to the root. You are now supposed to extend your module with a function `compute_rates_decimal`, which computes the convergence rates achieved with your implementation of `Halley` (for the given problem).

   The implementation of `compute_rates_decimal` should involve the `decimal` module (you search for the right documentation!), to better handle very small errors that may enter the rate computations. For comparison, you should also compute the rates without using the `decimal` module. Test and compare with several parameter values.

**Hint** The logarithms in the rate calculation might require some extra consideration when you use the `decimal` module.
Filename: `Halleys_method.py`.

**Exercise 7.7: Fixed Point Iteration**
A nonlinear algebraic equation $f(x) = 0$ may be solved in many different ways, and we have met some of these in this chapter. Another, very useful, solution approach is to first re-write the equation into $x = \phi(x)$ (this re-write is not unique), and then formulate the iteration

$$x_{n+1} = \phi(x_n), \quad n = 0, 1, \ldots ,$$

with some starting value $x_0$. If $\phi(x)$ is continuous, and if $\phi(x_n)$ approaches $\alpha$ as $x_n$ approaches $\alpha$ (i.e., we get $\alpha = \phi(\alpha)$ as $n \to \infty$), the iteration is called a *fixed point iteration* and $\alpha$ is referred to as a *fixed point* of the mapping $x \to \phi(x)$. Clearly, if a fixed point $\alpha$ is found, $\alpha$ will also be a solution to the original equation $f(x) = 0$.

In this exercise, we will briefly explore the fixed point iteration method by solving

$$x^3 + 2x = e^{-x}, \quad x \in [-2, 2] .$$

For comparison, however, you will first be asked to solve the equation by Newton's method (which, in fact, can be seen as fixed point iteration[8]).

a) Write a program that solves this equation by Newton's method. Use $x = 1$ as your starting value. To better judge the printed answer found by Newton's method, let the code also plot the relevant function on the given interval.
b) The given equation may be rewritten as $x = \frac{e^{-x} - x^3}{2}$. Extend your program with a function `fixed_point_iteration`, which takes appropriate parameters, and uses fixed point iteration to find and return a solution (if found), as well as the number of iterations required. Use $x = 1$ as starting value.

[8] Check out https://en.wikipedia.org/wiki/Fixed_point_iteration.

When the program is executed, the original equation should be solved both with Newton's method and via fixed point iterations (as just described). Compare the output from the two methods.

Filename: `fixed_point_iteration.py`.

**Exercise 7.8: Solve Nonlinear Equation for a Vibrating Beam**
An important engineering problem that arises in a lot of applications is the vibrations of a clamped beam where the other end is free. This problem can be analyzed analytically, but the calculations boil down to solving the following nonlinear algebraic equation:

$$\cosh\beta\cos\beta = -1,$$

where $\beta$ is related to important beam parameters through

$$\beta^4 = \omega^2\frac{\varrho A}{EI},$$

where $\varrho$ is the density of the beam, $A$ is the area of the cross section, $E$ is Young's modulus, and $I$ is the moment of the inertia of the cross section. The most important parameter of interest is $\omega$, which is the frequency of the beam. We want to compute the frequencies of a vibrating steel beam with a rectangular cross section having width $b = 25$ mm and height $h = 8$ mm. The density of steel is 7850 kg/m$^3$, and $E = 2\times10^{11}$ Pa. The moment of inertia of a rectangular cross section is $I = bh^3/12$.

a) Plot the equation to be solved so that one can inspect where the zero crossings occur.

**Hint** When writing the equation as $f(\beta) = 0$, the $f$ function increases its amplitude dramatically with $\beta$. It is therefore wise to look at an equation with damped amplitude, $g(\beta) = e^{-\beta}f(\beta) = 0$. Plot $g$ instead.

b) Compute the first three frequencies.

Filename: `beam_vib.py`.

# Solving Ordinary Differential Equations

# 8

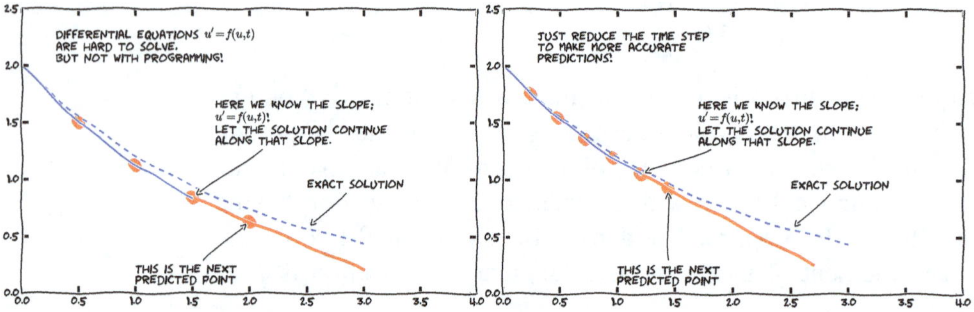


Differential equations constitute one of the most powerful mathematical tools to understand and predict the behavior of dynamical systems in nature, engineering, and society. A dynamical system is some system with some state, usually expressed by a set of variables, that evolves in time. For example, an oscillating pendulum, the spreading of a disease, and the weather are examples of dynamical systems. We can use basic laws of physics, or plain intuition, to express mathematical rules that govern the evolution of a system in time. These rules take the form of *differential equations*.

You are probably well experienced with equations, at least equations like $ax + b = 0$ and $ax^2 + bx + c = 0$, where $a$, $b$ and $c$ are constants. Such equations are known as *algebraic equations*, and the unknowns are *numbers*. In a differential equation, the unknown is a *function*, and a differential equation will usually involve this function and one or more of its derivatives. When this function depends on a single independent variable, the equation is called an *ordinary differential equation* (ODE, plural: ODEs), which is different from a *partial differential equation* (PDE, plural: PDEs), in which the function depends on several independent variables (Chap. 9). As an example, $f'(x) = f(x)$ is a simple ODE (asking if there is any function $f$ such that it equals its derivative—you might remember that $e^x$



S. Linge, H. P. Langtangen, *Programming for Computations - Python*,
Texts in Computational Science and Engineering 15,
https://doi.org/10.1007/978-3-030-16877-3_8

is a candidate).[1] This is also an example of a *first-order* ODE, since the highest derivative appearing in the equation is a first derivative. When the highest derivative in an ODE is a second derivative, it is a *second-order* ODE, and so on (a similar terminology is used also for PDEs).

**Order of ODE versus order of numerical solution method**

Note that an ODE will have an *order* as just explained. This order, however, should not be confused with the *order* of a numerical solution method applied to solve that ODE. The latter refers to the convergence rate of the numerical solution method, addressed at the end of this chapter. We will present several such solution methods in this chapter, being first-order, second-order or fourth-order, for example (and a first-order ODE might, in principle, be solved by any of these methods).

The present chapter[2] starts out preparing for ODEs and the Forward Euler method, which is a first-order method. Then we explain in detail how to solve ODEs numerically with the Forward Euler method, both *single (scalar)* first-order ODEs and *systems* of first-order ODEs. After the "warm-up" application—filling of a water tank—aimed at the less mathematically trained reader, we demonstrate all the mathematical and programming details through two specific applications: population growth and spreading of diseases. The first few programs we write, are deliberately made very simple and similar, while we focus the computational ideas.

Then we turn to oscillating mechanical systems, which arise in a wide range of engineering situations. The differential equation is now of second order, and the Forward Euler method does not perform too well. This observation motivates the need for other solution methods, and we derive the Euler-Cromer scheme, the second- and fourth-order Runge-Kutta schemes, as well as a finite difference scheme (the latter to handle the second-order differential equation directly without reformulating it as a first-order system). The presentation starts with undamped free oscillations and then treats general oscillatory systems with possibly nonlinear damping, nonlinear spring forces, and arbitrary external excitation. Besides developing programs from scratch, we also demonstrate how to access ready-made implementations of more advanced differential equation solvers in Python.

As we progress with more advanced methods, we develop more sophisticated and reusable programs. In particular, we incorporate good testing strategies, which allows us to bring solid evidence of correct computations. Consequently, the beginning—with water tank, population growth and disease modeling examples—has a very gentle learning curve, while that curve gets significantly steeper towards the end of our section on oscillatory systems.

---

[1] Note that the notation for the derivative may differ. For example, $f'(x)$ could equally well be written as just $f'$ (where the dependence on x is to be understood), or as $\frac{df}{dx}$.

[2] The reader should be aware of another excellent easy-to-read text by the late Prof. Langtangen, "Finite Difference Computing with Exponential Decay Models" (Springer, open access, 2016, https://www.springer.com/gp/book/9783319294384). It fits right in with the material on ODEs and PDEs of the present book.

## 8.1 Filling a Water Tank: Two Cases

If "ordinary differential equation" is not among your favorite expressions, then this section is for you.

Consider a 25 L tank that will be filled with water in two different ways. In the first case, *the water volume that enters the tank per time* (rate of volume increase) is piecewise constant, while in the second case, it is continuously increasing.

For each of these two cases, we are asked to develop a code that can predict (i.e., compute) how the total water volume $V$ in the tank will develop with time $t$ over a period of 3 s. Our calculations must be based on the information given: the initial volume of water (1L in both cases), and the volume of water entering the tank per time.

### 8.1.1 Case 1: Piecewise Constant Rate

In this simpler case, there is initially 1 L of water in the tank, i.e.,

$$V(0) = 1\,\mathrm{L},$$

while the rates of volume increase are given as:

$$\begin{aligned} r &= 1\,\mathrm{L\,s^{-1}}, && 0\,\mathrm{s} < t < 1\,\mathrm{s}, \\ r &= 3\,\mathrm{L\,s^{-1}}, && 1\,\mathrm{s} \le t < 2\,\mathrm{s}, \\ r &= 7\,\mathrm{L\,s^{-1}}, && 2\,\mathrm{s} \le t \le 3\,\mathrm{s}. \end{aligned}$$

Before turning to the programming, we should work out the exact solution by hand for this problem, since that is rather straight forward. Such a solution will of course be useful for verifying our implementation. In fact, comparing program output to these hand calculations should suffice for this particular problem.

**Exact Solution by Hand** Our reasoning goes like this: For each of the given subintervals (on the time axis), the total volume $V$ of water in the tank will increase linearly. Thus, if we compute $V$ after 1, 2 and 3 s, we will have what we need. We get

$$\begin{aligned} V(0) &= 1\,\mathrm{L}, \\ V(1) &= 1\,\mathrm{L} + (1\,\mathrm{s})(1\,\mathrm{L\,s^{-1}}) = 2\,\mathrm{L}, \\ V(2) &= 2\,\mathrm{L} + (1\,\mathrm{s})(3\,\mathrm{L\,s^{-1}}) = 5\,\mathrm{L}, \\ V(3) &= 5\,\mathrm{L} + (1\,\mathrm{s})(7\,\mathrm{L\,s^{-1}}) = 12\,\mathrm{L}. \end{aligned}$$

We also have what is required for plotting the exact solution, since we can just tell Python to plot the computed $V$ values against $t$ for $t = 0, 1, 2, 3$, and let Python fill in the straight lines in between these points. Therefore, the exact solution is ready and we may proceed to bring our reasoning into code.

**Implementation and Performance** A simple implementation may read (rate_piecewise_constant.py):

```
import numpy as np
import matplotlib.pyplot as plt

a = 0.0;   b = 3.0                        # time interval
N = 3                                     # number of time steps
dt = (b - a)/N                            # time step (s)
V_exact = [1.0, 2.0, 5.0, 12.0]           # exact volumes (L)
V = np.zeros(4)                           # numerically computed volume (L)
V[0] = 1                                  # initial volume
r = np.zeros(3)                           # rates of volume increase (L/s)
r[0] = 1; r[1] = 3; r[2] = 7

for i in [0, 1, 2]:
    V[i+1] = V[i] + dt*r[i]

time = [0, 1, 2, 3]
plt.plot(time, V, 'bo-', time, V_exact, 'r')
plt.title('Case 1')
plt.legend(['numerical','exact'], loc='upper left')
plt.xlabel('t (s)')
plt.ylabel('V (L)')
plt.show()
```

As you can see, we have included the exact (hand computed) solution in the code, so that it gets plotted together with the numerical solution found by the program. The time step dt will become 1 s here, and running the code, produces the plot seen in Fig. 8.1. We note that the numerical and exact solution can not be distinguished in the plot.

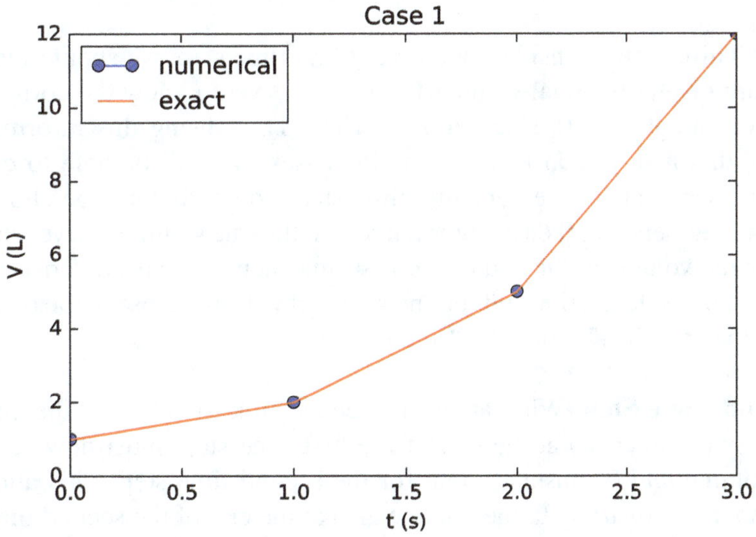


Fig. 8.1 Water volume in a tank as it develops with piecewise constant rate of volume increase

### 8.1.2 Case 2: Continuously Increasing Rate

This case is more tricky. As in the previous case, there is 1 L of water in the tank from the start. When the tank fills up, however, the rate of volume increase, $r$, is *always* equal to the current volume of water, i.e., $r = V$ (in units of $\mathrm{L\,s^{-1}}$). So, for example, at the time when there is 2 L in the tank, water enters the tank at $2\,\mathrm{L\,s^{-1}}$, when there is 2.1 L in the tank, water comes in at $2.1\,\mathrm{L\,s^{-1}}$, and so on. Thus, contrary to what we had in Case 1, $r$ is not constant for any period of time within the 3 s interval, it increases continuously and gives us a steeper and steeper curve for $V(t)$. Writing this up as for Case 1, the information we have is

$$V(0) = 1\,\mathrm{L},$$

and, for the rate (in $\mathrm{L\,s^{-1}}$),

$$r(t) = V(t), \qquad 0\,\mathrm{s} < t \leq 3\,\mathrm{s}\,.$$

Let us, for simplicity, assume that we also are given the exact solution in this case, which is $V(t) = e^t$. This allows us to easily check out the performance of any computational idea that we might try.

So, how can we compute the development of $V$, making it compare favorably to the given solution?

**An Idea** Clearly, we will be happy with an *approximately* correct solution, as long as the error can be made "small enough". In Case 1, we effectively computed connected straight line segments that matched the true development of $V$ because of piecewise constant $r$ values. Would it be possible to do something similar here in Case 2, i.e., compute straight line segments and use them as an *approximation* to the true solution curve? If so, it seems we could benefit from a very simple computational scheme! Let us pursue this idea further to see what comes out of it.

**The First Time Step** Considering the very first time step, we should realize that, since we are given the initial volume $V(0) = 1\,\mathrm{L}$, we do know the correct volume *and* correct rate at $t = 0$, since $r(t) = V(t)$. Thus, using this information and *pretending* that $r$ stays constant as time increases, we will be able to compute a straight line segment for the very first time step (some $\Delta t$ must be chosen). This straight line segment will then become tangent to the true solution curve when $t = 0$. The computed volume at the end of the first time step will have an error, but if our time step is not too large, the straight line segment will stay close to the true solution curve and the error in $V$ should be "small".

**The Second Time Step** What about the second time step? Well, the volume we computed (with an error) at the end of the first time step, must now serve as the starting volume *and* ("constant") rate for the second time step. This allows us to compute an *approximation* to the volume also at the end of the second time step. If errors are "small", also the second straight line segment should be close to the true solution curve.

**What About the Errors?** We realize that, in this way, we can work our way all along the total time interval. Immediately, we suspect that the error may grow with the number of time steps, but since the total time interval is not too large, and since we may choose a *very* small time step on modern computers, this could still work!

**Implementation and Performance** Let us write down the code, which by choice gets very similar to the code in Case 1, and see how it performs. We realize that, for our strategy to work, the time steps should not be too large. However, during these initial investigations of ours, our aim is first and foremost to check out the computational idea. So, we pick a time step $\Delta t = 0.1$ s for a first try. A simple version of the code (rate_exponential.py) may then read:

```
import numpy as np
import matplotlib.pyplot as plt

a = 0.0;  b = 3.0                        # time interval
N = 30                                   # number of time steps
dt = (b - a)/N                           # time step (s)
V = np.zeros(N+1)                        # numerically computed volume (L)
V[0] = 1                                 # initial volume

for i in range(0, N, 1):
    V[i+1] = V[i] + dt*V[i]              # ...r is V now

time_exact = np.linspace(a, b, 1000)
V_exact = np.exp(time_exact)             # make exact solution (for plotting)
time = np.linspace(0, 3, N+1)
plt.plot(time, V, 'bo-', time_exact, V_exact, 'r')
plt.title('Case 2')
plt.legend(['numerical','exact'], loc='upper left')
plt.xlabel('t (s)')
plt.ylabel('V (L)')
plt.show()
```

To plot the exact solution, we just picked 1000 points in time, which we consider "large enough" to get a representative curve. Compared to the code for Case 1, some more flexibility is introduced here, using `range` and `N` in the `for` loop header. Running the code gives the plot shown in Fig. 8.2.

This looks promising! Not surprisingly, the error grows with time, reaching about 2.64 L at the end. However, the time step is not particularly small, so we should expect much more accurate computations if $\Delta t$ is reduced. We skip showing the plots,[3] but if we increase `N` from 30 to 300, the maximum error drops to 0.30 L, while an `N` value of $3 \cdot 10^6$ gives an error of $3 \cdot 10^{-5}$ L. It seems we are on to something!

[3] With smaller time steps, it becomes inappropriate to use filled circles on the graph for the numerical values. Thus, in the plot command, one should change `bo-` to, e.g., only `b`.

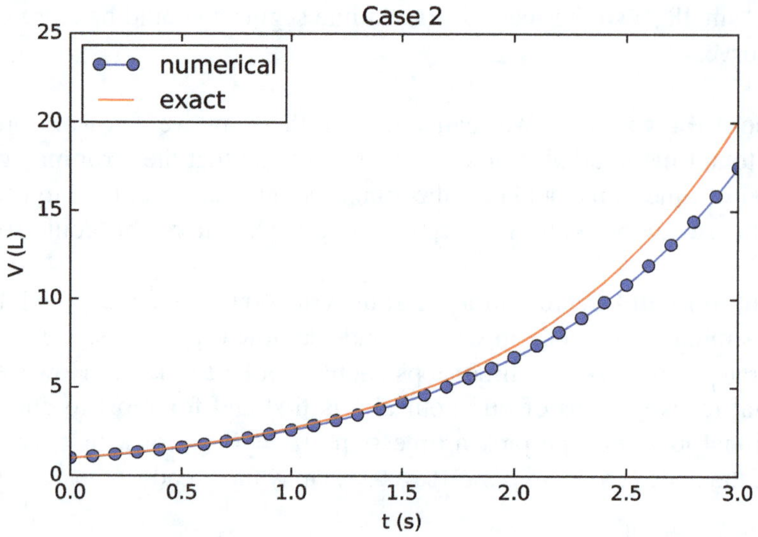


**Fig. 8.2** Water volume in a tank as it develops with constantly increasing rate of volume change ($r = V$). The numerical computations use piecewise constant rates as an approximation to the true rate

The similar code structures used for Case 1 and Case 2 suggests that a more general (and improved) code may be written, applicable to both cases. As we move on with our next example, population growth, we will see how this can be done.

### 8.1.3 Reformulating the Problems as ODEs

Typically, the problems we solved in Case 1 and Case 2, would rather have been presented in "more proper mathematical language" as ODEs.

**Case 1** When the rates were piecewise constant, we could have been requested to solve

$$V'(t) = 1\,\mathrm{L\,s^{-1}}, \qquad 0\,\mathrm{s} < t < 1\,\mathrm{s},$$
$$V'(t) = 3\,\mathrm{L\,s^{-1}}, \qquad 1\,\mathrm{s} \le t < 2\,\mathrm{s},$$
$$V'(t) = 7\,\mathrm{L\,s^{-1}}, \qquad 2\,\mathrm{s} \le t \le 3\,\mathrm{s},$$

with

$$V(0) = 1\,\mathrm{L},$$

where $V(0)$ is known as an *initial condition*.

**Case 2** With a continuously increasing rate, we could have been asked to solve

$$V'(t) = V(t), \qquad V(0) = 1\,\text{L}, \qquad 0\,\text{s} < t \leq 3\,\text{s}.$$

This particular ODE is very similar to the ODE we will address when we next turn to population growth (in fact, it may be seen as a special case of the latter).

**The Forward Euler Method: A Brief Encounter** If we had proceeded to solve these ODEs by something called the *Forward Euler method* (or *Euler's method*), we could (if we wanted) have written the solution codes exactly as they were developed above! Thus, we have already used the essentials of Euler's method without stating it.

In the following sections, the Forward Euler method will be thoroughly explained and elaborated on, while we demonstrate how the approach may be used to solve different ODEs numerically.

## 8.2 Population Growth: A First Order ODE

Our first real taste of differential equations regards modeling the growth of some population, such as a cell culture, an animal population, or a human population. The ideas even extend trivially to growth of money in a bank.

Let $N(t)$ be the number of individuals in the population at time $t$. How can we predict the evolution of $N$ with time? Below we shall derive a differential equation whose solution is $N(t)$. The equation we will derive reads

$$N'(t) = rN(t), \tag{8.1}$$

where $r$ is a number. Note that although $N$ obviously is an integer in real life, we model $N$ as a real-valued function. We choose to do this, because the solutions of differential equations are (normally continuous) real-valued functions. An integer-valued $N(t)$ in the model would lead to a lot of mathematical difficulties. Also, talking about, e.g., 2.5 individuals is no problem in mathematics, even though we must be a bit careful when applying this in a practical setting!

You may know, or find out, that the solution $N(t) = Ce^{rt}$, where $C$ is any number. To make this solution unique, we need to fix $C$, which is done by prescribing the value of $N$ at some time, usually at $t = 0$. If $N(0)$ is given as $N_0$, we get $N(t) = N_0 e^{rt}$.

In general, a *differential equation model* consists of a *differential equation*, such as (8.1) *and* an *initial condition*, such as $N(0) = N_0$. With a known initial condition, the differential equation can be solved for the unknown function and the solution is unique.

It is very rare that we can find the solution of a differential equation as easy as the ODE in this example allows. Normally, one has to apply certain mathematical methods. Still, these methods can only handle some of the simplest differential equations. However, with numerical methods and a bit of programming, we can easily deal with almost any differential equation! This is exactly the topic of the present chapter.

### 8.2.1 Derivation of the Model

It can be instructive to show how an equation like (8.1) arises. Consider some population of an animal species and let $N(t)$ be the number of individuals in a certain spatial region, e.g. an island. We are not concerned with the spatial distribution of the animals, just the number of them in some region where there is no exchange of individuals with other regions. During a time interval $\Delta t$, some animals will die and some will be born. The numbers of deaths and births are expected to be proportional to $N$. For example, if there are twice as many individuals, we expect them to get twice as many newborns. In a time interval $\Delta t$, the net growth of the population will then be

$$N(t + \Delta t) - N(t) = \bar{b}N(t) - \bar{d}N(t),$$

where $\bar{b}N(t)$ is the number of newborns and $\bar{d}N(t)$ is the number of deaths. If we double $\Delta t$, we expect the proportionality constants $\bar{b}$ and $\bar{d}$ to double too, so it makes sense to think of $\bar{b}$ and $\bar{d}$ as proportional to $\Delta t$ and "factor out" $\Delta t$. That is, we introduce $b = \bar{b}/\Delta t$ and $d = \bar{d}/\Delta t$ to be proportionality constants for newborns and deaths independent of $\Delta t$. Also, we introduce $r = b - d$, which is the net rate of growth of the population per time unit. Our model then becomes

$$N(t + \Delta t) - N(t) = \Delta t\, rN(t)\,. \tag{8.2}$$

Equation (8.2) is actually a computational model. Given $N(t)$, we can advance the population size by

$$N(t + \Delta t) = N(t) + \Delta t\, rN(t)\,.$$

This is called a *difference equation*. If we know $N(t)$ for some $t$, e.g., $N(0) = N_0$, we can compute

$$\begin{aligned}
N(\Delta t) &= N_0 + \Delta t\, rN_0,\\
N(2\Delta t) &= N(\Delta t) + \Delta t\, rN(\Delta t),\\
N(3\Delta t) &= N(2\Delta t) + \Delta t\, rN(2\Delta t),\\
&\vdots\\
N((k+1)\Delta t) &= N(k\Delta t) + \Delta t\, rN(k\Delta t),
\end{aligned}$$

where $k$ is some arbitrary integer. A computer program can easily compute $N((k+1)\Delta t)$ for us with the aid of a little loop.

**The initial condition**

Observe that the computational formula cannot be started unless we have an initial condition!

The solution of $N' = rN$ is $N = Ce^{rt}$ for any constant $C$, and the initial condition is needed to fix $C$ so the solution becomes unique. However, from a mathematical point of view, knowing $N(t)$ at any point $t$ is sufficient as initial condition. Numerically, we more literally need an initial condition: we need to know a starting value at the left end of the interval in order to get the computational formula going.

In fact, we do not really need a computer in this particular case, since we see a repetitive pattern when doing hand calculations. This leads us to a mathematical formula for $N((k+1)\Delta t)$:

$$\begin{aligned}
N((k+1)\Delta t) &= N(k\Delta t) + \Delta t\, rN(k\Delta t) = N(k\Delta t)(1 + \Delta t\, r) \\
&= N((k-1)\Delta t)(1 + \Delta t\, r)^2 \\
&\vdots \\
&= N_0(1 + \Delta t\, r)^{k+1}\,.
\end{aligned}$$

Rather than using (8.2) as a computational model directly, there is a strong tradition for deriving a differential equation from this difference equation. The idea is to consider a very small time interval $\Delta t$ and look at the instantaneous growth as this time interval is shrunk to an infinitesimally small size. In mathematical terms, it means that we let $\Delta t \to 0$. As (8.2) stands, letting $\Delta t \to 0$ will just produce an equation $0 = 0$, so we have to divide by $\Delta t$ and then take the limit:

$$\lim_{\Delta t \to 0} \frac{N(t+\Delta t) - N(t)}{\Delta t} = rN(t)\,.$$

The term on the left-hand side is actually the definition of the derivative $N'(t)$, so we have

$$N'(t) = rN(t),$$

which is the corresponding differential equation.

There is nothing in our derivation that forces the parameter $r$ to be constant—it can change with time due to, e.g., seasonal changes or more permanent environmental changes.

**Detour: Exact mathematical solution**

If you have taken a course on mathematical solution methods for differential equations, you may want to recap how an equation like $N' = rN$ or $N' = r(t)N$ is solved. The *method of separation of variables* is the most convenient solution strategy in this case:

$$
\begin{aligned}
N' &= rN \\
\frac{dN}{dt} &= rN \\
\frac{dN}{N} &= rdt \\
\int_{N_0}^{N} \frac{dN}{N} &= \int_0^t rdt \\
\ln N - \ln N_0 &= \int_0^t r(t)dt \\
N &= N_0 \exp\left(\int_0^t r(t)dt\right),
\end{aligned}
$$

which for constant $r$ results in $N = N_0 e^{rt}$. Note that $\exp(t)$ is the same as $e^t$.

As will be described later, $r$ must in more realistic models depend on $N$. The method of separation of variables then requires to integrate $\int_{N_0}^{N} N/r(N)dN$, which quickly becomes non-trivial for many choices of $r(N)$. The only generally applicable solution approach is therefore a numerical method.

### 8.2.2 Numerical Solution: The Forward Euler (FE) Method

There is a huge collection of numerical methods for problems like (8.1), and in general any equation of the form $u' = f(u,t)$, where $u(t)$ is the unknown function in the problem, and $f$ is some known formula of $u$ and optionally $t$. In our case with population growth, i.e., (8.1), $u'(t)$ corresponds to $N'(t)$, while $f(u,t)$ corresponds to $rN(t)$.

We will first present a simple *finite difference method* solving $u' = f(u,t)$. The idea is fourfold:

1. Introduce $N_t + 1$ points in time, $t_0, t_1, \ldots, t_{N_t}$, for the relevant time interval. We seek the unknown $u$ at these points in time, and introduce $u^n$ as the numerical approximation to $u(t_n)$, see Fig. 8.3.
2. Utilize that the differential equation is valid at the mesh points.
3. Approximate derivatives by finite differences, see Fig. 8.4.
4. Formulate a computational algorithm that can compute a new value $u^n$ based on previously computed values $u^i$, $i < n$.

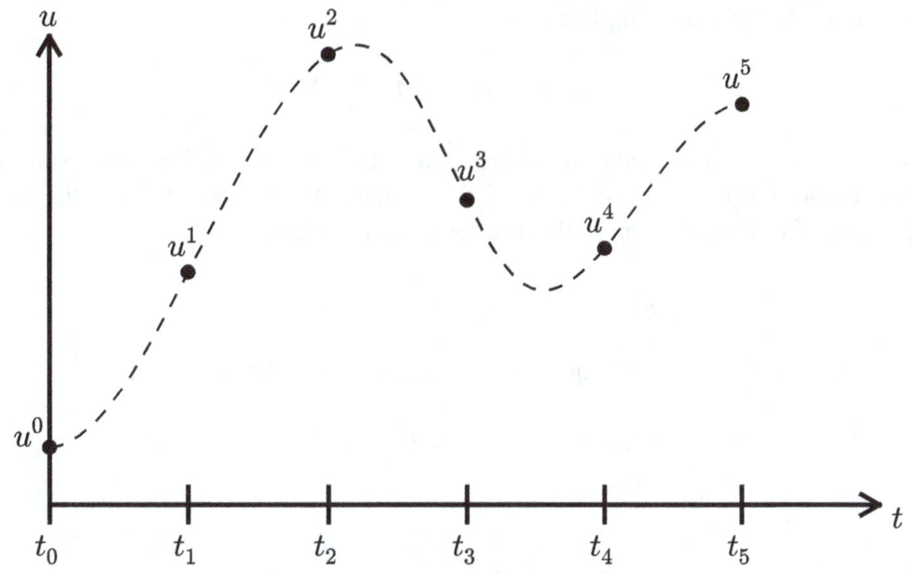


**Fig. 8.3** Mesh in time with corresponding discrete values (unknowns)

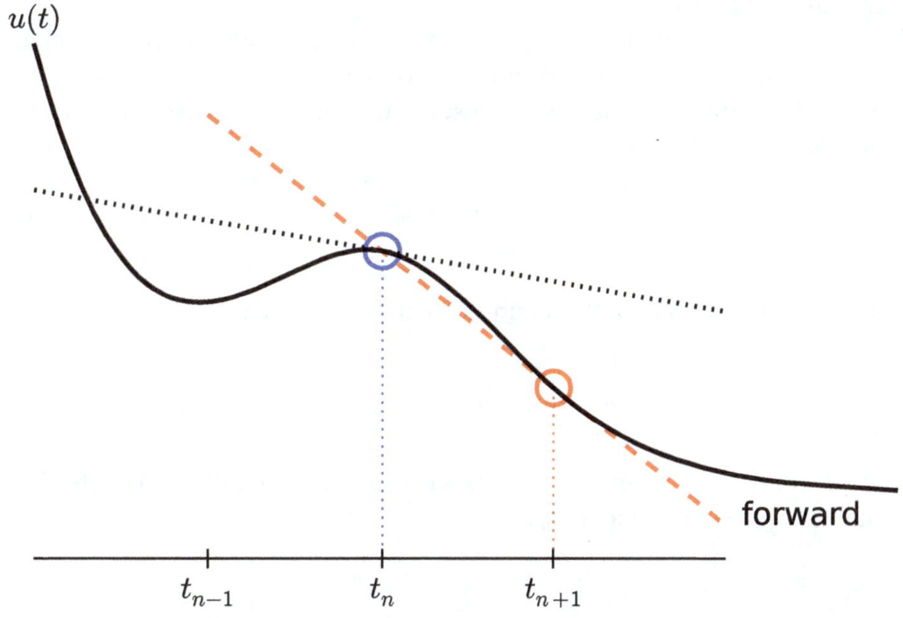


**Fig. 8.4** Illustration of a forward difference approximation to the derivative

The collection of points $t_0, t_1, \ldots, t_{N_t}$ is called a *mesh* (or *grid*), while the corresponding $u^n$ values[4] collectively are referred to as a *mesh function*.

Let us use an example to illustrate the given steps. First, we introduce the mesh, which often is *uniform*, meaning that the spacing between mesh points $t_n$ and $t_{n+1}$

---

[4] To get an estimate of $u$ in between the mesh points, one often assumes a straight line relationship between computed $u^n$ values. Check out *linear interpolation*, e.g., on Wikipedia (https://en.wikipedia.org/wiki/Linear_interpolation).

is constant. This property implies that

$$t_n = n\Delta t, \quad n = 0, 1, \ldots, N_t\,.$$

Second, the differential equation is supposed to hold at the mesh points. Note that this is an approximation, because the differential equation is originally valid for all real values of $t$. We can express this property mathematically as

$$u'(t_n) = f(u^n, t_n), \quad n = 0, 1, \ldots, N_t\,.$$

For example, with our model equation $u' = ru$, we have the special case

$$u'(t_n) = ru^n, \quad n = 0, 1, \ldots, N_t,$$

or

$$u'(t_n) = r(t_n)u^n, \quad n = 0, 1, \ldots, N_t,$$

if $r$ depends explicitly on $t$.

Third, derivatives are to be replaced by finite differences. To this end, we need to know specific formulas for how derivatives can be approximated by finite differences. One simple possibility is to use the definition of the derivative from any calculus book,

$$u'(t) = \lim_{\Delta t \to 0} \frac{u(t + \Delta t) - u(t)}{\Delta t}\,.$$

At an arbitrary mesh point $t_n$ this definition can be written as

$$u'(t_n) = \lim_{\Delta t \to 0} \frac{u^{n+1} - u^n}{\Delta t}\,.$$

Instead of going to the limit $\Delta t \to 0$ we can use a small $\Delta t$, which yields a computable approximation to $u'(t_n)$:

$$u'(t_n) \approx \frac{u^{n+1} - u^n}{\Delta t}\,.$$

This is known as a *forward difference* since we go forward in time ($u^{n+1}$) to collect information in $u$ to estimate the derivative. Figure 8.4 illustrates the idea. The error of the forward difference is proportional to $\Delta t$ (often written as $\mathcal{O}(\Delta t)$, but we will not use this notation in the present book).

We can now plug in the forward difference in our differential equation sampled at the arbitrary mesh point $t_n$:

$$\frac{u^{n+1} - u^n}{\Delta t} = f(u^n, t_n), \tag{8.3}$$

or with $f(u, t) = ru$ in our special model problem for population growth,

$$\frac{u^{n+1} - u^n}{\Delta t} = ru^n \,. \tag{8.4}$$

If $r$ depends on time, we insert $r(t_n) = r^n$ for $r$ in this latter equation.

The fourth step is to derive a computational algorithm. Looking at (8.3), we realize that if $u^n$ should be known, we can easily solve with respect to $u^{n+1}$ to get a formula for $u$ at the next time level $t_{n+1}$:

$$u^{n+1} = u^n + \Delta t f(u^n, t_n) \,. \tag{8.5}$$

Provided we have a known starting value, $u^0 = U_0$, we can use (8.5) to advance the solution by first computing $u^1$ from $u^0$, then $u^2$ from $u^1$, $u^3$ from $u^2$, and so forth.

Such an algorithm is called a *numerical scheme* for the differential equation. It is often written compactly as

$$u^{n+1} = u^n + \Delta t f(u^n, t_n), \quad u^0 = U_0, \quad n = 0, 1, \ldots, N_t - 1 \,. \tag{8.6}$$

This scheme is known as the *Forward Euler scheme*, also called *Euler's method.*

In our special population growth model, we have

$$u^{n+1} = u^n + \Delta t\, r u^n, \quad u^0 = U_0, \quad n = 0, 1, \ldots, N_t - 1 \,. \tag{8.7}$$

We may also write this model using the problem-specific symbol $N$ instead of the generic $u$ function:

$$N^{n+1} = N^n + \Delta t\, r N^n, \quad N^0 = N_0, \quad n = 0, 1, \ldots, N_t - 1 \,. \tag{8.8}$$

The observant reader will realize that (8.8) is nothing but the computational model (8.2) arising directly in the model derivation. The formula (8.8) arises, however, from a detour via a differential equation and a numerical method for the differential equation. This looks rather unnecessary! The reason why we bother to derive the differential equation model and then discretize it by a numerical method is simply that the discretization can be done in many ways, and we can create (much) more accurate and more computationally efficient methods than (8.8) or (8.6). This can be useful in many problems! Nevertheless, the Forward Euler scheme is intuitive and widely applicable, at least when $\Delta t$ is chosen to be small.

**The numerical solution between the mesh points**

Our numerical method computes the unknown function $u$ at discrete mesh points $t_1, t_2, \ldots, t_{N_t}$. What if we want to evaluate the numerical solution between the mesh points? The most natural choice is to *assume* a linear variation between the mesh points, see Fig. 8.5. This is compatible with the fact that when we plot the array $u^0, u^1, \ldots$ versus $t_0, t_1, \ldots$, a straight line is automatically drawn between the discrete points (unless we specify otherwise in the plot command).

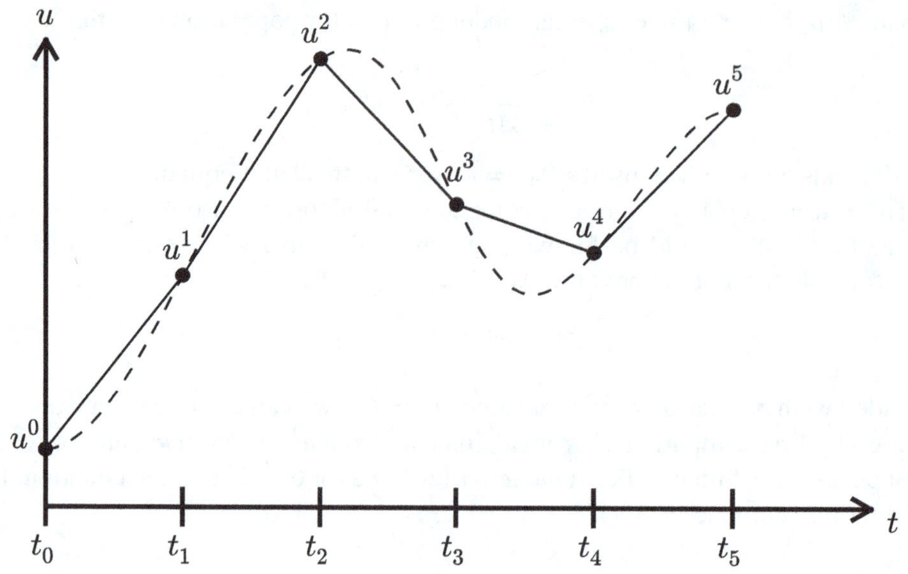


**Fig. 8.5** The numerical solution at points can be extended by linear segments between the mesh points

### 8.2.3 Programming the FE Scheme; the Special Case

Let us compute (8.8) in a program. The input variables are $N_0$, $\Delta t$, $r$, and $N_t$. Note that we need to compute $N_t$ new values $N^1, \ldots, N^{N_t}$. A total of $N_t + 1$ values are needed in an array representation of $N^n$, $n = 0, \ldots, N_t$.

Our first version of this program (growth1.py) is as simple as possible, and very similar to the codes we wrote previously for the water tank example:

```
import numpy as np
import matplotlib.pyplot as plt

N_0 = int(input('Give initial population size N_0: '))
r   = float(input('Give net growth rate r: '))
dt  = float(input('Give time step size: '))
N_t = int(input('Give number of steps: '))

t = np.linspace(0, N_t*dt, N_t+1)
N = np.zeros(N_t+1)

N[0] = N_0
for n in range(N_t):
    N[n+1] = N[n] + r*dt*N[n]

numerical_sol = 'bo' if N_t < 70 else 'b-'
plt.plot(t, N, numerical_sol, t, N_0*np.exp(r*t), 'r-')
plt.legend(['numerical', 'exact'], loc='upper left')
plt.xlabel('t'); plt.ylabel('N(t)')
filestem = 'growth1_{:d}steps'.format(N_t)
plt.savefig('{:s}.png'.format(filestem))
plt.savefig('{:s}.pdf'.format(filestem))
```

Note the compact assignment statement

```
numerical_sol = 'bo' if N_t < 70 else 'b-'
```

This is a one-line alternative to, e.g.,

```
if N_t < 70:
    numerical_sol = 'bo'
else:
    numerical_sol = 'b-'
```

Let us demonstrate a simulation where we start with 100 animals, a net growth rate of 10% (0.1) per time unit, which can be 1 month, and $t \in [0, 20]$ months. We may first try $\Delta t$ of half a month (0.5), which implies $N_t = 40$. Figure 8.6 shows the results. The solid line is the exact solution, while the circles are the computed numerical solution. The discrepancy is clearly visible. What if we make $\Delta t$ 10 times smaller? The result is displayed in Fig. 8.7, where we now use a solid line also for the numerical solution (otherwise, 400 circles would look very cluttered, so the program has a test on how to display the numerical solution, either as circles or a solid line). We can hardly distinguish the exact and the numerical solution. The computing time is also a fraction of a second on a laptop, so it appears that the Forward Euler method is sufficiently accurate for practical purposes. (This is not always true for large, complicated simulation models in engineering, so more sophisticated methods may be needed.)

It is also of interest to see what happens if we increase $\Delta t$ to 2 months. The results in Fig. 8.8 indicate that this is an inaccurate computation.

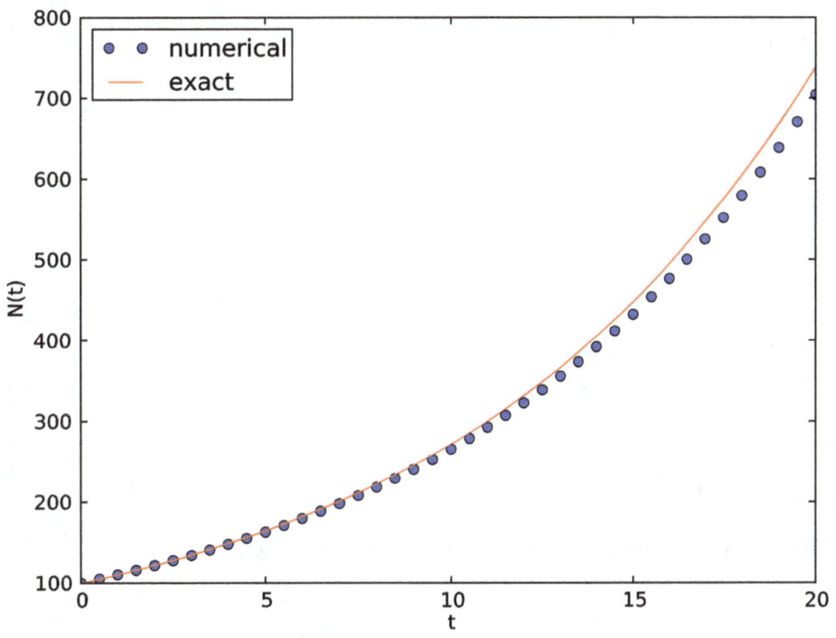


Fig. 8.6 Evolution of a population computed with time step 0.5 month

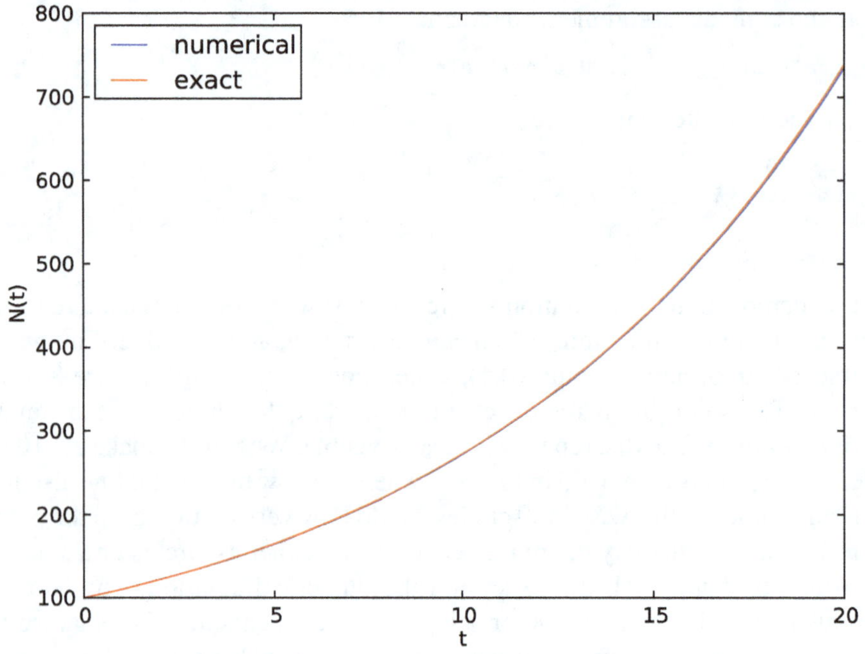


**Fig. 8.7** Evolution of a population computed with time step 0.05 month

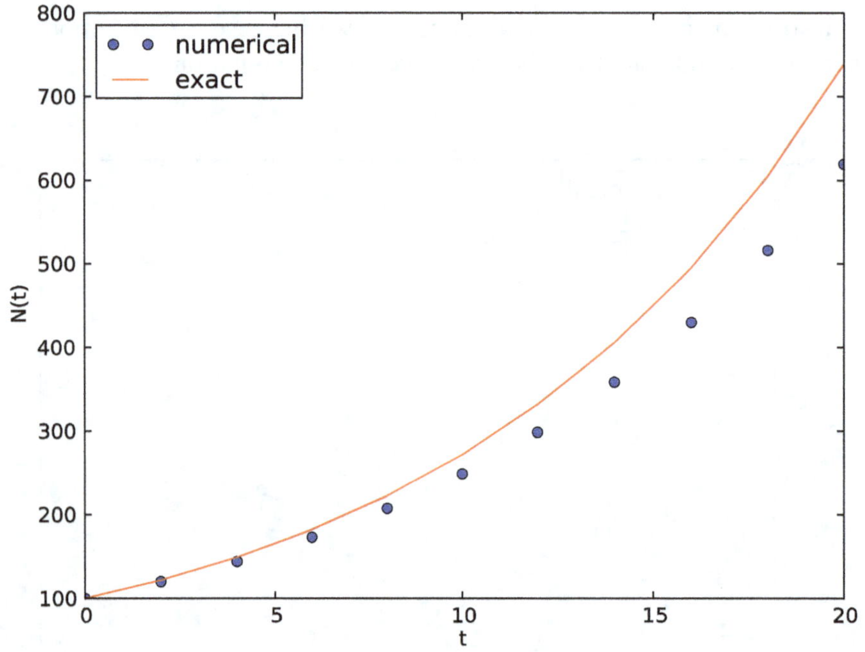


**Fig. 8.8** Evolution of a population computed with time step 2 months

### 8.2.4 Understanding the Forward Euler Method

The good thing about the Forward Euler method is that it gives an understanding of what a differential equation is and a geometrical picture of how to construct the solution. The first idea is that we have already computed the solution up to some time point $t_n$. The second idea is that we want to progress the solution from $t_n$ to $t_{n+1}$ as a straight line.

We know that the line must go through the solution at $t_n$, i.e., the point $(t_n, u^n)$. The differential equation tells us the slope of the line: $u'(t_n) = f(u^n, t_n) = ru^n$. That is, the differential equation gives a direct formula for the further *direction* of the solution curve. We can say that the differential equation expresses how the system ($u$) undergoes changes at a point.

There is a general formula for a straight line $y = ax + b$ with slope $a$ that goes through the point $(x_0, y_0)$: $y = a(x - x_0) + y_0$. Using this formula adapted to the present case, and evaluating the formula for $t_{n+1}$, results in

$$u^{n+1} = ru^n(t_{n+1} - t_n) + u^n = u^n + \Delta t\, ru^n,$$

which is nothing but the Forward Euler formula. You are now encouraged to do Exercise 8.2 to become more familiar with the geometric interpretation of the Forward Euler method.

### 8.2.5 Programming the FE Scheme; the General Case

Our previous program was just a simple main program without function definitions, tailored to a special differential equation. When programming mathematics, it is always good to consider a (large) class of problems and making a Python function to solve any problem that fits into the class. More specifically, we will make software for the class of differential equation problems of the form

$$u'(t) = f(u, t), \quad u = U_0,\ t \in [0, T],$$

for some given function $f$, and numbers $U_0$ and $T$. We also take the opportunity to illustrate what is commonly called a demo function. As the name implies, the purpose of such a function is solely to demonstrate how the function works (not to be confused with a test function, which does verification by use of `assert`). The Python function calculating the solution must take $f$, $U_0$, $\Delta t$, and $T$ as input, find the corresponding $N_t$, compute the solution, and return an array with $u^0, u^1, \ldots, u^{N_t}$ and an array with $t_0, t_1, \ldots, t_{N_t}$. The Forward Euler scheme reads

$$u^{n+1} = u^n + \Delta t f(u^n, t_n), \quad n = 0, \ldots, N_t - 1 .$$

The corresponding program may now take the form (file `ode_FE.py`):

```
import numpy as np
import matplotlib.pyplot as plt

def ode_FE(f, U_0, dt, T):
    N_t = int(round(T/dt))
    u = np.zeros(N_t+1)
    t = np.linspace(0, N_t*dt, len(u))
    u[0] = U_0
```

```
    for n in range(N_t):
        u[n+1] = u[n] + dt*f(u[n], t[n])
    return u, t

def demo_population_growth():
    """Test case: u'=r*u, u(0)=100."""
    def f(u, t):
        return 0.1*u

    u, t = ode_FE(f=f, U_0=100, dt=0.5, T=20)
    plt.plot(t, u, t, 100*np.exp(0.1*t))
    plt.show()

if __name__ == '__main__':
    demo_population_growth()
```

This program file, called `ode_FE.py`, is a reusable piece of code with a general `ode_FE` function that can solve any differential equation $u' = f(u, t)$ and a demo function for the special case $u' = 0.1u$, $u(0) = 100$. Observe that the call to the demo function is placed in a test block. This implies that the call is not active if `ode_FE` is imported as a module in another program, but active if `ode_FE.py` is run as a program.

The solution should be identical to what the `growth1.py` program produces with the same parameter settings ($r = 0.1$, $N_0 = 100$). This feature can easily be tested by inserting a print command, but a much better, automated verification is suggested in Exercise 8.2. You are strongly encouraged to take a "break" and do that exercise now.

**Remark on the Use of u as Variable**

In the `ode_FE` program, the variable `u` is used in different contexts. Inside the `ode_FE` function, `u` is an array, but in the `f(u,t)` function, as exemplified in the `demo_population_growth` function, the argument `u` is a number. Typically, we call `f` (in `ode_FE`) with the `u` argument as one element of the array `u` in the `ode_FE` function: `u[n]`.

### 8.2.6 A More Realistic Population Growth Model

Exponential growth of a population according the model $N' = rN$, with exponential solution $N = N_0 e^{rt}$, is unrealistic in the long run because the resources needed to feed the population are finite. At some point there will not be enough resources and the growth will decline. A common model taking this effect into account assumes that $r$ depends on the size of the population, $N$:

$$N(t + \Delta t) - N(t) = r(N(t))N(t)\,.$$

The corresponding differential equation becomes

$$N' = r(N)N\,.$$

The reader is strongly encouraged to repeat the steps in the derivation of the Forward Euler scheme and establish that we get

$$N^{n+1} = N^n + \Delta t\, r(N^n)N^n,$$

which computes as easy as for a constant $r$, since $r(N^n)$ is known when computing $N^{n+1}$. Alternatively, one can use the Forward Euler formula for the general problem $u' = f(u,t)$ and use $f(u,t) = r(u)u$ and replace $u$ by $N$.

The simplest choice of $r(N)$ is a linear function, starting with some growth value $\bar{r}$ and declining until the population has reached its maximum, $M$, according to the available resources:

$$r(N) = \bar{r}(1 - N/M)\,.$$

In the beginning, $N \ll M$ and we will have exponential growth $e^{\bar{r}t}$, but as $N$ increases, $r(N)$ decreases, and when $N$ reaches $M$, $r(N) = 0$ so there is no more growth and the population remains at $N(t) = M$. This linear choice of $r(N)$ gives rise to a model that is called the *logistic model*. The parameter $M$ is known as the *carrying capacity* of the population.

Let us run the logistic model with aid of the `ode_FE` function. We choose $N(0) = 100$, $\Delta t = 0.5$ month, $T = 60$ months, $r = 0.1$, and $M = 500$. The complete program, called `logistic.py`, is basically a call to `ode_FE`:

```
from ode_FE import ode_FE
import matplotlib.pyplot as plt

for dt, T in zip((0.5, 20), (60, 100)):
    u, t = ode_FE(f=lambda u, t: 0.1*(1 - u/500.)*u, \
                               U_0=100, dt=dt, T=T)
    plt.figure()  # Make separate figures for each pass in the loop
    plt.plot(t, u, 'b-')
    plt.xlabel('t'); plt.ylabel('N(t)')
    plt.savefig('tmp_{:g}.png'.format(dt))
    plt.savefig('tmp_{:g}.pdf'.format(dt))
```

Figure 8.9 shows the resulting curve. We see that the population stabilizes around $M = 500$ individuals. A corresponding exponential growth would reach $N_0e^{rt} = 100e^{0.1\cdot 60} \approx 40,300$ individuals!

What happens if we use "large" $\Delta t$ values here? We may set $\Delta t = 20$ and $T = 100$. Now the solution, seen in Fig. 8.10, oscillates and is hence qualitatively wrong, because one can prove that the exact solution of the differential equation is monotone.

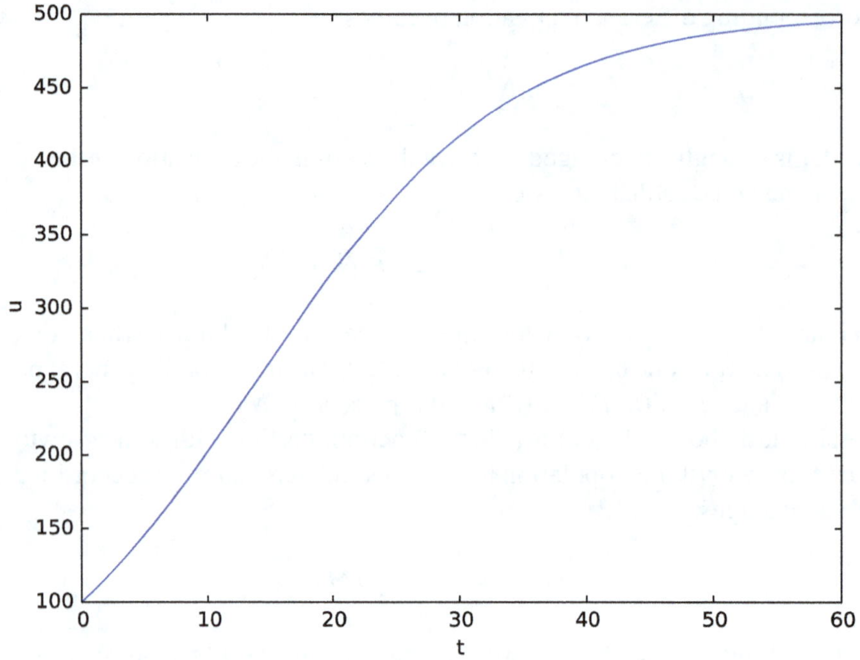


Fig. 8.9 Logistic growth of a population

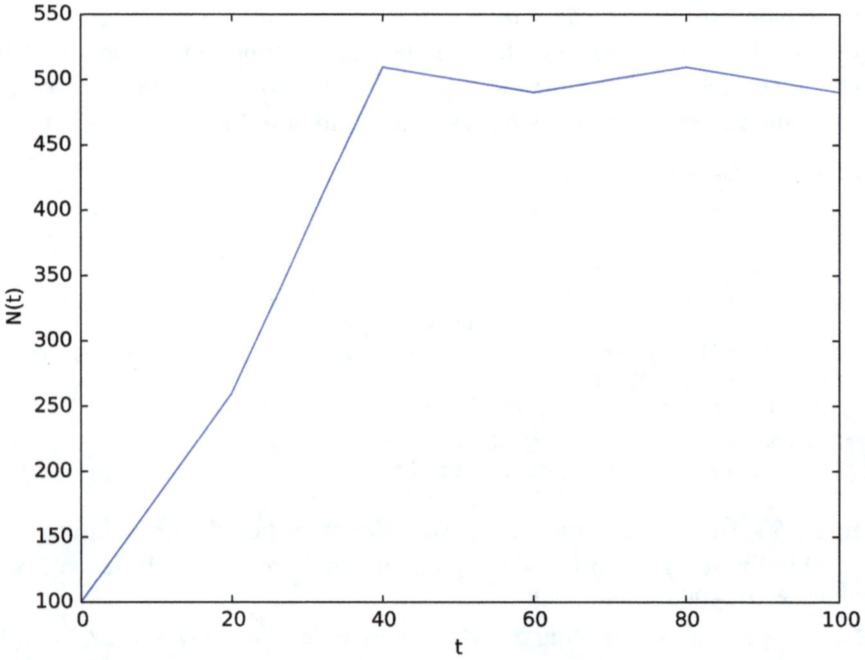


Fig. 8.10 Logistic growth with large time step

**Remark on the world population**

The number of people on the planet (http://en.wikipedia.org/wiki/Population_growth) follows the model $N' = r(t)N$, where the net reproduction $r(t)$ varies with time and has decreased since its top in 1990. The current world value of $r$ is 1.2%, and it is difficult to predict future values. At the moment, the predictions of the world population point to a growth to 9.6 billion before declining.

This example shows the limitation of a differential equation model: we need to know all input parameters, including $r(t)$, in order to predict the future. It is seldom the case that we know all input parameters. Sometimes knowledge of the solution from measurements can help estimate missing input parameters.

### 8.2.7 Verification: Exact Linear Solution of the Discrete Equations

How can we verify that the programming of an ODE model is correct? One way, is to compute convergence rates with a solver and confirm that the rates are according to expectations. We address convergence rates for ODE solvers later (in Sect. 8.5) and will then show how a corresponding test function for the `ode_FE` solver may be written.

The best verification method, however, is to find a problem where there are no unknown numerical approximation errors, because we can then compare the exact solution of the problem with the result produced by our implementation and expect the difference to be within a very small tolerance. We shall base a unit test on this idea and implement a corresponding *test function* (see Sect. 6.6.4) for automatic verification of our implementation.

It appears that most numerical methods for ODEs will exactly reproduce a solution $u$ that is linear in $t$. We may therefore set $u = at + b$ and choose any $f$ whose derivative is $a$. The choice $f(u,t) = a$ is very simple, but we may add anything that is zero, e.g.,

$$f(u,t) = a + (u - (at + b))^m.$$

This is a valid $f(u,t)$ for any $a$, $b$, and $m$. The corresponding ODE looks highly non-trivial, however:

$$u' = a + (u - (at + b))^m.$$

Using the general `ode_FE` function in `ode_FE.py`, we may write a proper test function as follows (in file `test_ode_FE_exact_linear.py`):

```
def test_ode_FE():
    """Test that a linear u(t)=a*t+b is exactly reproduced."""
```

```
def exact_solution(t):
    return a*t + b
def f(u, t):   # ODE
    return a + (u - exact_solution(t))**m

a = 4
b = -1
m = 6

dt = 0.5
T = 20.0

u, t = ode_FE(f, exact_solution(0), dt, T)
diff = abs(exact_solution(t) - u).max()
tol = 1E-15           # Tolerance for float comparison
success = diff < tol
assert success
```

As a measure of the error, we have here simply used the maximum error (picked out by a call to `max` and assigned to `diff`).

Recall that test functions should start with the name `test_`, have no arguments, and formulate the test as a boolean expression `success` that is `True` if the test passes and `False` if it fails. Test functions should make the test as `assert success` (here `success` can also be a boolean expression as in `assert diff < tol`).

Observe that we cannot compare `diff` to zero, which is what we mathematically expect, because `diff` is a floating-point variable that most likely contains small rounding errors. Therefore, we must compare `diff` to zero with a tolerance, here $10^{-15}$.

You are encouraged to do Exercise 8.3 where the goal is to make a test function for a verification based on comparison with hand-calculated results for a few time steps.

## 8.3 Spreading of Disease: A System of First Order ODEs

Our aim with this section is to show in detail how one can apply mathematics and programming to solve a system of first-order ODEs. We will do this as we investigate the spreading of disease. The mathematical model is now a system of three differential equations with three unknown functions. To derive such a model, we can use mainly intuition, so no specific background knowledge of diseases is required.

### 8.3.1 Spreading of Flu

Imagine a boarding school out in the country side. This school is a small and closed society. Suddenly, one or more of the pupils get the flu. We expect that the flu may spread quite effectively or die out. The question is how many of the pupils and the school's staff will be affected. Some quite simple mathematics can help us to achieve insight into the dynamics of how the disease spreads.

Let the mathematical function $S(t)$ count how many individuals, at time $t$, that have the possibility to get infected. Here, $t$ may count hours or days, for instance. These individuals make up a category called susceptibles, labeled as S. Another category, I, consists of the individuals that are infected. Let $I(t)$ count how many there are in category I at time $t$. An individual having recovered from the disease is assumed to gain immunity. There is also a small possibility that an infected will die. In either case, the individual is moved from the I category to a category we call the removed category, labeled with R. We let $R(t)$ count the number of individuals in the $R$ category at time $t$. Those who enter the $R$ category, cannot leave this category.

To summarize, the spreading of this disease is essentially the dynamics of moving individuals from the S to the I and then to the R category:

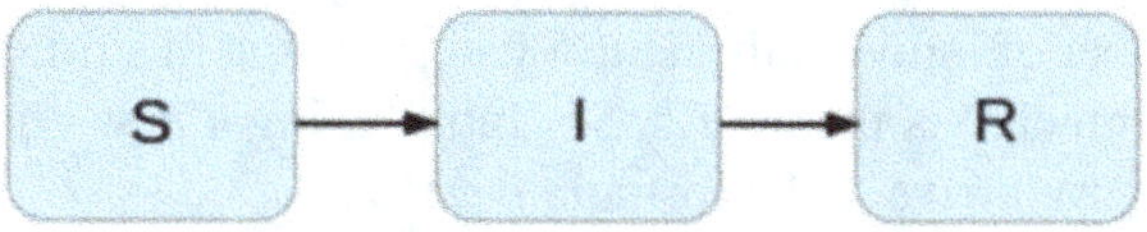


We can use mathematics to more precisely describe the exchange between the categories. The fundamental idea is to describe the changes that take place during a small time interval, denoted by $\Delta t$.

Our disease model is often referred to as a *compartment model*, where quantities are shuffled between compartments (here a synonym for categories) according to some rules. The rules express *changes* in a small time interval $\Delta t$, and from these changes we can let $\Delta t$ go to zero and obtain derivatives. The resulting equations then go from difference equations (with finite $\Delta t$) to differential equations ($\Delta t \to 0$).

We introduce a uniform mesh in time, $t_n = n\Delta t$, $n = 0, \ldots, N_t$, and seek $S$ at the mesh points. The numerical approximation to $S$ at time $t_n$ is denoted by $S^n$. Similarly, we seek the unknown values of $I(t)$ and $R(t)$ at the mesh points and introduce a similar notation $I^n$ and $R^n$ for the approximations to the exact values $I(t_n)$ and $R(t_n)$.

In the time interval $\Delta t$ we know that some people will be infected, so $S$ will decrease. We shall soon argue by mathematics that there will be $\beta \Delta t SI$ new infected individuals in this time interval, where $\beta$ is a parameter reflecting how easy people get infected during a time interval of unit length. If the loss in $S$ is $\beta \Delta t SI$, we have that the change in $S$ is

$$S^{n+1} - S^n = -\beta \Delta t S^n I^n \,. \tag{8.9}$$

Dividing by $\Delta t$ and letting $\Delta t \to 0$, makes the left-hand side approach $S'(t_n)$ such that we obtain a differential equation

$$S' = -\beta SI \,. \tag{8.10}$$

The reasoning in going from the difference equation (8.9) to the differential equation (8.10) follows exactly the steps explained in Sect. 8.2.1.

Before proceeding with how $I$ and $R$ develops in time, let us explain the formula $\beta \Delta t SI$. We have $S$ susceptibles and $I$ infected people. These can make up $SI$ pairs. Now, suppose that during a time interval $T$ we measure that $m$ actual pairwise meetings do occur among $n$ theoretically possible pairings of people from the S and I categories. The probability that people meet in pairs during a time $T$ is (by the empirical frequency definition of probability) equal to $m/n$, i.e., the number of successes divided by the number of possible outcomes. From such statistics we normally derive quantities expressed per unit time, i.e., here we want the probability per unit time, $\mu$, which is found from dividing by $T$: $\mu = m/(nT)$.

Given the probability $\mu$, the expected number of meetings per time interval of $SI$ possible pairs of people is (from basic statistics) $\mu SI$. During a time interval $\Delta t$, there will be $\mu SI\Delta t$ expected number of meetings between susceptibles and infected people such that the virus may spread. Only a fraction of the $\mu\Delta tSI$ meetings are effective in the sense that the susceptible actually becomes infected. Counting that $m$ people get infected in $n$ such pairwise meetings (say 5 are infected from 1000 meetings), we can estimate the probability of being infected as $p = m/n$. The expected number of individuals in the S category that in a time interval $\Delta t$ catch the virus and get infected is then $p\mu\Delta tSI$. Introducing a new constant $\beta = p\mu$ to save some writing, we arrive at the formula $\beta\Delta tSI$.

The value of $\beta$ must be known in order to predict the future with the disease model. One possibility is to estimate $p$ and $\mu$ from their meanings in the derivation above. Alternatively, we can observe an "experiment" where there are $S_0$ susceptibles and $I_0$ infected at some point in time. During a time interval $T$ we count that $N$ susceptibles have become infected. Using (8.9) as a rough approximation of how $S$ has developed during time $T$ (and now $T$ is not necessarily small, but we use (8.9) anyway), we get

$$N = \beta T S_0 I_0 \quad \Rightarrow \quad \beta = \frac{N}{T S_0 I_0} . \tag{8.11}$$

We need an additional equation to describe the evolution of $I(t)$. Such an equation is easy to establish by noting that the loss in the S category is a corresponding gain in the I category. More precisely,

$$I^{n+1} - I^n = \beta\Delta t S^n I^n . \tag{8.12}$$

However, there is also a loss in the I category because people recover from the disease. Suppose that we can measure that $m$ out of $n$ individuals recover in a time period $T$ (say 10 of 40 sick people recover during a day: $m = 10$, $n = 40$, $T = 24$ h). Now, $\gamma = m/(nT)$ is the probability that one individual recovers in a unit time interval. Then (on average) $\gamma\Delta tI$ infected will recover in a time interval $\Delta t$. This quantity represents a loss in the I category and a gain in the R category. We can therefore write the total change in the I category as

$$I^{n+1} - I^n = \beta\Delta t S^n I^n - \gamma\Delta t I^n . \tag{8.13}$$

The change in the R category is simple: there is always an increase got from the I category:

$$R^{n+1} - R^n = \gamma\Delta t I^n . \tag{8.14}$$

Since there is no loss in the R category (people are either recovered and immune, or dead), we are done with the modeling of this category. In fact, we do not strictly need Eq. (8.14) for $R$, but extensions of the model later will need an equation for $R$.

Dividing by $\Delta t$ in (8.13) and (8.14) and letting $\Delta t \rightarrow 0$, results in the corresponding differential equations

$$I' = \beta SI - \gamma I, \tag{8.15}$$

and

$$R' = \gamma I\,. \tag{8.16}$$

To summarize, we have derived three difference equations and three differential equations, which we list here for easy reference. The difference equations are:

$$S^{n+1} = S^n - \beta \Delta t S^n I^n, \tag{8.17}$$

$$I^{n+1} = I^n + \beta \Delta t S^n I^n - \gamma \Delta t I^n, \tag{8.18}$$

$$R^{n+1} = R^n + \gamma \Delta t I^n\,. \tag{8.19}$$

Note that we have isolated the new unknown quantities $S^{n+1}$, $I^{n+1}$, and $R^{n+1}$ on the left-hand side, such that these can readily be computed if $S^n$, $I^n$, and $R^n$ are known. To get such a procedure started, we need to know $S^0$, $I^0$, $R^0$. Obviously, we also need to have values for the parameters $\beta$ and $\gamma$.

The three differential equations are:

$$S' = -\beta SI, \tag{8.20}$$

$$I' = \beta SI - \gamma I, \tag{8.21}$$

$$R' = \gamma I\,. \tag{8.22}$$

This differential equation model (and also its discrete counterpart above) is known as an *SIR model*. The input data to the differential equation model consist of the parameter values for $\beta$ and $\gamma$, as well as the initial conditions $S(0) = S_0$, $I(0) = I_0$, and $R(0) = R_0$.

### 8.3.2 A FE Method for the System of ODEs

Let us apply the same principles as we did in Sect. 8.2.2 to discretize the differential equation system by the Forward Euler method. We already have a time mesh and time-discrete quantities $S^n$, $I^n$, $R^n$, $n = 0, \ldots, N_t$. The three differential equations are assumed to be valid at the mesh points. At the point $t_n$ we then have

$$S'(t_n) = -\beta S(t_n) I(t_n), \tag{8.23}$$

$$I'(t_n) = \beta S(t_n) I(t_n) - \gamma I(t_n), \tag{8.24}$$

$$R'(t_n) = \gamma I(t_n), \tag{8.25}$$

for $n = 0, 1, \ldots, N_t$. This is an approximation since the differential equations are originally valid at all times $t$ (usually in some finite interval $[0, T]$). Using forward finite differences for the derivatives results in an additional approximation,

$$\frac{S^{n+1} - S^n}{\Delta t} = -\beta S^n I^n, \tag{8.26}$$

$$\frac{I^{n+1} - I^n}{\Delta t} = \beta S^n I^n - \gamma I^n, \tag{8.27}$$

$$\frac{R^{n+1} - R^n}{\Delta t} = \gamma I^n. \tag{8.28}$$

As we can see, these equations are identical to the difference equations that naturally arise in the derivation of the model. However, other numerical methods than the Forward Euler scheme will result in slightly different difference equations.

### 8.3.3 Programming the FE Scheme; the Special Case

The computation of (8.26)–(8.28) can be readily made in a computer program `SIR1.py`:

```
import numpy as np
import matplotlib.pyplot as plt

# Time unit: 1 h
beta = 10./(40*8*24)
gamma = 3./(15*24)
dt = 0.1                # 6 min
D = 30                  # Simulate for D days
N_t = int(D*24/dt)      # Corresponding no of time steps

t = np.linspace(0, N_t*dt, N_t+1)
S = np.zeros(N_t+1)
I = np.zeros(N_t+1)
R = np.zeros(N_t+1)

# Initial condition
S[0] = 50
I[0] = 1
R[0] = 0

# Step equations forward in time
for n in range(N_t):
    S[n+1] = S[n] - dt*beta*S[n]*I[n]
    I[n+1] = I[n] + dt*beta*S[n]*I[n] - dt*gamma*I[n]
    R[n+1] = R[n] + dt*gamma*I[n]

fig = plt.figure()
l1, l2, l3 = plt.plot(t, S, t, I, t, R)
fig.legend((l1, l2, l3), ('S', 'I', 'R'), 'center right')
plt.xlabel('hours')
```

```
plt.savefig('tmp.pdf'); plt.savefig('tmp.png')
plt.show()
```

This program was written to investigate the spreading of flu at the mentioned boarding school, and the reasoning for the specific choices $\beta$ and $\gamma$ goes as follows. At some other school where the disease has already spread, it was observed that in the beginning of a day there were 40 susceptibles and 8 infected, while the numbers were 30 and 18, respectively, 24 h later. Using 1 h as time unit, we then have from (8.11) that $\beta = 10/(40 \cdot 8 \cdot 24)$. Among 15 infected, it was observed that 3 recovered during a day, giving $\gamma = 3/(15 \cdot 24)$. Applying these parameters to a new case where there is one infected initially and 50 susceptibles, gives the graphs in Fig. 8.11. These graphs are just straight lines between the values at times $t_i = i\Delta t$ as computed by the program. We observe that $S$ reduces as $I$ and $R$ grows. After about 30 days everyone has become ill and recovered again.

We can experiment with $\beta$ and $\gamma$ to see whether we get an outbreak of the disease or not. Imagine that a "wash your hands" campaign was successful and that the other school in this case experienced a reduction of $\beta$ by a factor of 5. With this lower $\beta$ the disease spreads very slowly so we simulate for 60 days. The curves appear in Fig. 8.12.

### 8.3.4 Outbreak or Not

Looking at the equation for $I$, it is clear that we must have $\beta SI - \gamma I > 0$ for $I$ to increase. When we start the simulation it means that

$$\beta S(0)I(0) - \gamma I(0) > 0,$$

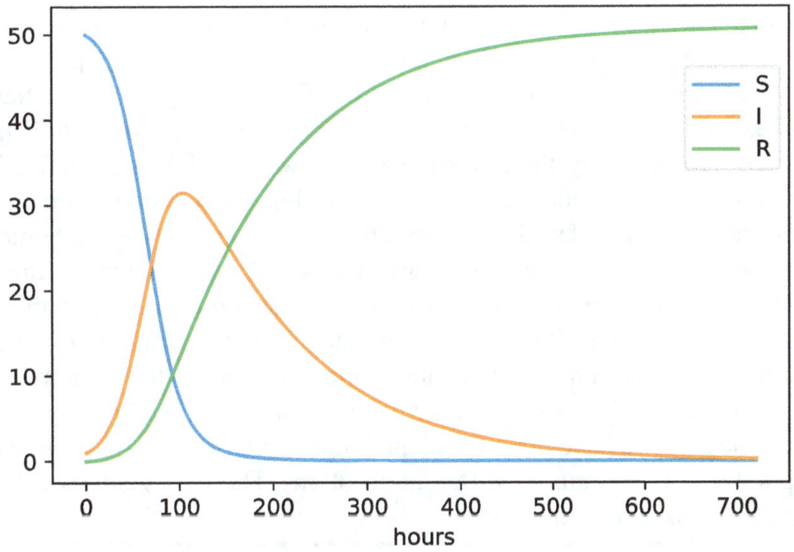


Fig. 8.11 Natural evolution of flu at a boarding school

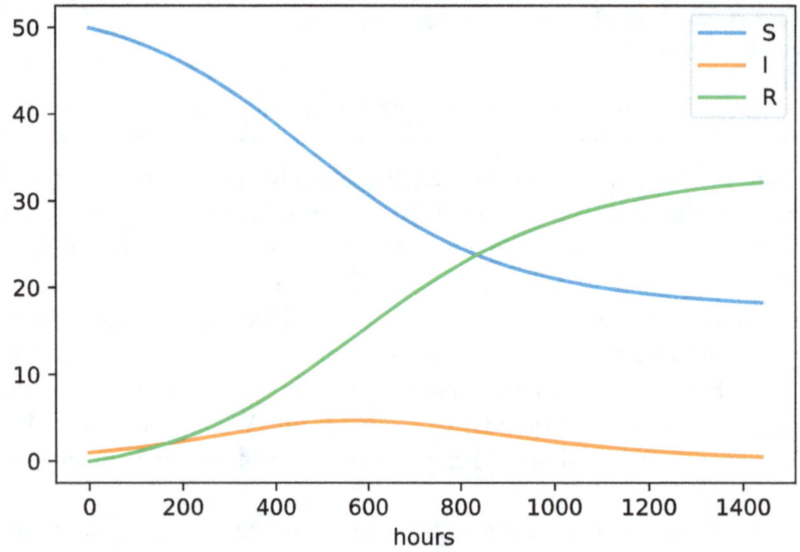


**Fig. 8.12** Small outbreak of flu at a boarding school ($\beta$ is much smaller than in Fig. 8.11)

or simpler

$$\frac{\beta S(0)}{\gamma} > 1 \tag{8.29}$$

to increase the number of infected people and accelerate the spreading of the disease. You can run the `SIR1.py` program with a smaller $\beta$ such that (8.29) is violated and observe that there is no outbreak.

**The power of mathematical modeling**

The reader should notice our careful use of words in the previous paragraphs. We started out with modeling a very specific case, namely the spreading of flu among pupils and staff at a boarding school. With purpose we exchanged words like pupils and flu with more neutral and general words like *individuals* and *disease*, respectively. Phrased equivalently, we raised the abstraction level by moving from a specific case (flu at a boarding school) to a more general case (disease in a closed society). Very often, when developing mathematical models, we start with a specific example and see, through the modeling, that what is going on of essence in this example also will take place in many similar problem settings. We try to incorporate this generalization in the model so that the model has a much wider application area than what we aimed at in the beginning. This is the very power of mathematical modeling: by solving one specific case we have often developed more generic tools that can readily be applied to solve seemingly different problems. The next sections will give substance to this assertion.

### 8.3.5 Abstract Problem and Notation

When we had a specific differential equation with one unknown, we quickly turned to an abstract differential equation written in the generic form $u' = f(u, t)$. We refer to such a problem as a *scalar ODE*. A specific equation corresponds to a specific choice of the formula $f(u, t)$ involving $u$ and (optionally) $t$.

It is advantageous to also write a system of differential equations in the same abstract notation,

$$u' = f(u, t),$$

but this time it is understood that $u$ is a vector of functions and $f$ is also vector. We say that $u' = f(u, t)$ is a *vector ODE* or *system of ODEs* in this case. For the SIR model we introduce the two 3-vectors, one for the unknowns,

$$u = (S(t), I(t), R(t)),$$

and one for the right-hand side functions,

$$f(u, t) = (-\beta SI, \beta SI - \gamma I, \gamma I)\,.$$

The equation $u' = f(u, t)$ means setting the two vectors equal, i.e., the components must be pairwise equal. Since $u' = (S', I', R')$, we get that $u' = f$ implies

$$\begin{aligned} S' &= -\beta SI, \\ I' &= \beta SI - \gamma I, \\ R' &= \gamma I\,. \end{aligned}$$

The generalized short notation $u' = f(u, t)$ is very handy since we can derive numerical methods and implement software for this abstract system and in a particular application just identify the formulas in the $f$ vector, implement these, and call functionality that solves the differential equation system.

### 8.3.6 Programming the FE Scheme; the General Case

In Python code, the Forward Euler step

$$u^{n+1} = u^n + \Delta t f(u^n, t_n),$$

being a scalar or a vector equation, can be coded as

```
u[n+1] = u[n] + dt*f(u[n], t[n])
```

both in the scalar and vector case. In the vector case, `u[n]` is a one-dimensional `numpy` array of length $m + 1$ holding the mathematical quantity $u^n$, and the Python function `f` must return a `numpy` array of length $m + 1$. Then the expression `u[n] + dt*f(u[n], t[n])` is an array plus a scalar times an array.

For all this to work, the complete numerical solution must be represented by a two-dimensional array, created by `u = zeros((N_t+1, m+1))`. The first index counts the time points and the second the components of the solution vector at one time point. That is, `u[n,i]` corresponds to the mathematical quantity $u_i^n$. When we use only one index, as in `u[n]`, this is the same as `u[n,:]` and picks out all the components in the solution at the time point with index `n`. Then the assignment `u[n+1] = ...` becomes correct because it is actually an in-place assignment `u[n+1, :] = ...`. The nice feature of these facts is that the same piece of Python code works for both a scalar ODE and a system of ODEs!

The `ode_FE` function for the vector ODE is placed in the file `ode_system_FE.py` and was written as follows:

```
import numpy as np
import matplotlib.pyplot as plt

def ode_FE(f, U_0, dt, T):
    N_t = int(round(T/dt))
    # Ensure that any list/tuple returned from f_ is wrapped as array
    f_ = lambda u, t: np.asarray(f(u, t))
    u = np.zeros((N_t+1, len(U_0)))
    t = np.linspace(0, N_t*dt, len(u))
    u[0] = U_0
    for n in range(N_t):
        u[n+1] = u[n] + dt*f_(u[n], t[n])
    return u, t
```

The line `f_ = lambda ...` needs an explanation. For a user, who just needs to define the $f$ in the ODE system, it is convenient to insert the various mathematical expressions on the right-hand sides in a list and return that list. Obviously, we could demand the user to convert the list to a `numpy` array, but it is so easy to do a general such conversion in the `ode_FE` function as well. To make sure that the result from `f` is indeed an array that can be used for array computing in the formula `u[n] + dt*f(u[n], t[n])`, we introduce a new function `f_` that calls the user's `f` and sends the results through the `numpy` function `asarray`, which ensures that its argument is converted to a `numpy` array (if it is not already an array).

Note also the extra parenthesis required when calling `zeros` with two indices.

Let us show how the previous SIR model can be solved using the new general `ode_FE` that can solve *any* vector ODE. The user's `f(u, t)` function takes a vector `u`, with three components corresponding to $S$, $I$, and $R$ as argument, along with the current time point `t[n]`, and must return the values of the formulas of the right-hand sides in the vector ODE. An appropriate implementation is

```
def f(u, t):
    S, I, R = u
    return [-beta*S*I, beta*S*I - gamma*I, gamma*I]
```

Note that the `S`, `I`, and `R` values correspond to $S^n$, $I^n$, and $R^n$. These values are then just inserted in the various formulas in the vector ODE. Here we collect the values in a list since the `ode_FE` function will anyway wrap this list in an array. We could, of course, returned an array instead:

```
def f(u, t):
    S, I, R = u
    return array([-beta*S*I, beta*S*I - gamma*I, gamma*I])
```

The list version looks a bit nicer, so that is why we prefer a list and rather introduce `f_ = lambda u, t: asarray(f(u,t))` in the general `ode_FE` function.

We can now show a function that runs the previous SIR example, while using the generic `ode_FE` function:

```
def demo_SIR():
    """Test case using a SIR model."""
    def f(u, t):
        S, I, R = u
        return [-beta*S*I, beta*S*I - gamma*I, gamma*I]

    beta = 10./(40*8*24)
    gamma = 3./(15*24)
    dt = 0.1                # 6 min
    D = 30                  # Simulate for D days
    N_t = int(D*24/dt)      # Corresponding no of time steps
    T = dt*N_t              # End time
    U_0 = [50, 1, 0]

    u, t = ode_FE(f, U_0, dt, T)

    S = u[:,0]
    I = u[:,1]
    R = u[:,2]
    fig = plt.figure()
    l1, l2, l3 = plt.plot(t, S, t, I, t, R)
    fig.legend((l1, l2, l3), ('S', 'I', 'R'), 'center right')
    plt.xlabel('hours')
    plt.show()

    # Consistency check:
    N = S[0] + I[0] + R[0]
    eps = 1E-12  # Tolerance for comparing real numbers
    for n in range(len(S)):
        SIR_sum = S[n] + I[n] + R[n]
        if abs(SIR_sum - N) > eps:
            print('*** consistency check failed: S+I+R={:g} != {:g}'\
                  .format(SIR_sum, N))

if __name__ == '__main__':
    demo_SIR()
```

Recall that the `u` returned from `ode_FE` contains all components ($S$, $I$, $R$) in the solution vector at all time points. We therefore need to extract the $S$, $I$, and $R$ values in separate arrays for further analysis and easy plotting.

Another key feature of this higher-quality code is the consistency check. By adding the three differential equations in the SIR model, we realize that $S' + I' + R' = 0$, which means that $S + I + R = \text{const}$. We can check that this relation holds by comparing $S^n + I^n + R^n$ to the sum of the initial conditions. Exercise 8.6 suggests another method for controlling the quality of the numerical solution.

### 8.3.7 Time-Restricted Immunity

Let us now assume that immunity after the disease only lasts for some certain time period. This means that there is transport from the R state to the S state:

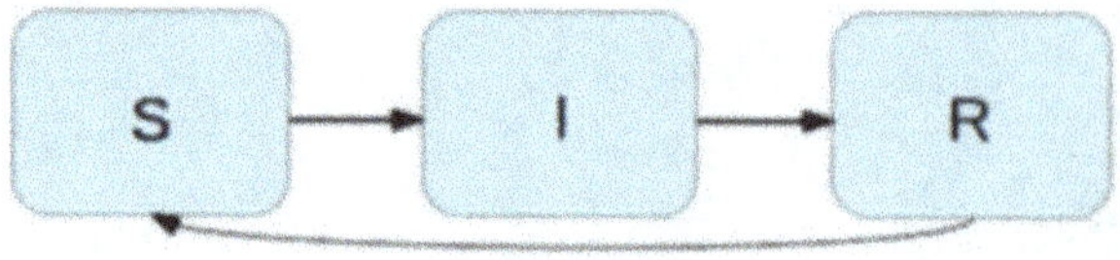


Modeling the loss of immunity is very similar to modeling recovery from the disease: the amount of people losing immunity is proportional to the amount of recovered patients and the length of the time interval $\Delta t$. We can therefore write the loss in the R category as $-\nu \Delta t R$ in time $\Delta t$, where $\nu^{-1}$ is the typical time it takes to lose immunity. The loss in $R(t)$ is a gain in $S(t)$. The "budgets" for the categories therefore become

$$S^{n+1} = S^n - \beta \Delta t S^n I^n + \nu \Delta t R^n, \tag{8.30}$$

$$I^{n+1} = I^n + \beta \Delta t S^n I^n - \gamma \Delta t I^n, \tag{8.31}$$

$$R^{n+1} = R^n + \gamma \Delta t I^n - \nu \Delta t R^n\,. \tag{8.32}$$

Dividing by $\Delta t$ and letting $\Delta t \to 0$ gives the differential equation system

$$S' = -\beta S I + \nu R, \tag{8.33}$$

$$I' = \beta S I - \gamma I, \tag{8.34}$$

$$R' = \gamma I - \nu R\,. \tag{8.35}$$

This system can be solved by the same methods as we demonstrated for the original SIR model. Only one modification in the program is necessary: adding `dt*nu*R[n]` to the `S[n+1]` update and subtracting the same quantity in the `R[n+1]` update:

```
for n in range(N_t):
    S[n+1] = S[n] - dt*beta*S[n]*I[n] + dt*nu*R[n]
    I[n+1] = I[n] + dt*beta*S[n]*I[n] - dt*gamma*I[n]
    R[n+1] = R[n] + dt*gamma*I[n] - dt*nu*R[n]
```

The modified code is found in the file `SIR2.py`.

Setting $\nu^{-1}$ to 50 days, reducing $\beta$ by a factor of 4 compared to the previous example ($\beta = 0.00033$), and simulating for 300 days gives an oscillatory behavior in the categories, as depicted in Fig. 8.13. It is easy now to play around and study how the parameters affect the spreading of the disease. For example, making the disease slightly more effective (increase $\beta$ to 0.00043) and increasing the average time to loss of immunity to 90 days lead to other oscillations, see Fig. 8.14.

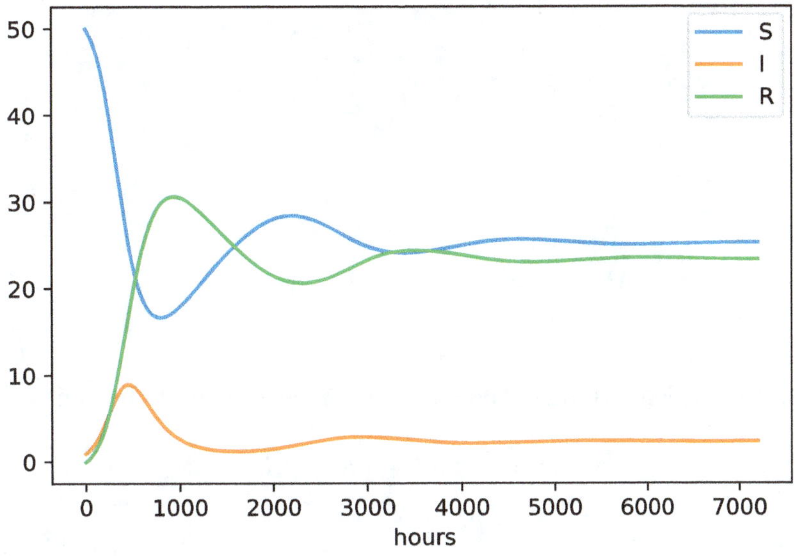


Fig. 8.13 Including loss of immunity

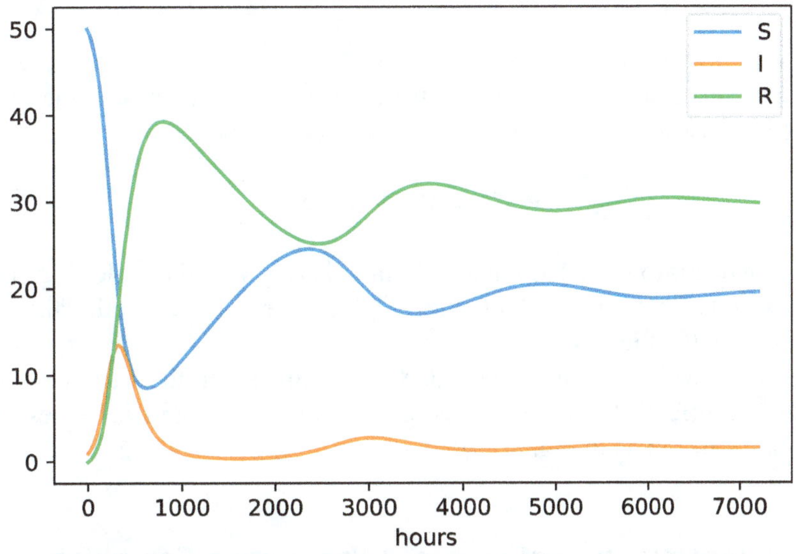


Fig. 8.14 Increasing $\beta$ and reducing $\nu$ compared to Fig. 8.13

### 8.3.8 Incorporating Vaccination

We can extend the model to also include vaccination. To this end, it can be useful to track those who are vaccinated and those who are not. So, we introduce a fourth category, V, for those who have taken a successful vaccination. Furthermore, we assume that in a time interval $\Delta t$, a fraction $p\Delta t$ of the S category is subject to a successful vaccination. This means that in the time $\Delta t$, $p\Delta t S$ people leave from the S to the V category. Since the vaccinated ones cannot get the disease, there is no impact on the I or R categories. We can visualize the categories, and the movement between them, as

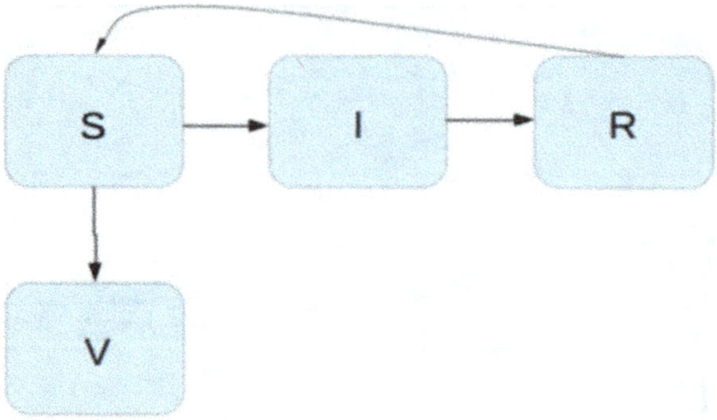


The new, extended differential equations with the $V$ quantity become

$$S' = -\beta SI + \nu R - pS, \tag{8.36}$$

$$V' = pS, \tag{8.37}$$

$$I' = \beta SI - \gamma I, \tag{8.38}$$

$$R' = \gamma I - \nu R\,. \tag{8.39}$$

We shall refer to this model as the SIRV model.

The new equation for $V'$ poses no difficulties when it comes to the numerical method. In a Forward Euler scheme we simply add an update

$$V^{n+1} = V^n + p\Delta t S^n\,.$$

The program needs to store $V(t)$ in an additional array `V`, and the plotting command must be extended with more arguments to plot `V` versus `t` as well. The complete code is found in the file `SIRV1.py`.

Using $p = 0.0005$ and $p = 0.0001$ as values for the vaccine efficiency parameter, the effect of vaccination is seen in Figs. 8.15 and 8.16, respectively. (other parameters are as in Fig. 8.13).

### 8.3.9 Discontinuous Coefficients: A Vaccination Campaign

What about modeling a vaccination campaign? Imagine that 6 days after the outbreak of the disease, the local health station launches a vaccination campaign. They reach out to many people, say 10 times as efficiently as in the previous (constant vaccination) case. If the campaign lasts for 10 days we can write

$$p(t) = \begin{cases} 0.005, & 6\cdot 24 \le t \le 15\cdot 24, \\ 0, & \text{otherwise} \end{cases}$$

Note that we must multiply the $t$ value by 24 because $t$ is measured in hours, not days. In the differential equation system, $pS(t)$ must be replaced by $p(t)S(t)$, and in this case we get a differential equation system with a term that is *discontinuous*. This

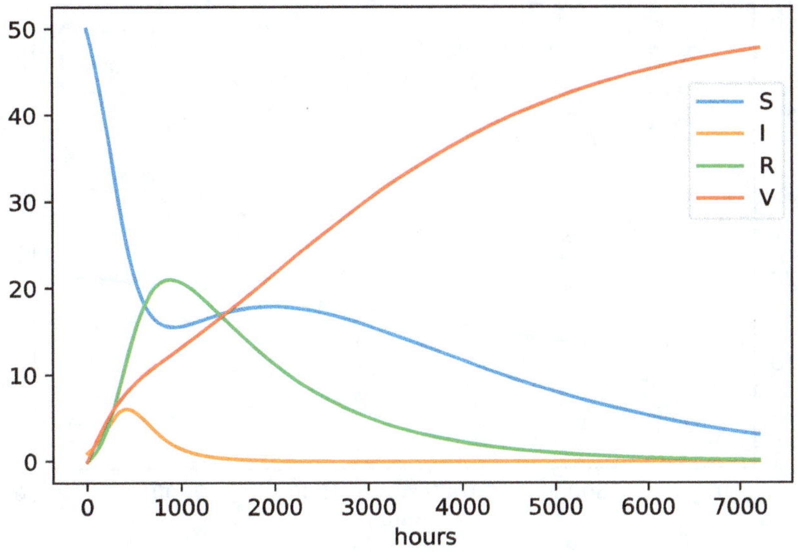


Fig. 8.15 The effect of vaccination: $p = 0.0005$

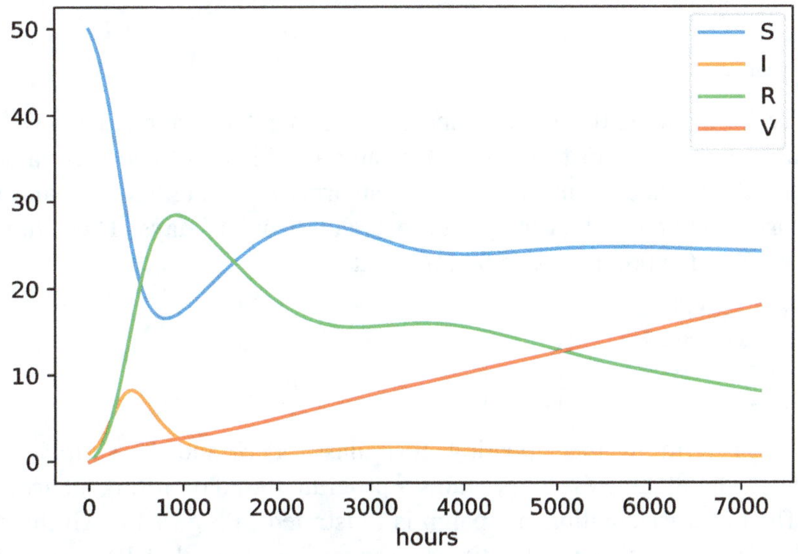


Fig. 8.16 The effect of vaccination: $p = 0.0001$

is usually quite a challenge in mathematics, but as long as we solve the equations numerically in a program, a discontinuous coefficient is easy to treat.

There are two ways to implement the discontinuous coefficient $p(t)$: through a function and through an array. The function approach is perhaps the easiest:

```
def p(t):
    return 0.005 if (6*24 <= t <= 15*24) else 0
```

Note the handy `if-else` construction in the return statement here. It is a one-line alternative to, for example,

```
if (6*24 <= t <= 15*24):
    return 0.005
```

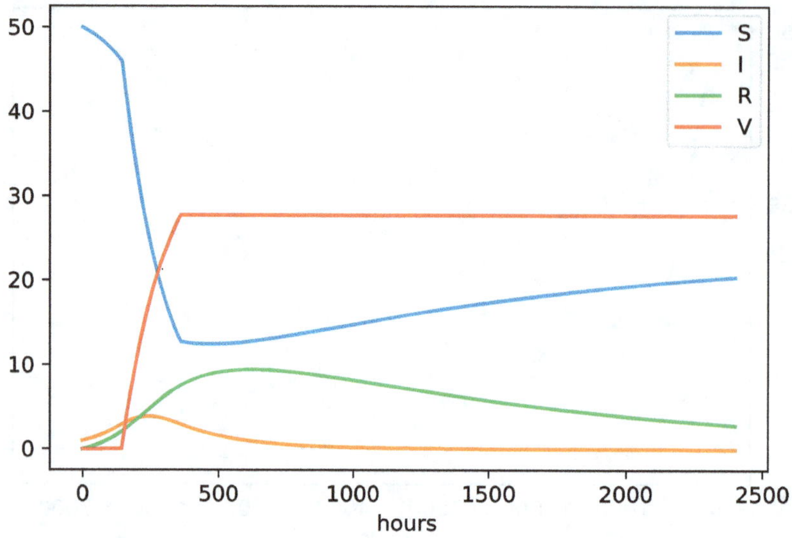


Fig. 8.17 The effect of a vaccination campaign

```
else:
    return 0
```

In the code for updating the arrays S and V, we then get a term p(t[n])*S[n].

Alternatively, we can instead let $p(t)$ be an array filled with correct values prior to the simulation. Then we need to allocate an array p of length N_t+1 and find the indices corresponding to the time period between 6 and 15 days. These indices are found from the time point divided by $\Delta t$. That is,

```
p = zeros(N_t+1)
start_index = 6*24/dt
stop_index = 15*24/dt
p[start_index:stop_index] = 0.005
```

The $p(t)S(t)$ term in the updating formulas for $S$ and $V$ simply becomes p[n]*S[n]. The file SIRV2.py contains a program based on filling an array p.

The effect of a vaccination campaign is illustrated in Fig. 8.17. All the data are as in Fig. 8.15, except that $p$ is ten times stronger for a period of 10 days and $p = 0$ elsewhere.

## 8.4 Oscillating 1D Systems: A Second Order ODE

Numerous engineering constructions and devices contain materials that act like springs. Such springs give rise to oscillations, and controlling oscillations is a key engineering task. We shall now learn to simulate oscillating systems.

As always, we start with the simplest meaningful mathematical model, which for oscillations is a second-order differential equation:

$$u''(t) + \omega^2 u(t) = 0, \tag{8.40}$$

where $\omega$ is a given physical parameter. Equation (8.40) models a one-dimensional system oscillating without damping (i.e., with negligible damping). One-dimensional here means that some motion takes place along one dimension only in some coordinate system. Along with (8.40) we need the two *initial conditions* $u(0)$ and $u'(0)$.

### 8.4.1 Derivation of a Simple Model

Many engineering systems undergo oscillations, and differential equations constitute the key tool to understand, predict, and control the oscillations. We start with the simplest possible model that captures the essential dynamics of an oscillating system. Some body with mass $m$ is attached to a spring and moves along a line without friction, see Fig. 8.18 for a sketch (rolling wheels indicate "no friction"). When the spring is stretched (or compressed), the spring force pulls (or pushes) the body back and work "against" the motion. More precisely, let $x(t)$ be the position of the body on the $x$ axis, along which the body moves. The spring is not stretched when $x = 0$, so the force is zero, and $x = 0$ is hence the equilibrium position of the body. The spring force is $-kx$, where $k$ is a constant to be measured. We assume that there are no other forces (e.g., no friction). Newton's second law of motion $F = ma$ then has $F = -kx$ and $a = \ddot{x}$,

$$-kx = m\ddot{x}, \tag{8.41}$$

which can be rewritten as

$$\ddot{x} + \omega^2 x = 0, \tag{8.42}$$

by introducing $\omega = \sqrt{k/m}$ (which is very common).

Equation (8.42) is a *second-order* differential equation, and therefore we need *two* initial conditions, one on the position $x(0)$ and one on the velocity $x'(0)$. Here

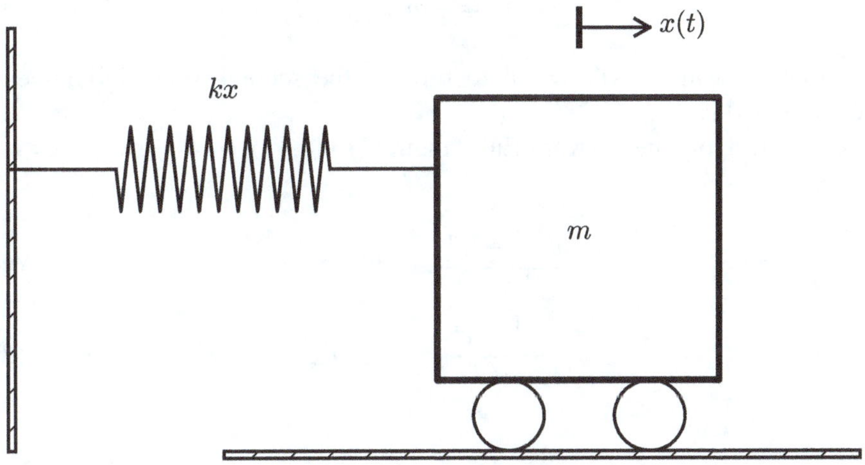


**Fig. 8.18** Sketch of a one-dimensional, oscillating dynamic system (without friction)

we choose the body to be at rest, but moved away from its equilibrium position:

$$x(0) = X_0, \quad x'(0) = 0\,.$$

The exact solution of (8.42) with these initial conditions is $x(t) = X_0 \cos \omega t$. This can easily be verified by substituting into (8.42) and checking the initial conditions. The solution tells us that such a spring-mass system oscillates back and forth as described by a cosine curve.

The differential equation (8.42) appears in numerous other contexts. A classical example is a simple pendulum that oscillates back and forth. Physics books derive, from Newton's second law of motion, that

$$mL\theta'' + mg \sin \theta = 0,$$

where $m$ is the mass of the body at the end of a pendulum with length $L$, $g$ is the acceleration of gravity, and $\theta$ is the angle the pendulum makes with the vertical. Considering small angles $\theta$, $\sin \theta \approx \theta$, and we get (8.42) with $x = \theta$, $\omega = \sqrt{g/L}$, $x(0) = \Theta$, and $x'(0) = 0$, if $\Theta$ is the initial angle and the pendulum is at rest at $t = 0$.

### 8.4.2 Numerical Solution

We have not looked at numerical methods for handling second-order derivatives, and such methods are an option, but we know how to solve first-order differential equations and even systems of first-order equations. With a little, yet very common, trick we can rewrite (8.42) as a first-order system of two differential equations. We introduce $u = x$ and $v = x' = u'$ as *two* new unknown functions. The two corresponding equations arise from the definition $v = u'$ and the original equation (8.42):

$$u' = v, \tag{8.43}$$

$$v' = -\omega^2 u\,. \tag{8.44}$$

(Notice that we can use $u'' = v'$ to remove the second-order derivative from Newton's second law.)

We can now apply the Forward Euler method to (8.43)–(8.44), exactly as we did in Sect. 8.3.2:

$$\frac{u^{n+1} - u^n}{\Delta t} = v^n, \tag{8.45}$$

$$\frac{v^{n+1} - v^n}{\Delta t} = -\omega^2 u^n, \tag{8.46}$$

resulting in the computational scheme

$$u^{n+1} = u^n + \Delta t\, v^n, \tag{8.47}$$

$$v^{n+1} = v^n - \Delta t\, \omega^2 u^n\,. \tag{8.48}$$

### 8.4.3 Programming the FE Scheme; the Special Case

A simple program for (8.47)–(8.48) follows the same ideas as in Sect. 8.3.3:

```
import numpy as np
import matplotlib.pyplot as plt

omega = 2
P = 2*np.pi/omega
dt = P/20
T = 3*P
N_t = int(round(T/dt))
t = np.linspace(0, N_t*dt, N_t+1)

u = np.zeros(N_t+1)
v = np.zeros(N_t+1)

# Initial condition
X_0 = 2
u[0] = X_0
v[0] = 0

# Step equations forward in time
for n in range(N_t):
    u[n+1] = u[n] + dt*v[n]
    v[n+1] = v[n] - dt*omega**2*u[n]

fig = plt.figure()
l1, l2 = plt.plot(t, u, 'b-', t, X_0*np.cos(omega*t), 'r--')
fig.legend((l1, l2), ('numerical', 'exact'), 'upper right')
plt.xlabel('t')
plt.savefig('tmp.pdf'); plt.savefig('tmp.png')
plt.show()
```

(See file `osc_FE.py`.)

Since we already know the exact solution as $u(t) = X_0 \cos \omega t$, we have reasoned as follows to find an appropriate simulation interval $[0, T]$ and also how many points we should choose. The solution has a period $P = 2\pi/\omega$. (The period $P$ is the time difference between two peaks of the $u(t) \sim \cos \omega t$ curve.) Simulating for three periods of the cosine function, $T = 3P$, and choosing $\Delta t$ such that there are 20 intervals per period gives $\Delta t = P/20$ and a total of $N_t = T/\Delta t$ intervals. The rest of the program is a straightforward coding of the Forward Euler scheme.

Figure 8.19 shows a comparison between the numerical solution and the exact solution of the differential equation. To our surprise, the numerical solution looks wrong. Is this discrepancy due to a programming error or a problem with the Forward Euler method?

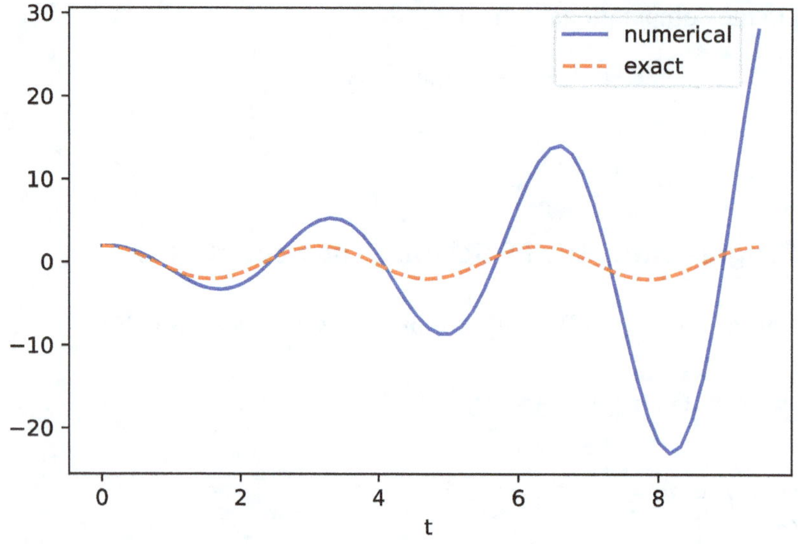


**Fig. 8.19** Simulation of an oscillating system

First of all, even before trying to run the program, you should sit down and compute two steps in the time loop with a calculator so you have some intermediate results to compare with. Using $X_0 = 2$, $dt = 0.157079632679$, and $\omega = 2$, we get $u^1 = 2$, $v^1 = -1.25663706$, $u^2 = 1.80260791$, and $v^2 = -2.51327412$. Such calculations show that the program is seemingly correct. (Later, we can use such values to construct a unit test and a corresponding test function.)

The next step is to reduce the discretization parameter $\Delta t$ and see if the results become more accurate. Figure 8.20 shows the numerical and exact solution for the cases $\Delta t = P/40, P/160, P/2000$. The results clearly become better, and the finest resolution gives graphs that cannot be visually distinguished. Nevertheless, the finest resolution involves 6000 computational intervals in total, which is considered quite much. This is no problem on a modern laptop, however, as the computations take just a fraction of a second.

Although 2000 intervals per oscillation period seem sufficient for an accurate numerical solution, the lower right graph in Fig. 8.20 shows that if we increase the simulation time, here to 20 periods, there is a little growth of the amplitude, which becomes significant over time. The conclusion is that the Forward Euler method has a fundamental problem with its growing amplitudes, and that a very small $\Delta t$ is required to achieve satisfactory results. The longer the simulation is, the smaller $\Delta t$ has to be. It is certainly time to look for more effective numerical methods!

### 8.4.4 A Magic Fix of the Numerical Method

In the Forward Euler scheme,

$$
\begin{aligned}
u^{n+1} &= u^n + \Delta t\, v^n, \\
v^{n+1} &= v^n - \Delta t\, \omega^2 u^n,
\end{aligned}
$$

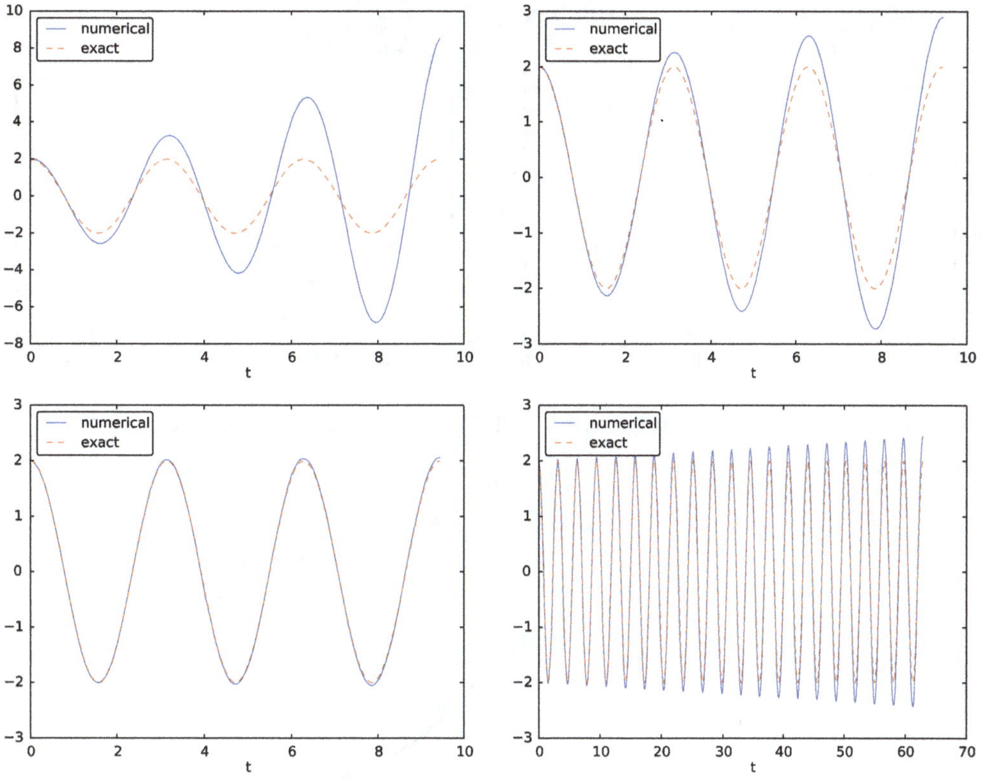


Fig. 8.20 Simulation of an oscillating system with different time steps. Upper left: 40 steps per oscillation period. Upper right: 160 steps per period. Lower left: 2000 steps per period. Lower right: 2000 steps per period, but longer simulation

we can replace $u^n$ in the last equation by the recently computed value $u^{n+1}$ from the first equation:

$$u^{n+1} = u^n + \Delta t\, v^n, \tag{8.49}$$

$$v^{n+1} = v^n - \Delta t\, \omega^2 u^{n+1}. \tag{8.50}$$

Before justifying this fix more mathematically, let us try it on the previous example. The results appear in Fig. 8.21. We see that the amplitude *does not grow*, but the phase is not entirely correct. After 40 periods (Fig. 8.21 right) we see a significant difference between the numerical and the exact solution. Decreasing $\Delta t$ decreases the error. For example, with 2000 intervals per period, we only see a small phase error even after 50,000 periods (!). We can safely conclude that the fix results in an excellent numerical method!

Let us interpret the adjusted scheme mathematically. First we order (8.49)–(8.50) such that the difference approximations to derivatives become transparent:

$$\frac{u^{n+1} - u^n}{\Delta t} = v^n, \tag{8.51}$$

$$\frac{v^{n+1} - v^n}{\Delta t} = -\omega^2 u^{n+1}. \tag{8.52}$$

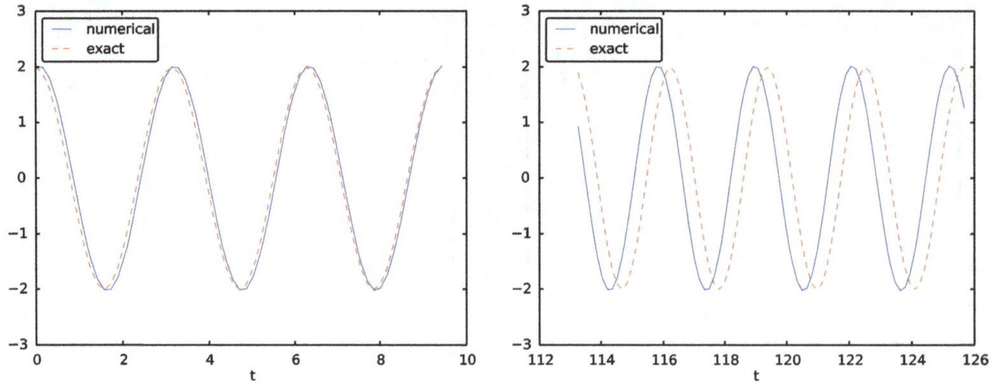


**Fig. 8.21** Adjusted method: first three periods (left) and period 36–40 (right)

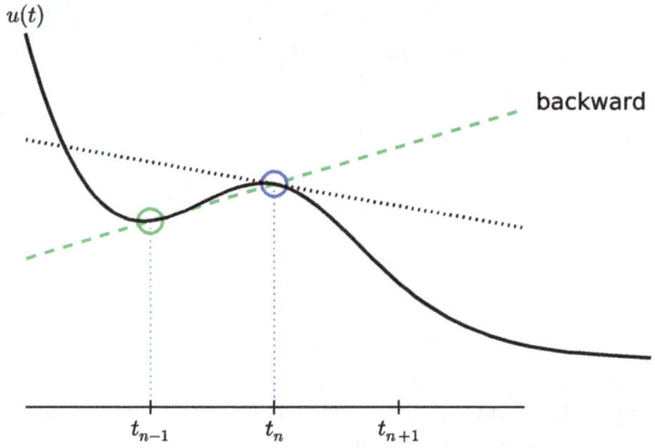


**Fig. 8.22** Illustration of a backward difference approximation to the derivative

We interpret (8.51) as the differential equation sampled at mesh point $t_n$, because we have $v^n$ on the right-hand side. The left-hand side is then a *forward difference* or Forward Euler approximation to the derivative $u'$, see Fig. 8.4. On the other hand, we interpret (8.52) as the differential equation sampled at mesh point $t_{n+1}$, since we have $u^{n+1}$ on the right-hand side. In this case, the difference approximation on the left-hand side is a *backward difference*,

$$v'(t_{n+1}) \approx \frac{v^{n+1} - v^n}{\Delta t} \quad \text{or} \quad v'(t_n) \approx \frac{v^n - v^{n-1}}{\Delta t} .$$

Figure 8.22 illustrates the backward difference. The error in the backward difference is proportional to $\Delta t$, the same as for the forward difference (but the proportionality constant in the error term has different sign). The resulting discretization method, seen in (8.52), is often referred to as a Backward Euler scheme (a first-order scheme, just like Forward Euler).

To summarize, using a forward difference for the first equation and a backward difference for the second equation results in a much better method than just using forward differences in both equations.

The standard way of expressing this scheme in physics is to change the order of the equations,

$$v' = -\omega^2 u, \tag{8.53}$$

$$u' = v, \tag{8.54}$$

and apply a forward difference to (8.53) and a backward difference to (8.54):

$$v^{n+1} = v^n - \Delta t\, \omega^2 u^n, \tag{8.55}$$

$$u^{n+1} = u^n + \Delta t\, v^{n+1}\,. \tag{8.56}$$

That is, first the velocity $v$ is updated and then the position $u$, using the most recently computed velocity. There is no difference between (8.55)–(8.56) and (8.49)–(8.50) with respect to accuracy, so how you order the original differential equations does not matter. The scheme (8.55)–(8.56) goes by the name Semi-implicit Euler,[5] or Euler-Cromer (a first-order method). The implementation of (8.55)–(8.56) is found in the file `osc_EC.py`. The core of the code goes like

```
u = zeros(N_t+1)
v = zeros(N_t+1)

# Initial condition
u[0] = 2
v[0] = 0

# Step equations forward in time
for n in range(N_t):
    v[n+1] = v[n] - dt*omega**2*u[n]
    u[n+1] = u[n] + dt*v[n+1]
```

**Explicit and implicit methods**

When we solve an ODE (linear or nonlinear) by the Forward Euler method, we get an explicit updating formula for the unknown at each time step, see, e.g., (8.6). Methods with this characteristic are known as *explicit*. We also have *implicit* methods. In that case, one or more algebraic equations must typically be solved for each time step. The Backward Euler method, for example, is such an implicit method (you will realize that when you do Exercise 8.24).

### 8.4.5 The Second-Order Runge-Kutta Method (or Heun's Method)

A very popular method for solving scalar and vector ODEs of first order is the second-order Runge-Kutta method (RK2), also known as Heun's method. The idea,

[5] http://en.wikipedia.org/wiki/Semi-implicit_Euler_method.

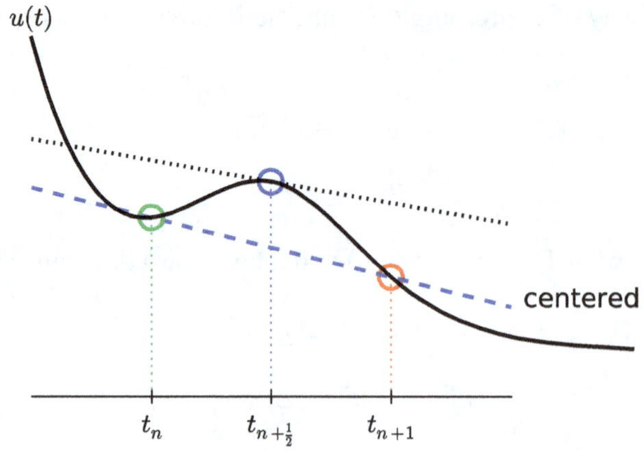


Fig. 8.23 Illustration of a centered difference approximation to the derivative

first thinking of a scalar ODE, is to form a *centered difference* approximation to the derivative between two time points:

$$u'(t_n + \frac{1}{2}\Delta t) \approx \frac{u^{n+1} - u^n}{\Delta t}.$$

The centered difference formula is visualized in Fig. 8.23. The error in the centered difference is proportional to $\Delta t^2$, one order higher than the forward and backward differences, which means that if we halve $\Delta t$, the error is more effectively reduced in the centered difference since it is reduced by a factor of four rather than two.

The problem with such a centered scheme for the general ODE $u' = f(u, t)$ is that we get

$$\frac{u^{n+1} - u^n}{\Delta t} = f(u^{n+\frac{1}{2}}, t_{n+\frac{1}{2}}),$$

which leads to difficulties since we do not know what $u^{n+\frac{1}{2}}$ is. However, we can approximate the value of $f$ between two time levels by the arithmetic average of the values at $t_n$ and $t_{n+1}$:

$$f(u^{n+\frac{1}{2}}, t_{n+\frac{1}{2}}) \approx \frac{1}{2}(f(u^n, t_n) + f(u^{n+1}, t_{n+1})).$$

This results in

$$\frac{u^{n+1} - u^n}{\Delta t} = \frac{1}{2}(f(u^n, t_n) + f(u^{n+1}, t_{n+1})),$$

which in general is a *nonlinear algebraic equation* for $u^{n+1}$ if $f(u, t)$ is not a linear function of $u$. To deal with the unknown term $f(u^{n+1}, t_{n+1})$, without solving nonlinear equations, we can approximate or predict $u^{n+1}$ using a Forward Euler step:

$$u^{n+1} = u^n + \Delta t f(u^n, t_n)\,.$$

This reasoning gives rise to the method

$$u^* = u^n + \Delta t f(u^n, t_n), \tag{8.57}$$

$$u^{n+1} = u^n + \frac{\Delta t}{2}(f(u^n, t_n) + f(u^*, t_{n+1}))\,. \tag{8.58}$$

The scheme applies to both scalar and vector ODEs.

For an oscillating system with $f = (v, -\omega^2 u)$ the file `osc_Heun.py` implements this method. The `demo` function in that file runs the simulation for 10 periods with 20 time steps per period. The corresponding numerical and exact solutions are shown in Fig. 8.24. We see that the amplitude grows, but not as much as for the Forward Euler method. However, the Euler-Cromer method performs better!

We should add that in problems where the Forward Euler method gives satisfactory approximations, such as growth/decay problems or the SIR model, the second-order Runge-Kutta method (Heun's method) usually works considerably better and produces greater accuracy for the same computational cost. It is therefore a very valuable method to be aware of, although it cannot compete with the Euler-Cromer scheme for oscillation problems. The derivation of the RK2/Heun scheme is also good general training in "numerical thinking".

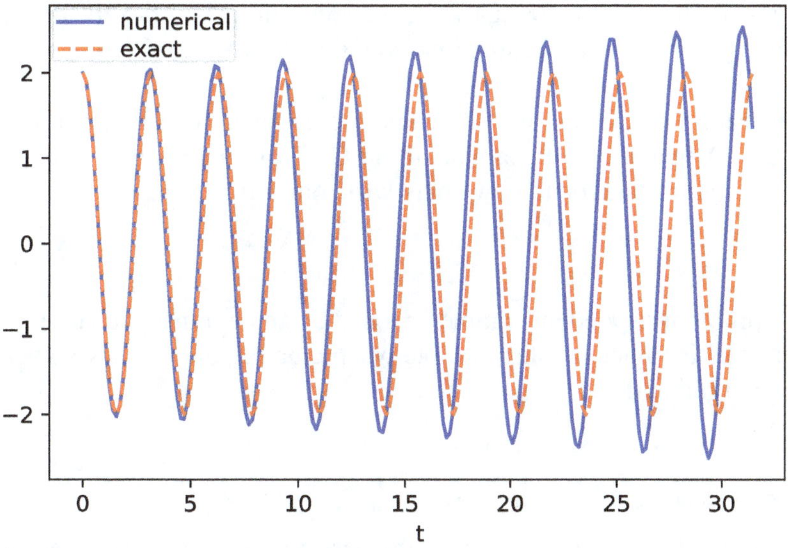


Fig. 8.24 Simulation of 10 periods of oscillations by Heun's method

### 8.4.6 Software for Solving ODEs

There is a jungle of methods for solving ODEs, and it would be nice to have easy access to implementations of a wide range of methods, especially the sophisticated and complicated *adaptive* methods that adjust $\Delta t$ automatically to obtain a prescribed accuracy. The Python package `Odespy` (https://github.com/thomasantony/odespy/tree/py36/odespy) gives easy access to a lot of numerical methods for ODEs.

**Odespy: Example with Exponential Growth** The simplest possible example on using Odespy is to solve $u' = u$, $u(0) = 2$, for 100 time steps until $t = 4$:

```
import odespy
import numpy as np
import matplotlib.pyplot as plt

def f(u, t):
    return u

method = odespy.Heun          # or, e.g., odespy.ForwardEuler
solver = method(f)
solver.set_initial_condition(2)
time_points = np.linspace(0, 4, 101)
u, t = solver.solve(time_points)
plt.plot(t, u)
plt.show()
```

In other words, you define your right-hand side function `f(u, t)`, initialize an Odespy `solver` object, set the initial condition, compute a collection of time points where you want the solution, and ask for the solution. If you run the code, you get the expected plot of the exponential function (not shown).

A nice feature of Odespy is that problem parameters can be arguments to the user's `f(u, t)` function. For example, if our ODE problem is $u' = -au + b$, with two problem parameters $a$ and $b$, we may write our `f` function as

```
def f(u, t, a, b):
    return -a*u + b
```

The extra, problem-dependent arguments `a` and `b` can be transferred to this function if we collect their values in a list or tuple when creating the Odespy solver and use the `f_args` argument:

```
a = 2
b = 1
solver = method(f, f_args=[a, b])
```

This is a good feature because problem parameters must otherwise be global variables—now they can be arguments in our right-hand side function in a natural way. Exercise 8.21 asks you to make a complete implementation of this problem and plot the solution.

**Odespy: Example with Oscillations** Using Odespy to solve oscillation ODEs like $u'' + \omega^2 u = 0$, reformulated as a system $u' = v$ and $v' = -\omega^2 u$, can be done with the following code:

```
import odespy
import numpy as np
import matplotlib.pyplot as plt

# Define the ODE system
# u' = v
# v' = -omega**2*u

def f(sol, t, omega=2):
    u, v = sol
    return [v, -omega**2*u]

# Set and compute problem dependent parameters
omega = 2
X_0 = 1
number_of_periods = 40
time_steps_per_period = 20
P = 2*np.pi/omega                      # length of one period
dt = P/time_steps_per_period           # time step
T = number_of_periods*P                # final simulation time

# Create Odespy solver object
odespy_method = odespy.RK2
solver = odespy_method(f, f_args=[omega])

# The initial condition for the system is collected in a list
solver.set_initial_condition([X_0, 0])

# Compute the desired time points where we want the solution
N_t = int(round(T/dt))                 # no of time intervals
time_points = np.linspace(0, T, N_t+1)

# Solve the ODE problem
sol, t = solver.solve(time_points)

# Note: sol contains both displacement and velocity
# Extract original variables
u = sol[:,0]
v = sol[:,1]

plt.plot(t, u, t, v)  # ...for a quick check on u and v
plt.show()
```

After specifying the number of periods to simulate, as well as the number of time steps per period, we compute the time step (`dt`) and simulation end time (`T`).

The two statements `u = sol[:,0]` and `v = sol[:,1]` are important, since our two functions $u$ and $v$ in the ODE system are packed together in one array inside the Odespy solver (the solution of the ODE system is returned from `solver.solve` as a two-dimensional array where the first column (`sol[:,0]`) stores $u$ and the second (`sol[:,1]`) stores $v$).

**Remark**

In the right-hand side function we write `f(sol, t, omega)` instead of `f(u, t, omega)` to indicate that the solution sent to `f` is a solution at time `t` where the values of $u$ and $v$ are packed together: `sol = [u, v]`. We might well use `u` as argument:

```
def f(u, t, omega=2):
    u, v = u
    return [v, -omega**2*u]
```

This just means that we redefine the name `u` inside the function to mean the solution at time `t` for the first component of the ODE system.

To switch to another numerical method, just substitute `RK2` by the proper name of the desired method. Typing `pydoc odespy` in the terminal window brings up a list of all the implemented methods. This very simple way of choosing a method suggests an obvious extension of the code above: we can define a list of methods, run all methods, and compare their $u$ curves in a plot. As Odespy also contains the Euler-Cromer scheme, we rewrite the system with $v' = -\omega^2 u$ as the first ODE and $u' = v$ as the second ODE, because this is the standard choice when using the Euler-Cromer method (also in Odespy):

```
def f(u, t, omega=2):
    v, u = u
    return [-omega**2*u, v]
```

This change of equations also affects the initial condition: the first component is zero and second is `X_0`, so we need to pass the list `[0, X_0]` to `solver.set_initial_condition`.

The function `compare` in `osc_odespy.py` contains the details:

```
def compare(odespy_methods,
            omega,
            X_0,
            number_of_periods,
            time_intervals_per_period=20):

    P = 2*np.pi/omega                     # length of one period
    dt = P/time_intervals_per_period
    T = number_of_periods*P

    # If odespy_methods is not a list, but just the name of
    # a single Odespy solver, we wrap that name in a list
    # so we always have odespy_methods as a list
    if type(odespy_methods) != type([]):
        odespy_methods = [odespy_methods]

    # Make a list of solver objects
    solvers = [method(f, f_args=[omega]) for method in
               odespy_methods]
    for solver in solvers:
        solver.set_initial_condition([0, X_0])
```

```
    # Compute the time points where we want the solution
    N_t = int(round(T/dt))
    time_points = np.linspace(0, N_t*dt, N_t+1)

    legends = []
    for solver in solvers:
        sol, t = solver.solve(time_points)
        v = sol[:,0]
        u = sol[:,1]

        # Plot only the last p periods
        p = 6
        m = p*time_intervals_per_period  # no time steps to plot
        plt.plot(t[-m:], u[-m:])
        plt.hold('on')
        legends.append(solver.name())
        plt.xlabel('t')
    # Plot exact solution too
    plt.plot(t[-m:], X_0*np.cos(omega*t)[-m:], 'k--')
    legends.append('exact')
    plt.legend(legends, loc='lower left')
    plt.axis([t[-m], t[-1], -2*X_0, 2*X_0])
    plt.title('Simulation of {:d} periods with {:d} intervals per period'\
              .format(number_of_periods, time_intervals_per_period))
    plt.savefig('tmp.pdf'); plt.savefig('tmp.png')
    plt.show()
```

A new feature in this code is the ability to plot only the last p periods, which allows us to perform long time simulations and watch the end results without a cluttered plot with too many periods. The syntax `t[-m:]` plots the last `m` elements in `t` (a negative index in Python arrays/lists counts from the end).

We may compare Heun's method (i.e., the RK2 method) with the Euler-Cromer scheme:

```
compare(odespy_methods=[odespy.Heun, odespy.EulerCromer],
        omega=2, X_0=2, number_of_periods=20,
        time_intervals_per_period=20)
```

Figure 8.25 shows how Heun's method (blue line) has considerable error in both amplitude and phase already after 14–20 periods (upper left), but using three times as many time steps makes the curves almost equal (upper right). However, after 194–200 periods the errors have grown (lower left), but can be sufficiently reduced by halving the time step (lower right).

With all the methods in Odespy at hand, it is now easy to start exploring other methods, such as backward differences instead of the forward differences used in the Forward Euler scheme. Exercise 8.22 addresses that problem.

Odespy contains quite sophisticated adaptive methods where the user is "guaranteed" to get a solution with prescribed accuracy. There is no mathematical guarantee, but the error will for most cases not deviate significantly from the user's tolerance that reflects the accuracy. A very popular method of this type is the Runge-Kutta-Fehlberg method, which runs a fourth-order Runge-Kutta method and uses a fifth-order Runge-Kutta method to estimate the error so that $\Delta t$ can be adjusted to keep the error below a tolerance. This method is also widely known as `ode45`, because that is the name of the function implementing the method in Matlab. We can

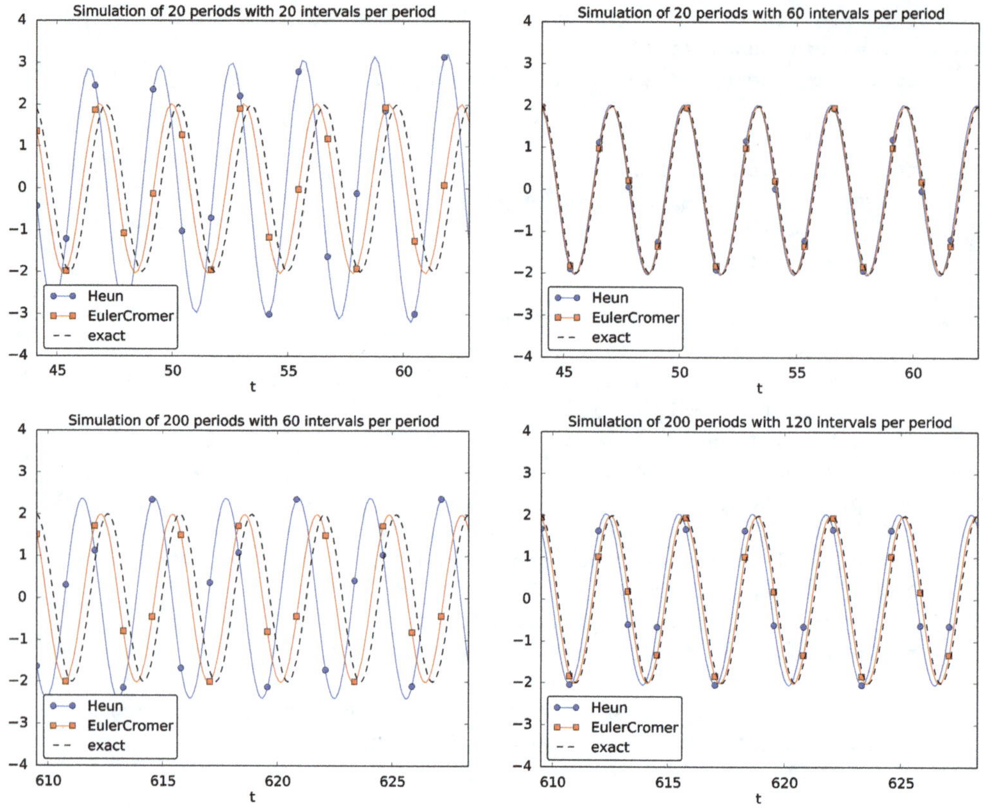


Fig. 8.25 Illustration of the impact of resolution (time steps per period) and length of simulation

easily test the Runge-Kutta-Fehlberg method as soon as we know the corresponding Odespy name, which is `RKFehlberg`:

```
compare(odespy_methods=[odespy.EulerCromer, odespy.RKFehlberg],
        omega=2, X_0=2, number_of_periods=200,
        time_intervals_per_period=40)
```

Note that the `time_intervals_per_period` argument refers to the time points where we want the solution. These points are also the ones used for numerical computations in the `odespy.EulerCromer` solver, while the `odespy.RKFehlberg` solver will use an unknown set of time points since the time intervals are adjusted as the method runs. One can easily look at the points actually used by the method as these are available as an array `solver.t_all` (but plotting or examining the points requires modifications inside the `compare` method).

Figure 8.26 shows a computational example where the Runge-Kutta-Fehlberg method is clearly superior to the Euler-Cromer scheme in long time simulations, but the comparison is not really fair because the Runge-Kutta-Fehlberg method applies about twice as many time steps in this computation and performs much more work per time step. It is quite a complicated task to compare two so different methods in a fair way so that the computational work versus accuracy is scientifically well reported.

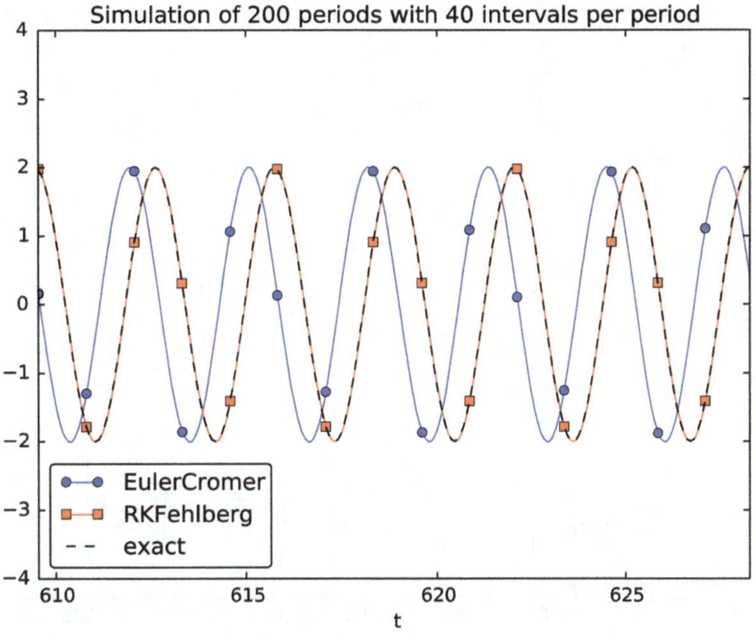


Fig. 8.26 Comparison of the Runge-Kutta-Fehlberg adaptive method against the Euler-Cromer scheme for a long time simulation (200 periods)

### 8.4.7 The Fourth-Order Runge-Kutta Method

The fourth-order Runge-Kutta method (RK4) is clearly the most widely used method to solve ODEs. Its power comes from high accuracy even with not so small time steps.

**The Algorithm** We first just state the four-stage algorithm:

$$u^{n+1} = u^n + \frac{\Delta t}{6}\left(f^n + 2\hat{f}^{n+\frac{1}{2}} + 2\tilde{f}^{n+\frac{1}{2}} + \bar{f}^{n+1}\right), \tag{8.59}$$

where

$$\hat{f}^{n+\frac{1}{2}} = f(u^n + \frac{1}{2}\Delta t f^n, t_{n+\frac{1}{2}}), \tag{8.60}$$

$$\tilde{f}^{n+\frac{1}{2}} = f(u^n + \frac{1}{2}\Delta t \hat{f}^{n+\frac{1}{2}}, t_{n+\frac{1}{2}}), \tag{8.61}$$

$$\bar{f}^{n+1} = f(u^n + \Delta t \tilde{f}^{n+\frac{1}{2}}, t_{n+1}). \tag{8.62}$$

**Application** We can run the same simulation as in Figs. 8.19, 8.21, and 8.24, for 40 periods. The 10 last periods are shown in Fig. 8.27. The results look as impressive as those of the Euler-Cromer method.

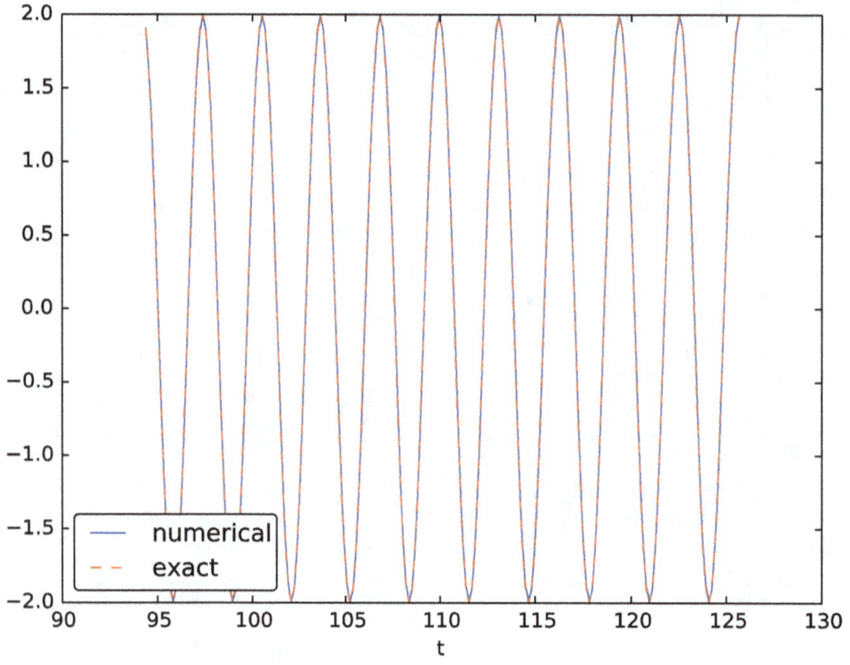


Fig. 8.27 The last 10 of 40 periods of oscillations by the fourth-order Runge-Kutta method

**Implementation** The stages in the fourth-order Runge-Kutta method can easily be implemented as a modification of the `osc_Heun.py` code. Alternatively, one can use the `osc_odespy.py` code by just providing the argument `odespy_methods=[odespy.RK4]` to the `compare` function.

**Derivation** The derivation of the fourth-order Runge-Kutta method can be presented in a pedagogical way that brings many fundamental elements of numerical discretization techniques together. It also illustrates many aspects of the "numerical thinking" required for constructing approximate solution methods.

We start with integrating the general ODE $u' = f(u, t)$ over a time step, from $t_n$ to $t_{n+1}$,

$$u(t_{n+1}) - u(t_n) = \int_{t_n}^{t_{n+1}} f(u(t), t)dt\,.$$

The goal of the computation is $u(t_{n+1})$ (written $u^{n+1}$), while $u(t_n)$ (written $u^n$) is the most recently known value of $u$. The challenge with the integral is that the integrand involves the unknown $u$ between $t_n$ and $t_{n+1}$.

The integral can be approximated by the famous Simpson's rule[6]:

$$\int_{t_n}^{t_{n+1}} f(u(t), t)dt \approx \frac{\Delta t}{6}\left(f^n + 4f^{n+\frac{1}{2}} + f^{n+1}\right).$$

The problem with this formula is that we do not know $f^{n+\frac{1}{2}} = f(u^{n+\frac{1}{2}}, t_{n+\frac{1}{2}})$ and $f^{n+1} = (u^{n+1}, t_{n+1})$ as only $u^n$ is available and only $f^n$ can then readily be computed.

To proceed, the idea is to use various approximations for $f^{n+\frac{1}{2}}$ and $f^{n+1}$ based on using well-known schemes for the ODE in the intervals $[t_n, t_{n+\frac{1}{2}}]$ and $[t_n, t_{n+1}]$. Let us split the integral into four terms:

$$\int_{t_n}^{t_{n+1}} f(u(t), t)dt \approx \frac{\Delta t}{6}\left(f^n + 2\hat{f}^{n+\frac{1}{2}} + 2\tilde{f}^{n+\frac{1}{2}} + \bar{f}^{n+1}\right),$$

where $\hat{f}^{n+\frac{1}{2}}$, $\tilde{f}^{n+\frac{1}{2}}$, and $\bar{f}^{n+1}$ are approximations to $f^{n+\frac{1}{2}}$ and $f^{n+1}$ that can utilize already computed quantities. For $\hat{f}^{n+\frac{1}{2}}$ we can simply apply an approximation to $u^{n+\frac{1}{2}}$ based on a Forward Euler step of size $\frac{1}{2}\Delta t$:

$$\hat{f}^{n+\frac{1}{2}} = f(u^n + \frac{1}{2}\Delta t f^n, t_{n+\frac{1}{2}}) \tag{8.63}$$

This formula provides a prediction of $f^{n+\frac{1}{2}}$, so we can for $\tilde{f}^{n+\frac{1}{2}}$ try a Backward Euler method to approximate $u^{n+\frac{1}{2}}$:

$$\tilde{f}^{n+\frac{1}{2}} = f(u^n + \frac{1}{2}\Delta t \hat{f}^{n+\frac{1}{2}}, t_{n+\frac{1}{2}}). \tag{8.64}$$

With $\tilde{f}^{n+\frac{1}{2}}$ as an approximation to $f^{n+\frac{1}{2}}$, we can for the final term $\bar{f}^{n+1}$ use a midpoint method (or central difference, also called a Crank-Nicolson method) to approximate $u^{n+1}$:

$$\bar{f}^{n+1} = f(u^n + \Delta t \hat{f}^{n+\frac{1}{2}}, t_{n+1}). \tag{8.65}$$

We have now used the Forward and Backward Euler methods as well as the centered difference approximation in the context of Simpson's rule. The hope is that the combination of these methods yields an overall time-stepping scheme from $t_n$ to $t_n$+1 that is much more accurate than the individual steps which have errors proportional to $\Delta t$ and $\Delta t^2$. This is indeed true: the numerical error goes in fact like $C\Delta t^4$ for a constant $C$, which means that the error approaches zero very quickly as we reduce the time step size, compared to the Forward Euler method (error $\sim \Delta t$),

6 http://en.wikipedia.org/wiki/Simpson's_rule.

the Euler-Cromer method (error $\sim \Delta t$) or the second-order Runge-Kutta, or Heun's, method (error $\sim \Delta t^2$).

Note that the fourth-order Runge-Kutta method is fully explicit so there is never any need to solve linear or nonlinear algebraic equations, regardless of what $f$ looks like. However, the stability is conditional and depends on $f$. There is a large family of *implicit* Runge-Kutta methods that are unconditionally stable, but require solution of algebraic equations involving $f$ at each time step. The Odespy package has support for a lot of sophisticated *explicit* Runge-Kutta methods, but not yet implicit Runge-Kutta methods.

### 8.4.8 More Effects: Damping, Nonlinearity, and External Forces

Our model problem $u'' + \omega^2 u = 0$ is the simplest possible mathematical model for oscillating systems. Nevertheless, this model makes strong demands to numerical methods, as we have seen, and is very useful as a benchmark for evaluating the performance of numerical methods.

Real-life applications involve more physical effects, which lead to a differential equation with more terms and also more complicated terms. Typically, one has a damping force $f(u')$ and a spring force $s(u)$. Both these forces may depend nonlinearly on their argument, $u'$ or $u$. In addition, environmental forces $F(t)$ may act on the system. For example, the classical pendulum has a nonlinear "spring" or restoring force $s(u) \sim \sin(u)$, and air resistance on the pendulum leads to a damping force $f(u') \sim |u'|u'$. Examples on environmental forces include shaking of the ground (e.g., due to an earthquake) as well as forces from waves and wind.

With three types of forces on the system: $F$, $f$, and $s$, the sum of forces is written $F(t) - f(u') - s(u)$. Note the minus sign in front of $f$ and $s$, which indicates that these functions are defined such that they represent forces acting *against* the motion. For example, springs attached to the wheels in a car are combined with effective dampers, each providing a damping force $f(u') = bu'$ that acts against the spring velocity $u'$. The corresponding physical force is then $-f$: $-bu'$, which points downwards when the spring is being stretched (and $u'$ points upwards), while $-f$ acts upwards when the spring is being compressed (and $u'$ points downwards).

Figure 8.28 shows an example of a mass $m$ attached to a potentially nonlinear spring and dashpot, and subject to an environmental force $F(t)$. Nevertheless, our general model can equally well be a pendulum as in Fig. 8.29 with $s(u) = mg\sin\theta$ and $f(\dot{u}) = \frac{1}{2}C_D A\varrho\dot{\theta}|\dot{\theta}|$ (where $C_D = 0.4$, $A$ is the cross sectional area of the body, and $\varrho$ is the density of air).

Newton's second law for the system can be written with mass times acceleration on the left-hand side and the forces on the right-hand side:

$$mu'' = F(t) - f(u') - s(u)\,.$$

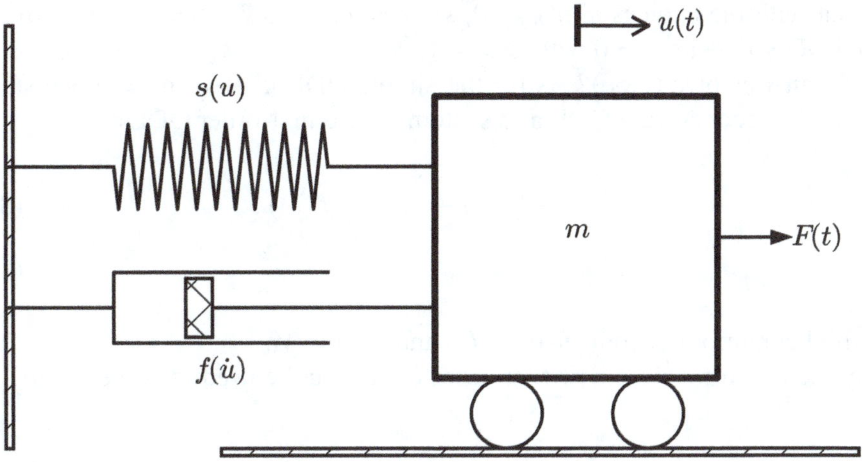


Fig. 8.28 General oscillating system

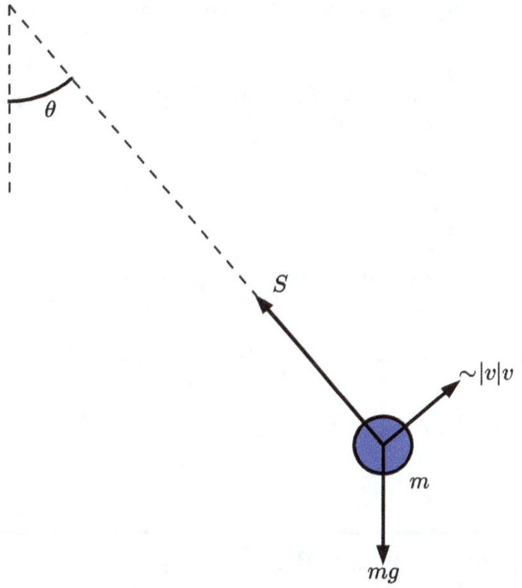


Fig. 8.29 A pendulum with forces

This equation is, however, more commonly reordered to

$$mu'' + f(u') + s(u) = F(t) \,. \tag{8.66}$$

Because the differential equation is of second order, due to the term $u''$, we need two initial conditions:

$$u(0) = U_0, \quad u'(0) = V_0 \,. \tag{8.67}$$

Note that with the choices $f(u') = 0$, $s(u) = ku$, and $F(t) = 0$ we recover the original ODE $u'' + \omega^2 u = 0$ with $\omega = \sqrt{k/m}$.

How can we solve (8.66)? As for the simple ODE $u'' + \omega^2 u = 0$, we start by rewriting the second-order ODE as a system of two first-order ODEs:

$$v' = \frac{1}{m}\left(F(t) - s(u) - f(v)\right), \tag{8.68}$$

$$u' = v\,. \tag{8.69}$$

The initial conditions become $u(0) = U_0$ and $v(0) = V_0$.

Any method for a system of first-order ODEs can be used to solve for $u(t)$ and $v(t)$.

**The Euler-Cromer Scheme** An attractive choice from an implementational, accuracy, and efficiency point of view is the Euler-Cromer scheme where we take a forward difference in (8.68) and a backward difference in (8.69):

$$\frac{v^{n+1} - v^n}{\Delta t} = \frac{1}{m}\left(F(t_n) - s(u^n) - f(v^n)\right), \tag{8.70}$$

$$\frac{u^{n+1} - u^n}{\Delta t} = v^{n+1}, \tag{8.71}$$

We can easily solve for the new unknowns $v^{n+1}$ and $u^{n+1}$:

$$v^{n+1} = v^n + \frac{\Delta t}{m}\left(F(t_n) - s(u^n) - f(v^n)\right), \tag{8.72}$$

$$u^{n+1} = u^n + \Delta t v^{n+1}\,. \tag{8.73}$$

**Remark on the ordering of the ODEs**

The ordering of the ODEs in the ODE system is important for the extended model (8.68)–(8.69). Imagine that we write the equation for $u'$ first and then the one for $v'$. The Euler-Cromer method would then first use a forward difference for $u^{n+1}$ and then a backward difference for $v^{n+1}$. The latter would lead to a *nonlinear* algebraic equation for $v^{n+1}$,

$$v^{n+1} + \frac{\Delta t}{m} f(v^{n+1}) = v^n + \frac{\Delta t}{m}\left(F(t_{n+1}) - s(u^{n+1})\right),$$

if $f(v)$ is a nonlinear function of $v$. This would require a numerical method for nonlinear algebraic equations to find $v^{n+1}$, while updating $v^{n+1}$ through a forward difference gives an equation for $v^{n+1}$ that is linear and trivial to solve by hand.

The file `osc_EC_general.py` has a function `EulerCromer` that implements this method:

```
def EulerCromer(f, s, F, m, T, U_0, V_0, dt):
    import numpy as np
    N_t = int(round(T/dt))
    print('N_t:', N_t)
    t = np.linspace(0, N_t*dt, N_t+1)

    u = np.zeros(N_t+1)
    v = np.zeros(N_t+1)

    # Initial condition
    u[0] = U_0
    v[0] = V_0

    # Step equations forward in time
    for n in range(N_t):
        v[n+1] = v[n] + dt*(1./m)*(F(t[n]) - f(v[n]) - s(u[n]))
        u[n+1] = u[n] + dt*v[n+1]
    return u, v, t
```

**The Fourth Order Runge-Kutta Method** The RK4 method just evaluates the right-hand side of the ODE system,

$$(\frac{1}{m}(F(t) - s(u) - f(v)), v)$$

for known values of $u$, $v$, and $t$, so the method is very simple to use regardless of how the functions $s(u)$ and $f(v)$ are chosen.

### 8.4.9 Illustration of Linear Damping

We consider an engineering system with a linear spring, $s(u) = kx$, and a viscous damper, where the damping force is proportional to $u'$, $f(u') = bu'$, for some constant $b > 0$. This choice may model the vertical spring system in a car (but engineers often like to illustrate such a system by a horizontally moving mass, like the one depicted in Fig. 8.28). We may choose simple values for the constants to illustrate basic effects of damping (and later excitations). Choosing the oscillations to be the simple $u(t) = \cos t$ function in the undamped case, we may set $m = 1$, $k = 1$, $b = 0.3$, $U_0 = 1$, $V_0 = 0$. The following function implements this case:

```
def linear_damping():
    import numpy as np
    b = 0.3
    f = lambda v: b*v
    s = lambda u: k*u
    F = lambda t: 0

    m = 1
    k = 1
```

```
U_0 = 1
V_0 = 0

T = 12*np.pi
dt = T/5000.

u, v, t = EulerCromer(f=f, s=s, F=F, m=m, T=T,
                      U_0=U_0, V_0=V_0, dt=dt)
plot_u(u, t)
```

The `plot_u` function is a collection of plot commands for plotting $u(t)$, or a part of it. Figure 8.30 shows the effect of the $bu'$ term: we have oscillations with (an approximate) period $2\pi$, as expected, but the amplitude is efficiently damped.

**Remark about working with a scaled problem**

Instead of setting $b = 0.3$ and $m = k = U_0 = 1$ as fairly "unlikely" physical values, it would be better to *scale* the equation $mu'' + bu' + ku = 0$. This means that we introduce dimensionless independent and dependent variables:

$$\bar{t} = \frac{t}{t_c}, \quad \bar{u} = \frac{u}{u_c},$$

where $t_c$ and $u_c$ are characteristic sizes of time and displacement, respectively, such that $\bar{t}$ and $\bar{u}$ have their typical size around unity (which minimizes rounding errors). In the present problem, we can choose $u_c = U_0$ and $t_c = \sqrt{m/k}$. This gives the following scaled (or dimensionless) problem for the dimensionless quantity $\bar{u}(\bar{t})$:

$$\frac{d^2\bar{u}}{d\bar{t}^2} + \beta\frac{d\bar{u}}{d\bar{t}} + \bar{u} = 0, \quad \bar{u}(0) = 1,\ \bar{u}'(0) = 0, \quad \beta = \frac{b}{\sqrt{mk}}\,.$$

The striking fact is that there is only *one* physical parameter in this problem: the dimensionless number $\beta$. Solving this problem corresponds to solving the original problem (with dimensions) with the parameters $m = k = U_0 = 1$ and $b = \beta$. However, solving the dimensionless problem is more general: if we have a solution $\bar{u}(\bar{t};\beta)$, we can find the physical solution of a range of problems since

$$u(t) = U_0\bar{u}(t\sqrt{k/m};\,\beta)\,.$$

As long as $\beta$ is fixed, we can find $u$ for any $U_0$, $k$, and $m$ from the above formula! In this way, a time consuming simulation can be done only once, but still provide many solutions. This demonstrates the power of working with scaled or dimensionless problems.

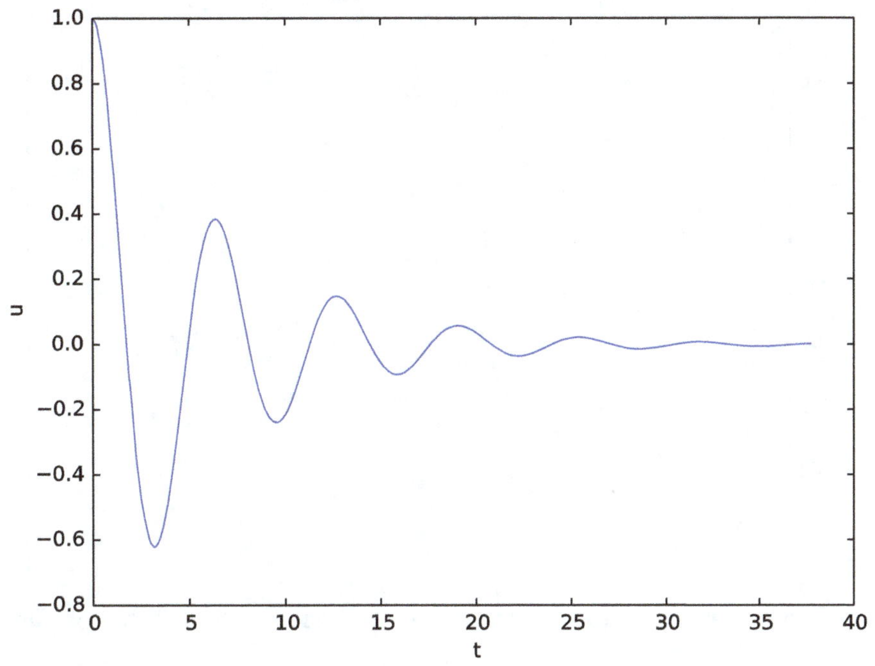


Fig. 8.30 Effect of linear damping

### 8.4.10 Illustration of Linear Damping with Sinusoidal Excitation

We now extend the previous example to also involve some external oscillating force on the system: $F(t) = A\sin(wt)$. Driving a car on a road with sinusoidal bumps might give such an external excitation on the spring system in the car ($w$ is related to the velocity of the car).

With $A = 0.5$ and $w = 3$,

```
import math
w = 3
A = 0.5
F = lambda t: A*math.sin(w*t)
```

we get the graph in Fig. 8.31. The striking difference from Fig. 8.30 is that the oscillations start out as a damped $\cos t$ signal without much influence of the external force, but then the free oscillations of the undamped system ($\cos t$) $u'' + u = 0$ die out and the external force $0.5\sin(3t)$ induces oscillations with a shorter period $2\pi/3$. You are encouraged to play around with a larger $A$ and switch from a sine to a cosine in $F$ and observe the effects. If you look this up in a physics book, you can find exact analytical solutions to the differential equation problem in these cases.

A particularly interesting case arises when the excitation force has the same frequency as the free oscillations of the undamped system, i.e., $F(t) = A\sin t$. With the same amplitude $A = 0.5$, but a smaller damping $b = 0.1$, the oscillations in Fig. 8.31 becomes qualitatively very different as the amplitude grows significantly larger over some periods. This phenomenon is called *resonance* and is exemplified in Fig. 8.32. Removing the damping results in an amplitude that grows linearly in time.

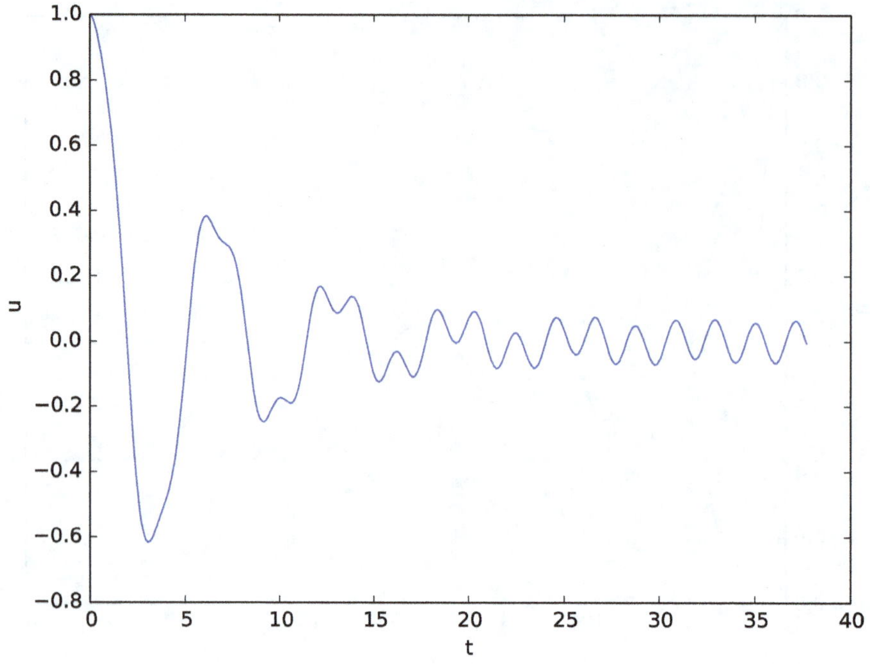


**Fig. 8.31** Effect of linear damping in combination with a sinusoidal external force

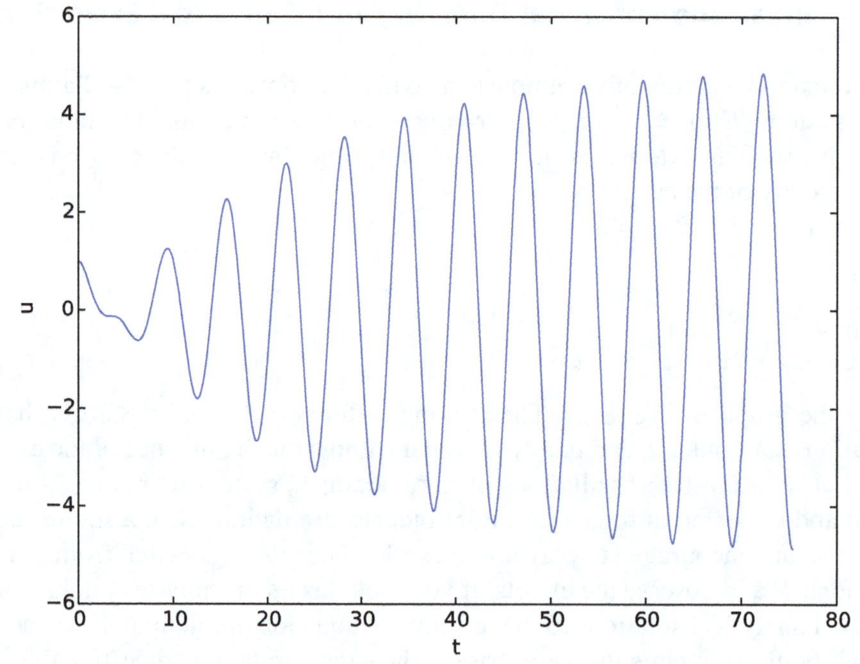


**Fig. 8.32** Excitation force that causes resonance

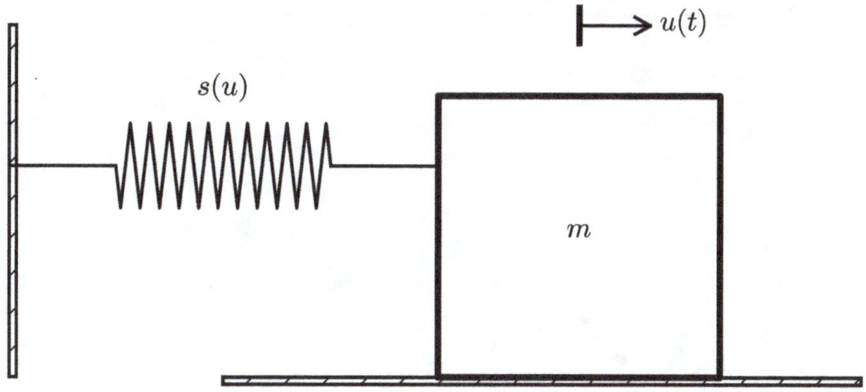


Fig. 8.33 Sketch of a one-dimensional, oscillating dynamic system subject to sliding friction and a spring force

### 8.4.11 Spring-Mass System with Sliding Friction

A body with mass $m$ is attached to a spring with stiffness $k$ while sliding on a plane surface. The body is also subject to a friction force $f(u')$ due to the contact between the body and the plane. Figure 8.33 depicts the situation. The friction force $f(u')$ can be modeled by Coulomb friction:

$$f(u') = \begin{cases} -\mu m g, & u' < 0, \\ \mu m g, & u' > 0, \\ 0, & u' = 0 \end{cases}$$

where $\mu$ is the friction coefficient, and $mg$ is the normal force on the surface where the body slides. This formula can also be written as $f(u') = \mu m g\,\mathrm{sign}(u')$, provided the signum function $\mathrm{sign}(x)$ is defined to be zero for $x = 0$ (`numpy.sign` has this property). To check that the signs in the definition of $f$ are right, recall that the actual physical force is $-f$ and this is positive (i.e., $f < 0$) when it works against the body moving with velocity $u' < 0$.

The nonlinear spring force is taken as

$$s(u) = -k\alpha^{-1}\tanh(\alpha u),$$

which is approximately $-ku$ for small $u$, but stabilizes at $\pm k/\alpha$ for large $\pm\alpha u$. Here is a plot with $k = 1000$ and $u \in [-0.1, 0.1]$ for three $\alpha$ values:

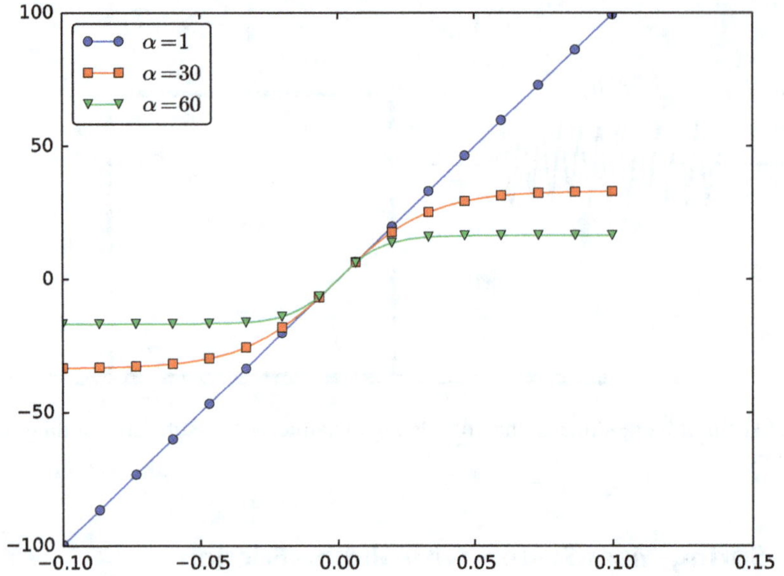


If there is no external excitation force acting on the body, we have the equation of motion

$$mu'' + \mu mg\,\mathrm{sign}(u') + k\alpha^{-1}\tanh(\alpha u) = 0\,.$$

Let us simulate a situation where a body of mass 1 kg slides on a surface with $\mu = 0.4$, while attached to a spring with stiffness $k = 1000\ \mathrm{kg/s^2}$. The initial displacement of the body is 10 cm, and the $\alpha$ parameter in $s(u)$ is set to 60 1/m. Using the `EulerCromer` function from the `osc_EC_general` code, we can write a function `sliding_friction` for solving this problem:

```
def sliding_friction():
    from numpy import tanh, sign

    f = lambda v: mu*m*g*sign(v)
    alpha = 60.0
    s = lambda u: k/alpha*tanh(alpha*u)
    F = lambda t: 0

    g = 9.81
    mu = 0.4
    m = 1
    k = 1000

    U_0 = 0.1
    V_0 = 0

    T = 2
    dt = T/5000.

    u, v, t = EulerCromer(f=f, s=s, F=F, m=m, T=T,
                          U_0=U_0, V_0=V_0, dt=dt)
    plot_u(u, t)
```

Running the `sliding_friction` function gives us the results in Fig. 8.34 with $s(u) = k\alpha^{-1}\tanh(\alpha u)$ (left) and the linearized version $s(u) = ku$ (right).

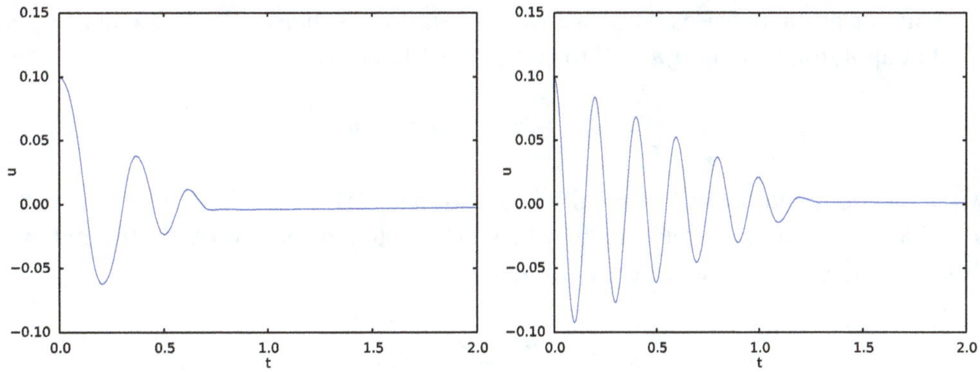


Fig. 8.34 Effect of nonlinear (left) and linear (right) spring on sliding friction

### 8.4.12 A Finite Difference Method; Undamped, Linear Case

We shall now address numerical methods for the second-order ODE

$$u'' + \omega^2 u = 0, \quad u(0) = U_0,\ u'(0) = 0,\ t \in (0, T],$$

*without* rewriting the ODE as a system of first-order ODEs. The primary motivation for "yet another solution method" is that the discretization principles result in a very good scheme, and more importantly, the thinking around the discretization can be reused when solving partial differential equations.

The main idea of this numerical method is to approximate the second-order derivative $u''$ by a finite difference. While there are several choices of difference approximations to first-order derivatives, there is one dominating formula for the second-order derivative:

$$u''(t_n) \approx \frac{u^{n+1} - 2u^n + u^{n-1}}{\Delta t^2}\,. \tag{8.74}$$

The error in this approximation is proportional to $\Delta t^2$. Letting the ODE be valid at some arbitrary time point $t_n$,

$$u''(t_n) + \omega^2 u(t_n) = 0,$$

we just insert the approximation (8.74) to get

$$\frac{u^{n+1} - 2u^n + u^{n-1}}{\Delta t^2} = -\omega^2 u^n\,. \tag{8.75}$$

We now assume that $u^{n-1}$ and $u^n$ are already computed and that $u^{n+1}$ is the new unknown. Solving with respect to $u^{n+1}$ gives

$$u^{n+1} = 2u^n - u^{n-1} - \Delta t^2 \omega^2 u^n\,. \tag{8.76}$$

A major problem arises when we want to start the scheme. We know that $u^0 = U_0$, but applying (8.76) for $n = 0$ to compute $u^1$ leads to

$$u^1 = 2u^0 - u^{-1} - \Delta t^2\omega^2 u^0, \tag{8.77}$$

where we do not know $u^{-1}$. The initial condition $u'(0) = 0$ can help us to eliminate $u^{-1}$—and this condition must anyway be incorporated in some way. To this end, we discretize $u'(0) = 0$ by a *centered difference*,

$$u'(0) \approx \frac{u^1 - u^{-1}}{2\Delta t} = 0\,.$$

It follows that $u^{-1} = u^1$, and we can use this relation to eliminate $u^{-1}$ in (8.77):

$$u^1 = u^0 - \frac{1}{2}\Delta t^2\omega^2 u^0\,. \tag{8.78}$$

With $u^0 = U_0$ and $u^1$ computed from (8.78), we can compute $u^2$, $u^3$, and so forth from (8.76). Exercise 8.25 asks you to explore how the steps above are modified in case we have a nonzero initial condition $u'(0) = V_0$.

**Remark on a simpler method for computing $u^1$**

We could approximate the initial condition $u'(0)$ by a forward difference:

$$u'(0) \approx \frac{u^1 - u^0}{\Delta t} = 0,$$

leading to $u^1 = u^0$. Then we can use (8.76) for the coming time steps. However, this forward difference has an error proportional to $\Delta t$, while the centered difference we used has an error proportional to $\Delta t^2$, which is compatible with the accuracy (error goes like $\Delta t^2$) used in the discretization of the differential equation.

The method for the second-order ODE described above goes under the name Störmer's method or Verlet integration.[7] It turns out that this method is mathematically equivalent with the Euler-Cromer scheme (!). Or more precisely, the general formula (8.76) is equivalent with the Euler-Cromer formula, but the scheme for the first time level (8.78) implements the initial condition $u'(0)$ slightly more accurately than what is naturally done in the Euler-Cromer scheme. The latter will do

$$v^1 = v^0 - \Delta t\omega^2 u^0, \quad u^1 = u^0 + \Delta t v^1 = u^0 - \Delta t^2\omega^2 u^0,$$

[7] http://en.wikipedia.org/wiki/Verlet_integration.

which differs from $u^1$ in (8.78) by an amount $\frac{1}{2}\Delta t^2\omega^2 u^0$.

Because of the equivalence of (8.76) with the Euler-Cromer scheme, the numerical results will have the same nice properties such as a constant amplitude. There will be a phase error as in the Euler-Cromer scheme, but this error is effectively reduced by reducing $\Delta t$, as already demonstrated.

The implementation of (8.78) and (8.76) is straightforward in a function (file `osc_2nd_order.py`):

```
import numpy as np

def osc_2nd_order(U_0, omega, dt, T):
    """
    Solve u'' + omega**2*u = 0 for t in (0,T], u(0)=U_0 and u'(0)=0,
    by a central finite difference method with time step dt.
    """
    Nt = int(round(T/dt))
    u = np.zeros(Nt+1)
    t = np.linspace(0, Nt*dt, Nt+1)

    u[0] = U_0
    u[1] = u[0] - 0.5*dt**2*omega**2*u[0]
    for n in range(1, Nt):
        u[n+1] = 2*u[n] - u[n-1] - dt**2*omega**2*u[n]
    return u, t
```

### 8.4.13 A Finite Difference Method; Linear Damping

A key issue is how to generalize the scheme from Sect. 8.4.12 to a differential equation with more terms. We start with the case of a linear damping term $f(u') = bu'$, a possibly nonlinear spring force $s(u)$, and an excitation force $F(t)$:

$$mu'' + bu' + s(u) = F(t), \quad u(0) = U_0,\ u'(0) = 0,\ t \in (0, T]\,. \tag{8.79}$$

We need to find the appropriate difference approximation to $u'$ in the $bu'$ term. A good choice is the *centered difference*

$$u'(t_n) \approx \frac{u^{n+1} - u^{n-1}}{2\Delta t}\,. \tag{8.80}$$

Sampling the equation at a time point $t_n$,

$$mu''(t_n) + bu'(t_n) + s(u^n) = F(t_n),$$

and inserting the finite difference approximations to $u''$ and $u'$ results in

$$m\frac{u^{n+1} - 2u^n + u^{n-1}}{\Delta t^2} + b\frac{u^{n+1} \quad u^{n-1}}{2\Delta t} + s(u^n) = F^n, \tag{8.81}$$

where $F^n$ is a short notation for $F(t_n)$. Equation (8.81) is linear in the unknown $u^{n+1}$, so we can easily solve for this quantity:

$$u^{n+1} = (2mu^n + (\frac{b}{2}\Delta t - m)u^{n-1} + \Delta t^2(F^n - s(u^n)))(m + \frac{b}{2}\Delta t)^{-1}\,. \quad (8.82)$$

As in the case without damping, we need to derive a special formula for $u^1$. The initial condition $u'(0) = 0$ implies also now that $u^{-1} = u^1$, and with (8.82) for $n = 0$, we get

$$u^1 = u^0 + \frac{\Delta t^2}{2m}(F^0 - s(u^0))\,. \quad (8.83)$$

In the more general case with a nonlinear damping term $f(u')$,

$$mu'' + f(u') + s(u) = F(t),$$

we get

$$m\frac{u^{n+1} - 2u^n + u^{n-1}}{\Delta t^2} + f(\frac{u^{n+1} - u^{n-1}}{2\Delta t}) + s(u^n) = F^n,$$

which is a *nonlinear algebraic equation* for $u^{n+1}$ that must be solved by numerical methods. A much more convenient scheme arises from using a backward difference for $u'$,

$$u'(t_n) \approx \frac{u^n - u^{n-1}}{\Delta t},$$

because the damping term will then be known, involving only $u^n$ and $u^{n-1}$, and we can easily solve for $u^{n+1}$.

The downside of the backward difference compared to the centered difference (8.80) is that it reduces the order of the accuracy in the overall scheme from $\Delta t^2$ to $\Delta t$. In fact, the Euler-Cromer scheme evaluates a nonlinear damping term as $f(v^n)$ when computing $v^{n+1}$, and this is equivalent to using the backward difference above. Consequently, the convenience of the Euler-Cromer scheme for nonlinear damping comes at a cost of lowering the overall accuracy of the scheme from second to first order in $\Delta t$. Using the same trick in the finite difference scheme for the second-order differential equation, i.e., using the backward difference in $f(u')$, makes this scheme equally convenient and accurate as the Euler-Cromer scheme in the general nonlinear case $mu'' + f(u') + s(u) = F$.

## 8.5 Rate of Convergence

In this chapter, we have seen how the numerical solutions improve as the time step $\Delta t$ is reduced, just like we would expect. Thinking back on numerical computation of integrals (Chap. 6), we experienced the same when reducing the sub-interval size $h$, i.e., computations became more accurate. Not too surprising then, the asymptotic error models are similar, and the convergence rate is computed in essentially the same way (except that the error computation requires some more consideration with the methods of the present chapter). Let us look at the details.

### 8.5.1 Asymptotic Behavior of the Error

For numerical methods that solve ODEs, it is known that when $\Delta t \to 0$, the approximation error[8] usually behaves like

$$E = C\,(\Delta t)^r\,, \tag{8.84}$$

for positive constants $C$ and $r$. The constant $r$ is known as the *convergence rate*, and its value will depend on the method ($r$ could be 1, 2 or 4, for example). A method with convergence rate $r$ is said to be an $r$-th order method, and we understand that the larger the $r$ value, the quicker the error $E$ drops when the time step $\Delta t$ is reduced.

### 8.5.2 Computing the Convergence Rate

Consider a set of experiments, $i = 0, 1, \ldots$, each depending on a discretization parameter $\Delta t_i$ that typically is halved from one experiment to the next. For each experiment, a corresponding error $E_i$ is computed. We may then estimate $r$ ($C$ is not really interesting) from two experiments:

$$E_{i-1} = C\Delta t_{i-1}^r$$
$$E_i = C\Delta t_i^r\,.$$

We eliminate $C$ by, e.g., dividing the latter equation by the former, and proceed to solve for $r$:

$$r = \frac{\ln(E_i/E_{i-1})}{\ln(\Delta t_i/\Delta t_{i-1})}\,.$$

Clearly, $r$ will vary with the pair of experiments used in the above formula, i.e., the value of $i$. Thus, what we actually compute, is a sequence of $r_{i-1}$ values ($i = 1, 2, \ldots$), where each $r_{i-1}$ value is computed from two experiments $(E_i, \Delta t_i)$ and $(E_{i-1}, \Delta t_{i-1})$. Since the error model is asymptotic (i.e., valid as $\Delta t \to 0$), the $r$ value corresponding to the smallest $\Delta t$ value will be the best estimate of the convergence rate.

**But How Do We Compute the Error $E_i$?** When we previously addressed the computing of convergence rates for numerical integration methods (trapezoidal and

[8] As will be addressed below, there are several options for how to quantify this error.

midpoint methods), the error was a single number for each choice of $n$, i.e., the number of sub-intervals. With each $\Delta t_i$ now, however, there is basically one error *for each point in the mesh* (remember: we compute an approximation to a *function* now, not a single number, as we did with integrals)! What we would like to have, is a single number $E_i$ that we could refer to as "the error" of the corresponding experiment.

There are different ways to arrive at $E_i$, and we might reason as follows. For each of our experiments, at each point in the mesh, there will be a difference (generally not zero) between the true solution and our computed approximation. The collection of all these differences makes up an error mesh function, having values at the mesh points only. Also, with a total of $N_t$ time steps, there will be $N_t + 1$ points in the time mesh ($N_t$ increases when $\Delta t$ decreases, for a fixed time interval $[0, T]$). Thus, for each $\Delta t_i$, the error mesh function comprises $N_t + 1$ function values $e^n$, $n = 0, 1, \ldots, N_t$. Now, one simple way to get to $E_i$, is to use the maximum of all $e^n$ values,[9] comparing absolute values. In fact, we did that previously in `test_ode_FE_exact_linear.py` (Sect. 8.2.7).

Other alternatives utilize a constructed error function $e(t)$, being a *continuous* function of time. The function $e(t)$ may be generated from the error mesh function by simply connecting successive $e^n$ values with straight lines. With $e(t)$ in place, one may choose to use the $L^2$ *norm* (read "L-two norm") of $e(t)$,

$$\|e\|_{L^2} = \sqrt{\int_0^T e(t)^2 dt}\,, \tag{8.85}$$

for $E_i$. The $L^2$ norm has nice mathematical properties and is much used. When computing the integral of the $L^2$ norm, we may use the trapezoidal method, and let the integration points coincide with the mesh points. Because of the straight lines composing $e(t)$, the integral computation will then become exact (within machine precision). Thus, assuming a uniform mesh, we can proceed to write (8.85) as

$$\|e\|_{L^2} \approx \sqrt{\Delta t\left(\frac{1}{2}(e_0) + \frac{1}{2}(e_{N_t}) + \sum_{n=1}^{N_t-1}(e_n)^2\right)}\,, \tag{8.86}$$

Finally, we make yet another approximation, by simply disregarding the contributions from $e_0$ and $e_{N_t}$. This is acceptable, since these contributions go to zero as $\Delta t \to 0$. The resulting expression is called the *discrete* $L^2$ norm, and is denoted by $l^2$. In this way, we get the final and simpler expression[10] as

$$\|e_n\|_{l^2} = \sqrt{\Delta t \sum_{n=1}^{N_t-1}(e_n)^2}\,. \tag{8.87}$$

[9] This is referred to as the discrete ($L^\infty$) norm (read "L-infinity norm", but often called the "max norm") for the error mesh function $e^n$.

[10] We should add that, in this expression, $\Delta t$ may be switched with $\frac{T}{N_t}$, followed by dropping $T$, since this common scaling factor is independent of the vector values. Finally, it is usually preferred to use the length of the vector, i.e. $N_t + 1$ in stead of $N_t$.

With (8.87), we have a simple way of computing the error $E_i$, letting

$$E_i = \|e_n\|_{l^2} \, . \tag{8.88}$$

We are now in position to compute convergence rates, and write corresponding test functions, also for ODE solvers.

### 8.5.3 Test Function: Convergence Rates for the FE Solver

To illustrate, we write a simple test function for `ode_FE` that we implemented previously (Sect. 8.2.5). Applying the solver to a population growth model, the test function could be written:

```
def test_convergence_rates_ode_FE(number_of_experiments):
    """
    Test that the convergence rate with the ode_FE solver is 1.
    Use population growth model as test case.
    """
    U_0=100       # initial value
    T=20          # total time span
    dt = 2.0      # initial time step
    expected_rate_FE = 1.0

    def f(u, t):
        """Population growth, u' = a*u, with a = 0.1 here."""
        return 0.1*u
    def u_exact(t):
        return 100*np.exp(0.1*t)

    dt_values = []
    E_values = []
    for i in range(number_of_experiments):
        u, t = ode_FE(f=f, U_0=U_0, dt=dt, T=T)
        u_e = u_exact(t)  # get exact solution at time mesh points (in t)
        E = np.sqrt(dt*np.sum((u_e-u)**2))    # ...discrete L^2 norm

        dt_values.append(dt)
        E_values.append(E)
        dt = dt/2                       # Halving time step for next solve

    r = [np.log(E_values[i]/E_values[i-1])/
         np.log(dt_values[i]/dt_values[i-1])
         for i in range(1, number_of_experiments, 1)]
    #print(r)

    # Accept rate to 1 decimal place
    tol = 0.1
    assert abs(r[-1] - expected_rate_FE) < tol
    return
```

When `test_convergence_rates_ode_FE` is called, the `for` loop will execute `ode_FE` the number of times specified by the input parameter `number_of_experiments`. Each execution of `ode_FE` happens with half the time step of the previous execution. Errors (`E`) and time steps (`dt`) are stored in corresponding lists, so that convergence rates (r) can be computed after the loop. Observe, in the loop, how `ode_FE` returns (the solution `u` and) the time mesh `t`, which then is used as input to the `u_exact` function, causing the exact function values to also be computed *at* the very same mesh points as `u`.

The Forward Euler method is a first order method, so we should get $r$ near 1 as the time step becomes small enough. A call to this test function does indeed confirm (remove # in front of `print(r)`) that `r` comes very close to 1 as `dt` gets smaller.

## 8.6 Exercises

**Exercise 8.1: Restructure a Given Code**

Section 8.1.1 gives a code for computing the development of water volume $V$ in a tank. Restructure the code by introducing an appropriate function `compute_V` that computes and returns the volumes, and a function `application` that calls the former function and plots the result.

Note that your restructuring should not cause any change in program behavior, as experienced by a user of the program.

Filename: `restruct_tank_case1.py`.

**Exercise 8.2: Geometric Construction of the Forward Euler Method**

Section 8.2.4 describes a geometric interpretation of the Forward Euler method. This exercise will demonstrate the geometric construction of the solution in detail. Consider the differential equation $u' = u$ with $u(0) = 1$. We use time steps $\Delta t = 1$.

a) Start at $t = 0$ and draw a straight line with slope $u'(0) = u(0) = 1$. Go one time step forward to $t = \Delta t$ and mark the solution point on the line.
b) Draw a straight line through the solution point $(\Delta t, u^1)$ with slope $u'(\Delta t) = u^1$. Go one time step forward to $t = 2\Delta t$ and mark the solution point on the line.
c) Draw a straight line through the solution point $(2\Delta t, u^2)$ with slope $u'(2\Delta t) = u^2$. Go one time step forward to $t = 3\Delta t$ and mark the solution point on the line.
d) Set up the Forward Euler scheme for the problem $u' = u$. Calculate $u^1$, $u^2$, and $u^3$. Check that the numbers are the same as obtained in a)-c).

Filename: `ForwardEuler_geometric_solution.py`.

**Exercise 8.3: Make Test Functions for the Forward Euler Method**

The purpose of this exercise is to make a file `test_ode_FE.py` that makes use of the `ode_FE` function in the file `ode_FE.py` and automatically verifies the implementation of `ode_FE`.

a) The solution computed by hand in Exercise 8.2 can be used as a reference solution. Make a function `test_ode_FE_1()` that calls `ode_FE` to compute three time steps in the problem $u' = u$, $u(0) = 1$, and compare the three values $u^1$, $u^2$, and $u^3$ with the values obtained in Exercise 8.2.
b) The test in a) can be made more general using the fact that if $f$ is linear in $u$ and does not depend on $t$, i.e., we have $u' = ru$, for some constant $r$, the Forward Euler method has a closed form solution as outlined in Sect. 8.2.1: $u^n = U_0(1 + r\Delta t)^n$. Use this result to construct a test function `test_ode_FE_2()` that

runs a number of steps in `ode_FE` and compares the computed solution with the listed formula for $u^n$.

Filename: `test_ode_FE.py`.

**Exercise 8.4: Implement and Evaluate Heun's Method**

a) A second-order Runge-Kutta method, also known has Heun's method, is derived in Sect. 8.4.5. Make a function `ode_Heun(f, U_0, dt, T)` (as a counterpart to `ode_FE(f, U_0, dt, T)` in `ode_FE.py`) for solving a scalar ODE problem $u' = f(u, t)$, $u(0) = U_0$, $t \in (0, T]$, with this method using a time step size $\Delta t$.
b) Solve the simple ODE problem $u' = u$, $u(0) = 1$, by the `ode_Heun` and the `ode_FE` function. Make a plot that compares Heun's method and the Forward Euler method with the exact solution $u(t) = e^t$ for $t \in [0, 6]$. Use a time step $\Delta t = 0.5$.
c) For the case in b), find through experimentation the largest value of $\Delta t$ where the exact solution and the numerical solution by Heun's method cannot be distinguished visually. It is of interest to see how far off the curve the Forward Euler method is when Heun's method can be regarded as "exact" (for visual purposes).

Filename: `ode_Heun.py`.

**Exercise 8.5: Find an Appropriate Time Step; Logistic Model**
Compute the numerical solution of the logistic equation for a set of repeatedly halved time steps: $\Delta t_k = 2^{-k}\Delta t$, $k = 0, 1, \ldots$. Plot the solutions corresponding to the last two time steps $\Delta t_k$ and $\Delta t_{k-1}$ in the same plot. Continue doing this until you cannot visually distinguish the two curves in the plot. Then one has found a sufficiently small time step.

**Hint** Extend the `logistic.py` file. Introduce a loop over $k$, write out $\Delta t_k$, and ask the user if the loop is to be continued.

Filename: `logistic_dt.py`.

**Exercise 8.6: Find an Appropriate Time Step; SIR Model**
Repeat Exercise 8.5 for the SIR model.

**Hint** Import the `ode_FE` function from the `ode_system_FE` module and make a modified `demo_SIR` function that has a loop over repeatedly halved time steps. Plot $S$, $I$, and $R$ versus time for the two last time step sizes in the same plot.

Filename: `SIR_dt.py`.

**Exercise 8.7: Model an Adaptive Vaccination Campaign**
In the SIRV model with time-dependent vaccination from Sect. 8.3.9, we want to test the effect of an adaptive vaccination campaign where vaccination is offered

as long as half of the population is not vaccinated. The campaign starts after $\Delta$ days. That is, $p = p_0$ if $V < \frac{1}{2}(S^0 + I^0)$ and $t > \Delta$ days, otherwise $p = 0$.

Demonstrate the effect of this vaccination policy: choose $\beta$, $\gamma$, and $\nu$ as in Sect. 8.3.9, set $p = 0.001$, $\Delta = 10$ days, and simulate for 200 days.

**Hint** This discontinuous $p(t)$ function is easiest implemented as a Python function containing the indicated `if` test. You may use the file `SIRV1.py` as starting point, but note that it implements a time-dependent $p(t)$ via an array.

Filename: `SIRV_p_adapt.py`.

**Exercise 8.8: Make a SIRV Model with Time-Limited Effect of Vaccination**
We consider the SIRV model from Sect. 8.3.8, but now the effect of vaccination is time-limited. After a characteristic period of time, $\pi$, the vaccination is no more effective and individuals are consequently moved from the V to the S category and can be infected again. Mathematically, this can be modeled as an average leakage $-\pi^{-1}V$ from the V category to the S category (i.e., a gain $\pi^{-1}V$ in the latter). Write up the complete model, implement it, and rerun the case from Sect. 8.3.8 with various choices of parameters to illustrate various effects.
Filename: `SIRV1_V2S.py`.

**Exercise 8.9: Refactor a Flat Program**
Consider the file `osc_FE.py` implementing the Forward Euler method for the oscillating system model (8.43)–(8.44). The `osc_FE.py` code is what we often refer to as a flat program, meaning that it is just one main program with no functions. Your task is to *refactor* the code in `osc_FE.py` according to the specifications below. Refactoring, means to alter the inner structure of the code, while, to a user, the program works just as before.

To easily reuse the numerical computations in other contexts, place the part that produces the numerical solution (allocation of arrays, initializing the arrays at time zero, and the time loop) in a function `osc_FE(X_0, omega, dt, T)`, which returns `u, v, t`. Place the particular computational example in `osc_FE.py` in a function `demo()`. Construct the file `osc_FE_func.py` such that the `osc_FE` function can easily be reused in other programs. In Python, this means that `osc_FE_func.py` is a module that can be imported in other programs. The requirement of a module is that there should be no main program, except in the test block. You must therefore call `demo` from a test block (i.e., the block after `if __name__ == '__main__'`).
Filename: `osc_FE_func.py`.

**Exercise 8.10: Simulate Oscillations by a General ODE Solver**
Solve the system (8.43)–(8.44) using the general solver `ode_FE` described in Sect. 8.3.6. Program the ODE system and the call to the `ode_FE` function in a separate file `osc_ode_FE.py`.

Equip this file with a test function that reads a file with correct $u$ values and compares these with those computed by the `ode_FE` function. To find correct $u$

values, modify the program `osc_FE.py` to dump the `u` array to file, run `osc_FE.py`, and let the test function read the reference results from that file.
Filename: `osc_ode_FE.py`.

**Exercise 8.11: Compute the Energy in Oscillations**

a) Make a function `osc_energy(u, v, omega)` for returning the potential and kinetic energy of an oscillating system described by (8.43)–(8.44). The potential energy is taken as $\frac{1}{2}\omega^2 u^2$ while the kinetic energy is $\frac{1}{2}v^2$. (Note that these expressions are not exactly the *physical* potential and kinetic energy, since these would be $\frac{1}{2}mv^2$ and $\frac{1}{2}ku^2$ for a model $mx'' + kx = 0$.)

   Place the `osc_energy` in a separate file `osc_energy.py` such that the function can be called from other functions.
b) Add a call to `osc_energy` in the programs `osc_FE.py` and `osc_EC.py` and plot the *sum* of the kinetic and potential energy. How does the total energy develop for the Forward Euler and the Euler-Cromer schemes?

Filenames: `osc_energy.py`, `osc_FE_energy.py`, `osc_EC_energy.py`.

**Exercise 8.12: Use a Backward Euler Scheme for Population Growth**

We consider the ODE problem $N'(t) = rN(t)$, $N(0) = N_0$. At some time, $t_n = n\Delta t$, we can approximate the derivative $N'(t_n)$ by a *backward difference*, see Fig. 8.22:

$$N'(t_n) \approx \frac{N(t_n) - N(t_n - \Delta t)}{\Delta t} = \frac{N^n - N^{n-1}}{\Delta t},$$

which leads to

$$\frac{N^n - N^{n-1}}{\Delta t} = rN^n\,,$$

called the *Backward Euler scheme*.

a) Find an expression for the $N^n$ in terms of $N^{n-1}$ and formulate an algorithm for computing $N^n$, $n = 1, 2, \ldots, N_t$.
b) Implement the algorithm in a) in a function `growth_BE(N_0, dt, T)` for solving $N' = rN$, $N(0) = N_0$, $t \in (0, T]$, with time step $\Delta t$ (`dt`).
c) Implement the Forward Euler scheme in a function `growth_FE(N_0, dt, T)` as described in b).
d) Compare visually the solution produced by the Forward and Backward Euler schemes with the exact solution when $r = 1$ and $T = 6$. Make two plots, one with $\Delta t = 0.5$ and one with $\Delta t = 0.05$.

Filename: `growth_BE.py`.

**Exercise 8.13: Use a Crank-Nicolson Scheme for Population Growth**
It is recommended to do Exercise 8.12 prior to the present one. Here we look at the same population growth model $N'(t) = rN(t)$, $N(0) = N_0$. The time derivative $N'(t)$ can be approximated by various types of finite differences. Exercise 8.12 considers a backward difference (Fig. 8.22), while Sect. 8.2.2 explained the forward difference (Fig. 8.4). A *centered difference* is more accurate than a backward or forward difference:

$$N'(t_n + \frac{1}{2}\Delta t) \approx \frac{N(t_n + \Delta t) - N(t_n)}{\Delta t} = \frac{N^{n+1} - N^n}{\Delta t}\,.$$

This type of difference, applied at the point $t_{n+\frac{1}{2}} = t_n + \frac{1}{2}\Delta t$, is illustrated geometrically in Fig. 8.23.

a) Insert the finite difference approximation in the ODE $N' = rN$ and solve for the unknown $N^{n+1}$, assuming $N^n$ is already computed and hence known. The resulting computational scheme is often referred to as a *Crank-Nicolson* scheme.
b) Implement the algorithm in a) in a function `growth_CN(N_0, dt, T)` for solving $N' = rN$, $N(0) = N_0$, $t \in (0, T]$, with time step $\Delta t$ (`dt`).
c) Make plots for comparing the Crank-Nicolson scheme with the Forward and Backward Euler schemes in the same test problem as in Exercise 8.12.

Filename: `growth_CN.py`.

**Exercise 8.14: Understand Finite Differences via Taylor Series**
The Taylor series around a point $x = a$ can for a function $f(x)$ be written

$$\begin{aligned} f(x) &= f(a) + \frac{d}{dx}f(a)(x-a) + \frac{1}{2!}\frac{d^2}{dx^2}f(a)(x-a)^2 \\ &\quad + \frac{1}{3!}\frac{d^3}{dx^3}f(a)(x-a)^3 + \ldots \\ &= \sum_{i=0}^{\infty}\frac{1}{i!}\frac{d^i}{dx^i}f(a)(x-a)^i\,. \end{aligned}$$

For a function of time, as addressed in our ODE problems, we would use $u$ instead of $f$, $t$ instead of $x$, and a time point $t_n$ instead of $a$:

$$\begin{aligned} u(t) &= u(t_n) + \frac{d}{dt}u(t_n)(t-t_n) + \frac{1}{2!}\frac{d^2}{dt^2}u(t_n)(t-t_n)^2 \\ &\quad + \frac{1}{3!}\frac{d^3}{dt^3}u(t_n)(t-t_n)^3 + \ldots \\ &= \sum_{i=0}^{\infty}\frac{1}{i!}\frac{d^i}{dt^i}u(t_n)(t-t_n)^i\,. \end{aligned}$$

a) A forward finite difference approximation to the derivative $f'(a)$ reads

$$u'(t_n) \approx \frac{u(t_n + \Delta t) - u(t_n)}{\Delta t}\,.$$

We can justify this formula mathematically through Taylor series. Write up the Taylor series for $u(t_n + \Delta t)$ (around $t = t_n$, as given above), and then solve the expression with respect to $u'(t_n)$. Identify, on the right-hand side, the finite difference approximation *and* an infinite series. This series is then the error in the finite difference approximation. If $\Delta t$ is assumed small (i.e. $\Delta t << 1$), $\Delta t$ will be much larger than $\Delta t^2$, which will be much larger than $\Delta t^3$, and so on. The *leading order term* in the series for the error, i.e., the error with the least power of $\Delta t$ is a good approximation of the error. Identify this term.

b) Repeat a) for a backward difference:

$$u'(t_n) \approx \frac{u(t_n) - u(t_n - \Delta t)}{\Delta t}\,.$$

This time, write up the Taylor series for $u(t_n - \Delta t)$ around $t_n$. Solve with respect to $u'(t_n)$, and identify the leading order term in the error. How is the error compared to the forward difference?

c) A centered difference approximation to the derivative, as explored in Exercise 8.13, can be written

$$u'(t_n + \frac{1}{2}\Delta t) \approx \frac{u(t_n + \Delta t) - u(t_n)}{\Delta t}\,.$$

Write up the Taylor series for $u(t_n)$ around $t_n + \frac{1}{2}\Delta t$ and the Taylor series for $u(t_n + \Delta t)$ around $t_n + \frac{1}{2}\Delta t$. Subtract the two series, solve with respect to $u'(t_n + \frac{1}{2}\Delta t)$, identify the finite difference approximation and the error terms on the right-hand side, and write up the leading order error term. How is this term compared to the ones for the forward and backward differences?

d) Can you use the leading order error terms in a)–c) to explain the visual observations in the numerical experiment in Exercise 8.13?

e) Find the leading order error term in the following standard finite difference approximation to the second-order derivative:

$$u''(t_n) \approx \frac{u(t_n + \Delta t) - 2u(t_n) + u(t_n - \Delta t)}{\Delta t^2}\,.$$

**Hint** Express $u(t_n \pm \Delta t)$ via Taylor series and insert them in the difference formula.

Filename: `Taylor_differences.pdf`.

**Exercise 8.15: The Leapfrog Method**

We consider the general ODE problem $u'(t) = f(u, t)$, $u(0) = U_0$. To solve such an ODE numerically, the second order *Leapfrog method* approximates the derivative (at some time $t_n = n\Delta t$) by use of a *centered difference* over two time steps,

$$u'(t_n) \approx \frac{u(t_{n+1}) - u(t_{n-1})}{2\Delta t} = \frac{u^{n+1} - u^{n-1}}{2\Delta t}.$$

a) Replace the derivative in the ODE by the given centered difference approximation and show that this allows us to formulate:

$$u^{n+1} = u^{n-1} + 2\Delta t f(u^n, t_n), \qquad n = 1, 2, \ldots, N_t - 1,$$

with $u^0 = U_0$. Do we have the information we need to get the scheme started?

b) The problem you discovered in the previous question, may be fixed by using the Forward Euler method. However, the Leapfrog method is a second order method, while the Forward Euler method is first order.

Argue, with reference to the Taylor series (see, e.g., Exercise 8.14), why the Forward Euler method can be used without reducing the order of the overall scheme.

c) Implement the Leapfrog scheme in a function `leapfrog`. Make sure the function takes an appropriate set of input parameters, so that it is easy to import and use.

d) Write a function `compare_FE_leapfrog` that compares graphically the solutions produced by the Forward Euler and Leapfrog methods, when they solve the population growth model $u' = 0.1u$, with $u(0) = 100$. Let the total time span $T = 20$, and use a time step $dt = 2$. In the plot produced, include also the exact solution, so that the numerical solutions can be assessed.

e) Suggest a reasonable asymptotic error model before you write a proper test function `test_convergence_rates` that may be used to compute and check the convergence rates of the implemented Leapfrog method. However, the test function should take appropriate input parameters, so that it can be used also for other ODE solvers, in particular the `ode_FE` implemented previously.

Include your test function in a program, together with the two functions you defined previously (`leapfrog` and `compare_FE_leapfrog`). Write the code with a test block, so that it gets easy to either import functions from the module, or to run it as a program.

Finally, run the program (so that `compare_FE_leapfrog` gets called, as well as `test_convergence_rates` for both FE and Leapfrog) and confirm that it works as expected. In particular, does the plot look good, and do you get the convergence rates you expected for Forward Euler and Leapfrog?

Filename: `growth_leapfrog.py`.

**Exercise 8.16: The Runge-Kutta Third Order Method**

A general ODE problem $u'(t) = f(u, t)$, $u(0) = U_0$, may be solved numerically by the third order Runge-Kutta method. The computational scheme reads

$$u^{n+1} = u^n + \frac{\Delta t}{6}(k_1 + 4k_2 + k_3), \qquad n = 0, 1, \ldots, N_t - 1,$$
$$k_1 = f(u^n, t_n),$$
$$k_2 = f(u^n + \frac{\Delta t}{2}, t_n + \frac{\Delta t}{2}),$$
$$k_3 = f(u^n - \Delta t k_1 + 2\Delta t k_2, t_n + \Delta t),$$

with $u^0 = U_0$.

a) Implement the scheme in a function `RK3` that takes appropriate parameters, so that it is easy to import and use whenever needed.
b) Write a function `compare_FE_RK3` that compares graphically the solutions produced by the Forward Euler and RK3 methods, when they solve the population growth model $u' = 0.1u$, with $u(0) = 100$. Let the total time span $T = 20$, and use a time step $dt = 2$. In the plot produced, include also the exact solution, so that the numerical solutions can be assessed.
c) Suggest a reasonable asymptotic error model before you write a proper test function `test_convergence_rates` that may be used to compute and check the convergence rates of the implemented RK3 method. However, the test function should take appropriate input parameters, so that it can be used also for other ODE solvers, in particular the `ode_FE` implemented previously (if you already have written this test function when doing Exercise 8.15, you may prefer to import the function).

   Include your test function in a program, together with the two functions you defined previously (`RK3` and `compare_FE_RK3`). Write the code with a test block, so that it gets easy to either import functions from the module, or to run it as a program.

   Finally, run the program (so that `compare_FE_RK3` gets called, as well as `test_convergence_rates` for both FE and RK3) and confirm that it works as expected. In particular, does the plot look good, and do you get the convergence rates you expected for Forward Euler and RK3?

Filename: `runge_kutta_3.py`.

**Exercise 8.17: The Two-Step Adams-Bashforth Method**

Differing from the *single-step* methods presented in this chapter, we have the *multi-step* methods, for example the Adams-Bashforth methods. With the single-step methods, $u^{n+1}$ is computed by use of the solution from the previous time step, i.e. $u^n$. In multi-step methods, the computed solutions from *several* previous time steps, e.g., $u^n$, $u^{n-1}$ and $u^{n-2}$ are used to estimate $u^{n+1}$. How many time steps that are involved in the computing of $u^{n+1}$, and how the previous solutions are combined, depends on the method.[11] With multi-step methods, more than one starting value is required to get the scheme started. Thus, apart from the given initial condition, the remaining starting values must be computed. This is done by some other appropriate scheme (in such a way that the convergence rate of the overall scheme is not reduced).

Note that the Runge-Kutta methods are single-step methods, even if they use several *intermediate* steps (between $t_n$ and $t_{n+1}$) when computing $u^{n+1}$, using no other previous solution than $u^n$.

One of the simplest multi-step methods is the (second order) *two-step Adams-Bashforth method*. The computational scheme reads:

$$u^{n+1} = u^n + \frac{\Delta t}{2}\left(3f(u^n, t_n) - f(u^{n-1}, t_{n-1})\right),$$

for $n = 1, 2, \ldots, N_t - 1$, with $u^0 = U_0$.

a) Implement the scheme in a function `adams_bashforth_2` that takes appropriate parameters, so that it is easy to import and use whenever needed. Use a Forward Euler scheme to compute the missing starting value.
b) Write a function `compare_FE_AdamsBashforth2` that compares graphically the solutions produced by the Forward Euler and two-step Adams-Bashforth methods, when they solve the population growth model $u' = 0.1u$, with $u(0) = 100$. Let the total time span $T = 20$, and use a time step $dt = 2$. In the plot produced, include also the exact solution, so that the numerical solutions can be assessed.
c) Suggest a reasonable asymptotic error model before you write a proper test function `test_convergence_rates` that may be used to compute and check the convergence rates of the implemented AB2 method. However, the test function should take appropriate input parameters, so that it can be used also for other ODE solvers, in particular the `ode_FE` implemented previously (if you already have written this test function when doing Exercise 8.15, you may prefer to import the function).

   Include your test function in a program, together with the two functions you defined previously (`AB2` and `compare_FE_AdamsBashforth2`). Write the code with a test block, so that it gets easy to either import functions from the module, or to run it as a program.

   Finally, run the program (so that `compare_FE_AdamsBashforth2` gets called, as well as `test_convergence_rates` for both FE and AB2) and confirm that it works as expected. In particular, does the plot look good, and do you get the convergence rates you expected for Forward Euler and AB2?

Filename: `Adams_Bashforth_2.py`.

[11] Read more about multi-step methods, e.g., on Wikipedia (https://en.wikipedia.org/wiki/Linear_multistep_method).

### Exercise 8.18: The Three-Step Adams-Bashforth Method

This exercise builds on Exercise 8.17, so you better do that one first. Another multi-step method, is the *three-step Adams-Bashforth method.* This is a third order method with a computational scheme that reads:

$$u^{n+1} = u^n + \frac{\Delta t}{12}\left(23f(u^n, t_n) - 16f(u^{n-1}, t_{n-1}) + 5f(u^{n-2}, t_{n-2})\right).$$

for $n = 2, 3, \ldots, N_t - 1$, with $u^0 = U_0$.

a) Assume that someone implemented the scheme as follows:

```
def adams_bashforth_3(f, U_0, dt, T):
    """Third-order Adams-Bashforth scheme for solving first order ODE"""
    N_t = int(round(T/dt))
    u = np.zeros(N_t+1)
    t = np.linspace(0, N_t*dt, len(u))
    u[0] = U_0
    # Compute missing starting values
    u[1] = 100*np.exp(0.1*dt)
    u[2] = 100*np.exp(0.1*(2*dt))
    for n in range(1, N_t, 1):
        u[n+1] = u[n] + (dt/12)*(23*f(u[n], t[n]) - \
                                 16*f(u[n-1], t[n-1]) +\
                                 5*f(u[n-2], t[n-2]))
    return u, t
```

There is one (known!) bug here, find it! Try first by simply reading the code. If not successful, you may try to run it and do some testing on your computer.

Also, what would you say about the way that missing starting values are computed?

b) Repeat Exercise 8.17, using the given three-step method in stead of the two-step method.

   Note that with the three-step method, you need 3 starting values. Use the Runge-Kutta third order scheme for this purpose. However, check also the convergence rate of the scheme when missing starting values are computed with Forward Euler in stead.

Filename: `Adams_Bashforth_3.py`.

### Exercise 8.19: Use a Backward Euler Scheme for Oscillations

Consider (8.43)–(8.44) modeling an oscillating engineering system. This $2 \times 2$ ODE system can be solved by the *Backward Euler scheme*, which is based on discretizing derivatives by collecting information backward in time. More specifically, $u'(t)$ is approximated as

$$u'(t) \approx \frac{u(t) - u(t - \Delta t)}{\Delta t}.$$

A general vector ODE $u' = f(u, t)$, where $u$ and $f$ are vectors, can use this approximation as follows:

$$\frac{u^n - u^{n-1}}{\Delta t} = f(u^n, t_n),$$

which leads to an equation for the new value $u^n$:

$$u^n - \Delta t f(u^n, t_n) = u^{n-1}\,.$$

For a general $f$, this is a system of *nonlinear algebraic equations*.

However, the ODE (8.43)–(8.44) is *linear*, so a Backward Euler scheme leads to a system of two algebraic equations for two unknowns:

$$u^n - \Delta t v^n = u^{n-1}, \tag{8.89}$$

$$v^n + \Delta t \omega^2 u^n = v^{n-1}\,. \tag{8.90}$$

a) Solve the system for $u^n$ and $v^n$.
b) Implement the found formulas for $u^n$ and $v^n$ in a program for computing the entire numerical solution of (8.43)–(8.44).
c) Run the program with a $\Delta t$ corresponding to 20 time steps per period of the oscillations (see Sect. 8.4.3 for how to find such a $\Delta t$). What do you observe? Increase to 2000 time steps per period. How much does this improve the solution?

Filename: `osc_BE.py`.

**Remarks** While the Forward Euler method applied to oscillation problems $u'' + \omega^2 u = 0$ gives growing amplitudes, the Backward Euler method leads to significantly damped amplitudes.

**Exercise 8.20: Use Heun's Method for the SIR Model**
Make a program that computes the solution of the SIR model from Sect. 8.3.1 both by the Forward Euler method and by Heun's method (or equivalently: the second-order Runge-Kutta method) from Sect. 8.4.5. Compare the two methods in the simulation case from Sect. 8.3.3. Make two comparison plots, one for a large and one for a small time step. Experiment to find what "large" and "small" should be: the large one gives significant differences, while the small one lead to very similar curves.
Filename: `SIR_Heun.py`.

**Exercise 8.21: Use Odespy to Solve a Simple ODE**
Solve

$$u' = -au + b, \quad u(0) = U_0, \quad t \in (0, T]$$

by the Odespy software. Let the problem parameters $a$ and $b$ be arguments to the function specifying the derivative. Use 100 time intervals in $[0, T]$ and plot the solution when $a = 2, b = 1, T = 6/a$.
Filename: `odespy_demo.py`.

**Exercise 8.22: Set up a Backward Euler Scheme for Oscillations**
Write the ODE $u'' + \omega^2 u = 0$ as a system of two first-order ODEs and discretize these with backward differences as illustrated in Fig. 8.22. The resulting method is referred to as a Backward Euler scheme. Identify the matrix and right-hand side of the linear system that has to be solved at each time level. Implement the method, either from scratch yourself or using Odespy (the name is `odespy.BackwardEuler`). Demonstrate that contrary to a Forward Euler scheme, the Backward Euler scheme leads to significant non-physical damping. The figure below shows that even with 60 time steps per period, the results after a few periods are useless:
Filename: `osc_BE.py`.

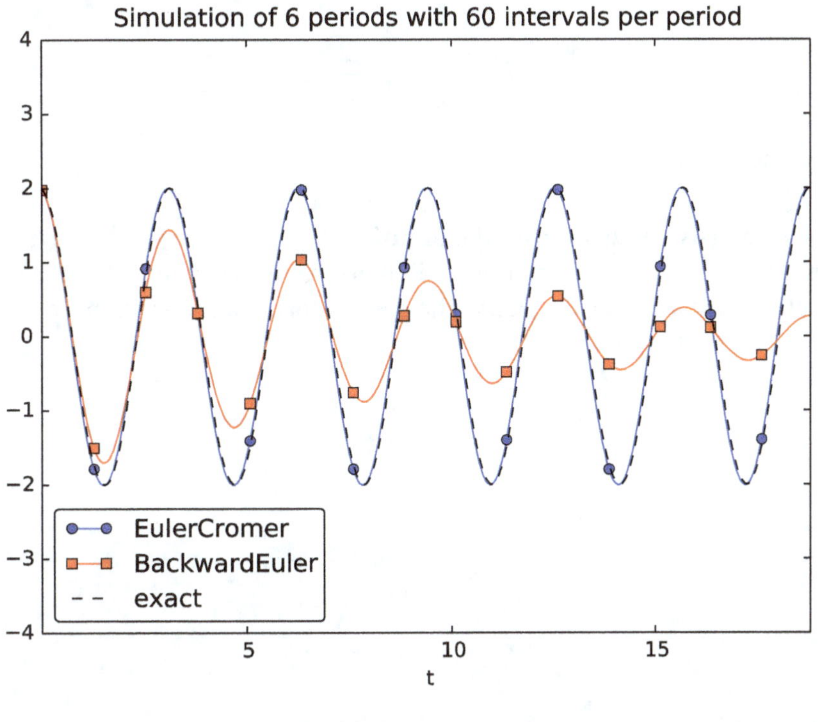


**Exercise 8.23: Set up a Forward Euler Scheme for Nonlinear and Damped Oscillations**
Derive a Forward Euler method for the ODE system (8.68)–(8.69). Compare the method with the Euler-Cromer scheme for the sliding friction problem from Sect. 8.4.11:

1. Does the Forward Euler scheme give growing amplitudes?
2. Is the period of oscillation accurate?
3. What is the required time step size for the two methods to have visually coinciding curves?

Filename: `osc_FE_general.py`.

**Exercise 8.24: Solving a Nonlinear ODE with Backward Euler**
Let $y$ be a scalar function of time $t$ and consider the nonlinear ODE

$$y' + y = ty^3,\ t \in (0, 4), \quad y(0) = \frac{1}{2}\,.$$

a) Assume you want to solve this ODE numerically by the Backward Euler method. Derive the computational scheme and show that (contrary to the Forward Euler scheme) you have to *solve a nonlinear algebraic equation* for each time step when using this scheme.
b) Implement the scheme in a program that also solves the ODE by a Forward Euler method. With Backward Euler, use Newton's method to solve the algebraic equation. As your initial guess, you have one good alternative, which one?
   Let your program plot the two numerical solutions together with the exact solution, which is known (e.g., from Wolfram Alpha) to be

$$y(t) = \frac{\sqrt{2}}{\sqrt{7e^{2t} + 2t + 1}}\,.$$

Filename: `nonlinBE.py`.

**Exercise 8.25: Discretize an Initial Condition**
Assume that the initial condition on $u'$ is nonzero in the finite difference method from Sect. 8.4.12: $u'(0) = V_0$. Derive the special formula for $u^1$ in this case.
Filename: `ic_with_V_0.pdf`.

Check for updates

# 9 Solving Partial Differential Equations

We now turn to the solving of differential equations in which the solution is a function that depends on several independent variables. One such equation is called a *partial differential equation* (PDE, plural: PDEs).

The subject of PDEs is enormous. At the same time, it is very important, since so many phenomena in nature and technology find their mathematical formulation through such equations. Knowing how to solve at least some PDEs is therefore of great importance to engineers. In an introductory book like this, nowhere near full justice to the subject can be made. However, we still find it valuable to give the reader a glimpse of the topic by presenting a few basic and general methods that we will apply to a very common type of PDE.

We shall focus on one of the most widely encountered partial differential equations: the diffusion equation, which in one dimension looks like

$$\frac{\partial u}{\partial t} = \beta \frac{\partial^2 u}{\partial x^2} + g\,.$$

The multi-dimensional counterpart is often written as

$$\frac{\partial u}{\partial t} = \beta \nabla^2 u + g\,.$$

We shall restrict the attention here to the one-dimensional case.

The unknown in the diffusion equation is a function $u(x, t)$ of space and time. The physical significance of $u$ depends on what type of process that is described by the diffusion equation. For example, $u$ is the concentration of a substance if the diffusion equation models transport of this substance by *diffusion*. Diffusion processes are of particular relevance at the microscopic level in biology, e.g., diffusive transport of certain ion types in a cell caused by molecular collisions. There is also diffusion of atoms in a solid, for instance, and diffusion of ink in a glass of water.

One very popular application of the diffusion equation is for heat transport in solid bodies. Then $u$ is the temperature, and the equation predicts how the temperature evolves in space and time within the solid body. For such applications,



S. Linge, H. P. Langtangen, *Programming for Computations - Python*,
Texts in Computational Science and Engineering 15,
https://doi.org/10.1007/978-3-030-16877-3_9

the equation is known as the *heat equation*. We remark that the temperature in a fluid is influenced not only by diffusion, but also by the flow of the liquid. If present, the latter effect requires an extra term in the equation (known as an advection or convection term).

The term $g$ is known as the *source term* and represents generation, or loss, of heat (by some mechanism) within the body. For diffusive transport, $g$ models injection or extraction of the substance.

We should also mention that the diffusion equation may appear after simplifying more complicated PDEs. For example, flow of a viscous fluid between two flat and parallel plates is described by a one-dimensional diffusion equation, where $u$ then is the fluid velocity.

A PDE is solved in some *domain* $\Omega$ in space and for a time interval $[0, T]$. The solution of the equation is not unique unless we also prescribe *initial and boundary conditions*. The type and number of such conditions depend on the type of equation. For the diffusion equation, we need one initial condition, $u(x, 0)$, stating what $u$ is when the process starts. In addition, the diffusion equation needs one boundary condition at each point of the boundary $\partial\Omega$ of $\Omega$. This condition can either be that $u$ is known or that we know the normal derivative, $\nabla u \cdot \boldsymbol{n} = \partial u/\partial n$ ($\boldsymbol{n}$ denotes an outward unit normal to $\partial\Omega$).

## 9.1 Example: Temperature Development in a Rod

Let us look at a specific application and how the diffusion equation with initial and boundary conditions then appears. We consider the evolution of temperature in a one-dimensional medium, more precisely a long rod, where the surface of the rod is covered by an insulating material. The heat can then not escape from the surface, which means that the temperature distribution will only depend on a coordinate along the rod, $x$, and time $t$. At one end of the rod, $x = L$, we also assume that the surface is insulated, but at the other end, $x = 0$, we assume that we have some device for controlling the temperature of the medium. Here, a function $s(t)$ tells what the temperature is in time. We therefore have a boundary condition $u(0, t) = s(t)$. At the other insulated end, $x = L$, heat cannot escape, which is expressed by the boundary condition $\partial u(L, t)/\partial x = 0$. The surface along the rod is also insulated and hence subject to the same boundary condition (here generalized to $\partial u/\partial n = 0$ at the curved surface). However, since we have reduced the problem to one dimension, we do not need this physical boundary condition in our mathematical model. In one dimension, we can set $\Omega = [0, L]$.

To summarize, the PDE with initial and boundary conditions reads

$$\frac{\partial u(x,t)}{\partial t} = \beta\frac{\partial^2 u(x,t)}{\partial x^2} + g(x,t), \qquad x \in (0,L), t \in (0,T], \tag{9.1}$$

$$u(0,t) = s(t), \qquad t \in (0,T], \tag{9.2}$$

$$\frac{\partial}{\partial x}u(L,t) = 0, \qquad t \in (0,T], \tag{9.3}$$

$$u(x,0) = I(x), \qquad x \in [0,L]\ . \tag{9.4}$$

Mathematically, we assume that at $t = 0$, the initial condition (9.4) holds and that the PDE (9.1) comes into play for $t > 0$. Similarly, at the end points, the boundary conditions (9.2) and (9.3) govern $u$ and the equation therefore is valid for $x \in (0, L)$.

**Boundary and initial conditions are needed!**

The initial and boundary conditions are extremely important. Without them, the solution is not unique, and no numerical method will work. Unfortunately, many physical applications have one or more initial or boundary conditions as unknowns. Such situations can be dealt with if we have measurements of $u$, but the mathematical framework is much more complicated.

What about the source term $g$ in our example with temperature distribution in a rod? $g(x,t)$ models heat generation inside the rod. One could think of chemical reactions at a microscopic level in some materials as a reason to include $g$. However, in most applications with temperature evolution, $g$ is zero and heat generation usually takes place at the boundary (as in our example with $u(0,t) = s(t)$).

### 9.1.1 A Particular Case

Before continuing, we may consider an example of how the temperature distribution evolves in the rod. At time $t = 0$, we assume that the temperature is 10 °C. Then we suddenly apply a device at $x = 0$ that keeps the temperature at 50 °C at this end. What happens inside the rod? Intuitively, you think that the heat generation at the end will warm up the material in the vicinity of $x = 0$, and as time goes by, more and more of the rod will be heated, before the entire rod has a temperature of 50 °C (recall that no heat escapes from the surface of the rod).

Mathematically, (with the temperature in Kelvin) this example has $I(x) = 283$ K, except at the end point: $I(0) = 323$ K, $s(t) = 323$ K, and $g = 0$. The figure below shows snapshots from two different times in the evolution of the temperature.

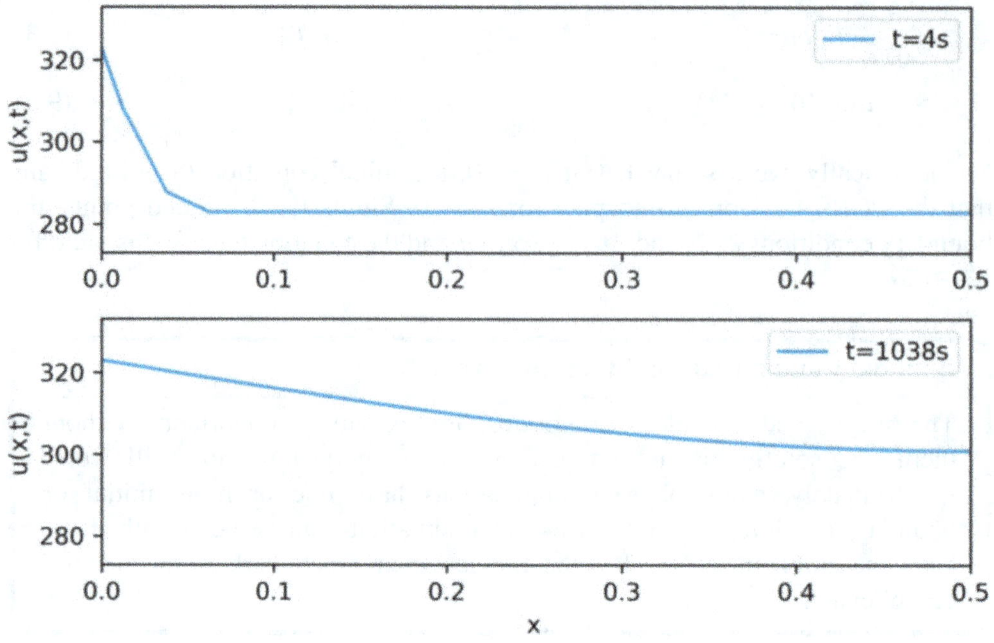


## 9.2 Finite Difference Methods

We shall now construct a numerical method for the diffusion equation. We know how to solve ODEs, so in a way we are able to deal with the time derivative. Very often in mathematics, a new problem can be solved by reducing it to a series of problems we know how to solve. In the present case, it means that we must do something with the spatial derivative $\partial^2/\partial x^2$ in order to reduce the PDE to ODEs. One important technique for achieving this, is based on finite difference discretization of spatial derivatives.

### 9.2.1 Reduction of a PDE to a System of ODEs

Introduce a spatial mesh in $\Omega$ with *mesh points*

$$x_0 = 0 < x_1 < x_2 < \cdots < x_N = L\,.$$

The space between two mesh points $x_i$ and $x_{i+1}$, i.e. the interval $[x_i, x_{i+1}]$, is called a *cell*. We shall here, for simplicity, assume that each cell has the same length $\Delta x = x_{i+1} - x_i$, $i = 0, \ldots, N-1$.

The PDE is valid at all spatial points $x \in \Omega$, but we may relax this condition and demand that it is fulfilled at the internal mesh points only, $x_1, \ldots, x_{N-1}$:

$$\frac{\partial u(x_i, t)}{\partial t} = \beta \frac{\partial^2 u(x_i, t)}{\partial x^2} + g(x_i, t), \quad i = 1, \ldots, N-1\,. \tag{9.5}$$

Now, at any point $x_i$ we can approximate the second-order derivative by a *finite difference*:

$$\frac{\partial^2 u(x_i, t)}{\partial x^2} \approx \frac{u(x_{i+1}, t) - 2u(x_i, t) + u(x_{i-1}, t)}{\Delta x^2}\,. \tag{9.6}$$

It is common to introduce a short notation $u_i(t)$ for $u(x_i, t)$, i.e., $u$ approximated at some mesh point $x_i$ in space. With this new notation we can, after inserting (9.6) in (9.5), write an approximation to the PDE at mesh point $(x_i, t)$ as

$$\frac{du_i(t)}{dt} = \beta \frac{u_{i+1}(t) - 2u_i(t) + u_{i-1}(t)}{\Delta x^2} + g_i(t), \quad i = 1, \ldots, N-1\,. \tag{9.7}$$

Note that we have adopted the notation $g_i(t)$ for $g(x_i, t)$ too.

What is (9.7)? This is nothing but a *system of ordinary differential equations* in $N-1$ unknowns $u_1(t), \ldots, u_{N-1}(t)$! In other words, with aid of the finite difference approximation (9.6), we have reduced the single PDE to a system of ODEs, which we know how to solve. In the literature, this strategy is called the *method of lines*.

We need to look into the initial and boundary conditions as well. The initial condition $u(x, 0) = I(x)$ translates to an initial condition for every unknown function $u_i(t)$: $u_i(0) = I(x_i)$, $i = 0, \ldots, N$. At the boundary $x = 0$ we need an ODE in our ODE system, which must come from the boundary condition at this point. The boundary condition reads $u(0, t) = s(t)$. We can derive an ODE from this equation by differentiating both sides: $u_0'(t) = s'(t)$. The ODE system above cannot be used for $u_0'$ since that equation involves some quantity $u_{-1}'$ outside the domain. Instead, we use the equation $u_0'(t) = s'(t)$ derived from the boundary condition. For this particular equation we also need to make sure the initial condition is $u_0(0) = s(0)$ (otherwise nothing will happen: we get $u = 283$ K forever).

We remark that a separate ODE for the (known) boundary condition $u_0 = s(t)$ is not strictly needed. We can just work with the ODE system for $u_1, \ldots, u_N$, and in the ODE for $u_0$, replace $u_0(t)$ by $s(t)$. However, these authors prefer to have an ODE for every point value $u_i$, $i = 0, \ldots, N$, which requires formulating the known boundary at $x = 0$ as an ODE. The reason for including the boundary values in the ODE system is that the solution of the system is then the complete solution at *all* mesh points, which is convenient, since special treatment of the boundary values is then avoided.

The condition $\partial u/\partial x = 0$ at $x = L$ is a bit more complicated, but we can approximate the spatial derivative by a centered finite difference:

$$\left.\frac{\partial u}{\partial x}\right|_{i=N} \approx \frac{u_{N+1} - u_{N-1}}{2\Delta x} = 0\,.$$

This approximation involves a fictitious point $x_{N+1}$ outside the domain. A common trick is to use (9.7) for $i = N$ and eliminate $u_{N+1}$ by use of the discrete boundary condition ($u_{N+1} = u_{N-1}$):

$$\frac{du_N(t)}{dt} = \beta\frac{2u_{N-1}(t) - 2u_N(t)}{\Delta x^2} + g_N(t)\,. \tag{9.8}$$

That is, we have a special version of (9.7) at the boundary $i = N$.

**What about simpler finite differences at the boundary?**

Some reader may think that a smarter trick is to approximate the boundary condition $\partial u/\partial x$ at $x = L$ by a one-sided difference:

$$\left.\frac{\partial u}{\partial x}\right|_{i=N} \approx \frac{u_N - u_{N-1}}{\Delta x} = 0\,.$$

This gives a simple equation $u_N = u_{N-1}$ for the boundary value, and a corresponding ODE $u'_N = u'_{N-1}$. However, this approximation has an error of order $\Delta x$, while the centered approximation we used above has an error of order $\Delta x^2$. The finite difference approximation we used for the second-order derivative in the diffusion equation also has an error of order $\Delta x^2$. Thus, if we use the simpler one-sided difference above, it turns out that we reduce the overall accuracy of the method.

We are now in a position to summarize how we can approximate the PDE problem (9.1)–(9.4) by a system of ordinary differential equations:

$$\frac{du_0}{dt} = s'(t), \tag{9.9}$$

$$\frac{du_i}{dt} = \frac{\beta}{\Delta x^2}(u_{i+1}(t) - 2u_i(t) + u_{i-1}(t)) + g_i(t), \quad i = 1, \ldots, N-1, \tag{9.10}$$

$$\frac{du_N}{dt} = \frac{2\beta}{\Delta x^2}(u_{N-1}(t) - u_N(t)) + g_N(t)\,. \tag{9.11}$$

The initial conditions are

$$u_0(0) = s(0), \tag{9.12}$$

$$u_i(0) = I(x_i), \quad i = 1, \ldots, N\,. \tag{9.13}$$

We can apply any method for systems of ODEs to solve (9.9)–(9.11).

### 9.2.2 Construction of a Test Problem with Known Discrete Solution

At this point, it is tempting to implement a real physical case and run it. However, PDEs constitute a non-trivial topic where mathematical and programming mistakes come easy. A better start is therefore to address a carefully designed test example where we can check that the method works. The most attractive examples for testing implementations are those without approximation errors, because we know exactly what numbers the program should produce. It turns out that solutions $u(x,t)$ that are linear in time and in space can be exactly reproduced by most numerical methods for PDEs. A candidate solution might be

$$u(x,t) = (3t + 2)(x - L)\,.$$

Inserting this $u$ in the governing equation gives

$$3(x - L) = 0 + g(x,t) \quad \Rightarrow \quad g(x,t) = 3(x - L)\,.$$

What about the boundary conditions? We realize that $\partial u/\partial x = 3t + 2$ for $x = L$, which breaks the assumption of $\partial u/\partial x = 0$ at $x = L$ in the formulation of the numerical method above. Moreover, $u(0,t) = -L(3t + 2)$, so we must set $s(t) = -L(3t + 2)$ and $s'(t) = -3L$. Finally, the initial condition dictates $I(x) = 2(x - L)$, but recall that we must have $u_0 = s(0)$, and $u_i = I(x_i)$, $i = 1, \ldots, N$: it is important that $u_0$ starts out at the right value dictated by $s(t)$ in case $I(0)$ is not equal this value.

First we need to generalize our method to handle $\partial u/\partial x = \gamma \neq 0$ at $x = L$. We then have

$$\frac{u_{N+1}(t) - u_{N-1}(t)}{2\Delta x} = \gamma \quad \Rightarrow \quad u_{N+1} = u_{N-1} + 2\gamma\Delta x,$$

which inserted in (9.7) gives

$$\frac{du_N(t)}{dt} = \beta\frac{2u_{N-1}(t) + 2\gamma\Delta x - 2u_N(t)}{\Delta x^2} + g_N(t)\,. \tag{9.14}$$

### 9.2.3 Implementation: Forward Euler Method

In particular, we may use the Forward Euler method as implemented in the general function `ode_FE` in the module `ode_system_FE` from Sect. 8.3.6. The `ode_FE` function needs a specification of the right-hand side of the ODE system. This is a matter of translating (9.9), (9.10), and (9.14) to Python code (in file `test_diffusion_pde_exact_linear.py`):

```
def rhs(u, t):
    N = len(u) - 1
    rhs = np.zeros(N+1)
    rhs[0] = dsdt(t)
```

```
    for i in range(1, N):
        rhs[i] = (beta/dx**2)*(u[i+1] - 2*u[i] + u[i-1]) + \
                 g(x[i], t)
    rhs[N] = (beta/dx**2)*(2*u[N-1] + 2*dx*dudx(t) -
                           2*u[N]) + g(x[N], t)
    return rhs

def u_exact(x, t):
    return (3*t + 2)*(x - L)

def dudx(t):
    return (3*t + 2)

def s(t):
    return u_exact(0, t)

def dsdt(t):
    return 3*(-L)

def g(x, t):
    return 3*(x-L)
```

Note that `dudx(t)` is the function representing the $\gamma$ parameter in (9.14). Also note that the `rhs` function relies on access to global variables `beta`, `dx`, `L`, and `x`, and global functions `dsdt`, `g`, and `dudx`.

We expect the solution to be correct regardless of $N$ and $\Delta t$, so we can choose a small $N$, $N = 4$, and $\Delta t = 0.1$. A test function with $N = 4$ goes like

```
def test_diffusion_exact_linear():
    global beta, dx, L, x  # needed in rhs
    L = 1.5
    beta = 0.5
    N = 4
    x = np.linspace(0, L, N+1)
    dx = x[1] - x[0]
    u = np.zeros(N+1)

    U_0 = np.zeros(N+1)
    U_0[0] = s(0)
    U_0[1:] = u_exact(x[1:], 0)
    dt = 0.1
    print(dt)

    u, t = ode_FE(rhs, U_0, dt, T=1.2)

    tol = 1E-12
    for i in range(0, u.shape[0]):
        diff = np.abs(u_exact(x, t[i]) - u[i,:]).max()
        assert diff < tol, 'diff={:.16g}'.format(diff)
        print('diff={:g} at t={:g}'.format(diff, t[i]))
```

With $N = 4$ we reproduce the linear solution exactly. This brings confidence to the implementation, which is just what we need for attacking a real physical problem next.

**Problems with reusing the rhs function**

The rhs function *must* take u and t as arguments, because that is required by the ode_FE function. What about the variables beta, dx, L, x, dsdt, g, and dudx that the rhs function needs? These are global in the solution we have presented so far. Unfortunately, this has an undesired side effect: we cannot import the rhs function in a new file, define dudx and dsdt in this new file and get the imported rhs to use these functions. The imported rhs will use the global variables, including functions, in its own module.

How can we find solutions to this problem? Technically, we must pack the extra data beta, dx, L, x, dsdt, g, and dudx with the rhs function, which requires more advanced programming considered beyond the scope of this text.

A class is the simplest construction for packing a function together with data, see the beginning of Chapter 7 in [11] for a detailed example on how classes can be used in such a context. Another solution in Python, and especially in computer languages supporting *functional programming*, is so called *closures*. They are also covered in Chapter 7 in the mentioned reference and behave in a magic way. The third solution is to allow an arbitrary set of arguments for rhs in a list to be transferred to ode_FE and then back to rhs. Appendix H.4 in [11] explains the technical details.

### 9.2.4 Animation: Heat Conduction in a Rod

Let us return to the case with heat conduction in a rod (9.1)–(9.4). Assume that the rod is 50 cm long and made of aluminum alloy 6082. The $\beta$ parameter equals $\kappa/(\varrho c)$, where $\kappa$ is the heat conduction coefficient, $\varrho$ is the density, and $c$ is the heat capacity. We can find proper values for these physical quantities in the case of aluminum alloy 6082: $\varrho = 2.7 \cdot 10^3\ \mathrm{kg/m^3}$, $\kappa = 200\ \frac{\mathrm{W}}{\mathrm{mK}}$, $c = 900\ \frac{\mathrm{J}}{\mathrm{Kkg}}$. This results in $\beta = \kappa/(\varrho c) = 8.2 \cdot 10^{-5}\ \mathrm{m^2/s}$. Preliminary simulations show that we are close to a constant steady state temperature after 1 h, i.e., $T = 3600$ s.

The rhs function from the previous section can be reused, only the functions s, dsdt, g, and dudx must be changed (see file rod_FE.py):

```
def dudx(t):
    return 0

def s(t):
    return 323

def dsdt(t):
    return 0

def g(x, t):
    return 0
```

Parameters can be set as

```
L = 0.5
beta = 8.2E-5
N = 40
x = np.linspace(0, L, N+1)
dx = x[1] - x[0]
u = np.zeros(N+1)

U_0 = np.zeros(N+1)
U_0[0] = s(0)
U_0[1:] = 283
```

Let us use $\Delta t = 1.0$. We can now call `ode_FE` and then make an animation on the screen to see how $u(x, t)$ develops in time:

```
from ode_system_FE import ode_FE
u, t = ode_FE(rhs, U_0, dt, T=1*60*60)

# Make movie
import os
os.system('rm tmp_*.png')
import matplotlib.pyplot as plt
plt.ion()
y = u[0,:]
lines = plt.plot(x, y)
plt.axis([x[0], x[-1], 273, s(0)+10])
plt.xlabel('x')
plt.ylabel('u(x,t)')
counter = 0
# Plot each of the first 100 frames, then increase speed by 10x
change_speed = 100
for i in range(0, u.shape[0]):
    print(t[i])
    plot = True if i <= change_speed else i % 10 == 0
    lines[0].set_ydata(u[i,:])
    if i > change_speed:
        plt.legend(['t={:.0f} 10x'.format(t[i])])
    else:
        plt.legend(['t={:.0f}'.format(t[i])])
    plt.draw()
    if plot:
        plt.savefig('tmp_{:04d}.png'.format(counter))
        counter += 1
    #time.sleep(0.2)
```

The plotting statements update the $u(x, t)$ curve on the screen. In addition, we save a fraction of the plots to files `tmp_0000.png`, `tmp_0001.png`, `tmp_0002.png`, and so on. These plots can be combined to ordinary video files. A common tool is `ffmpeg` or its sister `avconv`.

These programs take the same type of command-line options. To make a Flash video `movie.flv`, run[1]

```
Terminal

Terminal> ffmpeg -i tmp_%04d.png -r 4 -vcodec flv movie.flv
```

[1] You may read about using a *terminal* in Appendix A.

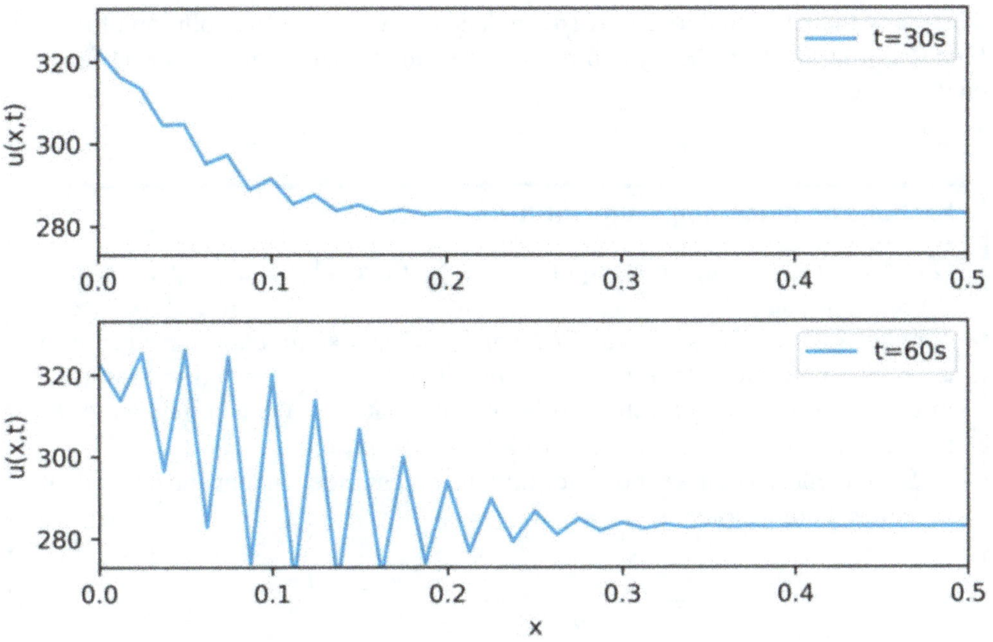


**Fig. 9.1** Unstable simulation of the temperature in a rod

The `-i` option specifies the naming of the plot files, and `-r` specifies the number of frames per second in the movie. On Mac, run `ffmpeg` instead of `avconv` with the same options. Other video formats, such as MP4, WebM, and Ogg can also be produced:

Terminal

```
Terminal> ffmpeg -i tmp_%04d.png -r 4 -vcodec libx264   movie.mp4
Terminal> ffmpeg -i tmp_%04d.png -r 4 -vcodec libvpx    movie.webm
Terminal> ffmpeg -i tmp_%04d.png -r 4 -vcodec libtheora movie.ogg
```

**An Unstable Solution** The results of a simulation start out as seen from the two snapshots in Fig. 9.1. We see that the solution definitely looks wrong. The temperature is expected to be smooth, not having such a saw-tooth shape. We say that this solution is *unstable*, meaning that it does not display the same characteristics as the true, physical solution. Even though we tested the code carefully in the previous section, it does not seem to work for a physical application!

**Why Is the Solution Unstable?** The problem is that $\Delta t$ is too large, making the solution *unstable*. It turns out that the Forward Euler time integration method puts a restriction on the size of $\Delta t$. For the heat equation and the way we have discretized it, this restriction can be shown to be [14]

$$\Delta t \leq \frac{\Delta x^2}{2\beta} . \tag{9.15}$$

This is called a *stability criterion*. With the chosen parameters, (9.15) tells us that the upper limit is $\Delta t = 0.9527439$, which is smaller than our choice above. Rerunning the case with a $\Delta t$ equal to $\Delta x^2/(2\beta)$, indeed shows a smooth evolution of $u(x,t)$. Find the program `rod_FE.py` and run it to see an animation of the $u(x,t)$ function on the screen.

**Scaling and dimensionless quantities**

Our setting of parameters required finding three physical properties of a certain material. The time interval for simulation and the time step depend crucially on the values for $\beta$ and $L$, which can vary significantly from case to case. Often, we are more interested in how the shape of $u(x,t)$ develops, than in the actual $u$, $x$, and $t$ values for a specific material. We can then simplify the setting of physical parameters by *scaling* the problem.

Scaling means that we introduce dimensionless independent and dependent variables, here denoted by a bar:

$$\bar{u} = \frac{u - u^*}{u_c - u^*}, \quad \bar{x} = \frac{x}{x_c}, \quad \bar{t} = \frac{t}{t_c},$$

where $u_c$ is a characteristic size of the temperature, $u^*$ is some reference temperature, while $x_c$ and $t_c$ are characteristic time and space scales. Here, it is natural to choose $u^*$ as the initial condition, and set $u_c$ to the stationary (end) temperature. Then $\bar{u} \in [0,1]$, starting at 0 and ending at 1 as $t \to \infty$. The length $L$ is $x_c$, while choosing $t_c$ is more challenging, but one can argue for $t_c = L^2/\beta$. The resulting equation for $\bar{u}$ reads

$$\frac{\partial \bar{u}}{\partial \bar{t}} = \frac{\partial^2 \bar{u}}{\partial \bar{x}^2}, \quad \bar{x} \in (0,1)\,.$$

Note that in this equation, there are *no physical parameters*! In other words, we have found a model that is independent of the length of the rod and the material it is made of (!).

We can easily solve this equation with our program by setting $\beta = 1$, $L = 1$, $I(x) = 0$, and $s(t) = 1$. It turns out that the total simulation time (to "infinity") can be taken as 1.2. When we have the solution $\bar{u}(\bar{x},\bar{t})$, the solution with dimension Kelvin, reflecting the true temperature in our medium, is given by

$$u(x,t) = u^* + (u_c - u^*)\bar{u}(x/L, t\beta/L^2)\,.$$

Through this formula we can quickly generate the solutions for a rod made of aluminum, wood, or rubber—it is just a matter of plugging in the right $\beta$ value.

The power of scaling is to reduce the number of physical parameters in a problem, and in the present case, we found one single problem that is independent of the material ($\beta$) and the geometry ($L$).

### 9.2.5 Vectorization

Occasionally in this book, we show how to speed up code by replacing loops over arrays by vectorized expressions. The present problem involves a loop for computing the right-hand side:

```
for i in range(1, N):
    rhs[i] = (beta/dx**2)*(u[i+1] - 2*u[i] + u[i-1]) + g(x[i], t)
```

This loop can be replaced by a vectorized expression with the following reasoning. We want to set all the inner points at once: `rhs[1:N-1]` (this goes from index `1` up to, but not including, `N`). As the loop index `i` runs from `1` to `N-1`, the `u[i+1]` term will cover all the inner `u` values displaced one index to the right (compared to `1:N-1`), i.e., `u[2:N]`. Similarly, `u[i-1]` corresponds to all inner `u` values displaced one index to the left: `u[0:N-2]`. Finally, `u[i]` has the same indices as `rhs`: `u[1:N-1]`. The vectorized loop can therefore be written in terms of slices:

```
rhs[1:N-1] = (beta/dx**2)*(u[2:N+1] - 2*u[1:N] + u[0:N-1]) +
             g(x[1:N], t)
```

This rewrite speeds up the code by about a factor of 10. A complete code is found in the file `rod_FE_vec.py`.

### 9.2.6 Using Odespy to Solve the System of ODEs

Let us now show how to apply a general ODE package like Odespy (see Sect. 8.4.6) to solve our diffusion problem. As long as we have defined a right-hand side function `rhs` this is very straightforward:

```
import odespy
import numpy as np

solver = odespy.RKFehlberg(rhs)
solver.set_initial_condition(U_0)

T = 1.2
N_t = int(round(T/dt))
time_points = np.linspace(0, T, N_t+1)
u, t = solver.solve(time_points)

# Check how many time steps are required by adaptive vs
# fixed-step methods
if hasattr(solver, 't_all'):
    print('# time steps:', len(solver.t_all))
else:
    print('# time steps:', len(t))
```

The very nice thing is that we can now easily experiment with many different integration methods. Trying out some simple ones first, like `RK2` and `RK4`, quickly reveals that the time step limitation of the Forward Euler scheme also applies to these more sophisticated Runge-Kutta methods, but their accuracy is better. However, the Odespy package offers also adaptive methods. We can then specify a much larger time step in `time_points`, and the solver will figure out the appropriate

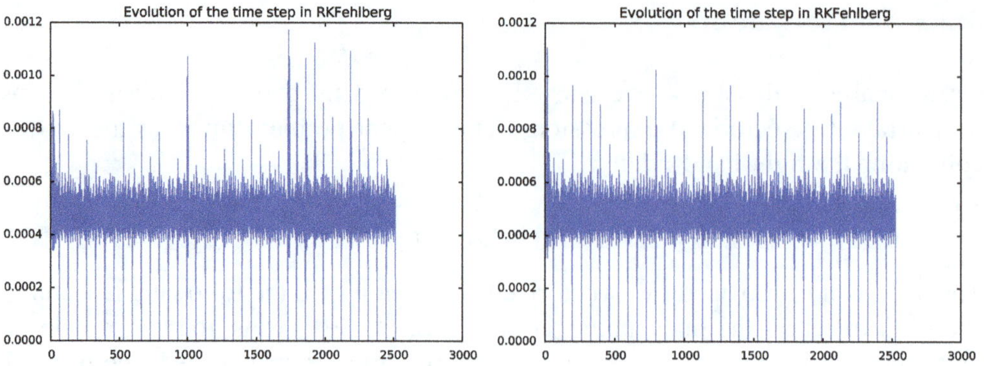


**Fig. 9.2** Time steps used by the Runge-Kutta-Fehlberg method: error tolerance $10^{-3}$ (left) and $10^{-6}$ (right)

step. Above we indicated how to use the adaptive Runge-Kutta-Fehlberg 4-5 solver. While the $\Delta t$ corresponding to the Forward Euler method requires over 8000 steps for a simulation, we started the `RKFehlberg` method with 100 times this time step and in the end it required just slightly more than 2500 steps, using the default tolerance parameters. Lowering the tolerance did not save any significant amount of computational work. Figure 9.2 shows a comparison of the length of all the time steps for two values of the tolerance. We see that the influence of the tolerance is minor in this computational example, so it seems that the blow-up due to instability is what governs the time step size. The nice feature of this adaptive method is that we can just specify when we want the solution to be computed, and the method figures out on its own what time step that has to be used because of stability restrictions.

We have seen how easy it is to apply sophisticated methods for ODEs to this PDE example. We shall take the use of Odespy one step further in the next section.

### 9.2.7 Implicit Methods

A major problem with the stability criterion (9.15) is that the time step becomes very small if $\Delta x$ is small. For example, halving $\Delta x$ requires four times as many time steps and eight times the work. Now, with $N = 40$, which is a reasonable resolution for the test problem above, the computations are very fast. What takes time, is the visualization on the screen, but for that purpose one can visualize only a subset of the time steps. However, there are occasions when you need to take larger time steps with the diffusion equation, especially if interest is in the long-term behavior as $t \to \infty$. You must then turn to *implicit methods* for ODEs. These methods require the solutions of *linear systems*, if the underlying PDE is linear, and systems of *nonlinear algebraic equations* if the underlying PDE is non-linear.

The simplest implicit method is the Backward Euler scheme, which puts no restrictions on $\Delta t$ for stability, but obviously, a large $\Delta t$ leads to inaccurate results. The Backward Euler scheme for a scalar ODE $u' = f(u, t)$ reads

$$\frac{u^{n+1} - u^n}{\Delta t} = f(u^{n+1}, t_{n+1}) \, .$$

This equation is to be solved for $u^{n+1}$. If $f$ is linear in $u$, it is a linear equation, but if $f$ is nonlinear in $u$, one needs approximate methods for nonlinear equations (Chap. 7).

In our case, we have a system of linear ODEs (9.9)–(9.11). The Backward Euler scheme applied to each equation leads to

$$\frac{u_0^{n+1} - u_0^n}{\Delta t} = s'(t_{n+1}), \tag{9.16}$$

$$\frac{u_i^{n+1} - u_i^n}{\Delta t} = \frac{\beta}{\Delta x^2}(u_{i+1}^{n+1} - 2u_i^{n+1} + u_{i-1}^{n+1}) + g_i(t_{n+1}), \tag{9.17}$$

$$i = 1, \ldots, N-1,$$

$$\frac{u_N^{n+1} - u_N^n}{\Delta t} = \frac{2\beta}{\Delta x^2}(u_{N-1}^{n+1} - u_N^{n+1}) + g_i(t_{n+1}). \tag{9.18}$$

This is a system of linear equations in the unknowns $u_i^{n+1}$, $i = 0, \ldots, N$, which is easy to realize by writing out the equations for the case $N = 3$, collecting all the unknown terms on the left-hand side and all the known terms on the right-hand side:

$$u_0^{n+1} = u_0^n + \Delta t\, s'(t_{n+1}), \tag{9.19}$$

$$u_1^{n+1} - \Delta t \frac{\beta}{\Delta x^2}(u_2^{n+1} - 2u_1^{n+1} + u_0^{n+1}) = u_1^n + \Delta t\, g_1(t_{n+1}), \tag{9.20}$$

$$u_2^{n+1} - \Delta t \frac{2\beta}{\Delta x^2}(u_1^{n+1} - u_2^{n+1}) = u_2^n + \Delta t\, g_2(t_{n+1}). \tag{9.21}$$

A system of linear equations like this, is usually written on matrix form $Au = b$, where $A$ is a coefficient matrix, $u = (u_0^{n+1}, \ldots, n_N^{n+1})$ is the vector of unknowns, and $b$ is a vector of known values. The coefficient matrix for the case (9.19)–(9.21) becomes

$$A = \begin{pmatrix} 1 & 0 & 0 \\ -\Delta t \frac{\beta}{\Delta x^2} & 1 + 2\Delta t \frac{\beta}{\Delta x^2} & -\Delta t \frac{\beta}{\Delta x^2} \\ 0 & -\Delta t \frac{2\beta}{\Delta x^2} & 1 + \Delta t \frac{2\beta}{\Delta x^2} \end{pmatrix}$$

In the general case (9.16)–(9.18), the coefficient matrix is an $(N+1) \times (N+1)$ matrix with zero entries, except for

$$A_{1,1} = 1 \tag{9.22}$$

$$A_{i,i-1} = -\Delta t \frac{\beta}{\Delta x^2}, \quad i = 2, \ldots, N-1 \tag{9.23}$$

$$A_{i,i+1} = -\Delta t \frac{\beta}{\Delta x^2}, \quad i = 2, \ldots, N-1 \tag{9.24}$$

$$A_{i,i} = 1 + 2\Delta t \frac{\beta}{\Delta x^2}, \quad i = 2, \ldots, N-1 \tag{9.25}$$

$$A_{N,N-1} = -\Delta t \frac{2\beta}{\Delta x^2} \tag{9.26}$$

$$A_{N,N} = 1 + \Delta t \frac{2\beta}{\Delta x^2} \tag{9.27}$$

If we want to apply general methods for systems of ODEs on the form $u' = f(u,t)$, we can assume a linear $f(u,t) = Ku$. The coefficient matrix $K$ is found from the right-hand side of (9.16)–(9.18) to be

$$K_{1,1} = 0 \tag{9.28}$$

$$K_{i,i-1} = \frac{\beta}{\Delta x^2}, \quad i = 2, \ldots, N-1 \tag{9.29}$$

$$K_{i,i+1} = \frac{\beta}{\Delta x^2}, \quad i = 2, \ldots, N-1 \tag{9.30}$$

$$K_{i,i} = -\frac{2\beta}{\Delta x^2}, \quad i = 2, \ldots, N-1 \tag{9.31}$$

$$K_{N,N-1} = \frac{2\beta}{\Delta x^2} \tag{9.32}$$

$$K_{N,N} = -\frac{2\beta}{\Delta x^2} \tag{9.33}$$

We see that $A = I - \Delta t\, K$.

To implement the Backward Euler scheme, we can either fill a matrix and call a linear solver, or we can apply Odespy. We follow the latter strategy. Implicit methods in Odespy need the $K$ matrix above, given as an argument `jac` (Jacobian of $f$) in the call to `odespy.BackwardEuler`. Here is the Python code for the right-hand side of the ODE system (`rhs`) and the $K$ matrix (`K`) as well as statements for initializing and running the Odespy solver `BackwardEuler` (in the file `rod_BE.py`):

```
def rhs(u, t):
    N = len(u) - 1
    rhs = zeros(N+1)
    rhs[0] = dsdt(t)
    for i in range(1, N):
        rhs[i] = (beta/dx**2)*(u[i+1] - 2*u[i] + u[i-1]) + \
                 g(x[i], t)
    rhs[N] = (beta/dx**2)*(2*u[i-1] + 2*dx*dudx(t) -
                           2*u[i]) + g(x[N], t)
    return rhs

def K(u, t):
    N = len(u) - 1
    K = zeros((N+1,N+1))
    K[0,0] = 0
    for i in range(1, N):
        K[i,i-1] = beta/dx**2
        K[i,i] = -2*beta/dx**2
        K[i,i+1] = beta/dx**2
    K[N,N-1] = (beta/dx**2)*2
```

```
    K[N,N] = (beta/dx**2)*(-2)
    return K
```

```
import odespy
solver = odespy.BackwardEuler(rhs, f_is_linear=True, jac=K)
solver = odespy.ThetaRule(rhs, f_is_linear=True, jac=K, theta=0.5)
solver.set_initial_condition(U_0)
T = 1*60*60
N_t = int(round(T/dt))
time_points = linspace(0, T, N_t+1)
u, t = solver.solve(time_points)
```

The file `rod_BE.py` has all the details and shows a movie of the solution. We can run it with any $\Delta t$ we want, its size just impacts the accuracy of the first steps.

**Odespy solvers apply dense matrices!**

Looking at the entries of the $K$ matrix, we realize that there are at maximum three entries different from zero in each row. Therefore, most of the entries are zeroes. The Odespy solvers expect dense square matrices as input, here with $(N + 1) \times (N + 1)$ elements. When solving the linear systems, a lot of storage and work are spent on the zero entries in the matrix. It would be much more efficient to store the matrix as a *tridiagonal* matrix and apply a specialized Gaussian elimination solver for tridiagonal systems. Actually, this reduces the work from the order $N^3$ to the order $N$.

In one-dimensional diffusion problems, the savings of using a tridiagonal matrix are modest in practice, since the matrices are very small anyway. In two- and three-dimensional PDE problems, however, one cannot afford dense square matrices. Rather, one *must* resort to more efficient storage formats and algorithms tailored to such formats, but this is beyond the scope of the present text.

## 9.3 Exercises

**Exercise 9.1: Simulate a Diffusion Equation by Hand**
Consider the problem given by (9.9), (9.10) and (9.14). Set $N = 2$ and compute $u_i^0$, $u_i^1$ and $u_i^2$ by hand for $i = 0, 1, 2$. Use these values to construct a test function for checking that the implementation is correct. Copy useful functions from `test_diffusion_pde_exact_linear.py` and make a new test function `test_diffusion_hand_calculation`.
Filename: `test_rod_hand_calculations.py`.

**Exercise 9.2: Compute Temperature Variations in the Ground**
The surface temperature at the ground shows daily and seasonal oscillations. When the temperature rises at the surface, heat is propagated into the ground, and the coefficient $\beta$ in the diffusion equation determines how fast this propagation is. It takes some time before the temperature rises down in the ground. At the surface, the

temperature has then fallen. We are interested in how the temperature varies down in the ground because of temperature oscillations on the surface.

Assuming homogeneous horizontal properties of the ground, at least locally, and no variations of the temperature at the surface at a fixed point of time, we can neglect the horizontal variations of the temperature. Then a one-dimensional diffusion equation governs the heat propagation along a vertical axis called $x$. The surface corresponds to $x = 0$ and the $x$ axis point downwards into the ground. There is no source term in the equation (actually, if rocks in the ground are radioactive, they emit heat and that can be modeled by a source term, but this effect is neglected here).

At some depth $x = L$ we assume that the heat changes in $x$ vanish, so $\partial u/\partial x = 0$ is an appropriate boundary condition at $x = L$. We assume a simple sinusoidal temperature variation at the surface:

$$u(0,t) = T_0 + T_a \sin\left(\frac{2\pi}{P}t\right),$$

where $P$ is the period, taken here as 24 h ($24 \cdot 60 \cdot 60$ s). The $\beta$ coefficient may be set to $10^{-6}$ m$^2$/s. Time is then measured in seconds. Set appropriate values for $T_0$ and $T_a$.

a) Show that the present problem has an analytical solution of the form

$$u(x,t) = A + Be^{-rx}\sin(\omega t - rx),$$

for appropriate values of $A$, $B$, $r$, and $\omega$.

b) Solve this heat propagation problem numerically for some days and animate the temperature. You may use the Forward Euler method in time. Plot both the numerical and analytical solution. As initial condition for the numerical solution, use the exact solution during program development, and when the curves coincide in the animation for all times, your implementation works, and you can then switch to a constant initial condition: $u(x,0) = T_0$. For this latter initial condition, how many periods of oscillations are necessary before there is a good (visual) match between the numerical and exact solution (despite differences at $t = 0$)?

Filename: `ground_temp.py`.

**Exercise 9.3: Compare Implicit Methods**

An equally stable, but more accurate method than the Backward Euler scheme, is the so-called 2-step backward scheme, which for an ODE $u' = f(u,t)$ can be expressed by

$$\frac{3u^{n+1} - 4u^n + u^{n-1}}{2\Delta t} = f(u^{n+1}, t_{n+1}).$$

The Odespy package offers this method as `odespy.Backward2Step`. The purpose of this exercise is to compare three methods and animate the three solutions:

1. The Backward Euler method with $\Delta t = 0.001$
2. The backward 2-step method with $\Delta t = 0.001$

3. The backward 2-step method with $\Delta t = 0.01$

Choose the model problem from Sect. 9.2.4.
Filename: `rod_BE_vs_B2Step.py`.

**Exercise 9.4: Explore Adaptive and Implicit Methods**
We consider the same problem as in Exercise 9.2. Now we want to explore the use of adaptive and implicit methods from Odespy to see if they are more efficient than the Forward Euler method. Assume that you want the accuracy provided by the Forward Euler method with its maximum $\Delta t$ value. Since there exists an analytical solution, you can compute an error measure that summarizes the error in space and time over the whole simulation:

$$E = \sqrt{\Delta x \Delta t \sum_i \sum_n (U_i^n - u_i^n)^2}\,.$$

Here, $U_i^n$ is the exact solution. Use the Odespy package to run the following implicit and adaptive solvers:

1. `BackwardEuler`
2. `Backward2Step`
3. `RKFehlberg`

Experiment to see if you can use larger time steps than what is required by the Forward Euler method and get solutions with the same order of accuracy.

**Hint** To avoid oscillations in the solutions when using the RKFehlberg method, the `rtol` and `atol` parameters to `RKFFehlberg` must be set no larger than 0.001 and 0.0001, respectively. You can print out `solver_RKF.t_all` to see all the time steps used by the RKFehlberg solver (if `solver` is the `RKFehlberg` object). You can then compare the number of time steps with what is required by the other methods.

Filename: `ground_temp_adaptive.py`.

**Exercise 9.5: Investigate the $\theta$ Rule**

a) The Crank-Nicolson method for ODEs is very popular when combined with diffusion equations. For a linear ODE $u' = au$ it reads

$$\frac{u^{n+1} - u^n}{\Delta t} = \frac{1}{2}(au^n + au^{n+1})\,.$$

Apply the Crank-Nicolson method in time to the ODE system for a one-dimensional diffusion equation. Identify the linear system to be solved.

b) The Backward Euler, Forward Euler, and Crank-Nicolson methods can be given a unified implementation. For a linear ODE $u' = au$ this formulation is known as the $\theta$ rule:

$$\frac{u^{n+1} - u^n}{\Delta t} = (1-\theta)au^n + \theta a u^{n+1}\,.$$

For $\theta = 0$ we recover the Forward Euler method, $\theta = 1$ gives the Backward Euler scheme, and $\theta = 1/2$ corresponds to the Crank-Nicolson method. The approximation error in the $\theta$ rule is proportional to $\Delta t$, except for $\theta = 1/2$ where it is proportional to $\Delta t^2$. For $\theta \geq 1/2$ the method is stable for all $\Delta t$.

Apply the $\theta$ rule to the ODE system for a one-dimensional diffusion equation. Identify the linear system to be solved.

c) Implement the $\theta$ rule with aid of the Odespy package. The relevant object name is `ThetaRule`:

```
solver = odespy.ThetaRule(rhs, f_is_linear=True, jac=K, theta=0.5)
```

d) Consider the physical application from Sect. 9.2.4. Run this case with the $\theta$ rule and $\theta = 1/2$ for the following values of $\Delta t$: 0.001, 0.01, 0.05. Report what you see.

Filename: `rod_ThetaRule.py`.

**Remarks** Despite the fact that the Crank-Nicolson method, or the $\theta$ rule with $\theta = 1/2$, is theoretically more accurate than the Backward Euler and Forward Euler schemes, it may exhibit non-physical oscillations as in the present example if the solution is very steep. The oscillations are damped in time, and decreases with decreasing $\Delta t$. To avoid oscillations one must have $\Delta t$ at maximum twice the stability limit of the Forward Euler method. This is one reason why the Backward Euler method (or a 2-step backward scheme, see Exercise 9.3) are popular for diffusion equations with abrupt initial conditions.

**Exercise 9.6: Compute the Diffusion of a Gaussian Peak**

Solve the following diffusion problem:

$$\frac{\partial u}{\partial t} = \beta\frac{\partial^2 u}{\partial x^2}, \qquad x \in (-1,1),\ t \in (0,T] \tag{9.34}$$

$$u(x,0) = \frac{1}{\sqrt{2\pi}\sigma}\exp\left(-\frac{x^2}{2\sigma^2}\right), \qquad x \in [-1,1], \tag{9.35}$$

$$\frac{\partial}{\partial x}u(-1,t) = 0, \qquad t \in (0,T], \tag{9.36}$$

$$\frac{\partial}{\partial x}u(1,t) = 0, \qquad t \in (0,T]\,. \tag{9.37}$$

The initial condition is the famous and widely used *Gaussian function* with standard deviation (or "width") $\sigma$, which is here taken to be small, $\sigma = 0.01$, such that the initial condition is a peak. This peak will then diffuse and become lower and wider. Compute $u(x, t)$ until $u$ becomes approximately constant over the domain.
Filename: `gaussian_diffusion.py`.

**Remarks** Running the simulation with $\sigma = 0.2$ results in a constant solution $u \approx 1$ as $t \to \infty$, while one might expect from "physics of diffusion" that the solution should approach zero. The reason is that we apply Neumann conditions as boundary conditions. One can then easily show that the area under the $u$ curve remains constant. Integrating the PDE gives

$$\int_{-1}^{1} \frac{\partial u}{\partial t} dx = \beta \int_{-1}^{1} \frac{\partial^2 u}{\partial x^2} dx\,.$$

Using the Gauss divergence theorem on the integral on the right-hand and moving the time-derivative outside the integral on the left-hand side results in

$$\frac{\partial}{\partial t} \int_{-1}^{1} u(x, t) dx = \beta \left[ \frac{\partial u}{\partial x} \right]_{-1}^{1} = 0.$$

(Recall that $\partial u/\partial x = 0$ at the end points.) The result means that $\int_{-1}^{1} u dx$ remains constant during the simulation. Giving the PDE an interpretation in terms of heat conduction can easily explain the result: with Neumann conditions no heat can escape from the domain so the initial heat will just be evenly distributed, but not leak out, so the temperature cannot go to zero (or the scaled and translated temperature $u$, to be precise). The area under the initial condition is 1, so with a sufficiently fine mesh, $u \to 1$, regardless of $\sigma$.

**Exercise 9.7: Vectorize a Function for Computing the Area of a Polygon**
Vectorize the implementation of the function for computing the area of a polygon in Exercise 5.6. Make a test function that compares the scalar implementation in Exercise 5.6 and the new vectorized implementation for the test cases used in Exercise 5.6.

**Hint** Notice that the formula $x_1 y_2 + x_2 y_3 + \cdots + x_{n-1} y_n = \sum_{i=0}^{n-1} x_i y_{i+1}$ is the dot product of two vectors, `x[:-1]` and `y[1:]`, which can be computed as `numpy.dot(x[:-1], y[1:])`, or more explicitly as `numpy.sum(x[:-1]*y[1:])`.

Filename: `polyarea_vec.py`.

**Exercise 9.8: Explore Symmetry**
One can observe (and also mathematically prove) that the solution $u(x, t)$ of the problem in Exercise 9.6 is symmetric around $x = 0$: $u(-x, t) = u(x, t)$. In such a case, we can split the domain in two and compute $u$ in only one half, $[-1, 0]$ or $[0, 1]$. At the symmetry line $x = 0$ we have the symmetry boundary condition

$\partial u/\partial x = 0$. Reformulate the problem in Exercise 9.6 such that we compute only for $x \in [0, 1]$. Display the solution and observe that it equals the right part of the solution in Exercise 9.6.
Filename: `symmetric_gaussian_diffusion.py`.

**Remarks** In 2D and 3D problems, where the CPU time to compute a solution of PDE can be hours and days, it is very important to utilize symmetry as we do above to reduce the size of the problem.

Also note the remarks in Exercise 9.6 about the constant area under the $u(x, t)$ curve: here, the area is 0.5 and $u \to 0.5$ as $t \to 0.5$ (if the mesh is sufficiently fine—one will get convergence to smaller values for small $\sigma$ if the mesh is not fine enough to properly resolve a thin-shaped initial condition).

**Exercise 9.9: Compute Solutions as $t \to \infty$**
Many diffusion problems reach a stationary time-independent solution as $t \to \infty$. The model problem from Sect. 9.2.4 is one example where $u(x, t) = s(t) = \text{const}$ for $t \to \infty$. When $u$ does not depend on time, the diffusion equation reduces to

$$-\beta u''(x) = f(x),$$

in one dimension, and

$$-\beta \nabla^2 u = f(x),$$

in 2D and 3D. This is the famous *Poisson* equation, or if $f = 0$, it is known as the *Laplace* equation. In this limit $t \to \infty$, there is no need for an initial condition, but the boundary conditions are the same as for the diffusion equation.

We now consider a one-dimensional problem

$$-u''(x) = 0, \ x \in (0, L), \quad u(0) = C, \ u'(L) = 0, \tag{9.38}$$

which is known as a *two-point boundary value problem*. This is nothing but the stationary limit of the diffusion problem in Sect. 9.2.4. How can we solve such a stationary problem (9.38)? The simplest strategy, when we already have a solver for the corresponding time-dependent problem, is to use that solver and simulate until $t \to \infty$, which in practice means that $u(x, t)$ no longer changes in time (within some tolerance).

A nice feature of implicit methods like the Backward Euler scheme is that one can take *one very long time step* to "infinity" and produce the solution of (9.38).

a) Let (9.38) be valid at mesh points $x_i$ in space, discretize $u''$ by a finite difference, and set up a system of equations for the point values $u_i$,$i = 0, \ldots, N$, where $u_i$ is the approximation at mesh point $x_i$.
b) Show that if $\Delta t \to \infty$ in (9.16)–(9.18), it leads to the same equations as in a).
c) Demonstrate, by running a program, that you can take one large time step with the Backward Euler scheme and compute the solution of (9.38). The solution is very boring since it is constant: $u(x) = C$.

Filename: `rod_stationary.py`.

**Remarks** If the interest is in the stationary limit of a diffusion equation, one can either solve the associated Laplace or Poisson equation directly, or use a Backward Euler scheme for the time-dependent diffusion equation with a very long time step. Using a Forward Euler scheme with small time steps is typically inappropriate in such situations because the solution changes more and more slowly, but the time step must still be kept small, and it takes "forever" to approach the stationary state. This is yet another example why one needs implicit methods like the Backward Euler scheme.

**Exercise 9.10: Solve a Two-Point Boundary Value Problem**
Solve the following two-point boundary-value problem

$$u''(x) = 2, \ x \in (0, 1), \quad u(0) = 0, \ u(1) = 1 .$$

**Hint** Do Exercise 9.9. Modify the boundary condition in the code so it incorporates a known value for $u(1)$.

Filename: `2ptBVP.py`.

# Installation and Use of Python

# A

This appendix addresses[1] a few issues related to the installation and use of Python on different platforms. In addition, the accessing of Python in the cloud is commented in brief.

## A.1 Recommendation: Install Anaconda and Odespy

If you install Anaconda, the only additional package you need for running all the software in the present book, is `Odespy`. The original version of `Odespy` was written in Python 2.7 by H.P. Langtangen and L. Wei (https://github.com/hplgit/odespy), but since the sad loss of Prof. Langtangen in October 2016, Thomas Anthony has made an updated version for Python 3.6 (https://github.com/thomasantony/odespy/tree/py36/odespy). In the present book, we use this version of `Odespy` to demonstrate how ordinary differential equations alternatively may be solved with ready-made software.

## A.2 Required Software

If you, for some reason, decide to install something else than Anaconda, you should know what software components that are required for running the programs in this book:

- Python[2] version 3.6 [24]
- Numerical Python[3] (NumPy) [18, 19] for array computing

[1] Some of the text is taken from the 4th edition of the book *A Primer on Scientific Programming with Python*, by H. P. Langtangen, published by Springer, 2014.
[2] http://python.org.
[3] http://www.numpy.org.



S. Linge, H. P. Langtangen, *Programming for Computations - Python*,
Texts in Computational Science and Engineering 15,
https://doi.org/10.1007/978-3-030-16877-3

- Matplotlib[4] [7, 8] for plotting
- IPython[5] [21, 22] for interactive computing
- SymPy[6] [2] for symbolic mathematics
- Spyder[7] if you want to write and run your programs as we (primarily) do in this book.

In addition, allthough not used herein, the following packages might be of interest to you (probably at some later stage, if you are a newbie):

- SciTools[8] [13] for add-ons to NumPy
- ScientificPython[9] [26] for add-ons to NumPy
- pytest[10] or nose[11] for testing programs
- pip[12] for installing Python packages
- Cython[13] for compiling Python to C
- SciPy[14] [9] for advanced scientific computing

**Converting a Python 2 Program to Python 3**

Python comes in two versions, version 2 and 3, and these are not fully compatible. However, for the programs in this book, the differences are very small, the major one being `print`, which in Python 2 is a statement like

```
print 'a:', a, 'b:', b
```

while in Python 3 it is a function call

```
print( 'a:', a, 'b:', b)
```

The code in this book is written in Python 3.6. However, you may come across code elsewhere that is written in Python 2, and you might prefer to have that code in Python 3. The good news, is that porting code from Python 2 to Python 3 is usually quite straight forward. One alternative, is to use the program `2to3`. Running `2to3 prog.py` will transform a Python 2 program `prog.py` to its Python 3 counterpart. One can also use tools like `future` or `six` to easily write programs that run under both Python 2 and 3. Also, the `futurize` program can automatically do this for you based on v2.7 code.

4 http://matplotlib.org.
5 http://ipython.org.
6 http://sympy.org.
7 https://github.com/spyder-ide/spyder.
8 https://github.com/hplgit/scitools.
9 http://starship.python.net/crew/hinsen.
10 http://pytest.org/latest/.
11 https://nose.readthedocs.org.
12 http://www.pip-installer.org.
13 http://cython.org.
14 http://scipy.org.

As alternatives to installing the software on your own laptop, you may:

1. Use a computer system at an institution where the software is installed. Such a system can also be used from your local laptop through remote login over a network.
2. Use a web service.

A system administrator can take the list of software packages and install the missing ones on a computer system.

Using a web service is straightforward, but has the disadvantage that you are constrained by the packages that you are allowed to install on the service. There are services (at the time of this writing) that suffice for basic scientific Python programming. However, for more complicated mathematical problems, you will need more sophisticated packages, more storage and more computer resources, which means that you will greatly benefit from having Python installed on your own computer.

## A.3 Anaconda and Spyder

Anaconda[15] is a free Python distribution (by Continuum Analytics) with hundreds of excellent Python packages, as well as Python itself, for doing a wide range of scientific computations.

The Integrated Development Environment (IDE) *Spyder* comes with Anaconda and is our recommended tool for writing and running Python programs, unless you prefer a plain text editor for the writing of programs and a terminal window (explained below, see Appendix A.4.3) for running them.

### A.3.1 Spyder on Mac

Spyder is started by typing `spyder` in a (new) Terminal application. If you get an error message *unknown locale*, you need to type the following line in the Terminal application, or preferably put the line in your `$HOME/.bashrc` Unix initialization file:

```
export LANG=en_US.UTF-8; export LC_ALL=en_US.UTF-8
```

### A.3.2 Installation of Additional Packages

Anaconda installs the `pip` tool that is handy for installing additional packages. In a Terminal application on Mac, or in a PowerShell terminal on Windows, write

Terminal
```
pip install --user packagename
```

[15] https://www.anaconda.com/distribution.

## A.4 How to Write and Run a Python Program

You have basically three choices to develop and test a Python program:

1. use an IDE like Spyder, which offers a window with a text editor and functionality to run programs and observe the output
2. use a text editor and a terminal window
3. use the Jupyter notebook

### A.4.1 Spyder

Spyder is a graphical application for developing and running Python programs, available on all major platforms. Spyder comes with Anaconda and some other pre-built environments for scientific computing with Python. On Ubuntu it is conveniently installed by `sudo apt-get install spyder`.

The left pane in Spyder contains a plain text editor and this is where you will write your programs. As a quick test, write and run the following little program (compare also with Fig. A.1). Click in the editor pane and write `print('Hello!')`. Save this to a file (`File` and `Save as` from the menu) called, e.g., `Spyder_test.py`. Then, choose *Run* from the *Run* pull-down menu, and observe the output `Hello!` in the lower right pane, which is where program output appears. The upper right pane (file explorer) allows you to view and manage files.

With different settings (can be changed via the menu), the appearance and functioning of the Spyder environment may be changed in many ways. Much more details about the Spyder environment can be found at https://www.spyder-ide.org/.

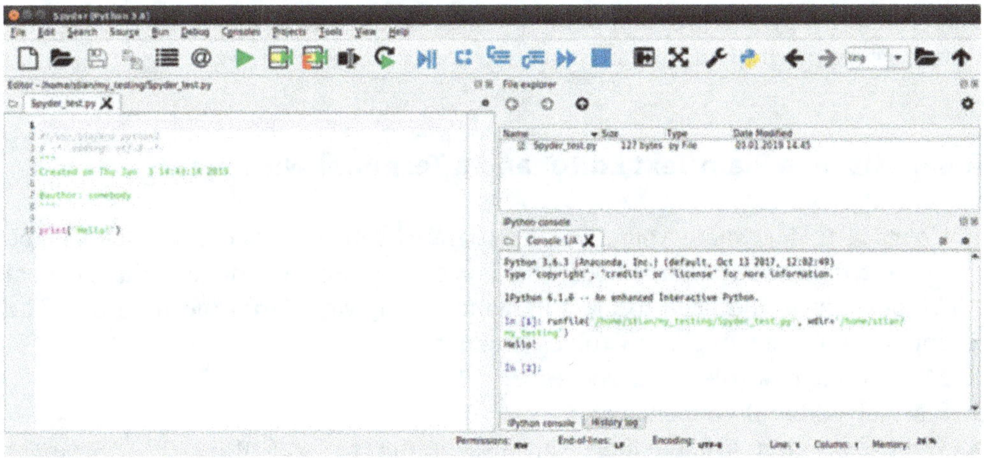

**Fig. A.1** The Spyder Integrated Development Environment with a simple program that prints `Hello!`

### A.4.2 Text Editors

The most widely used editors for writing programs are Emacs and Vim, which are available on all major platforms. Some simpler alternatives for beginners are

- Linux: Gedit
- Mac OS X: TextWrangler
- Windows: Notepad++

We may mention that Python comes with an editor called Idle, which can be used to write programs on all three platforms, but running the program with command-line arguments is a bit complicated for beginners in Idle so Idle is not my favorite recommendation.

Gedit is a standard program on Linux platforms, but all other editors must be installed in your system. This is easy: just google the name, download the file, and follow the standard procedure for installation. All of the mentioned editors come with a graphical user interface that is intuitive to use, but the major popularity of Emacs and Vim is due to their rich set of short-keys so that you can avoid using the mouse and consequently edit at higher speed.

### A.4.3 Terminal Windows

To run the Python program, you may use a *terminal window*. This is a window where you can issue Unix commands in Linux and Mac OS X systems and DOS commands in Windows. On a Linux computer, `gnome-terminal` is my favorite, but other choices work equally well, such as `xterm` and `konsole`. On a Mac computer, launch the application *Utilities—Terminal*. On Windows, launch *PowerShell*.

You must first move to the right folder using the `cd foldername` command. Then running a python program `prog.py` is a matter of writing `python prog.py`. Whatever the program prints can be seen in the terminal window.

### A.4.4 Using a Plain Text Editor and a Terminal Window

1. Create a folder where your Python programs can be located, say with name `mytest` under your home folder. This is most conveniently done in the terminal window since you need to use this window anyway to run the program. The command for creating a new folder is `mkdir mytest`.
2. Move to the new folder: `cd mytest`.
3. Start the editor of your choice.
4. Write a program in the editor, e.g., just the line `print('Hello!')`. Save the program under the name `myprog1.py` in the `mytest` folder.
5. Move to the terminal window and write `python myprog1.py`. You should see the word `Hello!` being printed in the window.

## A.5 Python with Jupyter Notebooks and Web Services

You can avoid installing Python on your machine by using a web service that allows you to write and run Python programs. One excellent such web service is *CoCalc* (https://cocalc.com/), previously known as *SageMathCloud*, which supports the use of *Jupyter notebooks* (and more).

Such notebooks are great, in particular for report writing, in that they allow text, mathematics, code and graphics to all be worked out in a single document. The code in the document can be developed, modified and run, producing updated plots that become part of a new version of the document (or report). You find the information you need at https://jupyter.org/.

# References


1. L. Baochuan, *Introduction to Numerical Methods* (2015), http://en.wikibooks.org/wiki/Introduction_to_Numerical_Methods
2. O. Certik et al., SymPy: Python library for symbolic mathematics. http://sympy.org/
3. S.D. Conte, C. de Boor, *Elementary Numerical Analysis–An Algorithmic Approach*, 3rd edn. (McGraw-Hill, New York, 1980)
4. I. Danaila, P. Joly, S.M. Kaber, M. Postel, *An Introduction to Scientific Computing* (Springer, Berlin, 2007)
5. C. Greif, U.M. Ascher, *A First Course in Numerical Methods*. Computational Science and Engineering (SIAM, Philadelphia, 2011)
6. D.W. Harder, R. Khoury, *Numerical Analysis for Engineering* (2015), https://ece.uwaterloo.ca/~dwharder/NumericalAnalysis/
7. J.D. Hunter, Matplotlib: a 2D graphics environment. Comput. Sci. Eng. **9**, 90–95 (2007)
8. J.D. Hunter et al., Matplotlib: Software package for 2D graphics, http://matplotlib.org/
9. E. Jones, T.E. Oliphant, P. Peterson, et al., SciPy scientific computing library for Python, http://scipy.org
10. J. Kiusalaas. *Numerical Methods in Engineering with Python*, 2nd edn. (Cambridge Universtiy Press, Cambridge, 2014)
11. H.P. Langtangen, *A Primer on Scientific Programming with Python*, 5th edn. Texts in Computational Science and Engineering (Springer, Berlin, 2016)
12. H.P. Langtangen, DocOnce publishing platform, https://github.com/hplgit/doconce
13. H.P. Langtangen, J.H. Ring, SciTools: Software tools for scientific computing, https://github.com/hplgit/scitools
14. R. LeVeque, *Finite Difference Methods for Ordinary and Partial Differential Equations: Steady-State and Time-Dependent Problems* (SIAM, Philadelphia, 2007)
15. T. Lyche, J.-L. Merrien, *Exercises in Computational Mathematics with MATLAB* (Springer, Berlin, 2014)
16. C. Moler, *Numerical Computing with MATLAB* (SIAM, Philadelphia, 2004) http://se.mathworks.com/moler/chapters.html
17. S. Nakamura, *Numerical Analysis and Graphic Visualization with Matlab*, 2nd edn. (Prentice Hall, Upper Saddle River, 2002)
18. T.E. Oliphant, Python for scientific computing. Comput. Sci. Eng. **9**, 10–20 (2007)
19. T.E. Oliphant, et al., NumPy array processing package for Python, http://www.numpy.org




S. Linge, H. P. Langtangen, *Programming for Computations - Python*,
Texts in Computational Science and Engineering 15,
https://doi.org/10.1007/978-3-030-16877-3

20. S. Otto, J.P. Denier, *An Introduction to Programming and Numerical Methods in MATLAB* (Springer, Berlin, 2005)
21. F. Perez, B.E. Granger, IPython: a system for interactive scientific computing. Comput. Sci. Eng. **9**, 21–29 (2007)
22. F. Perez, B.E. Granger, et al., IPython software package for interactive scientific computing, http://ipython.org/
23. W.H. Press, S.A. Teukolsky, W.T. Vetterling, B.P. Flannery, *Numerical Recipes* (Cambridge University Press, Cambridge, 1992), http://www.nrbook.com/a/bookcpdf.php
24. Python programming language, http://python.org
25. G. Recktenwald, *Numerical Methods with MATLAB: Implementations and Applications* (Prentice-Hall, Upper Saddle River, 2000), http://web.cecs.pdx.edu/~gerry/nmm/
26. ScientificPython software package, http://starship.python.net/crew/hinsen
27. G. Sewell, *The Numerical Solution of Ordinary and Partial Differential Equations* (Wiley, Hoboken, 2005)
28. T. Siauw, A. Bayen, *An Introduction to MATLAB Programming and Numerical Methods for Engineers* (Academic Press, Cambridge, 2014), http://www.sciencedirect.com/science/book/9780124202283
29. L.N. Trefethen, *Spectral Methods in MATLAB* (SIAM, Philadelphia, 2000)
30. L.N. Trefethen, *Approximation Theory and Approximation Practice* (SIAM, Philadelphia, 2012)
31. T. Young, M.J. Mohlenkamp, *Introduction to Numerical Methods and MATLAB Programming for Engineers* (2015), https://www.math.ohiou.edu/courses/math3600/book.pdf

# Index








S. Linge, H. P. Langtangen, *Programming for Computations - Python*,
Texts in Computational Science and Engineering 15,
https://doi.org/10.1007/978-3-030-16877-3

## *Editorial Policy*

1. Textbooks on topics in the field of computational science and engineering will be considered. They should be written for courses in CSE education. Both graduate and undergraduate textbooks will be published in TCSE. Multidisciplinary topics and multidisciplinary teams of authors are especially welcome.
2. Format: Only works in English will be considered. For evaluation purposes, manuscripts may be submitted in print or electronic form, in the latter case, preferably as pdf- or zipped ps-files. Authors are requested to use the LaTeX style files available from Springer at: http://www.springer.com/authors/book+authors/helpdesk?SGWID=0-1723113-12-971304-0 (Click on ⟶ Templates ⟶ LaTeX ⟶ monographs)
   Electronic material can be included if appropriate. Please contact the publisher.
3. Those considering a book which might be suitable for the series are strongly advised to contact the publisher or the series editors at an early stage.

## *General Remarks*

Careful preparation of manuscripts will help keep production time short and ensure a satisfactory appearance of the finished book.

The following terms and conditions hold:

Regarding free copies and royalties, the standard terms for Springer mathematics textbooks hold. Please write to martin.peters@springer.com for details.

Authors are entitled to purchase further copies of their book and other Springer books for their personal use, at a discount of 33.3% directly from Springer-Verlag.

## *Series Editors*

# Texts in Computational Science and Engineering

1. H. P. Langtangen, *Computational Partial Differential Equations.* Numerical Methods and Diffpack Programming. 2nd Edition
2. A. Quarteroni, F. Saleri, P. Gervasio, *Scientific Computing with MATLAB and Octave.* 4th Edition
3. H. P. Langtangen, *Python Scripting for Computational Science.* 3rd Edition
4. H. Gardner, G. Manduchi, *Design Patterns for e-Science.*
5. M. Griebel, S. Knapek, G. Zumbusch, *Numerical Simulation in Molecular Dynamics.*
6. H. P. Langtangen, *A Primer on Scientific Programming with Python.* 5th Edition
7. A. Tveito, H. P. Langtangen, B. F. Nielsen, X. Cai, *Elements of Scientific Computing.*
8. B. Gustafsson, *Fundamentals of Scientific Computing.*
9. M. Bader, *Space-Filling Curves.*
10. M. Larson, F. Bengzon, *The Finite Element Method: Theory, Implementation and Applications.*
11. W. Gander, M. Gander, F. Kwok, *Scientific Computing: An Introduction using Maple and MATLAB.*
12. P. Deuflhard, S. Röblitz, *A Guide to Numerical Modelling in Systems Biology.*
13. M. H. Holmes, *Introduction to Scientific Computing and Data Analysis.*
14. S. Linge, H. P. Langtangen, *Programming for Computations* - A Gentle Introduction to Numerical Simulations with MATLAB/Octave.
15. S. Linge, H. P. Langtangen, *Programming for Computations* - A Gentle Introduction to Numerical Simulations with Python.
16. H.P. Langtangen, S. Linge, *Finite Difference Computing with PDEs* - A Modern Software Approach.
17. B. Gustafsson, *Scientific Computing - A Historical Perspective.*
18. J. A. Trangenstein, *Scientific Computing* - Vol. I. - Linear and Nonlinear Equations.
19. J. A. Trangenstein, *Scientific Computing* - Vol. II. - Eigenvalues and Optimization.
20. J. A. Trangenstein, *Scientific Computing* - Vol. III. - Approximation and Integration.

*For further information on these books please have a look at our mathematics catalogue at the following URL:* `www.springer.com/series/5151`

# Monographs in Computational Science and Engineering

1. J. Sundnes, G.T. Lines, X. Cai, B.F. Nielsen, K.-A. Mardal, A. Tveito, *Computing the Electrical Activity in the Heart.*

*For further information on this book, please have a look at our mathematics catalogue at the following URL:* `www.springer.com/series/7417`

# Lecture Notes in Computational Science and Engineering

1. D. Funaro, *Spectral Elements for Transport-Dominated Equations.*
2. H.P. Langtangen, *Computational Partial Differential Equations.* Numerical Methods and Diffpack Programming.
3. W. Hackbusch, G. Wittum (eds.), *Multigrid Methods V.*
4. P. Deuflhard, J. Hermans, B. Leimkuhler, A.E. Mark, S. Reich, R.D. Skeel (eds.), *Computational Molecular Dynamics: Challenges, Methods, Ideas.*
5. D. Kröner, M. Ohlberger, C. Rohde (eds.), *An Introduction to Recent Developments in Theory and Numerics for Conservation Laws.*
6. S. Turek, *Efficient Solvers for Incompressible Flow Problems.* An Algorithmic and Computational Approach.
7. R. von Schwerin, ***M**ulti **B**ody **S**ystem **SIM**ulation.* Numerical Methods, Algorithms, and Software.
8. H.-J. Bungartz, F. Durst, C. Zenger (eds.), *High Performance Scientific and Engineering Computing.*
9. T.J. Barth, H. Deconinck (eds.), *High-Order Methods for Computational Physics.*
10. H.P. Langtangen, A.M. Bruaset, E. Quak (eds.), *Advances in Software Tools for Scientific Computing.*
11. B. Cockburn, G.E. Karniadakis, C.-W. Shu (eds.), *Discontinuous Galerkin Methods.* Theory, Computation and Applications.
12. U. van Rienen, *Numerical Methods in Computational Electrodynamics.* Linear Systems in Practical Applications.
13. B. Engquist, L. Johnsson, M. Hammill, F. Short (eds.), *Simulation and Visualization on the Grid.*
14. E. Dick, K. Riemslagh, J. Vierendeels (eds.), *Multigrid Methods VI.*
15. A. Frommer, T. Lippert, B. Medeke, K. Schilling (eds.), *Numerical Challenges in Lattice Quantum Chromodynamics.*
16. J. Lang, *Adaptive Multilevel Solution of Nonlinear Parabolic PDE Systems.* Theory, Algorithm, and Applications.
17. B.I. Wohlmuth, *Discretization Methods and Iterative Solvers Based on Domain Decomposition.*
18. U. van Rienen, M. Günther, D. Hecht (eds.), *Scientific Computing in Electrical Engineering.*
19. I. Babuška, P.G. Ciarlet, T. Miyoshi (eds.), *Mathematical Modeling and Numerical Simulation in Continuum Mechanics.*
20. T.J. Barth, T. Chan, R. Haimes (eds.), *Multiscale and Multiresolution Methods.* Theory and Applications.
21. M. Breuer, F. Durst, C. Zenger (eds.), *High Performance Scientific and Engineering Computing.*
22. K. Urban, *Wavelets in Numerical Simulation.* Problem Adapted Construction and Applications.
23. L.F. Pavarino, A. Toselli (eds.), *Recent Developments in Domain Decomposition Methods.*

24. T. Schlick, H.H. Gan (eds.), *Computational Methods for Macromolecules: Challenges and Applications.*

25. T.J. Barth, H. Deconinck (eds.), *Error Estimation and Adaptive Discretization Methods in Computational Fluid Dynamics.*

26. M. Griebel, M.A. Schweitzer (eds.), *Meshfree Methods for Partial Differential Equations.*

27. S. Müller, *Adaptive Multiscale Schemes for Conservation Laws.*

28. C. Carstensen, S. Funken, W. Hackbusch, R.H.W. Hoppe, P. Monk (eds.), *Computational Electromagnetics.*

29. M.A. Schweitzer, *A Parallel Multilevel Partition of Unity Method for Elliptic Partial Differential Equations.*

30. T. Biegler, O. Ghattas, M. Heinkenschloss, B. van Bloemen Waanders (eds.), *Large-Scale PDE-Constrained Optimization.*

31. M. Ainsworth, P. Davies, D. Duncan, P. Martin, B. Rynne (eds.), *Topics in Computational Wave Propagation.* Direct and Inverse Problems.

32. H. Emmerich, B. Nestler, M. Schreckenberg (eds.), *Interface and Transport Dynamics.* Computational Modelling.

33. H.P. Langtangen, A. Tveito (eds.), *Advanced Topics in Computational Partial Differential Equations.* Numerical Methods and Diffpack Programming.

34. V. John, *Large Eddy Simulation of Turbulent Incompressible Flows.* Analytical and Numerical Results for a Class of LES Models.

35. E. Bänsch (ed.), *Challenges in Scientific Computing – CISC 2002.*

36. B.N. Khoromskij, G. Wittum, *Numerical Solution of Elliptic Differential Equations by Reduction to the Interface.*

37. A. Iske, *Multiresolution Methods in Scattered Data Modelling.*

38. S.-I. Niculescu, K. Gu (eds.), *Advances in Time-Delay Systems.*

39. S. Attinger, P. Koumoutsakos (eds.), *Multiscale Modelling and Simulation.*

40. R. Kornhuber, R. Hoppe, J. Périaux, O. Pironneau, O. Wildlund, J. Xu (eds.), *Domain Decomposition Methods in Science and Engineering.*

41. T. Plewa, T. Linde, V.G. Weirs (eds.), *Adaptive Mesh Refinement – Theory and Applications.*

42. A. Schmidt, K.G. Siebert, *Design of Adaptive Finite Element Software.* The Finite Element Toolbox ALBERTA.

43. M. Griebel, M.A. Schweitzer (eds.), *Meshfree Methods for Partial Differential Equations II.*

44. B. Engquist, P. Lötstedt, O. Runborg (eds.), *Multiscale Methods in Science and Engineering.*

45. P. Benner, V. Mehrmann, D.C. Sorensen (eds.), *Dimension Reduction of Large-Scale Systems.*

46. D. Kressner, *Numerical Methods for General and Structured Eigenvalue Problems.*

47. A. Boriçi, A. Frommer, B. Joó, A. Kennedy, B. Pendleton (eds.), *QCD and Numerical Analysis III.*

48. F. Graziani (ed.), *Computational Methods in Transport.*

49. B. Leimkuhler, C. Chipot, R. Elber, A. Laaksonen, A. Mark, T. Schlick, C. Schütte, R. Skeel (eds.), *New Algorithms for Macromolecular Simulation.*

50. M. Bücker, G. Corliss, P. Hovland, U. Naumann, B. Norris (eds.), *Automatic Differentiation: Applications, Theory, and Implementations.*

51. A.M. Bruaset, A. Tveito (eds.), *Numerical Solution of Partial Differential Equations on Parallel Computers.*

52. K.H. Hoffmann, A. Meyer (eds.), *Parallel Algorithms and Cluster Computing.*

53. H.-J. Bungartz, M. Schäfer (eds.), *Fluid-Structure Interaction.*

54. J. Behrens, *Adaptive Atmospheric Modeling.*

55. O. Widlund, D. Keyes (eds.), *Domain Decomposition Methods in Science and Engineering XVI.*

56. S. Kassinos, C. Langer, G. Iaccarino, P. Moin (eds.), *Complex Effects in Large Eddy Simulations.*

57. M. Griebel, M.A Schweitzer (eds.), *Meshfree Methods for Partial Differential Equations III.*

58. A.N. Gorban, B. Kégl, D.C. Wunsch, A. Zinovyev (eds.), *Principal Manifolds for Data Visualization and Dimension Reduction.*

59. H. Ammari (ed.), *Modeling and Computations in Electromagnetics: A Volume Dedicated to Jean-Claude Nédélec.*

60. U. Langer, M. Discacciati, D. Keyes, O. Widlund, W. Zulehner (eds.), *Domain Decomposition Methods in Science and Engineering XVII.*

61. T. Mathew, *Domain Decomposition Methods for the Numerical Solution of Partial Differential Equations.*

62. F. Graziani (ed.), *Computational Methods in Transport: Verification and Validation.*

63. M. Bebendorf, *Hierarchical Matrices.* A Means to Efficiently Solve Elliptic Boundary Value Problems.

64. C.H. Bischof, H.M. Bücker, P. Hovland, U. Naumann, J. Utke (eds.), *Advances in Automatic Differentiation.*

65. M. Griebel, M.A. Schweitzer (eds.), *Meshfree Methods for Partial Differential Equations IV.*

66. B. Engquist, P. Lötstedt, O. Runborg (eds.), *Multiscale Modeling and Simulation in Science.*

67. I.H. Tuncer, Ü. Gülcat, D.R. Emerson, K. Matsuno (eds.), *Parallel Computational Fluid Dynamics 2007.*

68. S. Yip, T. Diaz de la Rubia (eds.), *Scientific Modeling and Simulations.*

69. A. Hegarty, N. Kopteva, E. O'Riordan, M. Stynes (eds.), *BAIL* 2008 – *Boundary and Interior Layers.*

70. M. Bercovier, M.J. Gander, R. Kornhuber, O. Widlund (eds.), *Domain Decomposition Methods in Science and Engineering XVIII.*

71. B. Koren, C. Vuik (eds.), *Advanced Computational Methods in Science and Engineering.*

72. M. Peters (ed.), *Computational Fluid Dynamics for Sport Simulation.*

73. H.-J. Bungartz, M. Mehl, M. Schäfer (eds.), *Fluid Structure Interaction II - Modelling, Simulation, Optimization.*

74. D. Tromeur-Dervout, G. Brenner, D.R. Emerson, J. Erhel (eds.), *Parallel Computational Fluid Dynamics 2008.*

75. A.N. Gorban, D. Roose (eds.), *Coping with Complexity: Model Reduction and Data Analysis.*

76. J.S. Hesthaven, E.M. Rønquist (eds.), *Spectral and High Order Methods for Partial Differential Equations.*
77. M. Holtz, *Sparse Grid Quadrature in High Dimensions with Applications in Finance and Insurance.*
78. Y. Huang, R. Kornhuber, O.Widlund, J. Xu (eds.), *Domain Decomposition Methods in Science and Engineering XIX.*
79. M. Griebel, M.A. Schweitzer (eds.), *Meshfree Methods for Partial Differential Equations V.*
80. P.H. Lauritzen, C. Jablonowski, M.A. Taylor, R.D. Nair (eds.), *Numerical Techniques for Global Atmospheric Models.*
81. C. Clavero, J.L. Gracia, F.J. Lisbona (eds.), *BAIL 2010 – Boundary and Interior Layers, Computational and Asymptotic Methods.*
82. B. Engquist, O. Runborg, Y.R. Tsai (eds.), *Numerical Analysis and Multiscale Computations.*
83. I.G. Graham, T.Y. Hou, O. Lakkis, R. Scheichl (eds.), *Numerical Analysis of Multiscale Problems.*
84. A. Logg, K.-A. Mardal, G. Wells (eds.), *Automated Solution of Differential Equations by the Finite Element Method.*
85. J. Blowey, M. Jensen (eds.), *Frontiers in Numerical Analysis – Durham 2010.*
86. O. Kolditz, U.-J. Gorke, H. Shao, W. Wang (eds.), *Thermo-Hydro-Mechanical-Chemical Processes in Fractured Porous Media – Benchmarks and Examples.*
87. S. Forth, P. Hovland, E. Phipps, J. Utke, A. Walther (eds.), *Recent Advances in Algorithmic Differentiation.*
88. J. Garcke, M. Griebel (eds.), *Sparse Grids and Applications.*
89. M. Griebel, M.A. Schweitzer (eds.), *Meshfree Methods for Partial Differential Equations VI.*
90. C. Pechstein, *Finite and Boundary Element Tearing and Interconnecting Solvers for Multiscale Problems.*
91. R. Bank, M. Holst, O. Widlund, J. Xu (eds.), *Domain Decomposition Methods in Science and Engineering XX.*
92. H. Bijl, D. Lucor, S. Mishra, C. Schwab (eds.), *Uncertainty Quantification in Computational Fluid Dynamics.*
93. M. Bader, H.-J. Bungartz, T. Weinzierl (eds.), *Advanced Computing.*
94. M. Ehrhardt, T. Koprucki (eds.), *Advanced Mathematical Models and Numerical Techniques for Multi-Band Effective Mass Approximations.*
95. M. Azaïez, H. El Fekih, J.S. Hesthaven (eds.), *Spectral and High Order Methods for Partial Differential Equations ICOSAHOM 2012.*
96. F. Graziani, M.P. Desjarlais, R. Redmer, S.B. Trickey (eds.), *Frontiers and Challenges in Warm Dense Matter.*
97. J. Garcke, D. Pflüger (eds.), *Sparse Grids and Applications – Munich 2012.*
98. J. Erhel, M. Gander, L. Halpern, G. Pichot, T. Sassi, O. Widlund (eds.), *Domain Decomposition Methods in Science and Engineering XXI.*
99. R. Abgrall, H. Beaugendre, P.M. Congedo, C. Dobrzynski, V. Perrier, M. Ricchiuto (eds.), *High Order Nonlinear Numerical Methods for Evolutionary PDEs - HONOM 2013.*
100. M. Griebel, M.A. Schweitzer (eds.), *Meshfree Methods for Partial Differential Equations VII.*

101. R. Hoppe (ed.), *Optimization with PDE Constraints - OPTPDE 2014.*

102. S. Dahlke, W. Dahmen, M. Griebel, W. Hackbusch, K. Ritter, R. Schneider, C. Schwab, H. Yserentant (eds.), *Extraction of Quantifiable Information from Complex Systems.*

103. A. Abdulle, S. Deparis, D. Kressner, F. Nobile, M. Picasso (eds.), *Numerical Mathematics and Advanced Applications - ENUMATH 2013.*

104. T. Dickopf, M.J. Gander, L. Halpern, R. Krause, L.F. Pavarino (eds.), *Domain Decomposition Methods in Science and Engineering XXII.*

105. M. Mehl, M. Bischoff, M. Schäfer (eds.), *Recent Trends in Computational Engineering - CE2014.* Optimization, Uncertainty, Parallel Algorithms, Coupled and Complex Problems.

106. R.M. Kirby, M. Berzins, J.S. Hesthaven (eds.), *Spectral and High Order Methods for Partial Differential Equations - ICOSAHOM'14.*

107. B. Jüttler, B. Simeon (eds.), *Isogeometric Analysis and Applications 2014.*

108. P. Knobloch (ed.), *Boundary and Interior Layers, Computational and Asymptotic Methods – BAIL 2014.*

109. J. Garcke, D. Pflüger (eds.), *Sparse Grids and Applications – Stuttgart 2014.*

110. H. P. Langtangen, *Finite Difference Computing with Exponential Decay Models.*

111. A. Tveito, G.T. Lines, *Computing Characterizations of Drugs for Ion Channels and Receptors Using Markov Models.*

112. B. Karazösen, M. Manguoğlu, M. Tezer-Sezgin, S. Göktepe, Ö. Uğur (eds.), *Numerical Mathematics and Advanced Applications - ENUMATH 2015.*

113. H.-J. Bungartz, P. Neumann, W.E. Nagel (eds.), *Software for Exascale Computing - SPPEXA 2013-2015.*

114. G.R. Barrenechea, F. Brezzi, A. Cangiani, E.H. Georgoulis (eds.), *Building Bridges: Connections and Challenges in Modern Approaches to Numerical Partial Differential Equations.*

115. M. Griebel, M.A. Schweitzer (eds.), *Meshfree Methods for Partial Differential Equations VIII.*

116. C.-O. Lee, X.-C. Cai, D.E. Keyes, H.H. Kim, A. Klawonn, E.-J. Park, O.B. Widlund (eds.), *Domain Decomposition Methods in Science and Engineering XXIII.*

117. T. Sakurai, S. Zhang, T. Imamura, Y. Yusaku, K. Yoshinobu, H. Takeo (eds.), *Eigenvalue Problems: Algorithms, Software and Applications, in Petascale Computing*. EPASA 2015, Tsukuba, Japan, September 2015.

118. T. Richter (ed.), *Fluid-structure Interactions.* Models, Analysis and Finite Elements.

119. M.L. Bittencourt, N.A. Dumont, J.S. Hesthaven (eds.), *Spectral and High Order Methods for Partial Differential Equations ICOSAHOM 2016.*

120. Z. Huang, M. Stynes, Z. Zhang (eds.), *Boundary and Interior Layers, Computational and Asymptotic Methods BAIL 2016.*

121. S.P.A. Bordas, E.N. Burman, M.G. Larson, M.A. Olshanskii (eds.), *Geometrically Unfitted Finite Element Methods and Applications.* Proceedings of the UCL Workshop 2016.

122. A. Gerisch, R. Penta, J. Lang (eds.), *Multiscale Models in Mechano and Tumor Biology*. Modeling, Homogenization, and Applications.

123. J. Garcke, D. Pflüger, C.G. Webster, G. Zhang (eds.), *Sparse Grids and Applications - Miami 2016.*

*For further information on these books please have a look at our mathematics catalogue at the following URL:* www.springer.com/series/3527

www.ingramcontent.com/pod-product-compliance
Lightning Source LLC
Chambersburg PA
CBHW080250030726
47593CB00009B/2432
* 9 7 8 1 0 1 3 2 7 3 3 8 4 *